The Making of Knowledge in Composition

in Composition

Portrait of an Emerging Field

The Making of Knowledge in Composition

Portrait of an Emerging Field

Stephen M. North
State University of New York
at Albany

BOYNTON/COOK PUBLISHERS
HEINEMANN
PORTSMOUTH, NH

For Liz, Matthew, Patricia, and David

Boynton/Cook Publishers
A Division of
Heinemann Educational Books, Inc.
70 Court Street, Portsmouth, NH 03801
Offices and agents throughout the world

Library of Congress Cataloguing-in-Publication Data

North, Stephen M.
  The making of knowledge in composition.

  1. English language—Rhetoric—Study and teaching—
Methodology. 2. English language—Composition and
exercises—Study and teaching—Methodology. I. Title.
PE1404.N67 1987   808'.042'07   87-5141
ISBN 0-86709-151-7

Printed in the United States of America.

88   89   90   91   10   9   8   7   6   5   4   3   2

Preface

I think it might be useful, by way of preface, to explain where this book comes from. I like to identify myself as a member of the first generation of English teaching professionals whose primary allegiance is to the teaching of writing: people who, by both training and professional choice, see themselves not simply as knowing something about composition, but whose academic identity derives from their membership in the field they call Composition. To be sure, as a check of *Dissertation Abstracts International* will reveal, some members of earlier academic generations had identified the teaching of writing as a major feature of their professional training, a few in English departments, more in schools of education. And, of course, a good many people—the majority of the field's members—although trained in traditional literary studies, have come either by accident, coercion, or choice to make Composition a career priority. But few have been able to do both, for the simple reason that, with very few exceptions, there were no graduate programs in Composition before the mid-1970s. Composition, described so often as the "ghetto" or the "stepchild" of English departments, was something that had to be taught—or, perhaps, endured. But it was not perceived as a discipline or a field, as a subject matter suitable for graduate study.

About the time I reached graduate school in 1973, though, the forces which were to change that perception—forces I have tried to trace in this book—had come to a head. Suddenly it was possible, if still not entirely advisable, to seek an advanced degree in English with Composition, and not literary studies, as one's primary field. My introduction to Composition, one I expect was pretty typical, came via the time-honored ritual: being assigned, lost soul, new T.A., to teach a section of Freshman English. The three months that followed were as frustrating and confusing as any in my life. I was—and, worse, felt—so terribly ignorant, so remarkably inept, that my choices were clear and simple: either find out what there was to know about doing this, and get better, or else walk away. Ten years, maybe even five years earlier, I would have walked. But the teaching of writing was not what it had been. Nothing else in English compared with the excitement, the absolute fervor, of a Composition fired by what was declared to be a national literacy crisis.

My own emblem of the time is of an intense, sweat-drenched Carl Klaus of Iowa, tie askew, addressing a standing-room-only crowd at the 1976 Conference on College Composition and Communication on "Public Opinion and Professional Belief." It wasn't so much what he said—in the years since, I have come to disagree with much of that talk's substance—but how he said it, and how I heard it! That unbearably hot Philadelphia hotel conference room crackled for me with the energy of a revival meeting. In a style so deliberate as to be almost awkward, and for that very reason all the more impassioned, he held out an irresistible invitation. There were no professional teachers of writing, he said. Even after 20 or 30 years of experience, no one—himself included—could claim that title; experience was not enough. But there could be such a thing, and they were needed, badly. Or, as it seemed to me then, I was needed, badly. Nothing I had studied—not Chaucer or the Transcendentalists, not Wordsworth or Coleridge or Blake—had made me an offer anything like this, and I was clearly not alone. For those of us who saw in this invitation an opportunity, and seized it, it was an exciting time indeed.

Looking back, I suppose it was that excitement, the uncritical enthusiasm of the new recruit, that blinded me to any problems in my new object of loyalty. My field was Composition, the study of the doing, learning, and teaching of writing. It had a name, an organization, a journal, even its share of celebrity members. It held conventions, for heaven's sake. That was enough for me; it must be for real. Not only that, but it was going to rescue me from my ignorance and ineptitude in the classroom. Somebody out there had studied the problem of how writing could best be taught and learned, and I was now to be privy to that knowledge. My days of frustration were over.

In other words, it wasn't until I actually began trying to use some of what my new field offered that I began to notice that maybe my hopes were too high, that it wasn't going to be that easy. It was true, as I had believed, that people knew, or claimed to know, about writing, and especially about how best to teach it. At any rate, they knew more—or declared what they knew with more authority—than

I did. The trouble was that the things they knew didn't seem to hang together very well. It wasn't just that there was no unanimity on important issues; I knew from literary studies that unanimity was no great virtue. But it began to seem as if the field didn't have a core or a center: there seemed to be no way to frame its central problems, nor any method by which to set about trying to resolve them. The closest anyone came at the time to offering an elemental, and so central, opposition, was the "product vs. process" slogan. But then, as now, it was very hard to get a handle on what that opposition might entail. Like "conservative vs. liberal" or "hawk vs. dove," it seemed to identify political tendencies within some specific context; the terms themselves had no fixed or absolute value, no field-wide definition. It got to be positively alarming: those terms could mean whatever anybody wanted. As a result, their opposition was more useful for generating the kind of rhetoric that marks street corner debate than the kinds of discourse one expects from serious inquiry: fervent, energetic, entertaining, sometimes even raucous—but not, in the end, productive in any clear way.

In practical terms, this centerless-ness meant that I ended up with what amounted to a loosely organized catalogue of classroom options, everything from curricular models that would tell me what to do in every class all semester to hundreds, even thousands, of pedagogical bits and pieces from which I could build my own courses: freewriting and sentence-combining, casebooks and Comp-Lab, talk-write and tagmemics, and on and on and on. I was naturally disappointed that things couldn't be simpler—teaching was obviously going to remain a struggle—but I managed, about 1978, to arrive at a solution that satisfied me as a practitioner. Since I couldn't sort out my students on the basis of what my newly chosen field told me I knew, I decided I would have to do it the other way around: sort out what my field told me I knew on the basis of my students, picking and choosing what seemed to make the most sense for any particular learner at any given time.[1]

And, despite some obvious logistical difficulties, that solution would probably have worked indefinitely, especially since I came to do most of my work in a writing center, where such tailoring is the norm. Unfortunately, my professional role continued to change, so that my problems with the field's nagging lack of definition didn't go away. I found myself not only having to add to the fund of Composition knowledge via my own research, but to initiate others into the field as well: to teach graduate courses, sponsor directed readings, and serve on dissertation and examination committees. The research part I have managed tolerably well, although methodology—the matter of what *counts* as knowledge in Composition and why—has turned out to be a far more nettlesome one than I might have liked. Where the problems really hit home, though, were in my initiatory roles. I was consistently troubled when it came to assembling and organizing reading lists: what should be included, and why? Even more troublesome was establishing how the works that finally made the lists were connected. I could make sure candidates read enough of the right individual works to get them through publishers' cocktail parties, but where was the core? What held this professional literature together?

The whole matter reached a kind of crisis point, finally, during the oral doctoral examination of a graduate student in our program. He and I had worked closely for a year on the Composition portion of his exam list, covering all the works carefully, and, where possible, making connections among them. As far as we could manage, he knew what I knew. And on the examination itself, it was clear he knew the individual works, and knew them well. But I asked, as did the other examiners (who knew relatively little about Composition), questions which demanded, in the answer and probe format of that exam, an overview, a synthesis, that the student simply didn't have— or, more accurately, that Composition as a field seemed not to have. What is the relationship between the claims, say, of Peter Elbow and those of Linda Flower and John Hayes? Is there a logical hierarchy of knowledge in the field? A method of establishing one? What *do* people know about the teaching of writing that they didn't know fifty or a hundred years ago, and how do they know it? The examination was a disaster; that student, who had also become my friend, failed. And I had failed him.

That portion of this story has a happy ending. The student took the examination again, framing our questions this time by first sketching out his own version of the shape of the field, and he passed. But the experience—his pain, and mine for him—had brought home to me what I had known from the beginning, but managed to dodge: that I had pledged my allegiance to a field I never really understood and which, so far as I have been able to tell, no one else understands very well either. The questions are relatively simple, but the answers come hard: What exactly is this field called Composition? Where does it come from? How does it work? Where is it going?[2]

In a sense, then, I have been working on this book for some ten years, since at least that hot night in Philadelphia. In part, I have written it for my fellow Composition professionals, predecessors and contemporaries alike. This is, I think, who we have been, who we are, and how we got to be this way. I have written it for those who might come after us, as well, the successors not only to the student that I was, but to the student I failed so miserably. That shouldn't have happened, and it won't happen again. And, who knows, the book may even have some impact on readers outside of Composition, providing them with a glimpse of what we do they might not otherwise get.

But finally, and however peculiar it sounds, this is a book I have written for myself. The blind enthusiasm and naive faith that were mine as a new recruit to Composition will no longer serve. The development of further commitment, of a mature loyalty, requires a new perspective—one based on a broader and deeper knowledge, yes, but even more on a deliberate and critical consciousness. This book represents my search for that perspective. It is a search that I have found, and that I believe many readers will find, often painful; it just plain isn't easy to look hard at what you believe, and to discover the very narrow limits of what you know. What has kept me going is that promise of a better commitment: my determination that only by coming to know the field, whatever its flaws, can I serve it better. It is in the spirit of that commitment that I offer this book now. I hope it will sustain its readers, too.

□

I have had a great deal of support in putting this book together. Several friends and colleagues read all or parts of the manuscript and offered responses that gave me new perspectives on how the words worked: Lil Brannon, Penny Dugan, Mark Hurlbert, Ted Jennings, Richard Jenseth, Sharon Roy, and Meg Seckendorf. Michael Green took time he didn't have to talk about statistical matters. Robert Connors was kind enough to share a most intriguing and useful essay on historical inquiry in Composition.

I also need to acknowledge three people who listened and counseled: Rudy Nelson, who was there at the beginning, and very patient with a brash student; Gerry DiCarlo, who listened to what must often have seemed my ravings at their worst; and especially Cy Knoblauch, who not only read the manuscript, but kept his office door open to me all these past two years. Finally, there was Bob Boynton, who read and listened and counseled and was still willing to take a chance on a first-book writer.

Contents

Introduction

This is a book about how knowledge is made in the field that has come to be called Composition. As such, it is different, on the one hand, from the kinds of essay collections that attempt to frame or showcase the field's various kinds of inquiry for the use of other investigators: Gary Tate's *Teaching Composition: 10 Bibliographical Essays*, for example, Lee Odell and Charles Cooper's *Research on Composing: Points of Departure*; or, more recently, Richard Beach and Lillian Bridwell's *New Directions in Composition Research*, Peter Mosenthal, Lynne Tamor, and Sean Walmsley's *Research on Writing*, or George Hillocks, Jr.'s *Research on Written Composition*. On the other hand, it is different too from the books that make the results of those various kinds of inquiry accessible to teachers, the sort of theory-into-practice works: anthologies like Richard Graves's *Rhetoric and Composition*, or surveys like William Irmscher's *Teaching Expository Writing*, or David Foster's *A Primer for Writing Teachers*. Those books essentially deal with *what* people claim to know about the doing, teaching, and learning of writing; this one, by contrast, is concerned primarily with *how* they claim to know it. Specifically, it is concerned with what I shall be calling *modes of inquiry* —the whole series of steps an inquirer follows in making a contribution to a field of knowledge—as they operate within *methodological communities*: groups of inquirers more or less united by their allegiance to one such mode, to an agreed-upon set of rules for gathering, testing, validating, accumulating and distributing what they regard as knowledge.[1]

These two notions deserve some elaboration. First, modes of inquiry are not to be confused with the various research *techniques*

1

their practitioners might use. Counting T-units, unearthing old text-books, analyzing composing-aloud protocols, taking field notes—these and any other means for handling information are potentially available for any given mode, albeit with reservations that will become clear as we proceed. But their significance—how these techniques and their results come to *mean* for any particular investigation—is not inherent in the techniques themselves, but a function of community standards.

Second, I want to be clear about just what this notion of a methodological community means. Paul Diesing, whose *Patterns of Discovery in the Social Sciences* influenced this study in ways that will become increasingly clear, offers this useful description:

> A community is located by finding people who interact regularly with one another in their work. They read and use each other's ideas, discuss each other's work, and sometimes collaborate. They have common friends, acquaintances, intellectual ancestors, and opponents, and thus locate themselves at roughly the same point in sociometric space. Their interaction is facilitated by shared beliefs and values—goals, myths, terminology, self-concepts—which make their work mutually intelligible and valuable. Although they do not all use exactly the same procedure in their work, there is a great deal of similarity, and the differences are accepted as variant realizations of the same values (pp. 17–18).

What is especially important about such a conception is that *it leaves room for individuals to belong to—to be fluent knowledge-makers in—more than one such community.* So, for example, Chapter 7 will feature Janet Emig as a leading member of what I call the Clinicians' community for the work reported in her *The Composing Processes of Twelfth Graders*; but she will also figure prominently in Chapter 4, "The Philosophers," for writings like "The Tacit Tradition: The Inevitability of a Multi-Disciplinary Approach to Writing Research." Thus, while most members of the field do give their primary allegiance to one community or another, my placement of them, almost always in terms of specific investigations, will be by way of illustration, not restriction.

The book's central purpose, then, is to describe these modes, and to account for the emergence of these communities in Composition. For reasons to be offered in the first chapter, the field's modern origins can most usefully be traced to the early 1960s. Its development thereafter can best be characterized as a kind of methodological land-rush. Impelled by widely proclaimed arguments that, even after half a century of English teaching in America, very little was known about composition, group after group of investigators, each equipped with some different mode of inquiry, some new way of making knowledge, has scrambled to stake their claim to a portion of what they have perceived to be essentially virgin territory. If there was anything to be known about teaching and learning writing, these inquirers planned to find it out.

As a result, during the past twenty years or so Composition has grown tremendously—has, really, *become* a field. But while this growth has been exciting, it has often seemed chaotic and patternless as well, and has had at least two major liabilities. The first is that the new investigators have tended to trample roughshod over the claims of previous inquirers, especially the "indigenous" population that I will call the Practitioners. In other words, much of what especially teachers, and to a lesser extent writers, have claimed to know about writing has been ignored, discounted, or ridiculed—so that, despite their overwhelming majority, they have been effectively disenfranchised as knowledge-makers in their own field.

Second, the growth of methodological awareness has not kept pace with this scramble for the power and prestige that go with being able to say what constitutes knowledge. Investigators often seem unreflective about their own mode of inquiry, let alone anyone else's. The predictable result within methodological communities has been disorder: investigators are wont to claim more for their work than they can or should. Between communities, it has produced a kind of inflation: in the absence of a critical consciousness capable of discriminating more carefully, the various kinds of knowledge produced by these modes of inquiry have been piled up uncritically, helter-skelter, with little regard to incompatabilities. The result has been an accumulated knowledge of a relatively impressive size, but one that lacks any clear coherence or methodological integrity. Composition's collective fund of knowledge is a very fragile entity.

This study deals with this development in six major sections. Section I (Ch. 1) is a historical sketch, outlining the forces that can account for the institution of Composition as a discrete field within the larger discipline of English, and which at the same time created the conditions leading to the methodological scramble. Each of the next three sections examines one cluster of the communities that has emerged in response to those conditions. These clusters are rough groupings, held together by the kind of question that drives its constituent communities. Broadly speaking, then, the Practitioners (Ch. 2) want to know What do we do? the Scholars (Ch. 3-5) try to discover What does it mean? and the Researchers (Chs. 6-9) ask What happened (or happens)? Within these sections, each methodological community is treated in a separate chapter, with a review of its beginnings in the field, an analysis of its assumptions and procedures, and a consideration of the kind of knowledge it produces. There are eight in all: Practitioners, Historians, Philosophers, Critics, Experimentalists, Clinicians, Formalists, and Ethnographers.

In the fifth section (Chs. 10–11) I deal with what can be called the dynamics of inquiry: what has happened when the knowledge produced by the modes of inquiry presented in the previous eight chapters has been brought together—what methodological communities have gained power, how, why, and to what effect? And the sixth and final section (Ch. 12) deals with possible futures. That is, given the forces operating within—and without—Composition, it is an attempt to sketch out the likely scenarios for its future as a knowledge-making field.

A Note on the Method of This Study

In a section of *Patterns of Discovery in the Social Sciences* with a very similar title, Paul Diesing reflects on his own approach:

> Anyone who discusses method must eventually face the question of what *his* method is. After some thought I have concluded that my method all along has been that of participant observation. My approach is essentially anthropological; I treat various methods as subcultures within the general culture of science, each subculture belonging to a community within the general society of social scientists. There are as many methods as there are distinguishable communities of scientists, and the boundaries of each method are those of the community that uses it (p. 17, his emphasis).

As my language will already have suggested, I am inclined to take a similar position. That is, having conceived of these various communities as constituting the "society" of Composition, and of each method—each mode of inquiry—as the subculture of one or another of them, I have tried here to make sense of what I have seen and done in my ten years of "living among" the people of Composition: languages and rituals, histories and mythologies, ontologies and epistemologies.

I don't want to push my claims about such a posture too far. I did not deliberately set out ten or so years ago to collect data as a participant observer, planning, someday, to produce an account like this. I was, rather, an initiate looking to join the society and one or more of its communities. And even in Diesing's study, the claim to this anthropological perspective must be regarded as partly metaphorical.

"Living among" social scientists or Composition professionals is not like moving into a Maori village. Neither he nor I claim to deal with what happens at professional conferences, or with the behind-the-scene politics by which grant and award decisions are made, or with the lives of particular members of any community as case studies. Rather, we deal with the public life of these societies, with the community subcultures as manifested primarily in their written records. There are some exceptions—in my study, for example, the Practitioners are described as having a predominantly oral culture—but by their very nature, institutionalized, geographically-dispersed, knowledge-making "societies" like the social sciences or Composition are scribal cultures, and must be studied primarily in their texts.

Still, however much my study, following Diesing's, might thus be considered fairly standard humanist scholarship—an extended essay developing rational arguments founded on textual evidence—I think it remains useful to conceive of it as gaining certain advantages from the influence of the anthropological perspective he describes. First, then, it represents an attempt to describe each methodological community *from the inside*: to account for each community's patterns of knowledge-making in a way that, ideally, its members will recognize and approve. Thus, it is not an attempt to measure the value of Practitioner knowledge, say, against Experimentalist standards, but to characterize—and indeed, value—each brand of knowledge on its own terms. The same holds true for criticisms of particular studies, too, or for the delineation of community problems; they are based as far as possible only on internal, community-specific standards.

At the same time, though, the portrait of Composition *as a whole* is the product of a single consciousness. The more standard practice would have been to invite individual essays from an "expert" member of each community. This approach would yield, in its way, accounts from the inside, but would leave the reader to provide any image of the whole. My object, by contrast, was to provide that image of the whole myself, to account for what I saw from the peculiar vantage of insider/outsider, participant/observer. To borrow from Clifford Geertz's *The Interpretation of Cultures* (to which I shall refer again in Ch. 9), I wanted "to clarify what goes on in such places, to reduce the puzzlement—what manner of men are these?—to which unfamiliar acts emerging out of unknown backgrounds naturally give rise" (p. 16). Whatever the disadvantages of such a method in loss of expertise—no one moving through eight methods is likely to be the leading authority on any one—they seemed to me easily outweighed by the advantages gained in coherence and breadth of vision. Instead of eight discrete accounts, each inevitably framed in terms of its author's particular methodological allegiance, the account of each community would here be informed by my experience in all of the others. The image of the larger whole, with all that it makes possible—comparisons between methods, accounts of their interaction, and so on—could therefore take shape within a single frame of reference, my multi-communal experience.

And finally, this study is best understood as anthropological in this participant-observation sense in terms of the authority it can claim. However persuasive this portrait of Composition may be, and however much I test it in consultation with my "hosts," the other people in the field, it remains my creation, a product of my peculiar vision. Diesing offers a caution that applies here:

> I am *not* claiming that there are exactly four sharply distinct methods in the social sciences, rather than three, six, or eight; rather, I am picking out four prominent locations in the terrain and contrasting them with one another. Each of the locations can serve not only as a guidepost but also as a point of departure for exploring the whole field of social science methods, and the field will look different whenever one begins from a different point of departure (p. 10).

The same must be true, clearly, of my study in relation to Composition—perhaps even truer, given the field's mixed humanist and social science heritage. The modes of inquiry I will describe are not *the* eight modes in the field, with neat and measurable boundaries that will look the same to any investigator. If this study supplies a kind of map, it is a map of an ever-shifting, ever-moving terrain, whose shape—as Diesing suggests—is a function of where you happen to be standing. Offering it, as I offer it here, marks the beginning of a dialogue, not the end. The measure of success for this book will be the extent to which readers, reassured at recognizing in some particular chapter their own perspectives—their own communal identity—will then be able, via the juxtaposition provided here, to see the field from other perspectives as well, and fashion for themselves a new vision of Composition.

I

A Historical Context

1

composition
Becomes Composition

Any date chosen to mark the beginning of "modern" Composition is bound to be arbitrary. One might, for example, consider 1873, the year Harvard first added an English composition requirement to its list of admissions standards. Even more promising, perhaps, would be 1949, the year that the Conference on College Composition and Communication, the group which has come to assume the power center of the new field, was constituted. And yet events in education generally, and English specifically, were such that the early 1960s call the most attention to themselves.

In a sense, there could be no Composition—academic field, capital "C"—before, say, 1958. Indeed, English as a whole, to borrow the distinction offered by Arthur Applebee in his *Tradition and Reform in the Teaching of English* was very much English-the-school-subject, and only just beginning, about the mid-1950s, to be considered as English-the-discipline (p. 194). The reform movement in secondary education was turning back a half-century of dominance by what had come to be called "progressive" education. In English as in other subjects, this represented a turning away from progressive concerns with "the immediate needs and the characteristics of the student," to be replaced with an "emphasis on long-term goals and the nature of the subject" (pp. 191–192). With this shift in emphasis came a change in the nature and location of authority over curricula, so that "liberal arts faculties became involved in curriculum reform in a way unparalleled since the late nineteenth century, when the college had also served as the model for the high school program" (p. 192).

9

The central tenet of this reform movement in English, articulated in the reports of the Basic Issues conferences of 1958, was that "English must be regarded as 'a fundamental liberal discipline,' a body of specific knowledge to be preserved and transmitted rather than a set of skills or an opportunity for guidance and individual adjustment" (p. 193). Thus, as Applebee explains, "College professors of English rather than of education or psychology became the body of expert opinion of most importance in curriculum development"; with the prospect, moreover, that since "the basis of the curriculum was felt to lie in the subject matter, such experts could provide guidance of a nearly universally applicable sort—in contrast with the dictum of the NCTE Commission on the English Curriculum [1956] that the curriculum must emanate from the needs of the student in his particular local community" (p. 193).

The drift of emphasis in Applebee's account is toward literary study. But the academic reform movement affected the whole of the English curriculum, and it was guided by the "tripod" metaphor for English studies, English conceived, that is, as consisting of three separate components: language, literature, and composition (p. 192). The catch, of course, for English as a whole and for each of these component "legs" was that they were and still are very hard to define in disciplinary terms, and especially as a body of content. In his "Afterword: The Problems Remaining," the first problem Applebee raises is that of English's peculiar mixed pedigree:

> This stress on content has been in part responsible for the uneasiness which teachers of English have traditionally felt about the definition of their subject matter. The Committee of Ten [1893–94] in effect brought together a number of disparate subjects, each with its own body of rules and formal subject matter, and called them "English." Beyond the cliché that each of these studies deals with language, they have no real unity *as subject matter*; attempts to interrelate them have been artificial and, for the most part, short-lived. Whether the model for the educational process has been growth in language, the four basic skills (reading, writing, listening, speaking), or the three basic disciplines (language, literature, and composition) some aspect of what teachers considered to be important has been lost, re-emerging to assert its own values and undercut the basis of the reconciliation. Inevitably, the edges of the subject have blurred and wavered, creating for the teacher of English a perpetual crisis of identity (pp. 245–246, his emphasis).

Nevertheless, the stakes in the academic reform movement were very high, and the pressure for unambiguous expertise considerable.

There had been periods of reform before, of course; they are one of the hallmarks of American education. But this time educational reform was perceived as a national issue with a new urgency—as, really, a Cold War crisis, a matter of national defense. To quote Applebee quoting Vice-Admiral Rickover: "Only massive upgrading of the scholastic standards of our schools will guarantee the future prosperity and freedom of the Republic" (p. 189). Moreover, Federal dollars—potentially lots of them—were involved. The National Defense Education Act of 1958 had provided money for educational reforms on an unprecedented scale: for research, for curriculum design and testing, for professional training. Unfortunately, the original legislation did not make provision for English, prompting the 1961 production of NCTE's *The National Interest and the Teaching of English*, "a publication that struck the national government so forcibly," argues John Gerber in "Explosion in English," delivered to NCTE in 1967, "that it appeared in toto in the published proceedings of the House Subcommittee on Labor and Education" (p. 4).

Now the "crisis" in math and science, heated by perceived technological demands, fanned by a rapidly rising birthrate, and ignited, at least symbolically, by Sputnik, could be officially extended to include English:

> Our political democracy can provide our youth with the conditions of liberty—abundance, freedom of action, an accessible system of schools. But the ability to think and write and read, and an intimate contact with ideals, beauty, and morality—all central in English studies—are needed to equip our citizens to use their freedom wisely. America is now a major world power. As never before our country must think about its responsibilities to mankind and about its need for citizens to meet these awesome responsibilities. Tomorrow's leaders must learn today whatever truth and beauty and wisdom our culture can provide. Only a quality education will prepare our youth for the test; only a balanced education will assure the quality needed. National interest demands vigorous leadership to improve all educational programs (*National Interest*, p. 136).

As Applebee observes, it was a "direct and shrewd presentation of the importance of English to the national welfare" (p. 199). If nothing else, it demonstrated that the English teaching profession could muster considerable rhetorical energy. Its most immediate impact, however, was not the extension of the NDEA to include English; that would not happen until 1964. Instead, Congress approved an extension of the Cooperative Research Program (originally established in 1954), to include English; this support took the form of an effort called Project English (for more on which see Applebee, Ch. 7).

Federal interest in English *per se* on this scale was relatively short-lived, but the momentum generated by the intense interest of these few years launched modern Composition. The broadest effects were on English teachers' self-perception as professionals. Applebee explains:

> As has been hinted several times in the course of this chapter, the major accomplishment of the period during which the English course was remolded on the academic model was the sense of the profession generated among teachers at all levels. The battle for federal funds, the attempt to provide an academic curriculum through the work of the various curriculum study centers, the summers of study in the CEEB and NDEA institutes, the renewed cooperation between NCTE and MLA— all contributed to the sense that teachers of English at all levels shared common problems (p. 213).

The impact of the reform movement was not, however, without its ironies. One of the concerns among reformers was that, of the three components of the tripod, literature was getting shortest shrift in terms of research dollars. It was less easily amenable to the "scientific" modes of inquiry favored for government support than either language or composition. It seems also to have been the case that, while it was dearest to the hearts of English teachers, its value was far less obvious to either researchers or bureaucrats, whereas language (which, via linguistics, had had some fairly visible training successes during the war) and composition were more obviously "useful." Albert Kitzhaber addresses this issue in a 1967 paper called "The Government and English Teaching." Trying to account for the wording of Commissioner of Education Sterling McMurrin's request that Project English money should go to support projects that would improve " 'reading and the written and oral usage of the English language,' " he offers the following:

> The Commissioner had a reason for this [the non-mention of literature]. In the first place, there was a distrust of literature, amounting almost to hostility, among some influential members of the Commissioner's own staff, who were, we might say, "skills-oriented." And this attitude was equally evident in Congress. The record of testimony shows that one Congressman was especially anxious to be assured that none of the money the Commissioner was requesting for English would be used "to teach novels and poems," an activity which, it was clear, the Congressman thought insane, possibly un-American. The Commissioner reassured him by saying that the money would be

used to teach only reading. And so it was that the Study Center proposal that we at Oregon submitted to USDE in that year bore the title "A Sequential Curriculum in Reading, Language, and Oral and Written Composition." We had, in effect, to bootleg literature into the curriculum those first years (pp. 136–137).

One obvious irony, then, was that while in the academy—in the English departments that were to stand as primary authorities on what English was—literature, and not composition or language, was then and remains the central concern, it could not attract the sought-after Federal support. A sort of corollary irony, perhaps not so obvious but more important here, was that composition, the "service" course, so long considered academic dirty work, *could* attract such money. Here were circumstances that stood to make composition teaching respectable and fundable—make it, almost by proclamation, Composition, with the capital C.

In effect, then, the academic reform movement demanded the existence of a post-secondary, English department-based expertise in all three legs of the tripod. The question was, who could claim composition? Literature was snapped up readily enough. Language seemed to have been ceded, as it were, to a burgeoning linguistics, although the debate over just how that increasingly "scientific" leg was going to stay attached to the tripod has still not ended. Composition was another matter. There were a few potential claimants. It had long been a topic of concern among practitioners at a variety of levels, though perhaps especially in secondary and post-secondary settings. Any issue of *English Journal*, for instance, was certain to have one or more articles on it. But these were written, except in rare cases, by people who thought of themselves as English teachers, not composition specialists, and in any case they were unlikely to be able to offer an academically respectable body of knowledge. There were also specialists who could make some claims to expertise—"educationists," as they were likely to be labeled, the sort of people who had conducted one or more of the 504 studies listed by Braddock, Lloyd-Jones, and Schoer in *Research in Written Composition*, people who designed curricula, created textbook series, and so on. But the expertise they claimed was of the wrong—i.e., "progressive education"—sort, inappropriate in that it was not disciplinary in the sense of deriving, by whatever means, from the body of knowledge that was English.

Hence, though these others obviously could and did contribute to the emergence of a more or less autonomous Composition, they could not offer it the necessary *academic* base, could not do what a Northrop Frye, say, could do for the literature leg: place their imprimatur on a system of knowledge-making that could then be called

Composition. Which left, as the one group that might be able to do so—however improbable it may have seemed—those lowliest members of the English academic community: those who taught and administered the freshman composition courses in colleges and universities.

In retrospect, there is a certain logic to such a turn of events. After more than half a century, these academics had finally organized, after a fashion. The Conference on College Composition and Communication, as I noted above, was founded as part of NCTE in 1949. This group could then, as now, claim an institutional power base of considerable potential. The freshman course was something nearly all of the rapidly increasing number of college students would take, and represented in many cases the largest chunk of an English department's budget. It is true, of course, that that power had remained only potential. Many of those who taught in such programs were not enfranchised members of English departments; and those who were— the directors, especially—necessarily treated their position as a stepping stone to some more worthwhile professional identity. Still, the lever was there.

Most important of all, though, these people may be said to have *needed* the chance this power vacancy in composition provided. If the generally enhanced professional status of English teachers Applebee describes had bypassed any group, it was this one. Composition stood to provide these second-class academic citizens with a way out of their academic "ghetto"—or, more accurately, a way to transform that ghetto, to make it a respectable neighborhood. This is not to say that they were necessarily ready or eager to take such a chance. The declaration of power in what amounted to a new field may have represented a great opportunity, but seizing power, claiming authority—even, as in this case, an authority no one else really wanted very badly—involved risk and responsibility, too. In this passage from "4C and Freshman English," an address to the CCCC in 1963, Albert Kitzhaber again—whose *Themes, Theories, and Therapy*, incidentally, the first book-length study of college writing, also appeared that year—scolds his peers for their timidity in assuming just such a leadership role:

> . . . in a field shot through with controversy, where so much is in confusion and where we are faced with so many important and difficult issues, 4C has rarely tried as an organization to introduce a degree of order into this chaos by taking a definite stand, then working to make this stand widely known and generally accepted throughout the profession. It has too seldom attempted to spearhead promising new trends or to condemn outworn practices, if either is controversial. (And what is there

in the teaching of writing, that is not controversial?) It has not, in other words, consistently exerted the kind of intelligent and courageous leadership in the profession that alone, I think, can justify its existence in the long run (p. 135).

Kitzhaber's challenge calls, in other words, for the exertion of authority over knowledge about composition: what it is, how it is made, who gets to say so and why. What made that so difficult a challenge to meet—the reason the "4C" had failed to exert such leadership—was that it never really had the means to do so: it had no such control over knowledge, no *mode of inquiry* by which such order might have been imposed, nor whose findings would have been acknowledged by the wider profession. The school subject, composition, consisted almost entirely of knowledge produced by Practitioner inquiry, knowledge I will describe in the next chapter as lore. And however useful or durable that knowledge might have been in the more than half-century of its effectively unchallenged dominance, the terms of the academic reform movement demanded something more—something, in short, that looked like acceptable, formal, academic inquiry.

□

We can therefore date the birth of modern Composition, capital C, to 1963. And what marks its emergence as a nascent academic field more than anything else is this need to replace practice as the field's dominant mode of inquiry. The same was true to some extent, of course, for all of the "reformed" English; granting priority to knowledge generated by the methods of the academy necessarily threatened to undermine the authority of the practitioner. This wasn't always a matter of frontal assault. For example, in his Introduction to the Proceedings of the 1962 conference on "Needed Research in the Teaching of English," Erwin Steinberg tries to temper what he fears will be construed as the ruthlessness of the collection's papers in this regard:

> Amid the profusion of questions raised at the conference and the flood of recommended research, some of the conferees, understandably, began to feel that nothing was known about the teaching of English, that, as one conferee put it, "it is all gap." The reader of this report, unless forewarned, may feel the same. Actually, much is known about the teaching of language, literature, and composition. Teaching, as a profession, goes back several thousand years, and the experiences and, more recently,

the research accumulated during that time have been widely published. . . . One need not be a research specialist to discover good teachers; one need only be a student (p. 2).

For Steinberg, the "many questions and recommended research projects, therefore, do not indicate a lack of knowledge," nor does he want to admit there is anything inimical to practical knowledge in the proposed inquiries:

> Sometimes they indicate a desire to buttress an art with science, to analyze and define the techniques of the skillful English teacher and the contents and patterns of good English courses and curriculums. With more exact knowledge available, colleges will be better able to prepare prospective teachers, and administrators and interested citizens will with more confidence be able to distinguish the better from the poorer programs (pp. 2–3).

But this assessment was more diplomatic than prophetic. The reform of English *would* be a top-down affair. Practitioner knowledge, however ancient or hard-won, would have to be supplanted. J. N. Hook, the first director of Project English, probably reflects the spirit of the times more accurately when he argues, in his address to the very same conference, that "in English teaching we have relied too long on our best guesses" (p. 7).

And in the new Composition, this stance would turn out to be, if anything, even more extreme. In that same year, 1962, the NCTE Executive Council formed an ad hoc Committee on the State of Knowledge about Composition, the purpose of which was " 'to review what is known and what is not known about the teaching and learning of composition and the conditions under which it is taught, for the purpose of preparing for publication a special scientifically based report on what is known in this area.' "[1] The document which resulted, *Research in Written Composition*, reflects nothing of Steinberg's optimism about how much is already known:

> Today's research in Composition, taken as a whole, may be compared to chemical research as it emerged from the period of alchemy: some terms are being defined usefully, a number of procedures are being refined, but the field as a whole is laced with dreams, prejudices, and makeshift operations. Not enough investigators are really informing themselves about the procedures and results of previous research before embarking on their own. Too few of them conduct pilot experiments and validate their measuring instruments before undertaking an investigation. Too many seem to be bent more on obtaining an advanced

degree or another publication than on making a genuine contribution to knowledge, and a fair measure of the blame goes to the faculty adviser or journal editor who permits or publishes such irresponsible work. And far too few of those who have conducted an initial piece of research follow it with further exploration or replicate the investigations of others (p. 5).

The explicit argument is clear enough. For these authors, the authority of an emerging Composition will derive from inquiry— "research"—modeled in method and rigor on research in the sciences. Measured against that standard, as the analogy suggests, the work of the first six decades of the century have been pathetic indeed. However, the implicit argument seems equally clear, and is even more important here. First, then, practical knowledge, the stuff of teachers' rooms, how-to articles, textbooks, and the like, doesn't count as research—at any rate, it is nowhere considered among the 504 studies Braddock et al. list, is not a portion of "what is known and what is not known about the teaching and learning of composition." Instead, the authors seem to imply, practice needs to be based on research. If that is true, though, then practice is in serious trouble indeed: If Composition research is to scientific inquiry what alchemy was to chemistry, then presumably current practice must be to "scientific" practice what "real" medicine is to witch doctoring. A practice based on "dreams, prejudices, and makeshift operations" is quite capable of doing as much harm as good.

It would be no great exaggeration to call *Research in Written Composition* the charter of modern Composition. With the image it fosters—of a sort of ur-discipline blindly groping its way out of the darkness toward the bright light of a "scientific" certainty—it sets the stage for what I have already characterized as the field's methodological land rush. Composition is declared to be essentially virgin territory; little is known, and even that little is of questionable value, the result of blundering or careless work. If old composition is to become new Composition; if the "profession," as its membership seemed ready to call it, is to take its rightful place in the academy, the dominance of practice and sloppy research would have to end. This was to be a new era, and it would demand new kinds of knowledge produced by new kinds of inquiry.

II

Practice as Inquiry

2

The Practitioners

It may seem odd, given the account of modern Composition's origins offered in the previous chapter, to turn immediately to a consideration of Practitioners as knowledge-makers. After all, the whole thrust of the academic reform movement was to remove authority over knowledge from the hands of those whose main source of such authority was their practice. And in Composition, where that authority had at any rate been exercised pretty much by default, the removal was effected quite successfully—so successfully, in fact, that we are by now, some twenty years later, largely unaccustomed to entertaining the notion of practice as a mode of inquiry at all, as involving a series of steps that result in a contribution to a field of knowledge. The more common conception of Practitioners has come to be rather more in keeping with the "emerging science" image Braddock et al. offer. In those terms, Practitioners are regarded essentially as technicians: Scholars and especially Researchers *make* knowledge; Practitioners apply it.

But this latter conception of practice has not come about overnight. However bald the declarations of ignorance about Composition made by people caught up in the fervor of those reform-oriented committees and conferences, the vast majority of the field's members were then, and remain now, Practitioners. Calling for new kinds of knowledge made in new ways was one thing; getting them was quite another. It takes time to identify new modes of inquiry, to acquire expertise in them, and then to find or create outlets in which to publish their results. They have emerged very slowly. Moreover, even as these alternate brands of knowledge have found their way into

Composition, they have not brought practice-as-inquiry to a grinding halt. The effect is better understood as a devaluation. Knowledge gained via practice hasn't disappeared. Instead, its credibility, its power vis-à-vis other kinds of knowledge, has gradually, steadily, diminished.

Thus, practice clearly was then, and remains now, not only a distinguishable mode of inquiry, but the one most widely pursued in the field. And in fact, some few Practitioners have always managed to maintain a certain extraordinary visibility and authority, usually by virtue of their power as writers within a Practitioner culture that is, as we shall see, primarily oral. These people can serve here as points of reference, emblems of Practitioner inquiry at its most visible. Some of the names from 1963 are still familiar now, though not always in the same role: Robert Gorrell, Walker Gibson, Priscilla Tyler, Harold Allen, Ken Macrorie, John Gerber, Josephine Miles, Richard Braddock, Paul Roberts, A. M. Tibbetts, Hans Guth, James McCrimmon. And there has been a steady line of new names since: Roger Sale, Donald Hall, Elizabeth Cowan, Donald Murray, William Coles, Mina Shaughnessy, John Schultz, Elaine Maimon, Peter Elbow, Muriel Harris, Toby Fulwiler—all Practitioners who, by virtue of some combination of eloquence and influence, attract a considerable following.

But these people also represent the exception, not the rule. Nor does visibility necessarily equal quality: these are the best known not necessarily the best, Practitioners. Practitioners are for the most part not highly visible in this way. They are rather, one might say, Composition's rank and file.[1] Day in and day out, thousands upon thousands of them work at Composition. They do so in a variety of settings: classrooms at all levels, some devoted exclusively to writing, some not; in writing labs and centers; as hired graders; as consultants in both academic and non-academic situations, and so on. In these settings, they are faced over and over again with variations on the problem of what to *do* about teaching writing: what sort of syllabus to construct for a seventh-grade class; what kind of writing to assign as a prelude to reading Poe; how to talk to a frightened college sophomore about a philosophy paper; how to respond to research papers on "The Maginot Line"; how to teach middle management people about readability. In the process, they draw on, and contribute to, a body of knowledge that I have come to call *lore*: the accumulated body of traditions, practices, and beliefs in terms of which Practitioners understand how writing is done, learned, and taught.

Eventually, it will be of considerable importance to this study to deal with the circumstances under which Practitioner inquiry has come to be devalued: to consider how this vast majority of Composition's membership should have come to be effectively disenfranchised as knowledge-makers, and what the implications of that devaluation might be. But that is getting ahead of the game. In this chapter I want simply to examine what lore is, and to account for how practice as inquiry works.

The Nature of Practitioner Knowledge: Lore

For some readers, perhaps, the term "lore" will have negative, even denigrative connotations. Lore is what witches know, or herbal healers, or wizards in fantasy fiction. It's exactly the sort of stuff, in fact, that the alchemy metaphor in *Research in Written Composition* warns us about, stuff that "scientific" inquiry would show to be a muddled combination of half-truths, myths, and superstitions. In that sense, lores in general would seem to be out of fashion in our time. On the other hand, Composition's lore is a body of knowledge very much like those accumulated among practitioners of other arts—art here being broadly conceived—like painting or parenting, to offer an unlikely pair. These bodies of knowledge are not "scientifically" rigorous, either. And while they can, like lore, be informed by other kinds of inquiry, including those of the various sciences, they cannot be supplanted by them. For example, analyses of ocular function can help inform us about how we "see" paintings, but they cannot tell a Picasso what to do with his brush; and while careful psychological studies might lead to a developmental model for children—Piaget comes to mind, of course—they cannot produce a formula for parental discipline, nor provide any substitute for an adeptness at reading a child's moods derived from affection and experience.

This is not to say that Practitioners' lore is without logic or form. Not at all. It is driven, first, by a pragmatic logic: It is concerned with what has worked, is working, or might work in teaching, doing, or learning writing. Second, its structure is essentially experiential. That is, the traditions, practices, and beliefs of which it is constituted are best understood as being organized within an experience-based framework: I will create my version of lore out of what has worked or might work—either in my own experience or in that of others—and I will understand and order it in terms of the circumstances under which it did so. In some of its more public manifestations—textbooks, syllabi, and the like—this structure tends to be obscured, usually in favor of some loosely topical organization (prewriting, writing, revision, editing; words, sentences, paragraphs, etc.). But, as we shall see below, such documents do not provide a very accurate image of lore. And indeed, textbook writers who are able to preserve some measure of this experiential structure in their work— Ken Macrorie or John Schultz, for instance—gain enormous popularity with Practitioners for precisely that reason. However quirky they may seem to other readers, to Practitioners they are operating within a clearly recognizable experiential framework, and so making perfect sense.

Lore's pragmatic logic and experience-based structure account for three of its most important functional properties. The first is that literally anything can become a part of lore. The only requirement for entry is that the idea, notion, practice, or whatever be nominated: some member of the community must claim that it worked, or seemed to work, or might work. Once this nomination is made—by formal publication, in a handout, or just in a hallway conversation— the item becomes a part of lore. No matter whether the nomination seems common-sensical, obvious, insightful, ludicrous—that children should write often, say, or that someone should read that writing, that it should be published, or that errors in it should be met with canings. The nature of a pragmatic logic makes disposition simple: once somebody says that it has worked or is working or might work, it is part of lore.

Lore's second functional property is just as important as this open-door policy, and no doubt equally curious to outsiders. It goes like this: While anything can become a part of lore, nothing can ever be dropped from it, either. There is simply no mechanism for it. Lore's various elements are not pitted against one another within the framework of some lore-specific dialectic, or checked and re-checked by Practitioner experiments, so that the weakest or least useful are eliminated. Indeed, lore can—and does—contain plenty of items that would, were they part of some other system, be contradictory: "Know what you want to say before you begin to write." "Write in order to find out what you want to say." "Never use the first person." "It's perfectly all right to use the first person." All Practitioners are aware, at some level, that what they know is chock full of such seeming contraries. What makes them acceptable, of course, is lore's experiential structure. Practitioners do not find themselves operating in the Experimentalist's neat world of dependent and independent variables, nor the Philosopher's dialectical oppositions. This place is messier; cause and effect are the objects of intuition, and shadowy at best. And in this messier world, experience regularly affirms seemingly contrary truths: What worked yesterday doesn't work today; what works in one class flops in another. That's how it is with arts, and there is never any accounting for exactly why. So it makes sense to keep around everything that *might* work, just in case. Indeed, for a pragmatic body of knowledge organized in terms of experience, the surprise would be that it did not embody such seeming contraries, not that it does.

The third functional property of lore has to do with the form of contributions to it—those made by Practitioners, but more importantly perhaps, those taken from other kinds of inquirers, from Researchers and Scholars. Because lore is fundamentally pragmatic, contributions to it have to be framed in practical terms, as knowledge about what to do; if they aren't, they will be changed. In effect, then, once a particular nomination is made the contributor gives up control over it: Practitioners can and will make it over in a way that suits their needs in a particular time and place. And not just once. Practitioners are always tinkering with things, seeing if they can't be made to work better.

Such tinkering with the contributions made by other Practitioners seldom seems terribly disturbing. Freewriting provides a good example. Peter Elbow's version of it in *Writing Without Teachers* is probably most familiar. For him, it is an absolutely non-stop activity, thinking on paper. At those junctures where the writer would ordinarily pause—stopping to reread what has been said, say—she is bound to keep writing, even just nonsense. Also, these writings are seen as part of a cycle. One reads the first such draft looking for a "center of gravity" that becomes the starting point for a second draft, which provides a basis for the third, and so on. In the model Elbow describes, the four hours that might produce a single finished paper by more conventional means here produces four drafts in succession.

But in practice, of course, this technique gets changed all the time: people will write more or less freely, but stop to reread what they have written; or they will insist on making careful sense, and so write very slowly; or they will use it only as a kind of journal writing, so that it never involves the cycle of successive drafts. In short, they will change what Elbow has offered to suit their needs. It may be that some Practitioners are purists in such matters, and so might object to such tinkering; but more of them, I think, being themselves rather used to the same sorts of transformations, would not.

Things are not so simple, however, when the contributions come from outside the Practitioner community. As I indicated in the Introduction, neither Scholarly nor Researcher inquiry is instrumental: neither is equipped to tell anyone what to do but only, to put it in epigrammatic form again, to suggest what things mean or what happens, respectively. Thus, even when (as we shall see is most often the case) the contributing Scholars or Researchers propose some practical implications for their offering, what tends to happen is that some or all of the contextual constraints that define the "imported" knowledge in its home community are ignored when Practitioners translate it into knowledge about what to do. A single example will serve to illustrate. In *The Development of Writing Abilities (11–18),* James Britton and his colleagues devise two classificatory schemes for assessing the 2122 student texts that constitute the data for their study. The first deals with audience, the apparent relationship between writer and reader. They developed four major categories: Self, Teacher, Wider Audience (known), and Unknown Audience. The second scheme delineates what they call "function categories," and its purpose is to distinguish "the principal functions of written utterances." Here they develop three major categories: the expressive (language close to the self); poetic (language as artifact); and transactional (language for doing business in the world).

Now, the purpose of the study was to describe the kinds of writing children do in school between the ages of eleven and eighteen, with an eye toward discovering some developmental pattern. In short, they wanted to know, as Researchers, what happens during those years. The rating schemes, then, were a device created to help with the description; specifically, they provided a set of "bins" into which a team of trained raters could sort those 2122 texts. For that purpose, they seemed to have worked fairly well, even though most of what the investigators learned as a result of the sorting did not necessarily confirm their expectations.[2]

The point here, in any case, is that although they are derived from an interesting and useful theory about the nature of language, these audience and function categories, as presented, constitute rating schemes, and nothing more: ways of sorting out a pile of papers, not kinds or genres of writing, readily identifiable because they contain universally recognizable features. When Britton and his team trained their "assessors," the people who did the sortings, they worked toward getting them to agree that when they were faced with certain textual features, or combinations thereof, they would classify a script in a certain category. That's all. And indeed, the length and specificity of their coding guides, and the relatively low inter-rater reliabilities their scorers managed (.682 and .635 for audience and function, respectively), suggest just how un-universal or non-generic those categories turned out, in practice, to be.[3]

But Practitioners have little need to do this kind of sorting. As a pair of rating scales, the audience and function categories are of little practical use: they don't tell anyone anything particularly useful about what to do. From a Practitioner's point of view, though, it isn't much of a jump from a rating scale to a curriculum guide—from a *de*-scriptive scheme to a set of *pre*-scriptions. Without any particular concern for the schemes' validities, then, or for the fact that in

Britton et al.'s sample, anyway, school writing turned out to be far narrower in its range than the investigators had hoped, so that most of the descriptors went little used, Practitioners have begun to assign "expressive" writing in their courses, or "poetic," or "transactional," and to assign these functions-cum-genres to be written for different audiences.

It is hard to say how much Britton and his colleagues are to be implicated in this development. Their last chapter ("Some Implications") rather suggests that schools would do well to conform more closely to the expectations embodied in their rating schemes, although of course they can offer no new arguments as to why that should be so. And I don't mean to suggest that this transformation is any great disaster, anyway. It has already shaken school curricula up some, and maybe that's a useful thing. Still, it is clearly a transmutation of the schemes as they were developed, and a good example of what can happen to Researcher or Scholarly knowledge when it becomes a part of lore.

☐

These three properties of lore are a source of considerable confusion and frustration for those whose loyalties lie with other modes of inquiry. They are especially daunting for would-be teacher trainers; judged against non-lore standards, Practitioners are bound to seem consistently undiscriminating, illogical, and sloppy. And yet lores in general, and Practitioners' lore in Composition specifically, are clearly very rich and powerful bodies of knowledge. I like to think of it in architectural terms, The House of Lore, as it were: a rambling, to my mind delightful old manse, wing branching off from wing, addition tacked to addition, in all sorts of materials—brick, wood, canvas, sheet metal, cardboard—with turrets and gables, minarets and spires, spiral staircases, rope ladders, pitons, dungeons, secret passageways— all seemingly random, yet all connected. Each generation of Practitioners inherits this pile from the one before, is ushered around some of what there is, and then, in its turn, adds on its own touches. Naturally, the structure is huge, sprawling. There are, after all, no provisions for tearing any of it down. Various portions of it can and almost certainly will be "forgotten" and "rediscovered" again and again. A wing abandoned by one generation will be resettled (and maybe refurbished) by another. And note, too, that there is nothing to rule out parallel discovery or re-invention, either; so the House of Lore has many rooms that look very much alike.

What I like about this image is the way it depicts lore's size, its absorbency, and the nature of its accumulated wealth and richness—

the pattern of lore's "progress." It also helps to illustrate the relationship between lore as a communally-held knowledge, on the one hand, and lore as individual knowledge, on the other. Thus, while we might say that lore has a shape, a front and back and so on, just where any Practitioner locates these depends entirely on where he or she enters, and on who—if anyone—does the showing around. There is no master plan, no controlling theory; each Practitioner's version of lore will have, as I have already explained, a unique experiential structure— will represent, to sustain the metaphor, a particular tour of the premises. In this sense, the Practitioners allow one another more individual latitude than any other inquirers in Composition. As in other communities, to be sure, members exercise some influence over one another, working to initiate the new or shape the old in various ways: methods courses, practica, in-service training, staffroom talk, articles, books, required texts, uniform syllabi, and so on. But whereas in other communities the greatest authority over what constitutes knowledge resides with the community—lies, in effect, with *public* knowledge—here it lies with the individual Practitioner, and *private* knowledge. The communal lore offers options, resources, and perhaps some directional pressure; but the individual, finally, decides what to do and whether (or how) it has worked—decides, in short, what counts as knowledge.

I don't want to exaggerate the practical extent of this autonomy. It is conceivable that a Practitioner could develop a teaching (or writing) style with minimal community contact—learn to write or teach writing in isolation from other Practitioners, more or less from scratch. It happens. Moreover, it is possible to become a Practitioner with little or no formal training. Indeed, despite some changes in professional preparation patterns, that almost certainly remains the norm. And, finally, nobody can tell a Practitioner how to approach lore's rambling potential—boldly, exploring every nook and cranny; carefully and cautiously, wary of deadends or other traps; or even reductively, finding a comfortable spot and staying there, refusing to learn any more. In all these ways, Practitioners can be said to be relatively free agents.

Nevertheless, the heart of the Practitioner community derives from a shared *institutional* experience. So, while it is true that each Practitioner's version of lore will assume a peculiar experiential structure, it is also true that for most Practitioners this version will be formed under conditions and circumstances that are widely shared, in the face of what are in many ways common demands. For although there have been and still are significant local, regional and grade-level variations in our schools, and despite the importance of proximity in determining influence on Practitioners— as we shall see shortly, lore is passed on mostly by talk and example, so that it tends to be most homogeneous within buildings, then districts, then regions, and so on. Still, to have taught writing in the United States over the past century is to have done so in the context of a really quite amazing institutional and logistical uniformity. Not only, then, must all Practitioners operate within a powerful set of what a colleague of mine likes to call "boundary conditions," constraints inherent in their art—so that, for example, they have been bound to pencil and paper as the primary medium of instruction—but a set of equally powerful institutional and logistical constraints as well, within an educational system that has become, for better or worse, increasingly uniform in terms of everything from teacher certification to curriculum to class size. To return one last time to my metaphor, these factors go a long way toward explaining why the lore of a nation full of Practitioners is a house—however rambling—and not a series of isolated settlements.

☐

Useful as the metaphor might be, though, lore is finally not a house, but a body of knowledge. And it is embodied not in rooms or wings, but in the more usual ways humans embody what they know, turning up in three primary forms: ritual, writing, and talk.

Ritual

First, then, are the rituals, those patterns of practice which acquire what amounts to a ceremonial status, and which get passed along mostly by example. They are easy enough to think of: the "Summer Vacation" essay; the codes for commentary; the assigning of modes of discourse; the position of the teacher in the room. Or consider what is perhaps the most obvious in a little more detail: the use of a red pen or pencil for commentary. Despite a good deal of bad press in the last few years, with all the references to "bloodied" papers, it would still seem to be the dominant choice. And yet few teachers, surely, have actually been told to use it, or forbidden, say, the editor's blue. Practitioners see it done, so they do it. It is part of the ritual, just one of many essentially ceremonial practices that drive and are driven by a mythic communal self-image: the weary but dedicated teacher, bi-focals on end of nose, cup of tea at hand, bent over piles of student themes long into the night, scrawling marginalia, coding corrections to some key on the inside cover of a handbook, marking in a meticulous script grades into the tiny boxed columns of the green, vinyl-covered gradebook—always in red.

And however much this mythic image and its constituent rituals may or may not jibe with who real, individual Practitioners are, or what they actually do, there are at least three good reasons for their durability. First, they form an important part of a Practitioner's identity, are the outward signs of community membership: When I do these things in this way, I declare myself a Practitioner. Second, these signs function for those outside the Practitioner community, too, providing much of the foundation for Practitioners' authority. Like the doctor's white coat and stethescope and palpitations, or the priest's vestments and gestures and incantations, these signs and behaviors acquire what amounts to a talismanic value. Students, their parents, administrators, legislators, and so on—these people have an investment in the Practitioners' mythic image, too. They need the piled papers, the red comments, the marginalia—need, in short, the rituals' ceremonial power.

Third and perhaps most important, these rituals also serve a logistical, practical function. Writing and the teaching of writing are activities as complex as any human beings undertake. All of what is involved cannot be articulated, let alone codified. Thus, a great deal of what one knows must not only be held but passed on as ritual knowledge: Nobody could ever explain all that there is to know or do, so we simply do as those before us have done. It is the way.

Writing

Obviously, a good bit of lore gets written down, too. The most public and visible of the writings are the textbooks, millions and millions of copies of them. As we shall see in Ch. 10, some recent commentators, most notably Richard Young and Maxine Hairston, have tended to treat these as complete articulations of what Practitioners know and do—the embodiment of what they most often call a "current-traditional rhetoric." In fact, though, while such books are clearly one feature of lore, they are far from identical with it. For the most part, they serve a catechetical function, and can be seen as an extension of the ritual power described above. That is, they provide the Practitioners' charges—students learning to write—with a simplified version of the articles of faith that purportedly underlie the literate community to which the students aspire. The grammars' drills on subject/verb agreement, then; the rhetorics' injunctions to be clear, unified, or concise; the readers' modeling of modes and styles—these represent lore formulated for one or another set of initiates, and they have approximately the same relationship to the full body of lore as the "Who made me?"/"God made me" sequences of the Baltimore Catechism have to the twenty-centuries old theology of the Catholic Church.

Hence, it isn't that these formulations are untrue, exactly. Rather, they offer, under cover of pedagogical necessity, a selective, simplified, inevitably distorted version of a far more complex body of knowledge about what it is to learn or do writing. They constitute a Practitioner's tool—again, with a certain talismanic power—but perform essentially as a kind of propaganda, one means by which to propagate the "faith" of literacy, as it were. This may be most obvious in the sorts of textbooks that have recently been so much under fire—*Warriner's*, for example, or the *Harbrace Handbook*.[4] Such books have traditionally prescribed the usages of the white middle and upper classes, for instance, and, insofar as they have dealt with it at all, offered an account of composing that is presumably "classical" in some sense, but that in any case seems to have little to do with how people actually go about writing. The confusions, contradictions, and complexities a fuller account of lore would require are not presented, nor are students encouraged to question what they are being taught, or why.

In reaction to this approach, other writers have offered other perspectives. One might look, for example, at Ken Macrorie's books, or Elbow's *Writing with Power* or Brannon, Knight, and Neverow-Turk's *Writers Writing*. Here, in more intimate, self-conscious personas, the monolith of correctness is recast in a less important form, and attention shifts to the act of writing. But of course the result is no less propaganda. The only difference is that an alternative set of political values is at work. To frame it in somewhat oversimplified terms, the "traditional" texts present writing as a matter of learning to conform, with an emphasis on decorum as a means of identifying individual with group; whereas the "non-traditional" books present it as a liberating activity, a means of defining individual as separate from group. The point here is that writing is necessarily more complex, and more variable, than either position can depict—encompasses both of them, and more. In either case, then, the users of such books are presented with proselytizers who differ only in their particular doctrinal allegiance: in short, with propaganda.[5]

Despite their visibility and considerable influence, though, textbooks are by no means all of written lore. One set of closely related documents is the teachers' guides which, while obviously limited in their scope by the approaches they are designed to help implement, are at least written for Practitioners, not students, and so offer a somewhat clearer view of lore than the textbooks themselves. In addition, a wide range of professional journals print varying amounts of Practitioner to Practitioner communication. *Exercise Exchange*, for example, is devoted exclusively to it; *Language Arts* runs a good deal. *College Composition and Communication* still runs a fair amount, although it has come to print less and less, especially over the past eight years or so (thereby promoting, I think, the emergence of alternative journals like *The Writing Instructor*). At the far end of the spectrum, journals like *Research in the Teaching of English* or *Written Communication* seem unlikely to print any lore at all.[6]

And last, there are the more workaday documents of the Practitioners' trade, the sorts of things the vast majority of Practitioners produce all the time: lesson plans, syllabi, and handouts; course, program, and grant proposals; and memos and notes of all kinds, including commentary on student work. Of all the written materials, these may be said to embody lore most fully and accurately. They reflect the knowing about what to *do* that is lore's essence.

Talk

Finally, though, the Practitioners' community is primarily an oral culture: Practitioners talk about what they know and don't know, about what they have done, are doing, and plan to do, all the time. They talk to one another, to their students, to administrators, to Scholars and Researchers, to spouses and friends, to anyone who will listen. They do so in all sorts of settings: in classrooms, of course, but also in offices, writing centers, teachers' rooms, hallways, cars, restaurants and cafeterias, conferences, restrooms, workshops. Whatever the value of ritual or writing, lore is manifested most often, and most fully, in the more ephemeral medium of the spoken word.

As is so often the case with oral cultures, this communal knowledge mostly takes story form. In a few instances, such stories may resemble the long, more or less formalized tales told and re-told by special storytellers—epics, as it were, that cast and recast essentially archetypal narratives, and so promote one or another version of the community's mythic self-image. Mina Shaughnessy, for example, seems to have played this role for Practitioner audiences, and her various versions of the Basic Writing story have become essentially apocryphal. By and large, though, Practitioner story telling is reciprocal: an exchange, a duet, not a solo; and sometimes, though not always, a dialogue. Listen to any group of Practitioners: I tell you what happened to me, you tell me what happened to you. The logic of such exchanges is, naturally, the experiential-associative one I described earlier: Something in your story—not even, necessarily, what you thought was central—reminds me of something I experienced, so I tell you about it. You are reminded in turn of something in your experience, and tell me; I tell about another experience, or reiterate the one already told with some variation, and so on.

That such stories should play a central role in the Practitioner community makes a good deal of sense. What better way, after all, to store and pass on knowledge about what to do than in the form of accounts of what has been or is being done? Hence, it is this talk that represents the community's lifeblood, its most vital essence. It is in these exchanges that lore is most alive.

Practice as Inquiry

We need to begin this section by defining pretty carefully when practice is and when it is not to be considered inquiry. The simple approach would be to say that practice is inquiry whenever it contributes to lore—only when, in short, it produces "new" knowledge. The catch is that in at least some phenomenological sense, Practitioners could be said to be facing new practical problems, and so making such "new" contributions, all the time. That is, they work with students who can be said to change from day to day, even hour to hour. The student for whom one prescribes a regimen of sentence-combining today is not exactly like any student ever assigned it before, and will not even be quite like today's "herself" tomorrow.

However, Practitioners themselves neither conceive of nor perform their work as though this were the case. For lore includes, as a part of its stock of common practices, beliefs, and traditions, a shared set of ways to perceive—to frame, if you will—situations. This should be neither surprising nor troubling. One of the usual purposes for any such body of knowledge is to make the otherwise overwhelming complexity of experience more manageable. That is bound to include not only organizing and limiting one's possible responses to situations, but organizing and limiting the range of one's possible perceptions of situations, as well. Practice is largely a matter of routine. Most of the time, then, Practitioners operate within the bounds of lore's known: they approach the matter of what to do by reducing the infinite number of potentially new situations into familiar terms, then handling them with familiar strategies.

As a result, practice becomes inquiry only

(a) when the situation cannot be framed in familiar terms, so that any familiar strategies will have to be adapted for use;

(b) when, although the situation is perceived as familiar, standard approaches are no longer satisfactory, and so new approaches are created for it; or

(c) when both situation and approach are non-standard.

A fairly dramatic example of (a) might be, as happened recently in our Writing Center, the appearance of a blind writer. There are other sightless writers in the world, of course, but Composition's lore is not replete with notions about what to do for them in terms of instruction. So far, though, our efforts have been to adapt our usual methods—which focus mostly on talk, anyway—to this writer's particular needs. We can find an example of (b) in any of the various approaches teachers have devised over the years in reaction to that inherited curricular chestnut, the research paper. The approach described by W. Keith Kraus in *Murder, Mischief, and Mayhem: A Process for Creative Research Papers*, for instance, gives students real unsolved crimes to work on via newspaper research. The problem thus remains the same—how to introduce students to these academic research activities—but the approach is new, the result of inquiry. As for (c), probably the most visible example is Mina Shaughnessy's *Errors and Expectations: A Guide for the Teacher of Basic Writing*, a book based on Shaughnessy's work at the City University of New York during the years following the advent of open admissions. Essentially, it documents her reaction to what she describes in her Preface as a kind of culture shock, a teacher facing students from backgrounds not only radically different from her own, but which would not seem to have prepared them in any way for college study. She needs to come to grips with this radically new situation, and to invent new ways to deal with it, as well.

How much of practice actually meets these conditions and qualifies as inquiry? I have no doubt whatever that the percentage is quite small. Working from my own experience, for instance, I would guess that for a full-load classroom teacher at the college level, handling something in the range of 120 students in three meetings per week, practice qualifies as inquiry less than ten percent of the time. The sheer logistics of this kind of teaching throw one back upon routine and ritual: a limited range of admissible situations to be met with a limited range of strategies. Under such circumstances, teaching is likely to become, at best, a craft—the ability to turn out a relatively high quality, albeit mostly uniform, product; and at worst, hack work, the rote production of work that is uniform only in its shoddiness. The time and energy required to respond to practice as inquiry are mostly devoured by the impossible numbers.

More favorable circumstances make higher percentages possible. This has long been implicitly recognized by organizations like NCTE and ADE, who offer guidelines on class size and teaching load that run pretty consistently below what many schools actually allow. But even ideal conditions don't guarantee that practice will qualify as inquiry all or even some of the time. Writing labs and centers, for example, are usually intended to provide individual attention that classrooms cannot. And yet there are many which operate strictly within the bounds of known lore, classifying students in terms of a fixed set of categories, then matching them up with some pre-designed instructional materials. Moreover, at the colleges and the universities where class sizes and teaching loads are usually the smallest, institutional priorities—in particular, a low regard, at least in terms of professional advancement, for teaching—undermine the chances that instructors will make the effort required to develop contributions to lore by this means. Indeed, the tradition in most large writing programs is to have teaching assistants do most of the teaching.

The irony in that practice, of course, is that the Practitioners in the best position to conduct inquiries are those least equipped to do so. You might think this is too harsh a judgment; that, since nearly all situations and strategies will be new to these Practitioner-initiates, they would be conducting inquiries all the time. But while this may occasionally be so, most of the time new teachers of Composition, like novices in any art, tend to operate timidly, teaching the way they have been taught. Piled on top of their own coursework, their teaching loads look as unmanageable to them as the full load of the high school teacher, and so they retreat quickly to whatever formulas they can find. And even when they are braver, opting for new ways of perceiving their students or experimenting with new strategies, their contributions to the community store of knowledge are most likely to be what I called in my "house" metaphor duplicate rooms: the sorts of things we are likely to characterize as those people need to learn the hard way. Such discoveries are crucial in their development, and important to the community as a whole, for they give lore the basis for a cross-generational resonance, a kind of depth. But depth is only one dimension, and a healthy lore needs breadth, too. Some part of that can come, as I suggested early on, from any source at all—guesses, notions, dreams, whatever. But most of it, and surely the most persuasive portions, derives from practice-as-inquiry; and for the bulk of that, the community relies on its more experienced members.

For the best of its lore, then, the Practitioner community must depend on those members who stay in the field long enough, under reasonably favorable conditions, and with sufficient motivation, to keep making their practice inquiry. These are relatively rare birds— people who defy the more usual career pattern: whose classroom successes don't lead them to become administrators of some kind; who don't "graduate" to teaching literature; who don't burn out in the face of impossible odds; and who resist the more substantial rewards of other kinds of inquiry—the prestige, say, of becoming a Scholar or Researcher. Many do it by combining activities. They are, for example, program directors who publish as Scholars, but who also manage to stay active in the classroom. And there are even some more or less "pure" Practitioners, too. Perhaps you know some:

professionals who get all the satisfaction they need from successfully practicing their art. The point here, in any case, is that making practice a form of inquiry is not easy to begin with, and that the conditions under which most Practitioners work make it very much harder.

□

In spite of these fairly grim odds, though, and allowing for adaptations to widely varying conditions, practice-as-inquiry does have an identifiable form. I have marked out six major steps:

1. Identifying a Problem
2. Searching for Cause(s)
3. Searching for Possible Solutions
4. Testing Solution in Practice
5. Validation
6. Dissemination

It would be mistaken to think of this as a neat, lock-step formula. In the first place, Practitioners are not all that methodologically self-conscious; this outline is my abstraction, not a feature of lore. Second, there is little pressure among Practitioners for anything resembling strict methodological uniformity. So whereas the Experimentalists, for instance, insist on replicability, Practitioners are satisfied with experience-based testimony. It helps, of course, if other Practitioners can relate to that experience. Findings that strike a familiar chord are likely to be more persuasive. But if I try something and say it works for me, that's the end of it. Nobody else has to try it for it to be accepted as part of lore.

So, while the inquiry of the Practitioner community as a whole can be characterized in terms of this pattern, individual investigations will play variations on it—change the order of these steps, vary their relative importance, or drop some altogether. A harried Practitioner, for example, may move rapidly through a trial and error sequence, entirely skipping any Search for Causes: from a tentative formulation of the problem to a possible solution, testing the solution, having it fail, trying another, having it fail, and so on until either a solution works, or, with possible solutions exhausted, the Practitioner has to go back and search for causes, reformulate the problem, or abandon it altogether. As we consider each step more closely, then, remember that the sequence represents a form, not a formula.

Identifying a Problem

All Practitioner work, inquiry or not, can be described in a fully non-perjorative sense as reactive: The Practitioner needs to decide what to do as a means to an end determined by someone or something else. Despite occasional claims about the intrinsic value of classroom activities, Practitioners themselves see their primary task as that of preparing their charges for some real or imagined exigencies (an exit exam, a portfolio submission, the next grade level, a college career, and so on) imposed from outside, beyond the bounds of their immediate relationship with the students.

Most of this work is, as I have already suggested, routine; Practitioners operate with varying skill according to what they already know. This routine generates a pretty powerful instructional inertia: Always pragmatic, Practitioners know that the best course is usually to stay with the tried and true. Hence, when Practitioners do identify a problem for inquiry, it is because that routine somehow fails them. Something in a situation creates a discomfiture and seems to demand a non-routine reaction: an ordinary situation seems extraordinary, or to demand extraordinary treatment, or both. In the classroom, for example, they are likely to react to something they see as amiss in student texts: the writing strikes the Practitioner as immature or lifeless; or it fails to "improve" after revisions; or there is not enough of it, and so on. Mina Shaughnessy's recollection of the origins of her *Errors and Expectations* dramatizes the moment of such an identification rather eloquently (invoking, it's worth noting in passing, an intriguing version of the Practitioners' mythic self-image):

> I remember sitting alone in the worn urban classroom where my students had just written their first essays and where I now began to read them, hoping to be able to assess quickly the sort of task that lay ahead of us that semester. But the writing was so stunningly unskilled that I could not begin to define the task nor even sort out the difficulties. I could only sit there, reading and re-reading the alien papers, wondering what had gone wrong and trying to understand what I at this eleventh hour of my students' academic lives could do about it (p. vii).

Naturally, events as institutionally cataclysmic as a sudden shift to open admissions are pretty uncommon, and the problems most Practitioners identify will be neither so grand in scope nor so dramatically motivated. In my own experience, for instance, this discomfiture has taken the form of a graduate student who, despite serious preparation, had been unable to pass her M.A. comprehensive exam in English in three tries. In another case, it was 30 students in an introductory literature class whose written responses to their reading were inexplicably detached from their personal lives. In both cases, I was, like Shaughnessy, led—or forced—to recognize that these were problems requiring solutions outside of my usual repertoire.

The process by which problems are thus identified, formulated, and refined obviously will not be uniform, but we can safely characterize its three major features. First, then, problems are usually not formulated with any great clarity or precision early on. Few Practitioners, even in retrospect, could summon the simple clarity of Shaughnessy's account. And during the inquiry itself, the process is usually both subtler and messier: far more a groping than a confident seizing, a muddling than a lightning flash of insight.

Second, it follows that however clearly the problem is articulated to begin with, it can and very likely will be reformulated as the investigation proceeds. Practitioner inquiry must be understood (to use a popular buzzword) as recursive: not a series of linear steps to much as an identifiable set of interrelated activities connected by a dominant but not exclusive sequentiality. Any of the other steps outlined above can not only affect the way the problem is framed and perceived, but even determine whether the inquiry continues or not—whether the problem is really a problem outside of my experience at all. A simple example: Suppose, in Searching for Causes with the introductory literature class I described above, I determined that half of them were functionally illiterate. Suddenly, the discomfiture I had identified with their apparent inability to relate their reading to their lives takes on a new form. It is superseded, in effect, by a new problem: that they can barely read what I asked them to read, let alone write about their responses. And this sort of transformation happens in practical inquiry all the time. Trying to frame one's shadowy and elusive sense of unease as a soluble problem is bound to be difficult, inexact work.

Third, and in keeping with the community's dominantly oral nature, the primary medium for this formulating and reformulating is talk—with colleagues, in particular. The object is to pin down the nature of the sense of unease by rendering it more and more articulable: "My students can't revise." "I don't have time to give each of my students adequate feedback." "My students aren't doing enough writing." Such talk isn't absolutely essential, of course. Writing can serve a similar function, as can reflection. Indeed, it may be that my sense of the talk's importance is distorted by its accessibility; in watching Practitioners at work, it is obviously easiest to construct a version of what is going on from what they say. Nevertheless, ten years of observation and participation lead me to be pretty adamant here: When Practitioners run into a situation that seems to fall outside of their ken, their first and most frequent reaction—*my* first re-action—is to talk about it.

When this talk is with other Practitioners, it comes as close as the Practitioner community ever gets to exerting the pressure over what ought and ought not constitute inquiry—pressures that are a regular feature of other communities. In the way that their reviews of the appropriate literature orient Experimentalists within their paradigm, then, or Philosophers within their dialectic, so this talk orients Practitioners within lore. When I come to you with my troubling situation, your knowledge of lore may cover this contingency that mine has not: "Oh sure, I had that student in my class last year. What's wrong is . . ." Or your response may simply confirm my own feelings: "Yes, that situation is outside of my knowledge of what to do, too." Then again, especially if you are what I think of as a really good Practitioner, you may respond with probes that help both of us define the problem more clearly: "Do you mean that the students don't connect their reading with their real lives, or only that the connections don't show up in their writing?"

You see the point. Our talk may lead me to discover that existing lore can handle the problem, and so scuttle my inquiry; or keep me on track, without real advancement; or keep me on track and, what is presumably better, help me move forward. I am not bound by these or any other responses. I need not, for example, worry—as I really must in other communities—that my findings won't be published if I should fail to follow your advice. Nevertheless, I think that in practice this talk does wield a considerable influence, bringing communal influence to bear on individual behavior, and—in that limited sense, anyway—making Practitioner inquiry more efficient.

Searching for Cause(s)

It is this step—or, more precisely, its relative location and importance in the process of inquiry—that most emphatically distinguishes Practitioner inquiry from other modes. After all, the inquiries of both Scholars and Researchers are, in a broad sense, geared to sift out causal connections from the chaos of experience: to *end* at causal connections, not begin there. For Practitioners, by contrast, the search for such connections is essentially preliminary: If information about the origin of an identified problem is going to help me decide what to do, I need to have it as soon as possible.

At the same time, because I am concerned about what to do that will work, and often have neither the time nor the inclination to figure out exactly why, there is a good chance that I won't take the search for causes all that seriously. In routine practice, of course, causes are part of the known. That is, standard problems are matched with standard sets of solutions. Somewhere in lore's past, causal connections may have been posited, but they tend to become vestigial. Practitioners need to know *what* to do, not necessarily—other than "It works"—*why*. This bedrock pragmatism is habit-forming. Practitioners tend to become habitually impatient with complicated causal analyses, which in turn makes them relatively cavalier about such analyses even for the purposes of inquiry. A causal connection, then, may be little more than a rapidly formed working hypothesis, a temporary bridge that makes the search for solutions possible. And in the end, no matter how extensive the search, causes, when posited, are not the end of inquiry, but only a means to that end.

This description of Practitioners' patterns of inquiry may not seem particularly flattering. We would probably prefer to think of Practitioners, or anyway of ourselves in our own practice, as more careful and methodical—in the way, say, traditional television doctors are: each student a unique individual with whom we become deeply involved, our inquiries eventually turning up some fundamental cause that leads us to an elegantly simple solution. Problem solved, case closed. And such an image is no doubt fostered by the accounts of Practitioner inquiry we see in print. So, for instance, Shaughnessy's *Errors and Expectations* has come to epitomize the practical investigator at work. Her prefatory question, you will recall, had two parts: What had gone wrong in her students writing, and what could she do about it? Plenty of writers have dealt with the second part; there are exercise books galore to attest to that. But no one had ever dealt with the first part in quite the way she did. Shaughnessy tries to discover, at unparalleled length and in unmatched detail, the *whys* for the peculiar texts turned out by the thousands of students she and her colleagues had to teach, and she claims to have found them. That claim is most reassuring.

We can see the same sort of phenomenon with a writer like Ken Macrorie. Indeed, admired as Shaughnessy has come to be, I expect even more Practitioners have been attracted by the clear simplicity of Macrorie's reasoning in such books as *Writing to Be Read*. There, for example, he identifies the problem in student writing that has motivated his search for solutions: "At times every young child makes memorable statements in writing or speaking. But as he advances in school, his language turns ever duller and emptier" (p. 2). Next, he looks for a cause for this progression towards dullness and emptiness, and finds it by a kind of deduction, determining what good writers do ("All good writers speak in honest voices and tell the truth" [p. 5]), and then deducing from that a kind of developmental model:

Part of growing up is learning to tell lies, big and little, sophisticated and crude, conscious and unconscious. The good writer
differs from the bad one in that he constantly tries to shake the
habit. He holds himself to the highest standard of truth telling.
Often he emulates children, who tell the truth so easily, partly
because they do not sense how truth will shock their elders
(p. 6).

The bad writers, then, must be those of us who succumb to this
learning to lie:

Any person trying to write honestly and accurately soon finds
he has already learned a hundred ways of writing falsely. As a
child he spoke and wrote honestly most of the time, but when
he reaches fifteen, honesty and truth come harder. The pressures on his ego are greater. He reaches for impressive language;
often it is pretentious and phony. He imitates the style of
adults, who are often bad writers themselves. They ask questions. So he asks questions in his writing: "Did you ever think
what might have happened to South Africa if the Boer War had
not been fought?" A false question. The writer knows most—
if not all—of his readers have not thought of this possibility.
However well meant—a false question (p. 6).

Problem: People write dull and empty prose. Cause: They have
learned to lie. What could be simpler?

The fact of the matter is, though, that while Shaughnessy's
psycho/social explanations or Macrorie's rather more glib developmental model contributes to what Practitioners claim to know about
the causes of problems in writing, neither is much good as a representation of practical inquiry in action. In both cases, hindsight, abetted
by the print medium, makes them too neat, strips them too much of
the clamor and chaos of the experience they purport to account for.
We have already seen that Practitioner's problems are hard to identify.
Once one moves outside the boundaries of routine formulations, it is
a struggle just to say with any clarity how we have been troubled in
reading a given text. Moving from there to explain what the causes of
such difficulties in the writer might be must be even more difficult:
How is a Practitioner to know what, in the infinite detail of teaching
or doing or learning writing, causes what? The causal chains Composition Practitioners deal with are of a kind very different from the
neatly definable clinical disorders a Marcus Welby faces. The simple
and elegant just don't turn up very often.

To get a somewhat more typical account of this search for
causes, then—albeit one still trapped, as it were, in prose—I want to
turn again to my own experience. The graduate student I described

above as preparing for her M.A. comprehensive exam worked with me for nearly 1½ years. To prepare her, we studied her failing exams, compared them to passing exams written by other people, had her write (and re-write) literally hundreds of practice exam questions, reviewed the material—in short, we tried every approach I could think of. I did identify what seemed to be a few significant textual patterns: answers developed in a form that reflected her progress through the text(s) in question rather than some conceptual or analytical organization; odd uses of critical terms; a tendency to not address questions. But these were symptoms, not causes. The real question was why: Why did she write answers in these ways? Exam pressure? Lack of understanding of the material? The genre of comprehensive exam writing? Or was she merely the victim of an unreliable grading system?

The instructional breakthrough seemed to come after about a year when, angry with me, and probably sick of the whole business, the student wrote a rather hostile analysis of Jonson's "To Penshurst." For the first time, her persona seemed to have the kind of authority that had been missing from all her other answers. And just a few months afterwards, she re-took the comprehensives, and passed— pretty handily, I gather. Why? What had changed? That shift in persona marked a significant turning point for both of us, but what exactly did it signify? That is, what cause or causes of her unsuccessful exam writing had our interaction, and her work, affected?

I saved everything she wrote, and I have her permission to try to figure out what happened. But I wonder how successful I can be. For all I know, she passed simply because she took the exam with a set of writers who made her look good by contrast. Or what if I am able to locate changes in textual patterns that I think are significant? Such patterns will not, as I suggested above, be tied to causes in any neat way; symptomatic changes in and of themselves are not all that revealing. But suppose that via this sort of retrospective analysis, I am able to make some causal guesses. The point here is that no matter how persuasive they are, they won't represent very accurately the half-formed guesses and cloudy intuitions that it seems to me I operated by as we worked together. I was making new guesses about cause on the fly all the time, and these would lead to new approaches. But we were both too bent on finding solutions to stop and seriously try to unravel the impossible complexities of just what was going "wrong." *What* to do had to take precedence over *why*. And this is the kind of cycle, played out rather dramatically in this atypically long and intense relationship, that I think characterizes Practitioner investigations: clear though they may be in retrospect, causes are seldom much more than cloudy, changeable hypotheses.

Searching for Possible Solutions

A practical investigation that survives to this point will have evolved from one of the original three motives for inquiry. That is, either a new problem will need to be matched with some old solution; an old problem will need a new solution; or a new problem will require a new solution. The most common form is the first. It's a logical consequence of what I called practical inertia: Practitioners will do whatever they can to stay within the bounds of the known. Even when what is clearly a problem demanding inquiry is forced upon them, they will try to handle it by turning to the same sources that inform their routine practice—reflection, talk, and written materials.

The search for new solutions to old problems is less common, though far from rare. The obvious difference is that the motivation for inquiry in this form almost has to be internal. For many Practitioners, it would constitute an almost profligate professional luxury; the pressures, and indeed, the urge, to be loyal to existing practices, even in the face of mediocre results can be overwhelming. And indeed, even when Practitioners do look for new solutions to old problems, they almost always remain pragmatically conservative. Great leaps to new procedures and the concomitant wholesale abandonments of old ways are simply too dangerous. Rather, they edge very carefully away from existing practices, looking for ways to introduce only as much variation as they think absolutely necessary. Earlier I mentioned the research paper, and Kraus's *Murder, Mischief, and Mayhem* as one variant approach. Such a book perfectly characterizes the tenor of most new Practitioner solutions. It does address the problem of student motivation by introducing so-called "real" research problems, but it is considerably less radical than, say, the "I-search" process proposed by Ken Macrorie in *Searching Writing*. And both of these seem more tame than the one that resulted in the widely celebrated Foxfire series, where "research" takes on an even more "real" meaning, with its large, goal-directed problems drawn from even further outside the academic context—framed in the students' community, not library books or newspapers, and where the results are actually published and sold.

The point, in any case, is that these approaches to teaching research writing represent increasingly daring departures from the more or less "classic" term paper tradition of historical, current events, or literary topics ("The Maginot Line," "Abortion," etc.), index cards, outlines, and bibliographical form. Even so, they remain very much recognizable variations on a single theme. Because they are so slow to change, Practitioners are sometimes perceived as being cynical or jaded, too little impressed by the variously presented

"breakthroughs" of other Practitioners, or of Scholars and Researchers. Some may be, of course. But what is more likely at work to
prompt such criticism is this pragmatic conservatism, a healthy skepticism that questions whether there can be anything all that new
under the composing sun; and which warns that, even if there were,
it would be folly to embrace anything too exotic, or anything which
demanded the rejection of too many other options. Sound practice is
not a patchwork of one-time guesses and far-out schemes. The House
of Lore may be rambling, but it's basically very sound.

All of which should go a long way toward explaining why the
third of the forms of practical inquiry—a new problem in need of a
new solution—should progress this far so very rarely. In many institutional settings, it has been and still is quite possible for a Practitioner to go through most of a career without being forced to face a
new problem. And when one does arise, every Practitioner instinct
will demand that it be solved with existing strategies. The cyclical
"Back to Basics" movements are a perfect example: when some portion of the population is perceived, for whatever reasons, to be less
than ideally literate, the first response is to run them through the
existing curriculum a second time—more slowly, perhaps, or under
some new constraints—but the curriculum will not be changed.

This kind of inquiry has been most likely to occur, then, at one
or the other end of the logistical scale. At one extreme, the new problem can assume proportions massive enough to break through both
pragmatic inertia and boundary conditions in the way it did for
Shaughnessy and her colleagues under open admissions. Here was a
new problem so dire that it threatened the very existence of the educational system and, perhaps more pertinent, the survival of the
Practitioners in it. Elegant though it is, *Errors and Expectations* is in
that sense the product of a desperation which, so far as I know, has
no equal in American post-secondary education.

At the other extreme are new problems presented in situations
where a Practitioner is able and/or encouraged to try new solutions.
The most obvious setting for this kind of inquiry is the writing center, where single writers can be given the kind of attention Shaughnessy gives to the generic needs of Basic Writers: the same long-term
definition of problems, the intense study of causes, the same freedom
to move outside of standard lore for ideas about how to proceed. A
good example of such an instance can be found in Mary Lamb's "Just
Getting the Words Down on Paper: Results from the Five-Minute
Writing Practice." Lamb finds that some of her students compose in
ways that seem to be counter-productive. In particular, they seem to
treat sentences as though they were, in a phrase she adapts from
Shaughnessy, "local trains, making many stops at jerky intervals"

(p. 2). She posits two possible causes for such habits. The first is that writers may be confusing speaking and writing strategies; since they can't take spoken words back, they treat written ones in much the same way. The other implicates drill work, which produces, she argues, rhythms and emphases very like the ones she observes in these students. After years of practice filling in blanks, or circling the correct word, or looking for misspellings, they have become accustomed to dealing with sentences in those terms.

Her solution to this problem is what she calls the "five-minute writing practice." It's simple enough. First, she sits down next to the writer, watching him write. Any time the writer stops, she asks why, and tries to discuss the reasons. As she develops some sense of which pauses seem to be productive and which don't, she begins to steer the writer, to "divert the student's attention away from the problems which are interfering with the writing" (p. 5). These five-minute sessions become a regular part of her tutorial routine, with the object of replacing old composing habits with new ones. The method is obviously still exploratory. Nonetheless, it represents what can happen: new problem, new solution, success.

□

I have said little here about details, about just how these searches for solutions, new or old, are conducted: Practitioners reflect, they talk, they read. How do they know what they are looking for? How do they know when they've found it? How long will a search for possible solutions continue? There are no simple answers to these questions. I don't think Practitioners *do* know, in any exact way, what they are looking for by way of solutions. They mostly expect to know it when they see it. They may know they have found it because it "feels" right—i.e., it makes sense in terms of their experience. Just as often, they will need to settle on something that may not seem perfect, but that will suffice; the presence of the writer demands that something be done. Thus a given search for possible solutions might continue indefinitely; but most often, some workable solution, some temporarily acceptable notion about what to do, will have to be accepted fairly early on.

As in any art, then, Practitioner inquiry is most often a combination of informed intuition and trial and error. In those terms, every attempted solution can be understood as a kind of probe, exploratory in the same sense as a painter's early sketches or a writer's successive drafts: ways of defining more fully the nature of the problem to be addressed, or of getting a better handle on its causes. And in that sense, no possible solution—however badly it fares in practice—can be deemed a complete failure.

Testing a Solution in Practice: Implementation and Evaluation

It seems as though this step ought to be the climax of Practitioner inquiry: At last, something is to be *done*. And I don't doubt that, insofar as they allow themselves such things, Practitioner fantasies here run along the same lines as the television doctor image I described above. My own favorites are usually some version of the miracle-cure scenario:

> Tommy is a chronic non-writer who can't compose fluently, seeming to get caught up all the time in what he is thinking, or in his fears, or in what he has already written. "Here, Tommy," I say. "Try just writing with this stylus on a sheet of paper with a carbon underneath so you can't be distracted by what you're writing." Tommy begins his awkward lefthanded scrawl, painfully hesitant at first, but then with greater and greater confidence; the music in the background—heavy with strings and French horn—swells. Sensing that he is becoming free from his crippling writer's block, Tommy composes faster and faster, obvious puzzlement giving way to broad smile. Tommy can write—and he likes it!
>
> An hour's worth of prose later, the two of us look at the six pages of scrawled under-sheet. The prose is a little wavy, the spacing not perfect—but it reads beautifully! "Oh, Dr. North, this is so much better! How can I ever thank you . . ."

Fantasies notwithstanding, though, implementing a solution in practice is less likely to be a moment of great exhilaration than the source of considerable frustration. However careful or thorough the inquiry that has framed the problem or investigated its causes; however sharp the intuitions that have guided the search for solutions; and however much the strategy has been tailored to suit specific situational needs—still, chances are pretty good that, one way or another, it will need to be modified further, or even dropped altogether. That such a solution has value as a probe can ease the frustration some, and seasoned Practitioners are perhaps most distinguishable by their greater patience. They have learned from experience that implementing a solution is seldom easy, and telling how well it has worked even harder, so that their tolerance for making adjustments is higher. But no Practitioner I know is fully immune.

These difficulties with getting a solution in place and then telling how well it works are obviously a result of the Practitioner's medium. Writers, either as individuals or groups, present a context for inquiry that is not only complex but unstable. The function of lore in routine practice, as I have already explained, is to frame both complexity and instability in manageable ways. Even there, of course, relatively few solutions work perfectly all the time, but failures are accounted for: if 10 out of every 100 students seem to get worse as a result of sentence combining practice, it's because they didn't work hard enough, or were handicapped in some way, or because such a result was to be expected. Whatever the reasons given—if any are considered at all—the point is that the approach itself is not faulted.

In practical inquiry, however, the investigator deliberately moves outside of that framework in some way, and so reopens her practice to both complexity and instability. Just getting the solution in place in the intended form can be troublesome. If nothing else, it will be new to the Practitioner, who will have to learn to handle it on the job. And even when the Practitioner is reasonably comfortable, there remains the considerable task of selling it to its prospective beneficiaries. Imagine yourself, for example, as one of Macrorie's students as he exhorts you to tell the truth in your writing, to shed the habits of lying you have acquired. Even if you understand his urgings, they may well run counter to everything you've ever learned about writing in school: What could such a man mean? What game is he playing? What does he *really* want? Surely many such solutions will evoke unexpected reactions just because they aren't business as usual. Introducing, say, the tagmemic heuristic to a novice writer is almost certain to cause at least temporary confusion. Introducing a radical degree of intensity to a freshman composition class—three hours of writing per day, let's say—will likely provoke anger and/or rebellion. We could multiply examples endlessly. It is just plain difficult to get people to do what you think is good for them, especially if what you ask them to do is new or unfamiliar.

As problematic as implementing solutions can be, though, evaluating them is even tougher. We have already seen how tentative Practitioners' causal analyses are bound to be. Evaluation poses the same difficulties. Among all the kinds of change that might occur in a given context, how is one to know which, if any, are the result of the trial solution? Lore provides routine practice with a variety of criteria for gauging change. The most common are the sort of text-based features described in many textbooks. These range from the very abstract and general to the fairly specific: coherence, unity, tone, attitude; length, neatness; number (and type) of misspellings, comma splices, unclear referents, confusing tense shifts, etc. They include the kind of spatio-logical criteria embodied in such notions as the five-paragraph theme: compositions arranged in five paragraphs of roughly equal length, the first an introduction with a clear thesis statement, three "body" paragraphs, and a conclusion. Some of these criteria, of course, have been pretty harshly criticized; in many circles, the whole notion of a "five-paragraph theme" is treated with derision, taken as a sure sign of a reductive conception of writing.

Even in routine practice, however, skilled Practitioners rely on a much wider range of indicators to gauge the effectiveness of their work, and these carry over into inquiry. Some of them are text-based, too, but they tend to be more subtle, more sophisticated. The popularly known criteria, catechetically reinforced by the textbooks, tend to treat writing as a simple dualistic code: a given usage is either "correct" or "incorrect," or a passage unified or not unified, clear and concise or unclear and verbose. In these terms, variations are essentially homogeneous—all "wrong," and more or less equally so. Seasoned Practitioners, though, learn to recognize in variation a more useful complexity, extracting from it information about the language habits of the writer who produced them: about development or dialect or rhetorical sophistication. Indeed, it was Shaughnessy's attempt to systematize her Practitioner vision in this sense that, more than anything else, makes *Errors and Expectations* such an important book. But this way of seeing writing was hardly Shaughnessy's invention. Practitioners have embraced her book for precisely the same reasons they embrace Macrorie's or Elbow's: because it strikes a familiar experiential chord. Before and since, with and without *Errors and Expectations*, skilled Practitioners have read their students' writing with the same kind of sophistication, seeing such features not as simple tests for determining which texts "have it" and which don't, but as clues about writers struggling in various ways to deal with a complex code. In gauging the effectiveness of their own trial solutions, then, these criteria—and this level of sophistication—inevitably come into play.

There are still other text-based indicators of change that might be explained as reactions to wholes rather than parts. Practitioners will talk about a student's or a class's writing as becoming "better organized," for example, or as having a clearer and more consistent sense of audience. In describing my work with the English graduate student, I said we both recognized her discovery of a more authoritative voice as a breakthrough. Such observations derive from reading, of course—they might be called in some sense "attributes" of texts, although the nature of their attribution would be a matter for considerable Scholarly debate. However we describe them, though, they are not qualities easily traceable to certain features in a text, or even to certain patterns of such features. Nevertheless, the authority of such judgments is very powerful: When I read my student's essay on "To Penshurst," I *knew* the voice was different. Under most circumstances, I think, skilled Practitioners will try to account for such reactions in terms the writer can best use, an effort that will almost surely involve textual features or patterns thereof, but they are seldom reducible to a simple accounting of such features. Certainly I tried in that case; doing so is a central feature of a writing center pedagogy, and the writer desperately wanted to know what I saw that she finally had got "right." But such accounting is bound to be difficult and complex. Despite their potency as indices of change, then, these more holistic responses tend to elude precise formulation.

And finally, Practitioners rely, to a degree that varies considerably with individual and situation, on feedback from the writers themselves: on what they say, on how they act. Here again, some signs will be more accessible than others. Writers may approach their tasks in new ways—take more time preparing to write, say, or produce two or three substantially different drafts. Or they may talk about writing more skillfully, making workshop responses that suggest a more subtle grasp of composing processes or textual matters. Much of the time, a Practitioner's "reading" of these changes will be as subtle as the holistic textual responses. No doubt there are identifiable "signals" or "stimuli" that might help account for such Practitioner judgments. After all, their "equipment" for making them is the same we all use in dealing with people, albeit sensitized for this specific purpose by training and experience. But what these signals are, how they are sent and received, even what their media are—these are not the direct concern of an inquiring Practitioner. So, for example, we could devise a Researcher investigation to search out one or more physical referents for a typical Practitioner expression like "I saw the lights go on . . ."—some combination, say, of eye contact, facial expression, retinal movement, and so on. The point here, though, is that whatever the findings of such a study, for Practitioner purposes what matters is not the parts, not a list of observable or measurable behaviors, but the whole: evaluation can depend upon whether the writer or writers "look" or "act" right.

When Practitioners try to gauge the effectiveness of trial solutions, then, they do so in terms of some combination of these textual and non-textual indicators. There is nothing magical in the process. Sometimes the trial solution will simply never get off the ground, will be ignored or rejected. It may have no discernible effect on the problem as framed. Or it may have some unexpected effect, either making the problem worse, or producing a beneficial effect where none was expected, as when sentence combining work has in some instances seemed to improve correctness. Most often, though, the solution will be judged a mixed success, effective at dealing with portions of the identified problem, less effective in other ways. Indeed, even when all indicators argue that the solution was a success—when, as in the case of my graduate student, both our intuitions *and* her passing of the exam argue that what we did worked—still, to the experienced Practitioner, the causal chain is not simple, and validation of any solution only tentative. Yes, I had adjured her to write with more sense of her own authority, and she did, and she passed. But I had also asked her to try many other things. Even more relevant, I had stumbled into making her angry—and maybe, by that simple accident, finally given her the kind of known adversarial audience she needed to create an aggressive persona. I see no way to know for sure what caused what. Whatever we did, it worked. As a Practitioner, I am satisfied.

Not surprisingly, the Practitioner community has always been most vulnerable to outside interference on this matter of evaluation. Those who have any stake in the larger society of Composition—the Scholars and Researchers, school administrators, and the general public—are all more willing to grant Practitioners autonomy in terms of the problems they define, the kinds of causal analyses they do, and the kinds of solutions they propose when it is clear that what the Practitioners do *works*. What these groups seem far less willing to grant, however, is the Practitioners' autonomy to determine, by their own means, just what does work. To accept the validation of practical inquiry—or, indeed, of routine practice—is to accept that Practitioners can see or sense or feel signs of change that outsiders, and even students, cannot: that things are happening that require both involvement and an appropriate sensitivity to perceive. That acceptance comes hard. Each group has its own bases for objecting. The Scholars and Researchers derive theirs from the methods of validation peculiar to their own modes of inquiry; the administrators and public mostly from their catechetical schooling in lore. Whatever their bases, the result is the same: a general erosion in Practitioner authority. It only makes sense. If Practitioners cannot be trusted as the best judges of what works and what doesn't, then they are not the best people to identify problems, either, or to trace causes—or, finally, to decide what to do. We will be dealing further with this erosion in Section V; by then other forces, other motives, will have come into play. But none of them will have a more central role in accounting for the decline of Practitioner knowledge than this matter of evaluation.[7]

Dissemination

Strictly speaking, Practitioner inquiry, like routine practice, could be said to end with Evaluation: either the solution works, in which case the inquirer goes on to identify a new problem; or it doesn't, in which case the investigation recycles (new trial solution, renewed search for causes, reframed problem) or is abandoned. In this sense, Practitioner inquiry is self-contained in a way that other modes of inquiry are not. Because it is primarily reflexive—geared toward directing the inquirer in what to do—it can perpetuate itself without recourse to community sanction. To become a part of the community's lore, though, inquirers must "publish" their findings in some way. Most such publishing, as with most Practitioner discourse, will be a matter of talk. And as with other parts of practical inquiry, this talk serves a reciprocal function. Not only does it inform the community about what has been done, then, but it helps the investigators assess it, too.

The various forms of Practitioner publication may be understood as ranging along a continuum. On one end is what we would be inclined to call the very informal, the talk most characteristic of Practitioner work in general—conversation in the hall or staffroom, over coffee in the cafeteria, and so on. Under most circumstances, this will be the most lor-ish form of Practitioner publication: experientially structured, pragmatically reasoned. It will also, in that same sense, be most powerfully reciprocal; the Practitioner's interlocutor(s) will respond in kind. At the other pole—in terms of oral publication, setting writing aside for the moment—are the highly formal, almost ritualized professional conference presentations. These will be least lor-ish. That is, their experiential structure will likely have been rearranged, so that events will have an abstracted linearity, problems and solutions neatly framed; and their pragmatic logic will probably have been distorted, so that solutions, successful or not, will tend to be presented as unambiguous. The resulting stylized monologue is also least reciprocal. Without the give and take of conversation, the investigator and his audience will have more difficulty creating or sustaining a shared experiential structure. Between these two extremes, of course, are a range of variations: discussions with supervisors, staff meeting presentations, in-service workshops, and the like.

Obviously the less formal kinds of talk are the most common; and they represent Practitioner knowledge at its most authentic. This is not to say that the formal presentations are of no value. At the very least, they represent an occasion for talking to colleagues in the audience about their work. Moreover, these stylized accounts of practice—like, say, the stylized versions of life we see on the stage or in the movies—can be entertaining, even inspiring. And if they manage to transcend the muddled details of workaday experience—well, they embody a more fundamental, again essentially mythic kind of truth. There is some danger, as there is for such forms in any sphere, that the visions they evoke will be mistaken for reality. For new Practitioners, especially, the Monday morning confrontation between visionary inspiration and who-shows-up can hurt. But those who survive, those who learn the lessons of pragmatism, manage to enjoy the vision with minimal pain: nothing they hear will sweep their world completely away, but they like a good story.

The most formal publishing option available to Practitioners, though, is to move out of talk altogether and into writing. I argued early on that the lore one finds in print could not be considered typical of either Practitioner knowledge in general or practical inquiry in particular. My reasons for that position should be even clearer now. As we have seen, a good bit of Practitioner inquiry will be conducted by beginners. This is surely essential work, and some of it will make its way into print—in local or specialized newsletters, for example, or journals like *The Gypsy Scholar*—but most of it will not, ending instead in practicum talk or seminars. We have seen, too, that textbooks represent less the results of Practitioner inquiry than a catechetical version of lore. And we can add here that many experienced Practitioners hold positions that don't reward written publication, or at any rate writing that deals with their practice in anything like lore form; or that they are too busy with their practice to stop and write about it; or that they are disinclined, for a whole range of other reasons, to concern themselves with writing for publication.

What's left, then, is the work of the writers I have been mentioning by way of example, along with that of maybe a few thousand or so Practitioners who have written with any comparable regularity or visibility over the past two-and-a-half decades. All of these writers, so far as I have been able to tell, make some effort to represent in their work both lore's experiential structure and its pragmatic logic. And, as I suggested earlier, it is the ability to do just that, especially in terms of the experiential structure, that makes writers like Macrorie or Elbow so widely accepted. Notions like Macrorie's learning-to-lie developmental sketch or Elbow's cooking and growing metaphor for writing work for Practitioners because they are grounded in a common experience and framed in the language of doing. We are certain we know what they mean—have written lies or worked through the cooking and growing.

But despite the efforts of these Practitioner writers, and their obvious influence, writing is, by definition, the medium least amenable to representing the results of Practitioner inquiry. Reciprocity, of course—the interaction which, like a gyroscope, serves to balance Practitioners in terms of structure and logic—is essentially impossible; this is the stylized monologue with a vengeance. The disclosure will inevitably drift away from the sharing of accounts of inquiry—the confusions, the tentativeness, the recursiveness, the muddied uncertainty about successes—toward a neater, more linear, more certain prescription. Moreover, the pressures to do so will be even greater than in the conference presentations. In the professional journals especially, but in books, too, Practitioners must compete for space with Scholars and Researchers, and write for audiences likely to be more diverse than a typical conference audience. The result is that written Practitioner knowledge very often gets presented with some of the trappings of Scholars' or Researchers' inquiry, with confusion on both sides over just what is being offered, and where its authority finally lies.

We have already considered one example of this in Shaughnessy's *Errors and Expectations*. There can be no question but that the book is, finally, practical. Its aim is to tell Practitioners what to do, and her authority rests primarily, I would argue, on our sense of her competence: We believe that what she did worked when she did it. But Shaughnessy goes to considerable lengths to track down causes for textual features, an effort far more typical of what I would describe as Hermeneutical than Practitioner inquiry. However valid or useful her explanations of those causes are—and I am inclined to say that her attitude is more valuable than any of her findings *per se*—that strategy has given the book a far wider acceptance among non-Practitioners than its suggestions about what to do alone would warrant.

Similar problems arise for the essays assembled in Ben McClelland and Timothy Donovan's *Eight Approaches to Teaching Composition*; I'll use Stephen Judy's "The Experiential Approach: Inner Worlds to Outer Worlds" to illustrate, but any of the essays would serve as well. As for Shaughnessy in her book, Judy's aim is to advise us about what to do. The essay tells what he believes about teaching writing and how these beliefs translate into what he does: workshops, assignments, class publications, and so on. And I find myself persuaded that what he does, when he does it, works. But while the essay's authority may be experiential and pragmatic, it tends to be framed in philosophical (or pseudo-philosophical) terms. So, for instance, Judy invokes the names of scholars and researchers from Composition and elsewhere: Piaget, Vygotsky, Langer, Jung, Britton, etc. He heads one early section "Major Premises." And this framework is based mostly on what he calls the "rubber triangle" of "thinking, experiencing, and languaging":

For most people, this rubber triangle is constantly growing and stretching. Every day the person—adult or child—has new experiences: seeing, tasting, hearing, reading, watching TV, and so on. Those experiences are internalized and in a language-based process synthesized to become part of the person's storehouse of experience. When one faces a new problem or concern, he or she draws on that storehouse and through the complicated activity labeled "thinking" (also a language-based process) comes up with "ideas" or "solutions." Finally, the person creates language about his or her ideas that both displays them for self-examination and allows them to be communicated to others. What gives this process its drive—its energy—is, first, that humans have an intrinsic need to sort through and understand their experiences, and second, that they need to share their perceptions with others (p. 38).

As we shall see in the next section, these tactics are very common among the inquirers I will call the Philosophers. They invoke the same sorts of names, use similar terminology, and raise similar issues. The difference here is that, given the title of the collection, and given the essay's overall reliance on accounts of his actual practices, Judy must be understood as being primarily interested in helping us to know what to do. Surely he does not present this "rubber triangle" metaphor as a matter for serious dialectical consideration, nor expect any serious response; certainly he himself never explores the complex issues it embodies. Indeed, far from providing a means of exploring those issues, it serves to package them, to hold their complexity at bay so that he can turn to practice. In that sense, the rubber triangle serves the same function as Macrorie's developmental lying model or Elbow's cooking and growing: these are lor-ish stories, parables almost, aimed at invoking a common experiential ground. The danger lies in the chance that readers—or writer, for that matter—will get caught up in the philosophical trappings, and forget that what he offers, despite those trappings, is not philosophy at all, but a kind of rationalization: an effort to make knowledge grounded in practice conform to the dictates of dialectical reasoning.

I don't want to lose the point here by belaboring it. Partly because of the medium, and partly because of pressure from institutions and other communities, when Practitioners report on their inquiry in writing, they tend to misrepresent both its nature and authority, moving farther and farther from their pragmatic and experiential power base. And the harder they try, it seems to me, the worse things get. They look more and more like bad Scholars or inadequate Researchers, and further undermine the public perception of Practitioner authority. Without question, the academic reflex to hold lore in low regard represents a serious problem in Composition, and Practitioners need to defend themselves—to argue for the value of what they know, and how they come to know it. For that very reason, though, they need to be more methodologically self-conscious than any of the other communities: to know the limits of the authority the other modes of inquiry can claim, on the one hand; but to know the limits of their own, as well, and work within them. In that direction, and not in any sort of methodological masquerade, lies the basis for a genuine credibility.

III

The Scholars
(Historians, Philosophers, and Critics)

III

The Scholars

In retrospect, it was probably inevitable that the knowledge-makers quickest off the mark to supplant lore as Composition's dominant form of knowledge should have been those who advocated the modes of inquiry clustered under this heading. True, the field's charter—*Research in Written Composition*, that is—may have ignored them; so far as I can tell, none of the 504 studies it lists would fit in this section. But the group claiming authority over the new field, you will recall, was primarily the membership of the Conference on College Composition and Communication. In the organization's early years, these were people who taught in and/or administered the freshman communications programs that had been its initial *raison d'etre*; and then, later, moving toward the early 1960s, their association was increasingly likely to be with a more narrowly defined freshman *writing* program. Whatever the nature of their programs, these were people trained in the traditions and methods of Western humanist thought. So despite the widespread faith in "scientific" modes of inquiry, it was only natural that this challenge to produce new kinds of knowledge about how writing is done, taught, and learned should lead some of them to fall back on that training, and turn to the Scholarly tradition and methods.

I have identified three distinct Scholarly modes of inquiry in Composition. The first I shall call Historical, and its users the Historians: those who work to provide a coherent past for the field. The second I shall call Philosophical, and its users the Philosophers, although their full title would have to be Philosophers of Composition. That is, while their effort, as for a philosopher in Philosophy proper, is to examine the nature of inquiry itself, their allegiance is finally to Composition and the nature of its inquiry. Thus, it is the Philosophers' task to examine the philosophical underpinnings of Composition. The third mode of inquiry I will call Hermeneutical, and its users, Critics. This mode, as the label suggests, deals with the interpretation of texts—is to Composition what the theory and practice of literary criticism is to literary studies. Just which texts are to be interpreted, for what purposes, and by what means are themselves among the key issues Hermeneutical inquiry faces.

These three modes belong in the same methodological cluster primarily because they share the humanist tradition's reliance on what can be broadly defined as dialectic—that is, the seeking of knowledge via the deliberate confrontation of opposing points of view. Also in keeping with that tradition, each is essentially text-based, although the kinds of texts they use, and the functions of those texts as part of the inquiry, differ considerably. We usually consider history in general a "first-order" kind of inquiry, defined at least as much by its subject matter as its method. That subject, the past, is sought within a body of texts, which provide a common ground for all Historians. They agree, that is, on the existence of those texts, but not on how they might be interpreted, on their significance. And indeed, to the extent that Historians can be said to offer a description of the empirical world—albeit a version of it as it was—they might be placed somewhere in the community of Researchers, much as History departments within colleges and universities seem to straddle the line between the Humanities and Social Sciences.

Philosophy, by contrast, is clearly a "second-order" inquiry, which has access to the findings of first-order inquiry, but has as its subject matter the activities of the first-order inquirers—in this case, the activities of Practitioners, Historians, Critics, the various kinds of Researchers in Composition and, of course, themselves. However, Philosophy never turns outward to "empirical" evidence to gather or test knowledge; it is, rather, the mind studying its own operations, the rational study of rational practices. For Historians, then, texts play two roles. On the one hand—and in this, they are like Researchers—texts are the raw materials from which they construct a portrait of the past; are, in some sense, the *objects* of study. On the other, texts (and the past they represent) can be, as for a Philosopher, not inquiry's object but its *medium*: various portions of, voices in, the continuing debate (or, for Historians, competing narratives) of which their own inquiries are a contemporary extension.

The Hermeneutical mode falls somewhere in between. It is probably best characterized, like History, as a first-order inquiry. It begins, as does Historical inquiry, with a text or set of texts, usually called a canon, to provide the common starting point for inquiry. And it is important—or has been important in most hermeneutical studies, although it hasn't come up much in Composition yet—to establish the authenticity and accuracy of that text or texts as physical objects. And yet, though one might therefore say that these texts are, as for Historians, the "objects" of study, they are not objects in quite the same sense. For a Historian, a text-as-object is a kind of evidence, a record—like the paleontologist's fossil—of some event in a series of events he wishes to understand. For the Critic, by contrast, it may be simplest to say that the text itself is, in some sense, the "event": that her concern is the relationship between that text and its writer(s), its reader(s), its language(s), and some version of the world (which includes, of course, other texts). Which of these relationships the Critic emphasizes, and by what means, are choices that are themselves part of the inquiry, and subject to later, dialectical scrutiny.

Three features of the methodological communities to which these modes of inquiry give rise are worth noting in advance. The first has to do with their collective size—or, rather, their lack of it. Given Composition's roots in practice, it is no surprise that there should be so many—a majority of—Practitioners; nor, given the relative novelty and scarcity of training in the requisite methods, that there should be proportionately few Researchers. But as I have already suggested, nearly all members of the field were trained, to some extent, *as* scholars, and yet there seem not to be very many more Scholars than Researchers. It may be that the explanation is fairly simple. In part, then, it may be that the traditionally low prestige of composition work in English departments will have encouraged even those who taught exclusively writing courses to spend whatever scholarly energies they might have elsewhere. Or it may be that the proportion of Scholars to Practitioners needs, in some sense, to remain small—that in any given academic society, it takes a great many people concerned about what to do to support even a few concerned about what the doing means, in a Scholarly sense. It may even be that, given the power of the image of composition-as-emerging-science, there is too little prestige attached to Scholarly inquiry to attract many recruits. Or, finally, it may be that most of those trained in that literary tradition, but who teach mostly writing, have translated what they learned about Scholarly method into a form they can use in the language and knowledge communities of their classrooms; that the mode of inquiry they were asked to master—the cycle of textual exegesis and dialectic—has become the basis for their practice. There have been some signs of an increase; as we shall see, the number of Scholarly studies, especially in book form, has grown fairly dramatically in the first half of the 1980s. Nevertheless, for whatever reasons, the Scholarly communities' active membership remains quite small.

The second feature, somewhat more problematic for my purposes, is the peculiar relationship between these communities and the others in Composition, especially the Practitioners. In their more regular academic forms—that is, as the disciplines of History, Philosophy, and Literary Studies (most prominently, although criticism obviously gets practiced elsewhere)—these modes of inquiry operate with a very powerful institutional insularity. Let me put it this way: Whatever role the American public might play in supporting scholarly activities, it does not look to those scholars for wisdom. It's a phenomenon fairly typical in our specialized culture. Historians write mostly to and for other Historians, Philosophers to and for other Philosophers, Critics to and for other Critics. Who but a scholar is likely to read Husserl, say, or Merleau-Ponty? These scholars don't operate entirely in isolation, of course; there is often a fair amount of exchange across disciplinary lines. Some of what they produce may be said to make its way into the larger culture, too: given our system of higher education, they will participate, albeit rather indirectly, in the training of teachers. And most ordinary citizens will study history in school, have a run-in with philosophy (although perhaps not until college), and suffer some exposure, however unwitting, to at least practical criticism. For the most part, though, these contacts can be regarded as incidental.

This has not been the case for the Scholars in Composition. For one thing, the society is on a much smaller scale. The "public" consists of the members of Composition, most of them Practitioners. And, no doubt in part because of that relative intimacy, they *are* willing to look to these Scholars for wisdom, for intellectual leadership, as it were. As a result, Composition's Scholars have never had much insularity, institutional or otherwise. Like their better insulated colleagues in the disciplines proper, they do write for one another; but they also write for, or at least very much aware of, an audience of outsiders, as well. The catch, of course—and what makes this situation problematic here—is that the presence of this second audience tends to affect the way that Scholarly inquiry is conducted and presented. This isn't automatically a bad thing. One might as easily argue that History, Philosophy, and Literary Studies proper have been corrupted by their insularity—have lost touch with reality by hiding in their ivory towers. Just the same, the situation in Composition is a tricky one, and part of my task in describing these communities will be to examine its effects on the nature of methodological authority.

Third and last, I think it important to point out that many of
the people I will identify here as belonging to one or the other of
these communities would call themselves by still another name:
Rhetorician. And indeed, much Scholarly work in Composition—
both early on and since—has made its way into the field under the
banner of "Rhetoric." The theme of the 1963 meeting of CCCC, for
example—that date once again—was "Toward a New Rhetoric." And
among the papers later printed (in the October 1963 edition of
College Composition and Communication) were these, presented by
as celebrated a trio as one is likely to find in the annals of Composition Scholarship: Wayne C. Booth's "The Rhetorical Stance";
Francis Christensen's "A Generative Rhetoric of the Sentence"; and
Edward P. J. Corbett's "The Usefulness of Classical Rhetoric"—
authors who also produced, as most readers will recognize, *The Rhetoric of Fiction, Notes Toward a New Rhetoric*, and *Classical Rhetoric
for the Modern Student*, respectively.

That Rhetoric should have been thus present as an influence in
CCCC is not surprising. It had, of course, been separated from literary studies as a discipline, and from most English departments institutionally, since 1914, when the "speech teachers" had walked out
of NCTE to form their own organization. The communications
courses launched in the late 1940s at the State University of Iowa,
Michigan State, and elsewhere were an attempt to reintegrate speaking and writing (and listening and reading) pedagogically; and the
organization to which they gave rise provided a context in which the
reintegration might occur in disciplinary and professional terms, too.
Somewhat ironically, the pedagogical connection rather failed. By
1960, the CCCC's Committee on Future Directions, headed by first
CCCC president John Gerber, was already officially emphasizing
"especially written discourse."[1] But the scholarly rapprochement
between Composition and Rhetoric had been made, and it has
proved quite durable.

What is particularly significant here, though, are the terms of
this rapprochement, and the way the Scholars who identify themselves with Rhetoric have insisted subtly but steadily on the distinction between the two fields. In common usage, the two terms are
sometimes used interchangeably: Rhetoric or Composition; and,
even more often, as a pair: Rhetoric and Composition (almost
always in that order). But for these self-declared Rhetoricians, that
pairing seems to represent a rather uneasy compromise. Difficult as
it has been to define Rhetoric in this century (indeed, trying to define it has been its adherents' major preoccupation), and however
institutionally diffuse its membership, they generally seem to prefer
to have it as their primary professional identification. James

Kinneavy's handling of the matter in *The Present State of Scholarship in Historical and Contemporary Rhetoric*—a book which he quite freely admits owes its existence in large part to the momentum of Composition—is representative. Writing on "Contemporary Rhetoric," Kinneavy cites "Rhetoric and the Teaching of Composition" as one of *sixteen* areas of interest among Rhetoricians. Hence, although he and most of the book's other contributors share Composition as a "major professional commitment," the message is clear: These are Rhetoricians specializing in Composition, not Composition specialists with an interest in Rhetoric.

I don't want to make too much of this semantic preference. I have not honored it here—have not, that is, labeled either this section nor a single chapter "The Rhetoricians." This is in part because the preference hasn't been shared widely enough; too many other Scholars—for instance Ann Berthoff and James Moffett, to name two I will feature—have shown either no interest in or even some aversion to it. Even more to the point, it is not much help methodologically. Rhetoric can be defined as an art to be mastered; or, as for these Scholars, the various manifestations of that art as practiced can be conceived as an object or field of study. But there is not, in this latter sense, any inherently Rhetorical mode of inquiry. As with Composition, any number of modes might be brought to bear. The Scholars I include in this section, then, are better understood as Historians, Philosophers, or Critics: those who seek knowledge about how rhetoric has been understood and practiced in the past; or who try to get at the theoretical underpinnings of rhetorical activity; or whose approach to textual interpretation has a rhetorical basis—in all three cases, of course, as such inquiries are relevant for Composition.

Still, I don't want to dismiss the preference altogether. The allegiance of Scholars like Corbett, Booth, Christensen, and Kinneavy; of Walter Ong, Louis Milic, Paul Rodgers, Virginia Burke, Winston Weathers, Donald Stewart, Frank D'Angelo; or, more recently, of Andrea Lunsford, Lisa Ede, S. Michael Halloran, C. H. Knoblauch, Robert Connors, James Berlin, and so on—their allegiance to something outside of Composition called Rhetoric marks a pattern we shall see repeated in other methodological communities. As new modes of inquiry compete for power in Composition, they need to prove themselves, and a chief means for doing so is to demonstrate their ties to some already legitimate academic enterprise. One such enterprise—and one that sells particularly well in English departments, where many of these inquirers have had to worry about their academic survival—is Rhetoric. Whereas Composition is conceived of pretty narrowly, usually as "mere" practice, Rhetoric is not only the crown of the classical trivium, but can arguably claim a tradition as deep and rich, maybe deeper and richer, than poetics. It is also concerned with practice, yes; but here it will more often be called *praxis*, which not only seems to have a broader and deeper intellectual resonance, but—well, to put it at its most cynical, *sounds* better, more scholarly, too. In short, Rhetorical inquiry into Composition may not be exactly mainstream literary studies. It may be hard, in fact, to say just what it is, or what the pairing of Rhetoric and Composition actually represents. No matter: Whatever it is, it stands as a more legitimate intellectual enterprise than just plain Composition.

We will see some form of this power-by-association in nearly all of these methodological communities. Investigators will claim philosophical ties, or hermeneutical, psychological, sociological, anthropological ones, and so on. Most of the time, the association holds benefits for both fields. So even though, in this particular pairing, Rhetoric may actually stand to gain the most—its current revival stemming in large part from this interest in writing—it has been good for Composition, too. It *does* sell in English departments, and so has provided Composition with some knowledge-making leverage there. At the same time, the kind of reluctance demonstrated by these Rhetoricians, their unwillingness to give up what might be called their dual citizenship—or, perhaps more accurately, their resident-alien-in-Composition-status—suggests a division of loyalty that does not bode well for Composition. In it may lie, as we shall see in Section V, the seeds of the field's dissolution.

3

The Historians

The Historian community in Composition grows out of the demand for a kind of knowledge that must be natural in any new field, knowledge about who and what has come before. Early on—that is, with what I shall refer to as the first generation of Composition Historians[1]—this impulse tended to emphasize, in a fairly narrow way, what might be called pedagogical history: the recovery and preservation of teaching practices from the past, and particularly those practices embodied in what is usually called the "classical" tradition, the body of Greco-Roman thought dominated by Aristotle, Plato, Cicero and Quintilian, but also traceable in its influence through the Middle Ages, Renaissance, and so on to the present. The paper I mentioned earlier from the 1963 meeting of CCCC, Edward P. J. Corbett's "The Usefulness of Classical Rhetoric," gives us a sense of the agenda for such inquiry:

> I do not claim that classical rhetoric will solve, once and for all, the manifold problems of the composition course, and I will not be trapped into the *non-sequitur* that because classical rhetoric had a long and honorable tradition it must be the best system ever devised for teaching students how to compose a discourse. But perhaps it deserves a chance to prove what it can do for our students. I imagine that some of you are chilled to the very marrow of your bones at the mere suggestion of a return to such a rigorous, disciplined system. But hasn't the cult of self-expression had a fair chance to prove itself in the classroom? How many creative writers have we produced? If we discover a

creative genius in our class, let us by all means give him free rein. But what most of our students need, even the bright ones, is careful, systematized guidance at every step in the writing process. Classical rhetoric can provide that kind of positive guidance. As F. R. Leavis has said, "Opportunities far from ideal are worth making the most of" (p. 164).

This kind of work is epitomized, and may well have reached its peak, in Corbett's own book, *Classical Rhetoric for the Modern Student*, but it can be found elsewhere: Richard E. Hughes' "The Contemporaneity of Classical Rhetoric"; Gayle B. Price's "A Case for a Modern Commonplace Book"; James C. Raymond's "Enthymemes, Examples, and Rhetorical Method"; Frank D'Angelo's "The Evolution of the Analytic *Topoi*: A Speculative Inquiry," and so on.

Strictly speaking, of course, these studies qualify only marginally as Historical inquiry; or, to put it more fairly, they represent only a relatively minor branch of the primary inquiry that is the history of Rhetoric. Writing *per se* simply was not a major concern of the rhetorical tradition, especially in this classical lineage, so that nearly all of these borrowings have had to be adapted for a different medium; notice even Corbett's caution in the passage above, where he uses the locution "compose a discourse." Moreover, in these studies anyway, the investigators tend, quite appropriately, to be less concerned with making major original contributions to any particular history—Rhetoric's or Composition's—than with making the already established findings of such inquiry accessible to a Composition audience.

Still, these efforts to recover a past for the new field have given rise, I think, not only to a more authentically Historical inquiry, but to one that, while not entirely divorced from Rhetorical history, nevertheless treats Composition as a movement worthy of study in its own right. The second generation of Historians, as it were, then, has focused more on what can be called Composition's *institutional* history. That is, instead of treating historical materials as sources of potentially useful practices, these investigators have begun to try to account for the political, economic, educational, and other forces that have affected writing instruction, especially (although not exclusively) in the United States, and for the most part since 1800.

It is a tribute to Corbett's intellectual vitality, although perhaps not all that surprising—his dissertation, after all, was on Hugh Blair, a major eighteenth-century figure—that he has had some impact here, as well, with studies on John Locke and John Henry Newman. But his influence has been exercised even more through his students— Robert Connors, Lisa Ede, and Andrea Lunsford, to name the three most prominent. And, in fact, a second figure from Composition's early days rather better prefigures this new emphasis: Albert Kitzhaber and, more specifically, his 1953 dissertation, "Rhetoric in American Colleges 1850-1900." It is Kitzhaber's study, for example, that James Berlin cites (along with Warren Guthrie's series in *Speech Monographs*, "The Development of Rhetorical Theory in America, 1635-1850") as having been of special usefulness for his monograph, *Writing Instruction in Nineteenth-Century American Colleges.* And that same influence, direct or indirect, can be seen in a number of other studies, too: John Michael Wozniak's *English Composition in Eastern Colleges 1850-1940*; Robert Connors' "The Rise and Fall of the Modes of Discourse"; Andrea Lunsford's "Essay Writing and Teachers' Responses in Nineteenth Century Scottish Universities" or Winifred Horner's "Rhetoric in the Liberal Arts: Nineteenth Century Scottish Universities"; Donald C. Stewart's edition of Fred Newton Scott's "Rhetoric Rediviva," and his further studies on the Scott era, "Two Model Teachers and the Harvardization of English Departments" and "The Status of Composition and Rhetoric in American Colleges, 1880-1902: An MLA Perspective"; Patrick Scott's "Jonathan Maxcy and the Aims of Early Nineteenth-Century Rhetorical Teaching," and so on.

All told, in two decades of inquiry, Composition's Historians have had some trouble getting underway; the body of work produced is not all that large, and much of it has emerged in pretty small pieces, appearing here and there, in fits and starts. But it has gradually gained momentum, so that over the past five years or so—since 1981, say, when Robert Connors' Braddock Award-winning "The Rise and Fall of the Modes of Discourse" appeared in *College Composition and Communication*, that pattern has been changing. More and more often, issues of professional journals like *College Composition and Communication* or *College English* or *Rhetoric Review* will feature one or more pieces of Historian inquiry. Equally significant has been the first appearance of longer studies, like Berlin's and Wozniak's and collections like Connors, Ede, and Lunsford's *Essays on Classical Rhetoric and Modern Discourse* and Murphy's *The Rhetorical Tradition and Modern Writing.* Not all of the essays in these latter two books are Historical inquiry—as their titles suggest, they are part of Rhetoric's effort to take advantage of Composition's current popularity—but enough are to make them important symbols of Historian momentum. How long this blossoming of Historical inquiry will last is hard to say. But for now, at any rate, a coherent history of Composition has begun to emerge.

The Nature of Historical Knowledge

Historical knowledge—I'll call it history, to keep things simple—
is fairly familiar to most of us, and so may not seem as exotic, as
huge or random or formless as Practitioner's lore. Its internal structure is a familiar and comfortable one: a narrative, a kind of story.
In the most basic sense, it is an account of how "events"— a term
that will have to serve here as a catch-all—have followed one another
in time. And at this most basic level, there is likely to be little disagreement among Historians about temporal sequence: Socrates'
work precedes Aristotle's, which precedes Quintilian's, which precedes Aquinas's; Campbell precedes Whately, who precedes Day, and
so on. This isn't always the case—one thinks of attempts to connect
the Plagues cited in Genesis with various geological phenomena, or
cases of debated authorship—but such disputes have not so far been
significant in Composition, and in any case are not always solvable
by Historian inquiry.

But a history is more than a catalogue of events in an agreed-
upon temporal order. The events of which it is constituted must be
connected, too: A history must follow a chrono-logic. At this
second level, of course, there is nothing close to unanimity among
Historians. Socrates precedes Aristotle, but what was the former's
influence on the latter? Do the Dialogues offer us an account of
what Socrates said, or are they just a convenient frame for Plato, a
way of gaining some authority for his work? And can we know what
Aristotle means in his Rhetoric? Can we trace the etymologies of
what seem to us to be his key terms, and make sense of them in
terms of Athenian culture? Can we determine how important his
rhetoric was in his time, as compared to, say, the rhetorics of various
Sophists? What, if anything, can be inferred about its relationship to
practices? These kinds of questions are inescapable in Historical inquiry because history must make sense, must be made to hang together by an infinitely complex web of cause/effect relationships.

There are thus two sets of fairly well established rules for introducing contributions to this narrative. One set deals with the
introduction of new events. For this purpose, a Historian needs
textual evidence of some kind—anything from carved tablets and
papyri to textbooks, diaries, lesson plans, old themes, newspaper
accounts—to support her claim for the occurrence of the event.
Obviously, some kinds of evidence are better than others (primary
vs. secondary sources, e.g.), and corroborative evidence is important
as well. It is in response to these rules that, as I suggested above, the
method of the Historian is closest to that of various Researchers: it
requires a tangible, physical record of some phenomenon from which

to begin. Of course, the direction of inquiry is never simply from "found" texts to interpretation. Indeed, a Historian might posit the occurrence of an event without or with only very weak textual evidence because the logic of his interpretation of events before and after seems to demand it, much as an astronomer predicts the discovery of a new planet by studying the behavior of other celestial bodies. This predicting may intensify the search for textual evidence in an effort to settle the matter, one way or another, but the event is still not granted full status. I know of no such prediction in Composition; but a former mentor of mine, a Chaucer scholar, was certain that Chaucer wrote in French—he was, after all, a court poet, and French was the language of the court. It was, and remains, an exciting idea, but there is as yet no sufficient textual evidence to support it.

The second set of rules, however, deals with the introduction of new or alternate connections between events: variant interpretations of the significance of some one event within the narrative, for example; or a new perspective on some whole section of the narrative in light of some new event. Here the method of the Historian more closely resembles that of the other Scholars, because a version of Scholarly dialectic takes over. In theory, I suppose, any connection or interpretation, however implausible or unlikely, could—as with practices in lore—be offered. But whereas in lore all nominations are accepted, in history all are at least potentially challengeable: the community has to agree that, in light of available evidence, the interpretation makes sense. The inquiry of practiced Historians, then, is usually constrained to some extent by what they expect their community will find unacceptable.

The Historian community is not, though, paradigmatic in the way that Thomas Kuhn suggests a natural science community might be. One version of the narrative, *the* history, does not hold sway and direct the work of "normal" history until it is overturned by accumulated anomalies. Quite the contrary: it is not only acceptable, but desirable—even necessary—that competing versions of the narrative be represented. The necessity for such opposition may not be so clear yet in a field as new as Composition. With so much territory still relatively unexplored, the inquiry so far has often in fact resembled early natural science research, with the emerging narrative confronted at every turn by events and texts that have not been dealt with before: the writings of and about a Fred Newton Scott, for example, or a Jonathan Maxcy. These pop up like anomalous phenomena, demanding a restructuring of the narrative without the immediate need for dialectic. But the number of such texts is presumably finite, and when they have been pretty well assembled, the making of Composition's history will by no means be over. At that point, dialectic will take over as its primary driving force.

There can be and are, of course, more or less dominant versions of the narrative, and those who hold them may acquire vested interests in their "rightness." It follows, as well, that competing versions will not always be welcomed by this establishment with open arms; the comforts of academic or communal prestige will compete with the rewards of inquiry. Again, though, because Composition is relatively new, there has been little major dissension of this kind. For the most part, then, indications so far suggest that for Composition's Historians the making of history, like the making of philosophy or textual criticism, is conceived as a never-ending debate, a cycle of interpretation and re-interpretation that does not stop even when no new events are forthcoming.

Historical Inquiry

Historical inquiry, reflecting these two sets of rules, might be said to be of two kinds, or to take place in two stages, the empirical and the interpretive. In the empirical stage or kind of inquiry, the Historian seeks simply to establish the "facts"—I use the term advisedly—from which she will work: to assemble and validate the texts which represent the events with and around which, in the interpretive stage, she will create a narrative. Obviously, the two stages are intimately connected, and not necessarily or neatly sequential. Interpretations are limited by the body of available texts, and the search for further texts—as in the example of my Chaucerian colleague—is as often as not guided by the needs of interpretation. With that interconnectedness in mind, we can represent the outline of Historical inquiry like this:

1. Identifying the Problem
   EMPIRICAL STAGE
2. Identifying Relevant Texts
3. Searching for Relevant Texts
4. Assembling and Validating Relevant Texts
   INTERPRETIVE STAGE
5. Seeking Pattern(s) in Texts
6. Explaining the Pattern(s): Creating a Narrative
7. Relating New Narrative to Existing Narratives: The Communal Dialectic
8. Dissemination to a Wider Audience

Identifying Problems

All Historical problems can be said to arise in the context of the overall narrative, out of some perceived gap or error in the history itself. One might almost expect that, as with other kinds of stories, Historians would simply begin at the beginning (whenever that might be) and work their way toward the present. But these Historians are not, of course, entirely autonomous—they are Historians of Composition. Part of their responsibility as members of that society is to emphasize those features of the field's history that they think both the other members of the society—the Practitioners, Researchers, and other Scholars—and those with whom that society deals—students, parents, school administrators, and so on—need.

Since Composition is a new field, there is a sense in which its Historians have been faced with nothing but gaps. As I have suggested, early inquiry was directed mostly by the needs of Practitioners—although one might also argue, I suppose, that in returning to classical Rhetoric, early investigators were also obeying an instinct to start at the beginning. Problems were cast as one or another version of "How did classical (Medieval, Renaissance, etc.) Rhetoric conceive and handle the problem of _____ ?"—a question to which Corbett's textbook is probably the fullest and most elegant answer. As I have also suggested, however, problems framed in this way lead to inquiry that is only marginally Historical, more often producing popularizations and/or adaptations from, rather than contributions to, a communal narrative.

The movement from what I have called pedagogical to institutional history, then, represents an important shift especially in terms of how problems for inquiry have been framed. As much as anything, this shift seems to be a function of a growing sense of authority—in the Historian community, which had grown somewhat larger, and in the field as a whole. The earlier form of inquiry, I think, reflects the low professional self-image that is part and parcel of the devaluation of lore: "Our present knowledge is dim and uncertain. Let us find models from a Golden Age that we might emulate them." There are still some elements of this self-image in the inquiry of the second generation—a tendency to create hero-figures, for example—but they have been somewhat muted. And coming to replace them are signs of an emerging critical self-consciousness that could only survive in a community more confident about its professional identity. The new question, then, has become something like this: "What has Composition been that it is what it is now?"—or, in its more pointed form, "Who have we been that we are who we are now?"

EMPIRICAL STAGE (Identification, Search, Assembly)

This portion of a Historian's work ought, I think, to be familiar enough in at least rough outline to most readers from their own research writing. The only actual account of it I have found in Composition is a very useful piece by Robert Connors called "Historical Inquiry in Composition" (delivered at CCCC, New York, 1984).[2] Here he outlines what I am calling Identification, Search, and Assembly:

> For a recent project on handbooks, for instance, it was important that I be aware of all important composition handbooks prior to 1940 or so. In order to do this I had to search all the library stacks under three different LC [Library of Congress] and Dewey classes, then supplement the resulting list of handbooks by cross-checking all author's names in the *NUC* [*National Union Catalog*], by doing call-number searches on the OCLC computer system, by searching the advertisements, "new books" lists, and book review pages of educational and NCTE journals going back to 1880. I then had to use the Inter-Library Loan system to get my hands on books that I needed to see. (There is no substitute for having a book in your hands.) [p. 16]

The major limitation in terms of how the community in general has handled this work so far is simply logistical: the body of materials so far assembled is pretty small, and Historians have yet to look all that hard for more. On just this issue, Connors points out Susan Miller's argument in "Is There a Text in This Class?" (a deliberate play on Stanley Fish's book of the same title) to the effect that most Historical inquiry to date, based as it has tended to be on textbooks and related published materials, has been more the history of publishing practices than of classrooms. Connors concedes the point, but contends that the *annales*-style inquiry Miller implicitly calls for cannot be usefully undertaken until "after the major currents of the age—important figures and theories—have been mapped out" (p. 11). But he wonders too, even after those major currents have been made clear, whether the kinds of materials one would need for such an approach can be found. Student texts, syllabi, assignments—these are not easily accessible, if they exist at all. Thus he ends up arguing that textbooks are, perforce, a Historian's "best reflection . . . of what was actually taught as the subject matter of composition, because *to do so was always their generic purpose*" (p. 15, his emphasis).

It remains to be seen how accurate an assessment this turns out to be. From the standpoint of standard library-based research, of course, it is probably pretty sound; even textbooks, as Connors points out, have not been a prime item in many collections. But there is little evidence as yet to suggest that Composition's Historians have tried other avenues: private collections, small town or school libraries, attics and garages; or the people themselves, teachers and students, either for written or oral material. Obviously there are students and teachers from such classes for at least as far back as fifty years, all of whom, to judge from published work, have gone untapped as resources. This is not a complaint about work done so far; the published and accessible sources have really only begun to be dealt with. But I think Susan Miller's observation is a good one; for Composition's history to be as good as it can be will demand a broader textual base.

Validation

Once the Historian has these materials in hand, he can begin the process that Connors calls, in keeping with traditional historian usage, "internal criticism":

> Internal criticism examines the sources with the intent of making sure that they're understood correctly. The historian must check the language and usage of sources to prevent misreading, eliminate corruptions or glosses, try to enter into the worlds and minds of the writers of her sources. For the handbook project, for instance, I had to make certain that I understood what the word "correctness" meant in 1870 and what it meant—something quite different—in 1915. I had to decide which of the books I had uncovered *were* genuine handbooks and which were something else—grammar books, or usage debates, or some other sort of text. I had to study the development of the term "grammar." I had to try to validate Albert Kitzhaber's contention that Edmund Wooley's *Handbook* of 1907 was the first composition handbook, and I had to attempt to understand whether all of A. S. Hill's talk about the "illiteracy" of American boys in 1890 would seem valid to us today. I had, in short, to study all my sources carefully in order to understand them correctly (pp. 16–17).

Validation covers roughly the same territory as "internal criticism." Sources must be examined to determine if they are what they promised to be—in this case, handbooks, and not something else. They must be examined to see that they are authentic, that the printed words are those of the reputed author, published at the reputed date. So, for example, a Historian may try to fix or authenticate the date of some text by referring to agreed-upon etymological data, or to substantiate claims about authorship by seeking references or stylistic patterns in the text that could tie it to other work in which date or authorship were better established. And it might include the checking of claims—like Kitzhaber's—about the textual corpus being studied, so long as they were judged to be empirically verifiable. Where Validation and internal criticism seem not to overlap, though—and this may be just a matter of loose or romantic phrasing on Connors' part—is in this matter of his entering "the worlds and minds of the writers" of his sources; and then, as a part of that process, trying to understand the meanings of what appear to be key terms (terms whose importance, in the case of Connors' study, seem to derive from their relevance—by whatever means that gets defined—for the present) as they may have been meant by the author (or read by the audience?). Establishing that "correctness" was a term current in both 1870 and 1915, trying to establish the breadth and variation of its usage in printed sources—these are legitimate concerns for Validation, rather like establishing the value of the dollar for the same period by examining records of what it might buy. But entering "worlds and minds"—imagining, as it were, what it felt like to have or spend such a dollar—these are better understood not as empirical, but as interpretive activities.

INTERPRETIVE STAGE

Searching for Patterns

Like all other forms of inquiry, historical inquiry is essentially a search for patterns that can be deemed meaningful—in this case, patterns of some kind(s) of features in the texts regarded as evidence of some events. In the Connors study we've been following, then, he had to sit down with all those textbooks and read them, searching for an identifiable pattern in some set of features: Do the textbooks get longer? Shorter? Do items appear, then disappear, then reappear again? Do they contain only usage and grammar prescriptions, or rhetorical advice, as well? Are there changes in the way they address students? The number of both features and patterns that might be examined is theoretically infinite, assuming the inquirer is willing, for instance, to examine the textbook writers' uses of each word, or search through every appearance of each letter searching for signs of wear in type fonts. And if such features of the handbooks seem not to change at all? That, of course, would be a pattern to be noted and explained, too.

It should be obvious, of course, that the investigator will always approach the assembled materials with some predisposition—explicit or implicit—about which sorts of features to look at and, too, about the kinds of patterns he expects to find; and that predisposition will inevitably affect not only what kinds of features he emphasizes, but what kinds of patterns he will "discover" among them. Further, it would be misleading to allow the sequential nature of my presentation to suggest that such inquiry, the thinking of a working Historian, is itself neatly sequential. From the moment a project is conceived, a Historian is likely to begin toying with versions of a narrative, establishing what might be loosely called working hypotheses. These hypotheses can take any form, from publicly delivered working papers to carefully recorded notebook entries to fleeting daydreams and fantasies. And they can concern any portion of the inquiry. Thus, a Historian might speculate in a journal, say, that she is setting out to find certain documents which she feels certain must exist; or tell a colleague that she is about to approach a set of texts with a pretty good idea of the kinds of patterns she will discover in them; or begin a whole project with the hope—only half-formulated, and as much a fantasy as anything else—that the explanation she creates for the patterns in the texts will run counter to all previously established versions, and so bring her professional recognition, or at least notoriety.

So far as I can discern, there is no explicit guidance from the community that directs Composition's Historians in identifying either what sorts of features ought to get their attention, or what kinds of patterns they ought to seek in them. Still, decisions about these, already directed to some extent by the way the problem has been framed, and again by the materials assembled, are further directed here by the same forces: (a) the interests of the community— that is, the drift of the prevailing narrative, when there is one; and (b) pressures from other Composition communities and from the larger culture. For example, in "Jonathan Maxcy and the Aims of Early Nineteenth-Century Rhetorical Teaching," an essay we'll come back to in the next section, Patrick Scott provides a particularly clear example of (a), for he seems to be explicitly reacting against the community's tendency to ignore or denigrate some early nineteenth-century American professors of rhetoric, especially with regard to the rise of literary studies. For (b), we have seen that Connors' major concern is with patterns in the presentation of certain terms in textbooks, terms which may also serve as indicators of changing attitudes toward how writing could best be taught—features, in short, that seem to him relevant to contemporary Practitioners, and among which he hopes to discern patterns from which may be drawn, as he is wont to say, "the lessons of history."

Such commitments to features or patterns are clearly not rock-bound. Early on, especially, the shape of either may not be very clear; and even when it is, other features and other patterns may well come into play. It is also worth pointing out that such predispositions are not to be considered a liability; these are not somehow dangerous biases. Dialectical inquiry, at least in its modern form, is based in part upon their existence. That is, the predispositions themselves are inescapable: Historians are no more "objective" than anyone else, and so are unlikely to produce anything like unanimity in terms of features or patterns or the ways they account for them. What the mode of inquiry provides is a way to harness that inevitable disagreement, a framework within which the intellectual energy inherent in their opposition can be used to work toward a narrative that has a dialectical, rather than objective, validity.

The kinds of limitations that characterize Composition's Historian inquiry here are an extension of those described in earlier sections, and spill over into the next two, as well. The tendency in most of the studies I have cited has been to focus on a very limited number of features relevant to a history of the *idea* of teaching writing, located in an intellectual context, with a few institutional coordinates, but pretty much stripped of place and time in other ways. Demographic concerns, geographic, economic, political (national, local, academic)—texts and textual features that might tell about these have not yet gotten much close attention. Who learned to write? How many of them were there? How much did their teachers get paid? What kind of living was that? Were these teachers politically active? In what ways? How did these things vary across the country?

And the patterns traced in this limited set of features have had their own, parallel sort of limitations. Two patterns have dominated. The first, corresponding to the earlier, pedagogical history, delineates the decline of the teaching of writing, or at least of Rhetoric, from past to present; what we know now is depicted as impoverished by what we have forgotten or lost. That is Corbett's perspective in the passage I quoted earlier, for example; and S. Michael Halloran is even more explicit about such costs in "Rhetoric in the American College Curriculum: The Decline of Public Discourse." The second pattern is characteristic of the contributions to institutional history. In nearly all of these lurks some notion of "progress": that is, the pattern traced tends to move from the bad toward the good, the latter being what we believe or do now. Berlin, for example, writing about the impact of the three nineteenth-century rhetorics he has examined in his monograph, argues that "it is heartening to realize that our attempts to improve our classroom performance are including the most promising [developments] from the past" (p. 91).

We will return to these patterns below, for they are integrally related to the problem of playing for two audiences. Here it is enough to say that both the relatively narrow range of relevant features and the tendency toward these rather coarse-grained patterns are understandable, although not inevitable, in a new historical undertaking. The inquiry has to begin somewhere.

Accounting for the Patterns: Creating a Narrative

Given the relatively narrow range of features and patterns the Historians have favored, it is only natural that most of their narratives to date—the accounts within which those patterns of features are connected—should favor the same broad sweep and smooth logic of progress and decline. Nearly all of the community's work, first and second generation alike, has consisted of what Connors says we "might reductively call 'kings and battles history'" (p. 11). That is, the focus is on what are conceived to be major figures—John Locke, Hugh Blair, Alexander Bain, Fred Newton Scott, and so on; and major periods, usually framed in terms of one or more such specific features—a practice (like responding to student writing), an issue (the relationship between Rhetoric and literary studies, e.g.), a concept (the modes of discourse), and so on. Obviously, a good deal necessarily gets left out of such accounts. They are, to shift to a more contemporary analogy, roughly equivalent to football highlight films. From three hours of footage, say, eight minutes may be chosen to tell the story. So it is here. With the few book-length studies offering a partial exception, whole centuries are covered in under twenty pages; detail is sacrificed for gains in dramatic power.

For the most part, then, studies have varied only in terms of emphasis—how much on battle, how much on king. Nearly all of the early pedagogical history, in its search for techniques, emphasizes the former; and the obvious examples of this major-period focus from the institutional perspective are the studies by Kitzhaber, Wozniak, and Berlin. Probably the best known example, though, is Connors' "The Rise and Fall of the Modes of Discourse." Connors explains both what he plans to do, and why:

> The classification of discourse into different types has been one of the continuing interests of rhetoricians since the classical period. Some of these classifications have been genuinely useful to teachers of discourse, but others have exemplified Butler's damning couplet, "all a rhetorician's rules / Teach nothing but to name his tools." To explore the question of what makes a

discourse classification useful or appealing to teachers, this
essay will examine the rise, reign, and fall of the most influential classification scheme of the last hundred years: the "forms"
or "modes" of discourse: Narration, Description, Exposition,
and Argument. More students have been taught composition
using the modes of discourse than any other classification system. The history of the modes is an instructive one; from the
time of their popularization in American rhetoric textbooks
during the late nineteenth century, through the absolute dominance they had in writing classrooms during the period 1895–
1930, and into the 1950's when they were finally superseded
by other systems, the modes of discourse both influenced and
reflected many of the important changes our discipline has seen
in the last century. Looking at the modes and their times may
also help us answer the question of what sorts of discourse
classifications are most useful for writing classes today (p. 444).

And the account he offers takes just the form he says it will. The five
subheadings tell the tale: "The Early Years: Introduction, Conflict,
and Acceptance"; "The Reign of the Modes"; "The Modes Under
Attack"; "Fall and Abandonment of the Modes"; "L'envoi—The
Modes as Plausible Fiction." In each section, to be sure, important
names come up: Campbell and Bain, Samuel Newman and "the re-
doubtable" John Genung, and so on. But the spotlight in this eleven-
page sweep of a century-long battle is decidedly on the modes
themselves.

The major-figure emphasis, by contrast, magnifies the role of
some actor or actors upon the stage of some such period, usually by
treating him or them (so far as I know, no woman has been dealt
with in this way) as somehow emblematic of the battle being waged.
This is the strategy favored by Donald C. Stewart, for example, in
"Two Model Teachers and the Harvardization of English Departments," in which he contrasts Francis Child, fourth Boylston Chair
of Rhetoric at Harvard, and Fred Newton Scott of the University of
Michigan; by Winifred Bryan Horner in "Rhetoric in the Liberal Arts:
Nineteenth Century Scottish Universities" which, despite its imposing
title, is a nine-page essay drawing almost exclusively on the work of
one George Jardine; and, too, by Patrick Scott in the essay I referred
to earlier, "Jonathan Maxcy and the Aims of Earth Nineteenth-
Century Rhetorical Teaching", and which we can consider here by
way of illustration.

Like Connors, Scott begins by roughly marking off the end
points of the period he plans to consider, describing it as falling between the "decline of purely classical rhetoric and the rise of modern

literary-historical study"—what he calls "the period of the compound titles." So we know that the battle, as it were, took place somewhere between 1790 and, say, 1875. Clearly, though, his primary concern is to present a coherent profile of Jonathan Maxcy as a corrective to what he sees as mistaken current historical notions about the period. That is, this account of Maxcy is to stand as proof that "far from mere rote-repetition of emptily elegant, belletristic, and rather outdated texts, early 'Rhetoric and Criticism' could, under a good professor, carry a sense of freshness and intellectual ambition that still fascinates" (p. 22). If Connors plans to work mostly with ground, Scott will deal mostly with figure.

In doing so, it should be noted, Scott moves a half-step closer to the kind of history implicit in Susan Miller's criticism, cited above: past an analysis of a set of textbooks to a clearer understanding of their classroom uses. We may know, he argues, a good deal about certain major text writers of the early nineteenth century, but that is not enough: ". . . Blair, Campbell, Kames and later Whately are well-known and have been the subject of modern analysis, but which of us would want our teaching to be judged solely from the textbooks we assign? What is far more difficult to recapture is the way such books were used, and the educational aims of those who assigned them" (p. 22). In other words, the gap in the narrative that frames his problem has to do with the nature of actual classroom practice during this period; and it is a gap he plans to begin filling with this single figure. To do so, of course, he needs a new set of texts, documents which will give him access to this practice in a way that the textbooks alone cannot. And he has found such a set: two "basic" biographies of Maxcy; a couple of college histories; the writings of a couple of Maxcy's former students; and, perhaps most important, the work of Maxcy himself:

> The subject of this paper, Jonathan Maxcy (1768–1820), never wrote a rhetoric text and so does not figure in modern histories of the subject. Throughout his nearly thirty years as a college president and rhetoric professor, he seems, like so many others of his generation, to have prescribed for his students the obvious, standard texts—Cicero, Blair's *Lectures on Rhetoric and Belles-Lettres*, and Kames' *Elements of Criticism.* Unlike most of his contemporaries, however, he published in 1817 a rationale for his subject, an introductory lecture on the *Philosophical Principles of Rhetorick and Criticism*; and this lecture, together with the extensive reading list he also had printed for his students, allows us to get behind the familiar catalogue of Scottish rhetorical texts to see something of the spirit in which they were being used by a practicing American college teacher (p. 22).

What we won't get from this investigation, clearly, is an account of the big picture; this is a micro, not a macro, approach. Its power derives, then, not from the way it has accounted for a pattern in some set of features traced over an imposing span of years, but from its account of them as concentrated in one emblematic figure:

> It is finally the explicitness and the intellectuality of his ped-agogic aims, I think, that are most impressive and provocative about Maxcy's lecture. The tributes of his younger colleagues after his death make it clear that he was always considered less a scholar than a teacher, and a textbook teacher at that. . . . But his emphasis on teaching did not mean an abandonment of intellectual aims. With all his limitations Maxcy knew the pur-pose of professing the compound subject of Rhetoric and Cri-ticism, and how it might be related to other subjects. After his death one of the student literary societies, the Clariosophic, erected a memorial, and its inscription recalled that Maxcy's teaching gifts had been *maxime . . . emolumento alumnis ad fingendos mores literarios vel castiganda judicia* ("of the greatest benefit to his students in fixing their literary habits and chasten-ing their judgement": LaBorde, p. 123; Hungerpiler, p. 39). In its awareness of critical methods and its sharply educational focus, that epitaph sums up much about the first generation who brought "rhetoric and belles-lettres" into the college cur-riculum. We do well, in questioning the MLA myth of our tribal origins, not to accept too readily the counter-myth of rhetorical purism or to forget the seriousness and ambition of Maxcy's period, the period of the compound titles (p. 30).

Relating the New Narrative to Existing Narratives: The Communal Dialectic

Up to this point in an investigation, the burden for establishing the integrity of the inquiry falls to the individual investigator. Of course, as in nearly all kinds of inquiry, there are various ways by which a Historian can enlist collegial help prior to formal publica-tion: conversation, letters, conference papers, exploratory articles, and so on. Useful as these can be, however, my guess is that they as often produce the stuff of footnotes as main arguments; and even when they play a more central role, appearing in the final product, say, as responses to anticipated objections, their net effect is to make the main workload heavier, not lighter.

In any case, a reasonably sound Historian will have by this time tested any proposed chunk of narrative in two directions. In one, it will have been tried against the texts and the discerned patterns for which it was generated—against, that is, the "empirical" data it purports to account for. Does it explain every feature of the pattern? Are there features—within the patterns, or outside of them—that don't fit, that belie the explanation? Can the explanation be adjusted to include these anomalies? And then, in the other direction, it will have been tested against the narrative, the larger history of which it proposes to become a part. Can it fit? Is it compatible with patterns and explanations already established for events preceding and following it, or with other, parallel events? If not, can the anomalies presented by the new material be accounted for?

The duration and intensity of this solo testing depend entirely on the individual Historian. An explanation that fails to account for half the features of a pattern can as easily be abandoned as adjusted, but if the Historian has a sense—call it intuition—that the explanation is somehow right, perhaps based in part on how well it fits with existing explanations, he may well stay with it, adjusting it and reexamining the features of the pattern, or the pattern itself, looking for a better fit. The same is obviously true for explanations that run counter to those already established. If the explanation makes a good match with the pattern, then the Historian may well stay with it despite—or, indeed, because of—the challenges it will presumably attract from his community. Eventually, though, the results of individual inquiry must be offered to the rest of the Historian community. And when it is, the workload—and the nature of the inquiry— change rather radically.

Formal publication, then, assumes a methodological importance for Historians, and for Scholars in general, not shared by either Practitioners or Researchers. More than in either of these others, publication marks not the end of inquiry, but a shift to a new stage of inquiry. I don't mean to suggest that there is no room for post-publication debate among Practitioners or Researchers. There clearly is, and it certainly serves a useful function. But such debate is not usually dialectical in a Scholarly sense, nor is it viewed as an essential extension of inquiry so much as somehow peripheral to it—as in reaction to past inquiry, or leading toward further inquiry. For Scholars, however, the communal debate is just such an extension. Indeed, as I have already suggested, the fundamental dynamic of the Scholarly community lies right here, in the tension it fosters among the idiosyncratic perceptions and interpretations of its individual members, and the forum it provides in which opposing positions can clash. In the Historian community, then, it is precisely this tension that metamorphoses what would be merely *stories* to produce, instead, *his*-tory.

Some of the post-publication debate of Historians can be empirical rather than dialectical, centering directly on the sufficiency of the texts that form the inquirer's data base. And, in fact, if that set of texts is found wanting—if the search for primary sources was not exhaustive enough, or if texts are included that don't belong—then the Historian's offering can simply be rejected, sent back to earlier stages of inquiry. It will not become part of the communal dialectic. I have not, however, come across any such instances in Composition.

Once that barrier has been overcome, though, any part of the inquiry is, at least in theory, open to questioning: Do other Historians agree that the pattern or patterns the inquirer has focused on are, in fact, there? Are there other patterns that the inquirer has ignored or played down that are relevant for the proffered strand of narrative? Does the explanation offered for the pattern make sense? What alternative explanations are available, and are they compatible? Indeed, even the definition used to establish the sufficiency of the textual base can be a subject for dialectic.

The truth of the matter, however, is that much of what I can say about such dialectic in the Historian community must remain "in theory." With the exception of the sort of general corrective stance taken by Patrick Scott, there has been very little public dialectic in the community to date. Consider, for example, the three historical essays clustered in the December 1981 issue of *College Composition and Communication* that included Connors' "Rise and Fall" piece. The first is Corbett's "John Locke's Contributions to Rhetoric" which, while from his later work, is still pretty typical of what I have characterized as first-generation Historian work. That is, having determined that Locke was influential in his time, Corbett has set out to recover him, as it were, and to "suggest to contemporary teachers of English, especially teachers of rhetoric and composition, that Locke can give them insights into the human psyche which can enhance their teaching" (p. 424). The essay is interesting and informative; Corbett accomplishes his purpose. Still, mostly because it is in this recovery mode, it is not part of any dialectic. Thus, while Corbett is careful to support his claims about Locke's importance by reference to other commentators—Kenneth MacLean and Wilbur Samuel Howell, for example—his object is not to take issue with their assessments, but simply to offer them as part of his justification for making Locke more generally accessible.

The same is essentially true for the second essay, Andrea Lunsford's "Essay Writing and Teachers' Responses in Nineteenth-Century Scottish Universities," albeit for different reasons. This is more clearly an example of what I have been calling second-generation Historical inquiry; Lunsford accounts for these nineteenth-century practices not to recover them, but to help us frame our own confusions. Still, there is no dialectic, no confrontation with other Historians. At the beginning of the essay, to be sure, Lunsford makes it clear—much as we have seen Scott do—that she plans to correct our "current stereotype of the nineteenth century classroom as a teacher-centered, product-oriented, usage-obsessed site of near torture for young students" (p. 434). Hence, like Scott, she creates a straw man of "current stereotype" as a point of opposition. But, also like Scott, that stereotype is never attributed to any specific scholarly source, and so it cannot generate dialectic. Indeed, working as she is from "archival holdings in Scottish universities," she makes no reference to any other commentators at all.

With the Connors essay, we do finally get a glimpse—albeit an almost furtive one—of what Historian dialectic might look like. Not from the essay itself: like Lunsford, Connors concentrates mostly on primary sources; and, like Corbett, when he does turn to a previous commentator—in this case, Alfred Kitzhaber's "Rhetoric in American Colleges, 1850-1900"—it is in search of support, not opposition. Once, then, Connors cites Kitzhaber to support his claim that "the terms we have come to call the modes were floating about in very general use during the period 1825-1870" (p. 444); a second time to support his choice of major textbook authors (p. 447); and a third time, quoting at length Kitzhaber's "damning" assessment of the modes' use, to set up his own explanation for their weakness (p. 453).

But Connors' account of the modes has not gone uncontested. Near the end of the essay, trying to explain how the modes could "rise to such power, hold it for so long and so absolutely, and then decline so rapidly," Connors offers the following explanation:

> At least part of the answer has to do with the relative vitality of the rhetorical tradition during the period 1870-1930, an era when hardly any progressive theoretical work was done in the field. Alexander Bain, Fred N. Scott, and perhaps Barrett Wendell are the greatest figures writing during the period and (except for Scott, whose influence was limited) they cannot stand beside Campbell in the eighteenth century or Burke in the twentieth. The modes became popular and stayed popular because they fit into the abstract, mechanical nature of writing instruction at the time, and they diminished in importance as other, more vital, ideas about writing appeared in the 1930's and after. Like the "dramatic unities" that ruled the drama of the seventeenth and eighteenth centuries until exploded by Samuel Johnson's common sense, the modes were only powerful so long as they were not examined for evidence of their usefulness (p. 453).

Now, even as an essentially non-historian reader, I am troubled by features of this explanation. For example, while it makes for a neat turn of phrase and an easy analogy, the notion that Johnson "exploded" what everyone ought to have known—had they had his "common sense"—were the useless unities makes me very uneasy. Such an explanation, applied to the modes or the unities, seems to me at once too broad and too neat.

And I think I detect a similar uneasiness, though rather less pointedly offered, in Sharon Crowley's "Counterstatement" response to Connors in the February 1984 issue of *CCC*. Crowley agrees that the "long adherence by composition text-writers to a patently artificial set of discourse classifications does require explanation," but hers is based on different reasons: "I think the answer to the puzzle is not to be found so much in the historical conditions surrounding nineteenth-century rhetoric as in the theoretical origin of the modes themselves." Crowley's alternative explanation, then, rests on the relationship between the modes—as presented, most influentially, by George Campbell—and "faculty psychology." That is, the modes derived their initial appeal and their staying power from a widespread, if not always explicitly stated, belief in their more or less direct connection to the way the mind works:

> If one accepts this model of the mind, as did Campbell and many of his contemporaries both on the Continent and in America, it is an easy leap to the supposition that a writer who wishes to appeal to one of the faculties, say, the will, can first devise a formal strategy which is peculiarly suited to moving the will of the reader, and further, that this strategy can be embodied in the finished text. That is, a leap is made from a discourse classification based on an author's possible range of intentions . . . to a classification which assumes that there are sets of formal textual features that distinguish kinds of texts from one another (p. 89).

I rather wish Professor Crowley had gone further. Like Connors, she implies—with her use of "patently artificial discourse classifications," for example—that an entire century's worth of theorists and teachers were, however understandable their excuses in terms of prevailing psychological theory, plain wrongheaded in following the modes . . . a wrongheadedness that now, in the bright light of progress, is perfectly obvious to us. That sort of seemingly un-selfconscious, even patronizing chrono-centrism seems to me terribly risky for Historical inquiry. Still, what she does is enough to illustrate the possibilities: in terms of Historical method as I've outlined it, she offers an alternative account for the pattern Connors describes by checking it against the larger narrative of which it is to be a part.

Thus, the modes' persistent appearances in nineteenth century texts can be better explained, she argues, by seeing them as grounded in some other, better established beliefs, rather than by the simple absence of competition.

I cite from these studies at this length simply to illustrate my point about the paucity of dialectic. In none of the three articles do the writers have occasion to dispute the claims of any other Historian. Nor, so far as I can tell, has anyone except Crowley disputed the claims made in any of them, although as the interval between Connors' essay and her "Counterstatement" suggests, such a dialectic moves rather slowly, and so responses may yet be forthcoming. And the same may be said for nearly all the Historian work I have reviewed. One reason for this shortage of controversy, as I suggested earlier, is that there is so much territory to cover; plenty of paths still guarantee solitude. It may also be a matter of inclination; members of so small a community may not want to threaten their unity with serious internal debate. My sense, though, is that the greater critical self-consciousness of the second generation will likely lead to a more powerful dialectic—if not in its own work, then surely when they begin to train generation number three.

Drawing Conclusions and Implications: Dissemination to a Wider Audience

As I suggested in introducing this Section, each Scholarly community has had to find a way to deal with the "public." It isn't hard to find a pattern in the work we've looked at. We have seen Patrick Scott, for example, conclude his study of Maxcy by arguing that "We do well, in questioning the MLA myth of our tribal origins, not to accept too readily the counter-myth of rhetorical purism or to forget the seriousness and ambition of Maxcy's period, the period of the compound titles" (p. 30). Corbett and Lunsford, too, in the essays we have just reviewed, move from some narrative to its implications for the present and future. Corbett's argument is representative, although perhaps milder in tone than average, of most first generation inquiry; he is basically saying "Try reading and emulating Locke," much as other essays adjure us to "Try enthymemes" or "Explore Aristotle's topics." Lunsford, here again more typical of second-generation work, wields her bit of narrative like a mirror, and directs us to take a careful look at ourselves:

> I have sketched here only one small part of the history of essay assignments and essay writing in nineteenth-century university classrooms; much more historical work needs to be done. But

my small study has led me to ask some very large questions. Just how far have we come in the 100 years since Bain retired from the chair at Aberdeen? On what historical and theoretical assumptions do we base *our* adherence to what we call "essay writing"? Do we today have a compelling theory of essay assignments and essay writing, one that will account for all parts of the act of composing, including the cognitive processes which underlie production as well as the system which evaluates it? When we conceive such a theory, we can justifiably claim an achievement (p. 442, her emphasis).

Simply contributing to the communal narrative, it would seem, is not quite enough; here is a need, bordering on compulsion, to draw for readers—presumably non-Historians—some moral from the story, some lesson from history. As I have suggested, this may be a matter of social obligation. The other communities in the society of Composition may require Historians to make this leap from their dialectically-refined narrative to the hurly-burly of the wider debate about what to do. Once again, it is Robert Connors who has dealt with the matter most self-consciously. "There is an inescapable component of value judgment in any historical interpretation," he argues near the end of "Historical Inquiry in Composition Studies," "and in my work—in most composition history that I've seen since Kitzhaber—that component is out in the open":

> To put it bluntly, composition historians have set themselves a propagandistic agenda as well as an informative agenda. We see ourselves as reformers as well as scholars; thus, when Don[ald C.] Stewart attacks A. S. Hill's formalism or I praise Porter Perrin's progressive rejection of drill-work we are making claims about composition today as well as about composition in 1885 or in 1930.
>
> This is, I believe, as it should be. The lessons of history have not yet been much applied in our field, and composition is not yet so stable, settled, or successful that it can pretend to scholarly neutrality. There are still large questions to be answered about our scope and ends and purpose, and our historical studies are brought to life by the service they can give in answering such questions (p. 18).

Again here, as so often, I find myself attracted to Connors' argument, both for its candor and its clarity. His assessment of the situation pretty much jibes with mine: this is a field whose members will look to the Historians for whatever guidance they can provide, and it certainly is possible—and has been, as Connors says, mostly the case—that Historians should adopt some version of the reformer role.

But I find myself made rather uneasy—again—by just what this propagandistic agenda entails. Clearly, as he argues earlier in the same passage, history is not a "quasi-scientific" mode of inquiry; in that sense, as I have already explained, scholarly neutrality isn't even a desideratum. So if what Connors means by a "propagandistic agenda" is a consistent and deliberate effort to favor one set of biases over another in these early investigations—identifying certain kinds of problems, favoring certain kinds of materials, leaning toward certain features and patterns, and the like—I am willing to sympathize. A small group of Historians cannot take on everything at once, and if they are convinced that temporarily favoring one emphasis rather than another will ensure the survival of their field, and so their communal dialectic, then perhaps they ought to follow that conviction. Later generations of Historians—and following this course, presumably, helps insure there will be some—can challenge that bias.

However, it is not clear, at least in "The Rise and Fall of the Modes of Discourse," that this is exactly what he has in mind. Really the only justification for taking such a position, it seems to me, is the promise that it will keep the communal dialectic alive. I don't mean this to sound naive. Obviously, narrative accounts of what has happened, and why, serve as instruments in power struggles all the time. Those who so use them seldom have any regard for dialectic. In that sense, a history is a story you make up to prove that you are right; if it is to be changed, it's because you need to justify some new set of actions. But Historical inquiry as I have tried to outline it here, and as I think Composition's Historians conceive of it, depends upon the interplay of a dialectic as free as possible from power plays outside the community. Individual Historians, then, will inevitably present accounts that justify one political or pedagogical position or another; but the community itself values, and indeed finally exists to promote, opposition.

The danger of even so self-aware a propagandist position as Connors', then, is that the fervor of reformation, with opposition only a distant possibility, will lead to claims that fall outside the boundaries of dialectical response, and so subvert the very inquiry the propagandist agenda is trying to perpetuate. Not to exaggerate: "The Rise and Fall of the Modes of Discourse" did win, as I have already mentioned, the Braddock Award as the best essay in *CCC* for 1981, and deservedly so. Connors demonstrates very ably how, given the evidence presented in the texts he has examined, the modes seem to have gone in and out of fashion. He suggests, too, how changes in theories of language and pedagogy, and their relationship, might account for the modes' eventual fall from favor. And we have seen, in Crowley's response, that his account leaves room for genuine dialectical opposition; that is, for questions which can be answered by further Historical inquiry.

But he makes other assertions, too. Following Kitzhaber's lead, for instance, he argues that the "weakness of the modes of discourse as a practical tool in the writing class was that they did not really help students to learn to write." He goes on:

> When we look closely at the nature of modal distinctions, it is not hard to see why: the modes classify and emphasize the product of writing, having almost nothing to do with the purpose for which the writer sat down, pen in hand. Modal distinctions are divorced from the composition process (p. 454).[3]

There is nothing wrong with such a claim. The position is an arguable one, and Connors also quotes from James Kinneavy's *A Theory of Discourse* by way of support. But surely it is not a position for which he has established any *historical* authority. When the modes were popular—as Connors has shown they were, at least in the texts he has studied—isn't it conceivable that they did help students learn to write? In short, except for what he sees as their fall from fashion, what historical evidence does he have for claiming that they had a "weakness" at all?

But he goes even further:

> The modes of discourse controlled a good part of composition teaching during one of rhetoric's least vigorous periods, offering in their seeming completeness and plausibility a schema of discourse that could be easily taught and learned. For years the fact that this schema did not help students learn to write better was not a concern, and even today the modes are accepted by some teachers despite their lack of a basis in useful reality. Our discipline has been long in knuckling from its eyes the sleep of the nineteenth and early twentieth centuries, and the real lesson of the modes is that we need always to be on guard against systems that seem convenient to teachers but that ignore the way writing is actually done (pp. 454–455).

The same questions arise here. On what basis has the supposition that the schema was a failure become "the fact"? By means of what unmentioned textual evidence is he able to say whether this purported failure was or was not "a concern," and to whom, or for how long? Or that teachers who use the modes today are so misguided, operating with a schema founded in a useless (?) reality? What can a Historical inquiry tell us about what constitutes a "useful" reality, or how writing is "actually done"?

These claims—and claims like them in the work of other

Historians—make for good propaganda; here, in particular, they do a nice job of setting up Connors' closing image, and the neat lesson of history. But they cannot carry, finally, the community's imprimatur, because they are not the product of Historical inquiry. Their presence here, though, at the end of an otherwise pretty careful Historical investigation, confuses the nature of their authority considerably, and in doing so, undermines the authority of the whole. To favor some interpretive bias in Historical inquiry is one thing. But to move outside the bounds of that inquiry in the name of reform, however subtly, is quite another. Down that road lies the demise of methodological integrity.

4

The Philosophers

Of all the methodological communities in this study, I have had the most difficulty accounting for the Philosophers'. This has been particularly frustrating because, in some ways, it seems to be the most accessible. It clearly represents one of Composition's most important groups. The impulse from which it springs—the impulse to account for, to frame, critique and analyze the field's fundamental assumptions and beliefs—is surely an elemental one, and has been a feature of Composition from its beginnings. It can also claim, I will argue, the largest population of the Scholarly communities and, behind the Practitioners, the second largest in the field.

At the same time, though, the Philosophical community can be very difficult to get a handle on. Much of the time, that elemental impulse to philosophize, as it were, has been mixed with the urge to proselytize: not simply to propose or account for some set of assumptions, but to urge them as *the* assumptions. The propagandistic agenda that Connors claims for Historical inquiry has been even more active here. To make matters worse, its population, while large, has also tended to be very unstable. The rapid growth of Composition as a whole has left a good many of its members trying out new places in it, with Practitioners, especially, looking for new and more prestigious identities. Given their backgrounds, the best first option for most of these movers is the Scholars' community; and since Philosophical inquiry, in an area still so new, is so wide open—requiring the least retraining, demanding access to no special materials, and offering the chance of relatively quick publication—many have given it a try. Not all that many stay. A few, frustrated by what they perceive as the limitations of Philosophical work, are drawn on to try other modes of inquiry. Most presumably return to whatever they did before, finding themselves uninterested in or not suited for the effort involved in sustained Philosophical inquiry. The resulting demographic pattern is rather like that of a marina: a small core of full-time residents; a larger group of longer-term types, who may stay as long as two or three years, or move in and out with some regularity; and lots of one-time, seasonal visitors who nevertheless— by sheet weight of numbers—leave their mark on the community. And so, even though we can say that the community has developed a stronger sense of its own identity—especially, like the Historians, in terms of a more potent critical self-consciousness—there are in fact enormous individual differences in the extent to which such a claim is true.

The result is that I have occasionally wondered whether it makes sense to claim that there is a community here founded on dialectic at all. The voices so often seem more zealous than reasonable, fervent than curious, converted than, in the best sense of the word, disinterested. They are sometimes rhetorically powerful, sometimes only shrill: Do they seek clarity—or influence? Is this dialectic —or deliberative rhetoric, albeit in a forum where nothing ever comes to a vote? And to add to the confusion, there seems not to be all that much listening going on. It stands to reason: in so unstable a population, a cumulative heritage is bound to develop rather slowly.

And yet I am convinced, as the existence of this chapter testifies, that somewhere within this welter of arguing voices, a genuine dialectic and a real Philosophical community are taking shape. Indeed, its first movements can be found well before 1963 whenever, in various issues of *CCC*, say, a writer moves beyond What do we do? to ask other questions: What is Composition? What does it mean to write? to learn to write? What assumptions guide our answers to such questions, and upon what preconditions do *they* rest? So, to choose just one example, in an article from the October 1950 issue, "The One-Legged, Wingless Bird of Freshman English," Kenneth Oliver reports on a workshop he attended whose purpose was to determine what the objectives of a college communications course ought to be. The workshop participants, he argues, fall into three groups, each of which he identifies by their basic—i.e., philosophical—positions: "communicators," those concerned with the immediate social purposes of language; the general semanticists, who aimed to make students astute information consumers; and the "traditional formalists," who tended to focus on how discourse was constructed, more or less regardless of content. The point, as his title suggests, is that these emphases, often held uncritically, tend to foster a crippled pedagogy

—to bind one leg or another, and to clip wings. In style, in tone, and even in conclusion ("There is still a need for pioneers") this admirably prefigures much of the debate to come.

After 1963, the movements of the Philosophical community can be seen as part of the reform of English as a whole: in the work of some of the Curriculum Study Centers funded by Project English, for example; or, in perhaps even more emblematic form, the Dartmouth Anglo-American Conference on the Teaching and Learning of English, where, in a month of debate, fifty participants managed to hammer out a list of eleven points which mix philosophy, politics, and pedagogy, as well as two books (John Dixon's *Growth Through English* and Herbert J. Muller's *The Uses of English*) and some thousand pages of working papers (*Working Papers of the Anglo-American Conference on the Teaching of English*).

But a specifically Composition-based debate begins to emerge, too. Much of the initial impetus, as I suggested earlier, stems from the effort to find or create in Rhetoric a basis for Composition—not so much, as in Corbett's early emphasis, to reclaim the classical tradition as a pedagogical system, but to invoke its voices as precursors in an ageless debate. Such is the ambition, for example, of Wayne Booth's "The Rhetorical Stance," or Robert Gorrell's "Very Like a Whale—A Report on Rhetoric." Perhaps the most pointed of those early proposals comes in Virginia Burke's 1965 essay, "The Composition-Rhetoric Pyramid":

> There is chaos today in the teaching of composition because since the turn of the century composition has lacked an informing discipline, without which no field can maintain its proper dimensions, the balance and proportion of its various parts or its very integrity. Consequently, the practice of composition has shrunk, has lost important elements, has become a victim of all manner of distortions (p. 5).

Control over this chaos, though, lies not in any simple reclamation of the classical tradition; if that tradition is to be useful at all, it will need "sifting and winnowing" (p. 3). The necessary philosophical foundation, then—the notion of the "friendly working together of theory and practice" she borrows from Donald L. Clark—cannot be generated either by "a flight into the past, nor by gathering up unexamined scraps from the banquet of the ancients, nor yet by devising a superficially impressive unity concocted of an uneasy syncretism of unsifted, often contradictory elements" (p. 4). The demand is for a new or reconstructed rhetorical theory, "one suited to today's needs" (p. 5), and able, when "re-established at the top of the composition-rhetoric pyramid, to inform and energize the teaching of composition at all levels" (p. 7).

The effort to lay the groundwork for a philosophy of Composition, however, has come to be even more broadly conceived. To be sure, there have been and continue to be contributions that can be characterized as more or less main-line rhetorical studies: Ross Winterowd's *Rhetoric: A Synthesis*; James Kinneavy's *A Theory of Discourse* which, though I actually deal with it in the next chapter because of its handling of texts, makes a substantial contribution to this Philosophical enterprise; John Warnock's "New Rhetoric and the Grammar of Pedagogy"; some of S. Michael Halloran's work, such as "On the End of Rhetoric, Classical and Modern"; Virginia Steinhoff's "The *Phaedrus* Idyll as Ethical Play: The Platonic Stance"; C. H. Knoblauch and Lil Brannon's *Rhetorical Traditions and the Teaching of Writing*; James L. Golden's "Plato Revisited: A Theory of Discourse for All Seasons" or John Gage's "An Adequate Epistemology for Composition: Classical and Modern Perspectives," and so on. The list is a long one.

But the influence of other disciplines, other traditions, other fields has been brought to bear. Psychology, for instance, shows up early on and influentially in Robert Zoellner's tremendously controversial "Talk-Write: A Behavioral Pedagogy for Composition"; Janice Lauer's "Heuristics and Composition" and James Moffett's *Teaching the Universe of Discourse*, about both of which I will have more to say later; Frank D'Angelo's *A Conceptual Theory of Rhetoric*; or, even more recently, Louise Wetherbee Phelps's "Foundations for a Modern Psychology of Composition." Since the mid-1950s, and well on into the 1960s, when it was hailed as the line of inquiry that would put the teaching of writing on a scientific footing at last, linguistics—and, later, psycholinguistics—have had a considerable impact. From its optimistic heyday, for example, see Harry Warfel's "Structural Linguistics and Composition"; in more sober times, Alton Becker and Richard Young's "Toward a Modern Theory of Rhetoric: A Tagmemic Contribution" is particularly visible; and this line of inquiry peaks—at least for the time being—in E. D. Hirsch's *The Philosophy of Composition* and George Dillon's powerful reply, *Constructing Texts*. And, predictably, both literary studies and philosophy proper have had their influences, as in Walter Ong's "The Writer's Audience is Always a Fiction," for example; Ann Berthoff's *The Making of Meaning*, among her other writings, with its invocations of William James, C. S. Peirce, Paulo Freire, and the like; or essays like Barrett Mandell's "The Writer Writing Is Not at Home" or Charles I. Schuster's "Mikhail Bakhtin as Rhetorical Theorist." And there have been infusions from other fields as well. Composition's Philosophers have been nothing if not eclectic.

Over two-and-a-half decades, this wide-ranging search for a
foundation, for some first principles, seems to have become both
more self-conscious and more reflexive. That is, the writers who have
served as the core of the community—Ann Berthoff first, perhaps,
but also Janet Emig and Richard Young, say, as well as some members of a very articulate second-generation—have become more careful and critical about what contributions from elsewhere might entail;
and, at the same time, turned their attention inward, as it were, trying to see what Composition already *is* before looking to see what it
might become. Perhaps the key essay in this development was Janet
Emig's "The Tacit Tradition: The Inevitability of a Multi-Disciplinary
Approach to Writing Research" in which she argues, in effect, that
one requirement for establishing Composition (although she actually
never uses that word) as a "discipline" (which she does use) is that it
claim an "intellectual tradition" and intellectual "ancestors." And
she proceeds to nominate a whole range of her own favorites: Thomas
Kuhn, George Kelly, John Dewey, Michael Polanyi, Susanne Langer,
Jean Piaget, Lev Vygotsky, A. R. Luria, and Eric Lenneberg.

But the general debate about the field's nature and heritage at
this more self-conscious level is picked up and carried on by Richard
Young in "Paradigms and Problems: Needed Research in Rhetorical
Invention"; Patricia Bizzell's "Thomas Kuhn, Scientism, and English
Studies"; Robert Connors' "Composition Studies and Science";
Michael Holzman's "Scientism and Sentence Combining"; Janice
Lauer's "Composition Studies: Dappled Discipline"; and James A.
Reither's "Writing and Knowing: Toward Redefining the Writing
Process," to name just a few. And, with an emphasis more particu-
larly on practice over the other modes of inquiry, there are studies
like Richard Young's (again) "Arts, Crafts, Gifts, and Knacks"; Paul
Kameen's "Rewording the Rhetoric of Composition"; and James
Berlin's "Contemporary Composition: The Major Pedagogical Theo-
ries," the central argument of which also plays a major role in his
Writing Instruction in Nineteenth-Century American Colleges.

I need to end this introductory sketch by offering as a caution
the complaint with which I began it. I have been able to trace this
pattern of development in Composition's Philosophical community
by picking and choosing my way through more than twenty years
of articles and books. Insofar as it represents an emerging coherence,
it is a legitimate account—one, at any rate, that I think the writers I
have characterized as being members of that community will recognize and, within limits, sanction.

However, as I observed at the outset, it would be a mistake to
conceive of the community's work as having been this narrow. As a
second-order inquiry, Philosophy derives its identity from its method,

not its subject matter, with the result, as we shall see ahead, that its practitioners are free to turn their attention to any issue whatever—a freedom even my short list suggests they have exercised pretty fully. And for every title I have listed, there are probably a half dozen or more that I have not. Nor, to be a little more critical, has it been this neat, this coherent. Sometimes the inquiries I have grouped under this heading have been painstakingly thorough, but just as often painfully careless. The community's interests have consistently run wider than they have deep; there has been a good deal more dabbling than dialectic. Thus, while it is possible to trace, as I have here, an emerging line of powerful inquiry, it is not yet clear to what extent the community itself is aware of, or has control over, that power.

The Nature of Philosophical Knowledge: The Great Debate

Philosophical knowledge has, I think, a certain simple elegance. We might say that both its logic and its form are dialectical. That is, although individual contributions are governed by the rules of inference—the movement from one or more premises to some conclusion —the body of knowledge of the community as a whole is held together by a specialized dia-logic: the dialectical opposition of competing inferential systems. Philosophical knowledge in this communal sense, then, takes the form of a free-ranging, never-ending debate— one of the topics of which, of course, is the rules by which it might be run.

What causes the most confusion for those outside a Philosophical community, presumably, is that this body of knowledge is not instrumental: the great debate does not lead to action. This property no doubt causes public relations problems for all sorts of philosophers. It's easy to imagine the misunderstanding of a public which assumes that a philosopher of Ethics is somebody who ought to be able to tell us what is right and what is wrong; and so here, too, a Philosopher of Composition ought to be able to figure out which are the best and which the worst ways to teach or research writing. But Philosophical inquiry doesn't work that way. It deals not with things in the world, hands on, directly—like Practitioners, or Experimental Researchers, or even Historians—but with the operations of reason, in this case by focusing on its manifestations in the Philosophers themselves, and in the activities of Composition's other inquirers. It cannot, for example, examine two systems for teaching writing and then declare one or the other more effective. What it can do is to try to trace a premises-to-conclusion line of reasoning that might account for each system, and examine their differences dialectically; or consider, in the same way, what might constitute the preconditions for deciding what "effective" means. But it cannot, finally, do the deciding. That's a problem for other modes of inquiry, each in its own way, to handle.

The usual response to any such account of its non-instrumental nature, of course, is a question about why: What makes Philosophical inquiry worth doing, Philosophical knowledge worth producing? Maybe the people who do it like it, but what good does it do anyone else—in this case, the society of Composition? Well, naturally, that has been a long-standing issue in the great debate, too; there is no easy answer. Probably the most facile is to say that this kind of inquiry is good at framing problems, at making them accessible in this way so that the other sorts of inquirers have a better sense of what they're involved in. That's pretty much the kind of sufferance Philosophical inquiry seems to have had in Composition so far. And I assume it has needed it. Even at its best, Philosophical knowledge can look to the uninitiated like a series of endless, ill-connected arguments that wander, often as not, onto topics that seem of minor importance.

But while that answer suffices for political purposes, I think it rather misses the point, or at least takes an unnecessarily reductive, utilitarian perspective. For what these arguments represent, no matter how imperfectly made, are the working out of basic, fundamentally opposed philosophical positions, world views, locked in the kind of opposition commonly called dialectical. As such they constitute, in our culture, anyway, more than 2000 years of struggle for— what shall we call it—a cultural self-consciousness? The tension generated by that dialectic-driven struggle, amplified by the tradition's continuity, provides the central dynamic of the Philosophers' community. And while the exact nature of its influence can be hard to determine, this connection with that ancient struggle represents a potent force for change in Composition as a whole.

One final feature of Philosophical knowledge has to do with the role that this tradition plays in the great debate. Because Philosophical inquiry is self-contained—that is, because it does not move outside of itself for verification—we can say that it takes place, even more than other dialectical modes, in the context of its own past: its history is also its medium. Progress in Philosophical inquiry is thus not conceived of as the steady weeding out of mistaken world views. However self-assured the rhetoric of a given Philosophical investigator, then—however strong the confidence that parallels what I called the Historians' chrono-centrism, that sense that what we know *now* is somehow better than what people have known before—the debate rages on. In Philosophical terms, Plato is not supplanted by

Aristotle, or Locke by Wittgenstein, or, in Composition *per se*, Moffett by Kinneavy, or Kinneavy by Hirsch. Instead, these are voices in the same, essentially timeless debate, contributions whose currency is not a function of their age. In this sense, the dialectic acquires—or, perhaps more accurately, is invested by its participants with—a life of its own, one that transcends the mortality of individual contributors. Among Composition's Philosophers, this importance of the past, always present to some extent in its ties to Rhetoric, has begun to become even more explicit in the growing preoccupation, exemplified in Emig's "Tacit Traditions," with just what sort of heritage the field can or ought to claim.

Philosophical Inquiry

I find it useful to think of modes of inquiry as consisting of what might be called private and public phases—portions, different in each community, which are and are not directly subject to community sanction. The public phase of Philosophical inquiry is easy enough to follow: argument plays off of argument, each response forcing an adjustment in the larger, underlying conceptual structure that supports whatever the visible thesis happens to be. Anyone can make an entry into this dialectic by offering—or responding to—an inferential chain. The private phase, however, the movements which lead to the publication of such inferential chains, is much harder to trace. The inquiry will not, after all, deal with any specific set of phenomena or data in the way the other modes do—will not depend, in any empirical way, on manipulating or observing or doing. To be sure, the Philosophers I have seen in action read, but some read more, some less. And they talk—again, some more than others—so that one might learn something about how the inquiry "works," in this sense, by listening. And of course they think, but information about how or when or in what forms, even if it were accessible, would hardly seem to provide the basis for generalizations. As in all fields of inquiry, I assume that there are Philosophers who, given some problem, methodically move from premises to arguments to conclusions; and others who seek out, intuitively, some attractive conclusion, and then set about seeking premises and arguments to support it, dropping the tentative conclusion only when they can no longer hope to salvage it. Sometimes these differences are reflected in the public inquiry, sometimes not. For my purposes, in any case, the method of Philosophical inquiry is finally identical with the public dialectic— the presentation and refutation of arguments—and not whatever private ruminations might precede and/or support it. Whether this is how practicing Philosophers "really" think is, here anyway, irrelevant. In its simplest form, then, that inquiry looks like this:

1. Identifying Problems
2. Establishing Premises
3. Making Argument(s): The Communal Dialectic
4. Drawing Conclusion(s): Dissemination to a Wider Audience

Some version of this elemental sequence holds whether the Philosopher is initiating or responding to an argument, taking on some fresh question or returning to an ancient one. And the sequence is repeated over and over again in sustained dialectic, with disagreement over conclusions or arguments or premises forming new assertions to be supported, argued, and so on. Strictly speaking, the mere presentation of an argument in this form makes its author at least temporarily a member of the Philosophical community. As it turns out, the majority of such arguments in Composition have so far failed to generate any direct response, and even fewer have been assimilated into any sustained dialectic. Nevertheless, each entrant presumably hopes to be recognized as entering or initiating such a debate, some longer-term inquiry, for it is only through such debate that sustained membership in the community is possible.

Identifying Problems

The most striking feature of Philosophical inquiry here, and one that outsiders and initiates find particularly frustrating, is that it has no internal means for discriminating among the particular problems it addresses—not in terms of relative importance or any other criteria: no Experimentalist paradigm, no Formalist model, not even the exigencies of practice. As I have already explained, Philosophical inquiry demands allegiance only to a mode, not a subject matter: what matters is *how* one investigates, not *what*. The absence of any such guide to priorities, however, is really of no concern to a community devoted to dialectic. For whatever the specific bone of contention might be, the process will always drive toward the ultimate goal: the construction, from what might be seen as these pieces or manifestations of it, of a coherent and inferentially systematic whole world view.

So, for example, an investigation might begin by addressing a problem like the one Kenneth A. Bruffee addresses in "Peer Tutoring and the 'Conversation of Mankind.' " He explains his purpose this way:

> This essay will sketch what seems to me to be the most persua-
> sive conceptual rationale for peer tutoring and will suggest what
> appear to be some of the larger implications of that rationale.
> The essay will begin by discussing the view of thought and lan-
> guage that seems to underlie peer tutoring. Then it will suggest
> what this view implies about how peer tutoring works. Finally,
> the essay will suggest what this concept of knowledge may sug-
> gest for studying and teaching the humanities (p. 4).

You can see what happens here. His central question is something
like this: What are the preconditions of the ideas that might underlie
the activity we call peer tutoring? From the perspectives of other
modes of inquiry, it seems pretty well restricted, nowhere near as
comprehensive as, say, "What is the nature of doing, learning, and
teaching writing?" But from a Philosophical perspective, the "size"
of the question in this sense is finally irrelevant: the larger issues are
always invoked. In order to answer this question, as Bruffee's outline
suggests, he will have to deal with certain premises about the nature
of discourse, about how we acquire and use language, about how
reading, talking, and writing are related, and so on; and these premises are part of some larger inferential system, a philosophical position. To the extent that not all of that system will be made explicit
in this one essay, we can say that this way of framing it makes the
investigation manageable: its author will work from the posited
premises to conclusions within the confines of how peer tutors
might function in the context of the humanities.

In the larger Philosophical scheme of things, though, these
boundaries are essentially arbitrary, and the problem's isolation, if
not illusory, is basically a matter of convenience. Imagine the slow
but inexorable collision between two glaciers. We could choose to
begin a description of them and their contact at any one of an infinite number of points, depending upon our interest. But if we are
committed to describing both glaciers and their full collision, our
choice of this first point—though it represents an inescapable decision—just won't matter that much, and in any case cannot be a
function of our inquiry: Just pick a spot, and go from there; it's all
attached. The analogy isn't perfect—it would be more accurate to
think of the glaciers as always in the process of construction, not
preformed—but I think it will serve here. From this perspective, the
"size" or "importance" of a Philosopher's point of entry into the
communal dialectic matters only insofar as it may or may not match
with the given investigator's ability—skill, endurance, interest, etc.—
to maintain control over the inferential structure to be built.

In the absence of communal guidance in terms of subject
matter, then, the Philosophical community's work has mostly been

shaped by the interests of its members, which has turned out most often to be practice. Indeed, I am inclined to believe that a fair amount of such inquiry has turned out to be Philosophical more or less by accident. An inquirer sets out to answer a practical question, but discovers that how the question gets answered depends on one's presuppositions, and ends up considering those—and thus philosophizing—instead. A classic example, perhaps *the* classic example in Composition, is James Moffett's *Teaching the Universe of Discourse*. For Moffett, this essentially theoretical work is a kind of byproduct of what he seems to regard as his primary, Practitioner work:

> It comprises essays written while I was preparing *A Student-Centered Language Arts Curriculum, Grades K-13: A Handbook for Teachers*, to which it is meant to be a companion volume. Whereas the handbook proposes in some detail an experimental curriculum made up of particular practices and assignments for different ages, the present book sketches a pedagogical theory of discourse that may provide both a fuller rationale for the curriculum, if the reader is familiar with it, and, quite independently, a set of ideas to help advance the current task of reconceiving education in the native language. These essays represent one teacher's efforts to theorize about discourse expressly for teaching purposes. Whereas much that is of value has been said about the subject recently and in the past, very little theory has originated in a concern for how one *learns* to discourse. What follows in these pages must, as an individual endeavor, be very imperfect; the ideas await correction and completion by other minds (p. xi, Moffett's emphasis).

Moffett seems uneasy beyond any conventional modesty about his undertaking here, at pains to maintain Practitioner status ("one teacher's efforts to theorize") and to restrict the range of the inquiry ("expressly for teaching purposes"). Nevertheless, the undertaking is clearly Philosophical: an argument in response to the question "How should discourse in English be taught in the schools to native speakers?" that considers not what should be done—for that, he has the *Curriculum*—but the preconditions of those understandings which might allow us to decide what to do. It is, in other words, an argument founded on a set of premises about the nature of discourse and development, designed to be tested not against execution, but in dialectic: "a set of ideas to help advance the current task of reconceiving education in the native language" that "await correction and completion by other minds."

This is not to say that all Philosophical inquiry has come about accidentally or reluctantly. Rather, there seem to me to be varying levels of methodological self-consciousness, levels not always easy to gauge through the haze of rhetorical strategies like Moffett's protests. The point to be made here is that the existence of this variation helps to account for the often serendipitous structure of the community's cumulative effort in its first two decades: to some extent it literally has come about by accident. At the same time, though, this ability of dialectic to absorb and eventually synthesize even such unself-conscious contributions explains why I should argue that there is a community at all—and why, especially given an increasing methodological awareness, it seems likely to have a more coherent future.

Establishing Premises

And what has been the major preoccupation of this rather loosely joined community of investigators? What else could it be but establishing premises: the process of assembling the foundations of full-fledged Philosophical positions. And the dominant strategy in this process has been one that I have come to think of, mostly without disparagement, as foraging. That is, the Composition Philosopher makes a foray into some field outside Composition itself, works to reach some degree of expertise in it, then returns ready to work out an argument about the nature of doing, learning, or teaching writing on the basis of the foraged premises. In some sense, of course, all philosophical premises are borrowed; or, more accurately, since the scope of philosophical inquiry is limited, the knowledge produced by any kind of inquiry is rightfully part of its sphere. But in Composition this borrowing has been such a distinctive activity that I think it warrants the special label.

Such activity seems natural enough, maybe even inevitable, in the formation of a new field. If investigators in other fields have tried to define, by whatever methodologies, what writing is, how it is done or learned, then it is only sensible to take advantage of their formulations, at least as points of departure. Thus, whether the forager has studied Piaget's careful clinical research, or the highly speculative work of Julian Jaynes, or the work of a linguist like Wallace Chafe, she is free to offer an argument that draws its premises from that work: "Let's suppose that what Piaget/Jaynes/Chafe says about the nature of consciousness is true," and then build from there. However, there is a fundamental Philosophical ground rule that needs to govern all such borrowings. To put it simply, there can be no privilege among them. The greatest problems arise, perhaps, with borrowings from various sciences; the urge is to treat such claims as "facts," not premises. But it can happen with borrowings from any method, and the error is the same, violating the fundamental tenet of dialectic: No premise is unassailable.

However, it is not so clear how carefully that rule has been followed. Let's return to Moffett, who illustrates as well as anyone what can go wrong. What he wants to do is provide a theoretical foundation for how discourse in English might—or, from his perspective, ought to—be taught to native speakers. And he has a plan:

> The most sensible strategy for determining a proper learning order in English, it seems to me, is to look for the main lines of child development and to assimilate to them, when fitting, the various formulations that scholars make about language and literature. This strategy is opposed to starting with some notions of structure derived from linguistics or literary criticism and trying to found a curriculum on them by negotiating a compromise between theory and the classroom facts of life. In other words, the sequence of psychological development should be the backbone of curriculum continuity, and logical formulations of the subject should serve only as an aid in describing this natural growth. Meshing learner and learned, in the case of a native language, is a matter of translating inner reality into the public terms of the subject (pp. 14–15).

The position he proposes here, at least in broad terms, has come to be a familar one: he wants to emphasize the nature of the learner, not the discourse. This is only one of several Philosophical positions he might have taken. So, for example, he might have argued that children will inevitably be made to fit themselves into some theoretical framework, and that it is therefore better to make that framework explicit; or that theory, rather than serving "only as an aid," should play no part at all in a language arts curriculum, on the grounds that it will always be intrusive and/or reductive; or that it should be introduced by individual teachers in individual ways on a classroom by classroom basis, and so on. Moreover, although he continues to exhibit the discomfiture of a Practitioner working at Philosophy, even going so far as to offer a peculiar disclaimer about the nature of the position he formulates ["The theory of discourse that makes up most of this chapter is meant to be utilized, not believed. I am after a strategic gain in concept" (p. 15).], it is clear that his object is to establish some authoritative premises: specifically, that "the sequence of psychological development should be the backbone of curriculum continuity."

The plan, however, has a problem:

> The chief difficulty with this strategy is the lack of information about how the thought and speech of children do in fact grow.

Whereas theories of grammar, rhetoric, and literature can flour-
ish in relative independence of psychological information, theories of child development depend largely on empirical research.
Most of what we know today about this development is vague,
controversial, and hard to translate into a curriculum. What I
would like to do here is piece together a theory of verbal and
cognitive growth in terms of the school subject, basing it partly
on present knowledge but definitely going beyond what can be
proven. A comprehensive rationale for a learning sequence in
language may never be provable, but the practices suggested
by the rationale can certainly be tested in schools for their
efficacy, and some hypothesis is necessary even to acquire more
knowledge. In our ignorance we still have to make assumptions
for further research and for an interim curriculum sequence
(p. 15).

For the purposes of the strategy I am trying to illustrate here
(i.e., foraging), the crucial question is this: In what sense are we to
take his use of the term "present knowledge"? In other words, what
are we to assume is the status of this knowledge imported from another field, this "vague, controversial, and hard to translate into a
curriculum" information gleaned from the "empirical research" on
child development? When he says that we need an "interim curriculum," does he mean that further research will offer the basis for a
final curriculum, or does he assume—as might be implicit in his guess
that a "comparative rationale . . . for a learning sequence in language
may never be provable"—that all curricula are bound to be "interim"?

You can see the importance of these questions for any accurate
representation of the Philosophical community, and they come up
pretty regularly when these investigators go foraging. As it turns out,
in the argument Moffett presents through the rest of *Teaching the
Universe of Discourse*, these theories taken from psychological research on child development *function* as sources for philosophical
premises. Still, his own attitude toward them remains somewhat
puzzling. He seems to want to grant them a special status because of
their empirical origins—seems to want, in effect, to make his argument Philosophical, but to make his premises into knowledge of a
different order, to make them unassailable.

If this is in fact the case—if his seeming to want special treatment for these imported premises is not more or less rhetorical, or
simply not carefully thought out—then perhaps he should not be
placed in the Philosophical community at all. Perhaps it would be
more appropriate to call Moffett, and all those other inquirers who
forage for similar purposes, something like Technicians or Curriculum

Engineers, with a role akin to those of technicians in the applied sciences. That is, it may be that the method they share, while resembling in most respects that of the Philosophers, has that one essential difference: that they consider the premises on which they base their arguments, derived from some other kind of inquiry, as unquestionable. Thus, the inferentially reasoned position such an inquirer advances is not to be tested dialectically, in conflict with other positions; but pragmatically or experimentally, by, as Moffett puts it, testing the practices "suggested by the rationale . . . in schools for their efficacy."

And yet, while this is an unmistakable tendency among Philosophical foragers, I am loath to make it the basis for a separate community. The ultimate danger, of course, is that carried to its fullest, most reductive extreme, the granting of such special status to any premises would finally scuttle the Philosophical enterprise: If certain premises are inviolate, then why not lines of argument? Conclusions? There seems, however, little chance of that happening. For one thing, though individual inquirers may flirt with such tendencies, they seldom seem to go all the way, as Moffett's recognition of the tentative relationship between a rationale and practices demonstrates: It *suggests* them, he says, not requires them. For another, even when the tendency is carried to greater extremes—as I think it is, for example, in E. D. Hirsch's *The Philosophy of Composition*—the Philosophical community will not let it happen, instead treating the attempt as either rhetorical excess or Philosophical error.

Making Argument(s): The Communal Dialectic

Given their preoccupation with establishing foraged premises, the majority of Philosophical arguments have followed a single pattern. They may or may not have had a title like "Recent Research in _____ and Its Implications for the Teaching of Writing," but that has usually been their general drift. The argument will then

(1) identify the problem—some gap in the current collective knowledge of Composition, suggesting the deleterious effects that ignorance has on practice, research, scholarship, or all three;

(2) identify criteria for adequate solutions to the problem, suggesting what sort of knowledge we need to fill the gap;

(3) establish some premises by offering the foraged knowledge;

(4) make arguments based on those premises, outlining some new way of looking at all or some part of Composition; and

(5) conclude by indicating the new positions's implications, and suggesting areas for further inquiry.

And, in fact, this represents perfectly sound Philosophical form for what have mostly been construed as first offerings—arguments, that is, that are not responding to positions previously spelled out by other members of the community, and so not framed yet in deliberately dialectical terms.

However, the shape of Philosophical argument becomes much clearer when it does assume a more clearly dialectical form, the back and forth of argument and counter-argument. Once a first argument has been made, then, a responder has two possible directions to move in (other than simply agreeing). First, she can look to the form of the argument, and test its validity: try to determine whether, in fact, the inferential chain by which it moves from premises to conclusions really works. If the argument proves invalid—if unacceptable conclusions have been drawn from acceptable premises, or if acceptable conclusions have been connected to acceptable premises by arguments that are not inferentially sound—the responder would demonstrate the formal error, and then either correct it or scrap the argument. Second, assuming the argument is formally sound, she may turn, as it were, to content, and see if she agrees with the argument's premises. If she does not, she cannot simply state her own objections —moral, practical, or whatever. Instead, the responder must offer arguments about why the maker of the initial argument should not want to hold onto one or more of the initial premises: demonstrate, that is, that these same premises would lead the original investigator to support a position he would not like.

The fullest and most careful instance of substantial dialectical confrontation in Composition, I think, can be found in George Dillon's *Constructing Texts: Elements of a Theory of Composition and Style*, and especially Ch. 1, "Biology and Convention, Bad and Good Writing," which is essentially a direct response to E. D. Hirsch's *The Philosophy of Composition*. Hirsch had drawn very heavily on psycholinguistics for his premises in that book. According to Dillon, though, Hirsch has been far too naive in his borrowings, placed too much faith in this science of language:

> Psycholinguists have been just as muddled as the rest of us, and it seems that their chief contribution to thinking about reading and writing at present is their growing awareness of their principal mistakes and false starts. If science tells us anything at present, it is, "Watch out for your assumptions" (p. 1)!

There are, he continues, "four faulty assumptions that must be avoided if there is to be any fruitful contact between psycholinguistics and English composition"—all of which, Dillon argues, Hirsch "tenaciously embraces":

- that reading is like listening, and writing like speaking;
- that reading proceeds bottom-to-top;
- that each unit of discourse should be self-contained and self-explanatory;
- that reading basically extracts propositional content (p. 1).

The chapter that follows explores these assumptions and Dillon's objections to them in some detail. "The result of holding all four of them" together, says Dillon,

> is a theory of "good writing," nowhere more clearly sketched than in *The Philosophy of Composition*: good writing, or style, is viewed as a property of sentences themselves, based on human psychological mechanisms and ultimately on biology. Good writing is writing that allows intake (extraction) of propositional content with the least effort on the reader's part. The rules of good writing can then be viewed as grounded in nature, and any anxiety that what the composition instructor teaches may be arbitrary and picayune, not to mention classist and sexist, can be laid to rest. "Writing" becomes a teachable skill and English composition a technology (pp. 17–18).

In short, what Dillon has done, in sound Philosophical fashion, is to work out from Hirsch's premises a position to which—as the tone of this passage begins subtly to suggest—Hirsch himself would presumably object. Dillon delivers the final stroke in his next paragraph, where he posits his own central premise:

> Against this view we set as a first principle that written discourses are governed by diverse and complex conventions, and that bad writing is a failure to meet a significant number of the reader's expectations. Like the other conventions that make up a culture, discourse conventions may ultimately be based in some biological necessity (say, drive reduction), but nobody, I suppose, would try to justify the rules governing a formal dinner party as those guaranteeing the most efficient intake of food given the relevant channel limitations. There is an ideology that attempts to ground social conventions and institutions, particularly existing ones, on biological realities: it is called Social Darwinism, and its chief architect was Herbert Spenser, the original proposer of channel limitations (p. 18).

As fine an example of such argument as this is, though, a perhaps more representative and, because more sustained, lively exchange takes place a few years earlier, in the pages of *College Composition and Communication* between Janice Lauer and Ann Berthoff.[1]

The issue is not unrelated: How can/should psychological research into heuristics be used in Composition? Lauer's initial essay is called "Heuristics and Composition," and it is a pretty standard piece of foraging. The major thrust of her argument is to claim a broader knowledge base for Composition, and it opens with this passage:

> Freshman English will never reach the status of a respectable intellectual discipline unless both its theorizers and its practitioners break out of the ghetto. Endless breastbeating, exchanges of despair, or scrambles after rhetorical gimmicks can result in little more than an ostrich solution . . . . Unless both the text-makers and the teachers of composition investigate beyond the field of English, beyond even the area of rhetorical studies for the solution to the composition problem, they will find themselves wandering in an endless maze (p. 80).

After another page or two of elaboration on the kinds of knowledge she thinks might be valuable, she ends by offering a bibliography of some two hundred items, most of them from psychology.

Berthoff responds in an essay called "The Problem of Problem Solving." Her reply is not formal; that is, she does not fault Lauer's logic. But she does have serious objections to her premises. She begins by quoting Lauer's "endless maze" passage, pairing it with a statement by Louis Kampf, whose essay in an earlier issue of *CCC* had claimed that "Composition courses should be eliminated . . . because they help to support an oppressive system." Both these arguments are mistaken, says Berthoff, because their premises are faulty. Kampf, a Marxist, concerns himself with the political dimensions of learning to write at the expense of the psychological; while Lauer, "with her narrow understanding of heuristics, virtually precludes from consideration all approaches but those sanctified by the technologists of learning," and so sells the political short:

> Indeed, each of these arguments can be faulted on psychological and political grounds, separately considered, but the important point is, I think, that neither Professor Kampf nor Sister Janice Lauer considers the crucial interdependency of psychological and political factors. In radical critics of education, from Jane Addams and Maria Montessori to I. A. Richards and Paulo Freire, what we may chiefly value is not their prescriptions but their understanding of this juncture, the necessary point of departure for any philosophy of education being the account offered of the relationship of society and knowledge (p. 91).

In other words, Berthoff asserts that Lauer has failed to fully consider the consequences inherent in her choice of foraging territory.

And she wants to show the reductive path down which such premises can lead:

> Teachers studying heuristics as understood by Sister Janice Lauer will soon discover that a theory of learning as problem-solving requires a view of language as signal code, a notion that converts meaning to "information," form to "medium," interpretation to "decoding," etc. By thus misconceiving of the human use of language, communication theory or, rather, pedagogy deriving from it falsely defines the forms of knowing. There is a fundamental failure to recognize that "the linguistic adult," in the current phrase, who comes to school is an *animal symbolicum* (p. 93).

Lauer's response ("Response to Ann E. Berthoff, 'The Problem of Problem Solving' ") attacks Berthoff on both formal and substantive grounds. So, she says, while Berthoff "laments the psychologists' polarizing of the creative and the intellectual," she is guilty of some polarizing of her own. This "Dichotomizing, especially unsubstantiated polarization," argues Lauer, is as reductive in Berthoff's hands as in any psychologist's. Worse, though, Berthoff is guilty of a "failure to make distinctions (not necessarily oppositions) and to reason logically." In one passage, says Lauer, Berthoff fails "to distinguish between [Jerome] Bruner's term, 'science,' and her own term, 'technology':

> Secondly, she has assumed that if scientific thinking is essentially problem solving, therefore problem solving is essentially scientific thinking. Hence her ability to conclude that if psychologists advocate problem solving, they are thereby narrowing learning to scientific thinking. *Non sequitur* (p. 99).

However, these formal errors, she seems to suggest, result from fears raised by a mistaken premise—Berthoff's belief, that is, that for composition teachers to look into fields outside of what she argues is their own tradition is to adopt dangerous and reductive notions about the relationship between knowledge and society. Such a premise, Lauer argues, commits Berthoff to consequences *she* won't like:

> This misinterpretation of Bruner as well as of my bibliography springs, I believe, from a sense of threat which is widespread— the fear of many humanists that they and their values will be gobbled up by the "scientists." Such a fear creates an atmosphere inimical to the changes needed to solve our very real educational problems. The effect of being too critical too soon of hypotheses is no hypotheses at all; it discourages potentially useful insights. I might have left out of the bibliography the

information theorists, Newell, Simon, and Shaw, as being less obviously useful than, say, the gestaltists, but they have contributions to make, or at least it is too soon to conclude that they don't. When confronted with difficult problems, as is the English teacher today, it is unwise to close off any sources of solution; not unless we enjoy the problems (pp. 99–100).

She does, however, in what seems to be a conciliatory gesture, offer to alter what she calls the "red flag" in her initial formulation, changing it to words she assumes Berthoff will approve. So now, instead of the hyperbolic claim that "teachers and textmakers" must investigate beyond English and rhetorical studies for "the solution to the composition problem," she amends her statement to say, more modestly, that they can find there "insight into the nature of the creative process of composition, 'the process of naming the world'" (p. 100).

Although Berthoff's next and last turn ("Response to Janice Lauer, 'Counterstatement'") acknowledges Lauer's gesture, she is still not satisfied in terms of the basic issues. She essentially reiterates, and to some extent expands on, her central argument, again seeking to demonstrate to Lauer that her allegiance to one of her premises commits her to a position she will not want to maintain. That is, Berthoff argues, while it is certainly possible for English teachers to seek insights in the findings of psychological research, to do so is, in effect, to buy into what she regards as psychology's sadly limited, reductive world view:

> Janice Lauer has genially removed "the red flag"—the term "problem solving"—but our disagreement over the alleged benefit to English teachers of research in "heuristics" as defined by psychologists is rather more than a quibble; it is a matter of concepts and premises and not of words only. Adding "creative" to "problem solving" doesn't really solve the problem of problem solving which is, as I see it, that those who reduce and limit the operation of the imagination in this way— psychologists who undertake to study "mentation" or problem solving or concept formation or creativity—leave out, in order to accumulate "meaningful data" and quantifiable results, the very factors which we as English teachers should be concerned with. The principal of these is the nature of language itself as an organ of growth, a speculative instrument, our means of creating and discovering those forms which are the bearers of meaning.
>
> English teachers who turn to psychologists for their pedagogical concepts and their epistemology, as they did at the

Dartmouth Conference, tend to develop assumptions about language which are diverting: they lead away from the questions of how the formative powers of language can be made available to our students (pp. 100–101).

The ball is back in Lauer's court. Her next move might have been to rephrase her objections to what she sees as Berthoff's "ostrich position" in such a way as to make the central issue—the relationship between the findings of various kinds of inquiry (like psychology) and practice—more accessible to further debate. But the ball, in fact, seems to have stayed in her court; I can find no continuation of the argument. Nevertheless, I think it serves its purpose here, illustrating the typical movement of dialectical inquiry; and illustrating the kind of movement—and the vigor, too—dialectical confrontation can take on.

Drawing Conclusions: Dissemination to a Wider Audience

The Philosophical community has not yet had an apologist as articulate as Robert Connors has been for the Historians, but I think what he says about his mode of inquiry works pretty well here, too. These investigators have been as concerned to be reformers as Philosophers. And the reasons are as understandable here as there. Dialectic, after all, doesn't ever end; positions are simply defined more and more precisely, perhaps more and more synthetically. But the great debate, at least as it has been conceived in a relative world, never breaks through to some Truth, nor does it overspill its boundaries to become instrumental. And yet the pressure from the larger society of Composition, as well as the attraction of gaining some power therein, make simple notions about disinterested inquiry seem not merely foolish, but irresponsible. *Someone* will harness various Philosophical positions as a means to political and pedagogical influence. Why shouldn't the Philosophers have some share in that influence? Moreover, like the Historians, they can rely on the restorative powers of a long-term commitment to dialectic to redress any imbalances they may create by deliberately working from premises that will lead to reform-oriented conclusions.

From my point of view, however, the problems raised by Philosophical reformism are much the same as for its Historical counterpart. As always, I want to avoid a naive view of the mode of inquiry. Philosophy does not get made in a vacuum; and, since the values and mores of the investigators will presumably influence their work whether they want them to or not (though even that can be a matter of Philosophical debate), I am sympathetic with efforts to orchestrate certain lines of argument in the name of sustaining the dialectic. But there is a difference between the exercise of such influence within the limits of the inquiry—as I say, in claiming certain traditions, or marshalling certain premises—and doing so in ways that are not methodologically sanctioned. We have already seen one way in which this can happen in the discussion of foraging, illustrated both in Moffett and, indirectly, in Hirsch: to grant certain premises special status, and so to claim that status for conclusions developed from them. Another variation, not all that different from the "lesson of history" notion, is to imply that a Philosophical position is a guide to action: to blur the distinction between considering the preconditions of the ideas we might use in deciding what to do and the deciding itself. Philosophical inquiry can do the former; it cannot do the latter.

The best illustration I know of the potential dangers of such a strategy can be seen in the presentation and reception of my colleagues C. H. Knoblauch and Lil Brannon's *Rhetorical Traditions and the Teaching of Writing*. That book's central argument, I think, represents a fine piece of Composition's Philosophical inquiry. In essence, it consists of the dialectical confrontation between two positions: what can be called a formalist (or perhaps "traditionalist") position against one that might be called epistemic. And the confrontation is presented in the context of what I've been calling the great debate, the authors delineating a philosophical heritage for each side: for the formalist, the classical tradition—Aristotle, Cicero, Quintilian, etc.; and for the epistemic, a new or "modern" rhetoric, its beginnings traceable in such writers as Descartes, Arnauld, and Bacon, later reaching maturity via Kant, Cassirer, de Saussure, Susanne Langer, and so on.

In setting up this confrontation, though, they begin with the following argument:

> As we see it, [teaching] methods derive from philosophical perspectives whether teachers wish to become philosophical about them or not—perspectives on language, on meaning, on communication, on learning, and on the ways of assisting learning, among others. Moreover, they frequently derive from differing perspectives which are opposed rather than complementary, for instance, mechanistic versus organic views of language. Most important, some perspectives are demonstrably preferable to others because they offer more accurate, more comprehensive, and more productive understanding of the nature of discourse and the development of verbal competence. We believe it's important for teachers to become conscious of the philosophical

dimensions of their work because nothing short of that consciousness will make instruction sensible and deliberate, the result of knowledge, not folklore, and of design, not just custom or accident (p. 2).

You can see why this is going to cause methodological trouble in a philosophical argument. True, they don't do what we have seen someone like Moffett do; they don't try to privilege the findings of some other mode of inquiry as premises. Instead, though, they try to privilege Philosophical inquiry itself. First, they want to make it empirical: Teaching methods—things people *do*—"derive" from philosophical perspectives. By itself, this is perhaps a little fuzzy; it isn't entirely clear how "derive" might be different from, say, "can be better understood in light of" or "are informed by," and the nature of such a difference might be crucial in Philosophical inquiry. Still, the empirical implication is there: If teaching methods derive from philosophical perspectives, then to study those perspectives is, in effect, to study the methods they give rise to.

Any ambiguity in Knoblauch and Brannon's intentions disappears, however, when they move to their second proposal. Some of these philosophical perspectives, they claim, "are demonstrably preferable to others because they offer more accurate, more comprehensive, and more productive understanding of the nature of discourse and the development of verbal competence." In other words, Philosophical inquiry, at least in this case, will not only be empirical but *instrumental*. It will directly help us choose our teaching methods because it can determine which of the method-generating philosophical perspectives best explains how the world really is. That, at least, is what the invoked criteria certainly suggest. To demonstrate which philosophical perspective most accurately explains the nature of discourse, for instance, is to demonstrate something empirical. In what other sense could accuracy be meaningful? It follows that, assuming we want to do the right thing—assuming, that is, that we don't want to use methods based on demonstrably inferior perspectives—we'll have no trouble deciding which perspective, and hence which derivative method, to choose.

Rhetorically, this position has the not-very-surprising effect of loading the dialectic with moral overtones, dressing out the philosophical perspectives as though they were characters in a sort of morality play. So the classical tradition, for example, while an "extraordinary achievement" (p. 22) in its time, is cast as the villain—"That Old Time Religion," its chapter is subtitled; while the modern tradition, which has "permanently displaced it" (p. 51), clearly comes off as the good guy. Again not surprisingly, this mode of presentation has clearly rankled in some quarters. John Gage, in a review of the book entitled "The 2000 Year Old Straw Man," explains his objections:

> To the extent that Knoblauch and Brannon's book does attempt to make us aware of the inadequacy of the assumptions about knowledge and discourse that prevail in current pedagogies, it is a compelling and necessary book. But it is seriously flawed in the *way* in which it argues this case, and if the book succeeds in opening up dialogue on this issue, I hope that it does not determine too narrowly the range of such talk. It risks doing so by making a straw man out of classical rhetoric, which Knoblauch and Brannon take to be a whole, unified system of composing with a single set of assumptions about knowledge, and by so doing they are able to dismiss it utterly from serious consideration. If the book fails to stimulate further debate about its central issues, it will be because this approach will simply prevent many people from taking it seriously. The authors intend their book to make some people angry, and there is nothing wrong with that. But I cannot see why they could have intended for people to take them as ill-informed and uncritical simply because they have chosen to be polemical. They deal in issues that need more rigorous argument, not more shrill rants (pp. 100–101, his emphasis).

I don't mean to suggest that Gage is right in everything he says. His is clearly the reaction of one of those he thinks the book is intended to anger, and he consequently responds more to its rhetorical form than its philosophical substance, and he often does so in kind. So, for example, *his* way of arguing that Knoblauch and Brannon "intended for people to take them as ill-informed and uncritical," whatever its level of irony, doesn't do much for his credibility. And later in the review, he seems to have a chip on his shoulder, taking exception when he really need not—stretching a Knoblauch and Brannon example about a "crotchety classicist" to fit his argument that theirs is a reductive we/they confrontation, or complaining that they think Aristotle "wrote a book called *Rhetorica* in Latin" because they follow a fairly standard convention for such a spelling.

Nevertheless, Gage's reaction is a revealing one. It may be, as he says, that some people will not take the book seriously because of what he sees as its polemical tendencies, and that's not good. Equally likely, and no better from a Philosophical perspective, is the chance that people *will* take it seriously, but uncritically: will be, as it were, converted. The dramatization of the philosophical positions presents a compelling emotional argument, and if Gage is maybe a little too sensitive about being identified as a "they," he is right on the mark about the appeal of the "we": the "we" are, Knoblauch and Brannon make it clear, "intellectually sophisticated teachers who make reasoned instructional choices within contexts provided by a modern philosophical perspective" (p. 98).

I want to be very clear, though, that it isn't the rhetorical power of the book that poses the methodological threat here; dialectical confrontations always involve choosing sides, debate is bound to get heated, and different writers will take different rhetorical tacks. The threat lies, rather, with the assertions about Philosophical inquiry that generate that rhetorical power in the first place—specifically, the philosophical status those assertions claim for the sides being chosen. In this confrontation, the formalist and epistemic positions are no longer simply manifestations of philosophical perspectives, to be hammered out in dialectic much as they have been for the previous 2000 years. Instead, they have a direct connection to method, are guides to action; and, since philosophical inquiry can demonstrate which of these guides is "preferable," there's no further need for dialectic. The confrontation is over, and the epistemic position has won.

The danger to Philosophical inquiry is clear: To move outside the bounds of method, whatever the short-term gains in reform— especially when, as here, the move finally threatens to subvert the power of a dialectic altogether—is to risk the demise of methodological integrity. As I suggested above, the impulse that drives such Scholarly reformism, the urge to make the world a better place, is surely understandable. But modes of inquiry are in some ways very restricting things; to accept what power they offer is to accept, as well, that there are things they cannot do—or at least, that they cannot do and still be themselves, sustained by the investment of the community of inquirers.

5

The Critics

By comparison with the fairly bustling communities described in the previous three chapters, the one presented here constitutes little more than a frontier settlement. The mode of inquiry itself is not an especially exotic one—is, in fact, the central *mode* of inquiry in literary studies. In keeping with the tradition of textual interpretation from which it derives, I will call it Hermeneutical, and its practitioners, the Critics. It has three major concerns: (a) establishing a body of texts, usually called a canon, for interpretation; (b) the interpretation of those texts; and (c) generating theories about (a) and (b)—that is, about what constitutes a canon, how interpretation should proceed, and to what end.

To say that this mode is little used in Composition is not to say that literary studies have not had an influence on the teaching of writing. After all, the vast majority of the field's members—surely 80 or 90%, anyway—have been trained in literary studies, and so in this Hermeneutical method: in its central cycle of interpretation and counter-interpretation, as well as attendant work in bibliography, textual studies, biography, stylistics, literary theory, and so on. Quite naturally, then, they have carried this enormous collective training into their new field. It has had a particular impact on practice, where literary texts have often been made central to writing courses as writing to respond to and/or writing to emulate. In addition, as we saw in the last chapter, literary theory has been a natural source for Composition's Philosophers, with borrowings from Longinus to Coleridge, Derrida to Bakhtin.

Despite both familiarity and influence, however, Hermeneutical inquiry has not been widely adopted as a way of *making knowledge* in Composition. So whereas Composition Scholars have responded to whatever impulse it is that calls for a history and a philosophy, there either has not been, or they have for the most part not responded to, any very strong concomitant impulse to create a Hermeneutics: to establish and interpret a specifically Composition-based canon. There are any number of ways to account for this phenomenon, and a full explanation would probably assemble some combination of them all. One simple possibility, for example, is that the method never seemed relevant: that people trained to operate within the rather narrow, belletristic canon of traditional English could see no knowledge-making application for that training in the mostly non-belletristic Composition. This would be more or less in keeping with the sort of historical-institutional account Winifred Bryant Horner offers in her "Introduction" to *Composition and Literature: Bridging the Gap*, where she traces the gradual widening of that "gap" in the rise to power of literary studies. And both of these would fit with my own, rather more immediate political explanation to the effect that this reluctance reflects Composition's need to establish a separate professional identity. As we saw in Ch. 1, the rise of Composition as a separate field came in response to a demand for an academy-based expertise. It may be that it was important for a group operating mostly out of very weak political positions in English departments to exercise an authority independent of their potentially overwhelming, co-existent literary studies. Hence the heavy initial investment in Researcher methodologies, the insistent focus on processes rather than products and, here, the reluctance to work with a method that might make them look derivative.

Whatever the reasons for it, the result of this general ambivalence is that those few who have adopted a Hermeneutical mode of inquiry find themselves inhabiting pretty lonely, isolated outposts—caught somewhere in the methodological no-man's land, if you will, between the often hostile Composition and Literary Studies. I count two such outposts, in fact. By far the more prominent is dominated by the looming presence of James Kinneavy's *A Theory of Discourse*. In this long and ambitious work, Kinneavy claims to be trying to "carve out" for Composition a "respectable domain in the field of English," and in a sense that is what he does (p. 2). But his major tactic, in fact, is to *redefine* the field of English, so that the Composition and Literature legs of the tripod metaphor come together in a broader category called "pragmatics," the study of texts. His subsequent reapportionment plan is a little unclear: Composition is renamed "discourse studies," and then either includes literary studies as one of its subsidiary interests (see, e.g., his chapter on "Literary Discourse"); or else it is to be distinguished from literary studies in that it deals with "the analysis of writing other than literary." In either case, the methodological point is the same: Kinneavy wants to claim a canonical turf for Composition/Discourse Studies, and to construct thereon "norms parallel in a sense to the techniques of new criticism" (p. 2). And that is a Hermeneutical proposal.

The other outpost is rather more obscure. As yet, it has almost no skyline, no looming presences, but rather a string of more modest contributions—a kind of trail edging gradually outward from Composition in the direction of literary studies. It begins with the Practitioner writings of people like Ken Macrorie and Kenneth Bruffee, both of whom propose that maybe student writers have a right to more textual authority than has traditionally been afforded them. It continues with Chapters 5 and 6 of Peter Elbow's *Writing Without Teachers*, where he presents guidelines for a "teacherless writing class": in effect, a practical (albeit quirky) hermeneutics for an interpretive community whose "canon" consists solely of its own productions. It appears again in work like Glenn Matott's "The Importance of Making Distinctions between Kinds of Writing"; John Schultz's story-workshop approach, most fully articulated in *Writing From Start to Finish*; Lil Brannon and C. H. Knoblauch's "On Students' Rights to Their Own Texts: A Model of Teacher Response," in which they begin by invoking I. A. Richards on the nature of writers' authority; and, in a slightly different way, *Student Writers at Work: The Bedford Prizes*, a published collection of prize-winning student writing.

Where this trail leads, its outermost point—for the moment, anyway—is my own study, "Writing in a Philosophy Class: Three Case Studies." In that investigation, I deliberately set out to take what seemed the logical next step in this gradual author-ization of student writing: I claim it as Composition's legitimate canonical turf, and spend about three-fifths of a forty-page essay interpreting the texts of three student writers. In doing so, I use essentially the same critical methodology I would use were it a study of Whitman, Thoreau, and Emerson, or any other trio of "major" figures. My basic rationale for this move is simple enough: Since the distinctions between Author and author, between Writing and writing are a matter of convention, of point of view, I am free to offer a different set of conventions, a new point of view.

I will have more to say about both Kinneavy's work and my own in the discussion that follows. Here I want simply to anticipate the objection that Hermeneutical inquiry doesn't warrant treatment— that two outposts do not a community make, and that to give them space roughly equal to the better established communities is to inflate their importance. I will admit to a certain bias in favor of this kind of investigation; of all my work in various modes of inquiry, I was most interested in these case studies. But my justification for including it is based rather more on its political importance. It has become increasingly fashionable to try to make connections between literary studies and Composition. Toward a general goal of maintaining a unified English, such a trend seems all to the good. But for the purposes of Composition's growing power as a field, a knowledge-making society, the terms of such a rapprochement—*how* the gap gets bridged—matters a great deal. And in the struggle over those terms, the fate of this Hermeneutical mode of inquiry, the one that literary studies calls its own, takes on considerable significance.

The Nature of Hermeneutical Knowledge

Assuming that my estimate about the training of Composition's membership is correct, the shape of Hermeneutical knowledge ought to be pretty familiar to most readers of a book like this. It is knowledge about the meaning of texts, derived from the act of reading, articulated as critical analysis, and refined by dialectic. Its structure is canonical; that is, it takes its shape from the texts upon which it is founded. And its logic, as in other Scholarly inquiry, is dialectical; that is, the central texts, serving as points of dialectical contact, provide the basis for the confrontation of more or less coherent and systematic opposed world views. It is, we might say, the mind studying its own operations in the peculiar realm of reading.

Like Historical inquiry, this Hermeneutical mode has two sets of rules, one empirical, the other interpretive. The former—generally thought of, perhaps, as editorial—governs the establishment of the text or texts to be interpreted, setting standards of sufficiency, authenticity, and accuracy. The second set deals with the introduction of an interpretation for community consideration. As in the other two communities, these are a version of Scholarly dialectic, here adapted for operating within the more restricted framework of a textual canon. Any new interpretation, then, will be tested by other inquirers both formally, to see whether it moves logically from premises to conclusions; and substantively, to see whether they agree with its premises.

Hermeneutical Inquiry

In its most basic form, then, Hermeneutical inquiry would go something like this:

1. Identifying Problem(s)
   EMPIRICAL STAGE
2. Identifying Relevant Text(s)
3. Searching for Text(s)
4. Assembling and Validating Text(s)
   INTERPRETIVE STAGE
5. Seeking Pattern(s) in the Text(s)
6. Explaining the Pattern(s): Generating an Interpretation
7. Relating New Interpretation to Existing Interpretations: The Communal Dialectic
8. Dissemination to a Wider Audience

This is pretty elemental stuff. Having established some focal text or texts, the Critic seeks patterns in them, attempts to interpret those patterns, and then offers the interpretations as arguments in a communal dialectic. When the inquiry shifts to what I called (c) above, a concern for theory, the investigation will—as we shall see with Kinneavy—focus less on the interpretation of individual texts, and instead treat the texts themselves as features in some larger, intertextual pattern.

Identifying Problem(s)

The means by which problems are identified for Hermeneutical inquiry can be seen as a sort of cross between the Historical and Philosophical modes. Like the Philosophical, then, the problems can be said to derive from the communal dialectic—as either beginning or responding to an argument. And in that sense, too, it doesn't really matter where the argument begins: debate over any one point will eventually be carried, by dialectic, to include the whole. Like Historical inquiry, though, Hermeneutical inquiry is bounded by textual evidence. You will recall that I have already made a distinction between these modes in terms of the *status* of those texts. Here, the texts are seen not as the referents to some outside events, but as constituting "events" themselves. Nevertheless, the effect on framing problems is the same: No text(s), no inquiry.

There is obviously a considerable difference between the problems Kinneavy and I frame in our respective studies. Mine is a more or less simple matter of Hermeneutical practice, practical criticism. In "Writing in a Philosophy Class: Three Case Studies," I assembled a set of primary texts that consisted of all the writings done by three students during the course of one semester in Philosophy 110, an introductory course designed as part of a writing-across-the-curriculum program. I also had two sets of secondary texts: the transcripts of three interviews with each student (beginning, middle, and end of course); and all the course materials (textbook, syllabus, teachers' comments). My research question, which I framed so as to set up a running comparison with a critical biography of Walt Whitman, was "How can we account for these fresh and startling voices?" That is, I wanted, as in a critical biography, to construct from my readings of these texts the consciousnesses that could have produced them: to explain the writers and their writings in terms of one another, and in a way that accounted for the peculiar milieu in which they worked.

Kinneavy's proposal, by contrast, not only has a wider, more theoretical scope, but would seem to have ties with a rather different, if somewhat fragmented, Composition tradition. In part, then, it might be seen as a logical extension of the longstanding tradition of "rhetorical readers" which, one might argue, are the practical precursors of a canon for Composition, even if the texts assembled therein received little professional attention, except maybe in teacher's guides. Perhaps more significant here, it also has connections with the tradition of what is usually called rhetorical criticism. Like other things rhetorical, this brand of inquiry has suffered an ambiguous institutional and disciplinary fate. So Wayne Booth's *The Rhetoric of Fiction*, to take an obvious title, has a clear place in literary studies; and indeed, in post-structuralist criticism, the idea that there could somehow be a purely "aesthetic"—and hence a-rhetorical—hermeneutics has become untenable. Whatever its general academic status, though, it has occasionally shown up in the Composition literature in the form of an explicative/interpretive essay: James Steel Smith's "H. G. Wells' Tonic," for instance, in the May 1962 *CCC*; James W. Nichols' "Julian Huxley: The Specialist as Rhetorician," in its February 1965 issue; or, more recently, and hence as a descendant, not precursor, of Kinneavy, S. Michael Halloran's excellent "The Birth of Molecular Biology: An Essay in the Rhetorical Criticism of Scientific Discourse" in the September 1984 *Rhetoric Review*.

As my reference to Kinneavy's study as a looming presence is intended to suggest, though, his ties to this tradition, interesting as they might be to trace, are finally not that important; his is an undertaking so ambitious, so out of proportion with anything before or since in Composition, that for now, anyway, it stands pretty much alone. And although he does use a few texts for illustrative purposes, his primary concern is not the interpretation of any particular texts, but the explication of a critical theory that will give shape to a

Composition-based hermeneutics, one that would help investigators know which texts ought to be interpreted, how, and to what end. In essence, he frames his problem when he explains what his title, *A Theory of Discourse*, promises to provide:

> A theory of discourse will then comprise an intelligible framework of different types of discourse with a treatment of the nature of each type, the underlying logic(s), the organizational structure of this type, and the stylistic characteristics of such discourse (pp. 4-5).

EMPIRICAL STAGE

Identifying Relevant Text(s) (Bibliography)

Searching for Text(s)

Assembling and Validating Text(s)

There has not been any really serious Empirical work in Composition, any substantial textual scholarship. Kinneavy appears to take the accuracy and authenticity of the few he uses—selections from *Statistics: A New Approach*, for example, or the Declaration of Independence—pretty much for granted. As we shall see, though, he has been called into question on essentially bibliographical grounds—for (a) having failed to deal with a sufficient number of texts and (b) for having chosen texts that are atypical of the types they purportedly represent. In my own study, I was as careful in my uses of all three sets as I thought the study warranted—searching for references across texts, determining which of two instructors wrote comments, checking my transcriptions of taped interviews. But I took no extraordinary precautions, and could easily enough have taken further steps to better guarantee accuracy and authenticity. It remains to be seen if concerns which have been so important in literary studies, where the attention given to the work of Authors has been in keeping with that once accorded to those assumed to have Divine origins, will play an equivalent part in Composition.

INTERPRETIVE STAGE

Seeking Patterns in Text(s)

As with Historical inquiry, there is no theoretical limit to the number either of the textual features an investigator addresses, nor the patterns of such features that might be deemed significant. Here, of course, they will acquire that significance not as a function of a communal narrative, but a dialectic; that is, they will be deemed meaningful by one or another interpretive sub-communities—sometimes called, albeit loosely, critical camps—each of which may be said to represent one of the world views whose confrontation drives the community's inquiry.

In the absence of such communities in Composition, though, Kinneavy and I were both pretty much on our own. My approach was to propose to account for the "fresh and startling voices" of my undergraduate writers by positing three of what I called "contexts," three ways of thinking about the universe of discourse in which these writers' words operated—"a Rhetorical context, an Intellectual/ Ethical context, and a disciplinary context":

> That is, we can understand these three writers as (a) students in a college classroom writing for (if not to) two teachers, with some purpose; (b) as, in a perhaps more fundamental sense, developing human beings at some point in a 1980's version of a liberal education, in some way "becoming" themselves intellectually and ethically, identifiable within the kind of developmental pattern outlined by William Perry in his *Forms of Intellectual and Ethical Development in the College Years* (Perry, 1968); and (c) more or less novice philosophers learning how to operate in the context of a discipline, Philosophy, whose boundaries are determined, for this term and these writings, by the teachers and the course (p. 14).

These, then, represented the basis for my critical interpretation. The features I focused on, and the patterns in which they were deemed meaningful, were those I found relevant within these contexts. As is the case in most critical studies, I offered no catalogue of either features or patterns; rather, these appear as called upon to support the line of argument that is my interpretation. So in terms of Rhetorical context, say, I would focus on choice of person, hints about a shared frame of reference, and the like. Having suggested that one student's relationship with her teacher-audience resembles what James Britton et al. call a "pupil to teacher/particular relationship," I offer the following as part of my evidence:

> From the very beginning of the course, she seems to see herself engaged in a dialogue with her instructors: She writes consistently, comfortably, in the first person. She uses fairly frequent, informal meta-comments ("Excuse me, I have to do some more reading."); asks questions ("How come there's no Reese [the instructor] entry?"); and assumes shared contexts ("When Prof asked in class . . . ") (p. 20).

I dealt with the other two contexts in the same way, looking for strings of features that seemed to me to reveal the writers' understanding of and attitudes toward knowledge and authority (Intellectual/Ethical); or examining their handling of philosophical vocabulary or strategies (Disciplinary). And where I could, I tried to make connections among these patterns, to see how my Rhetorical reading helped account for—or qualified—my Intellectual/Ethical one, and so on.

Given his theoretical purpose—his ambition to put together an "intelligible framework of different types of discourse"—Kinneavy is mainly interested in whole texts as features, among which the emergence of various patterns allows him to characterize types. As his reference to new criticism suggests, Kinneavy takes a formalist position rather different from my own author- and context-sensitive eclecticism. Specifically, he combines an insistence on the primacy of what he calls "aims"—those "certain purposes" which humans may achieve "in their use of language with one another" (p. 38)—with the conviction that, rather than assuming encoder (writer/speaker) or decoder (reader/listener) to be its "determinants," it "seems better to find the aim which is embodied in the text itself," albeit with some allowance made for "situation and culture":

> This means that a totality of effect is generated by the things talked about, the organization given the materials, the accompanying style, and so on. Other kinds of things talked about, other kinds of organizations, other styles generate other effects, different not only in degree but in kind. The effect of all these means (mode, art, meanings, grammar) is to generate a reaction of some kind of acceptance or rejection on the part of the normal decoder (p. 49).

Thus he proposes that the aim of any particular piece of discourse be founded upon the reaction of this "normal decoder" which, in the case of writing, would presumably be a "normal" reader like himself. For his macro-critical purpose—that is, for the purpose of arranging whole texts as features of an all-encompassing inter-textual pattern according to their dominant aims—this "reaction" supplies him with four kinds of discourse: reference, persuasive, literary, and expressive. For each he offers, as promised, an account of its nature, logic, organization, and style, in effect claiming that these are various strands of the overall intertextual pattern; that they emerge in a way that transcends the writing's specific communicative context; and so that they account for whatever constitutes the normative reaction.

Accounting for the Patterns: Creating an Interpretation

Given the different ways in which we frame our problems, and our different critical assumptions, my study and Kinneavy's necessarily arrive at very different kinds of interpretations. We have already seen that it is not to Kinneavy's purpose to deal closely with particular texts in and of themselves. Rather than studying the significance of the patterns of features in particular texts as a function of the communicative context in which they were written, he treats whole discourses as in some sense "features," and having traced in his readings of them, and in their treatment at the hands of other theorists, certain patterns, he explains or interprets those patterns by arguing that they derive from that principle he has defined as "aim": What or how they mean is seen primarily as a function of their location in his inter-textual scheme.

By contrast, I was concerned to determine what and how particular texts mean as a function of the communicative context in which they were written. For each of my writers, then, I offer what amounts to a mini-critical biography, portraits of them as writers in the peculiar milieu of their philosophy course. To do so, I deal with each of my contexts—Rhetorical, Ethical/Intellectual, and Disciplinary—in a separate section, in effect offering three interlocking readings that work toward the construction of the whole writer. Here, for example, is a passage from the end of the section on one writer, Alyson:

> In short, Alyson's dominant philosophical strategy is to work out, in problems based on her experience but framed by the Syllabus, the implications of her faith. She seems neither surprised (as we shall see is the case with Yvette) nor made more or less cynical (like Mark) by the reflection, in her textbook, of a relative world. Disabused of expectations of a simpler, more secure world by her family "tragedy," as she calls it, she has fashioned for herself a position the power of which, I think, she has yet to fully appreciate. What it gives her, in this philosophy course, anyway, is stability—not inflexibility, nor simplicity—but stability. Of all the comments written by her instructors in her journal, she seemed proudest of this one, and it might serve here as a summary: "You have an interesting way of taking a problem at its proper level of complexity. Bodes well for intellectual results" (p. 31).

By following this same procedure for all three writers, I am able to generate some contrastive perspective as well—each writer stands out in greater relief by comparison with the other two. Probably the simplest way to characterize the nature of this contrast is to offer a passage from a section called "Summary of the Cases." Having reiterated my critical purpose—that is, "to understand, via this textual interpretation, what each of these three writers made of his or her existence that others did not"—I argue that in this study I have framed that making in terms of "how the individual, through language, comes to grips with Authority as institutionalized in higher education":

> When we talk about writing as a means for learning for Alyson, Mark, and Yvette, then, it is in this sense: How have the four or five thousand words they wrote figured in the accommodations each has made with Authority as embodied in Phil. 110? For Alyson . . . Philosophy's Authority gets demoted, as it were, to a small "a"; she is already committed to a different, transcendent Absolute [Christianity]. Moreover, her structural solution makes it clear that she shares in this Authority herself: ". . . God exists within each one of us [so] we all possess some knowledge of truth." Thus the writing, to recall the word I used earlier, serves to affirm her own Authority. It is the means by which she articulates, clarifies, and even celebrates her own power.
>
> Yvette works out a very different arrangement. That "amazin' " discipline Philosophy, very much in the person of the professor, still has full Authority; in these matters of Philosophical reasoning she is the greenest of novices. For her, then, the writings . . . represent a means of acquiring some small share of that Authority for herself. She is an acolyte, and in her journal she attempts to mimic, by way of coming to control, the words of the empowered, although she doesn't get very far. Writing comes close here to incantation: Master the words, master the power (pp. 57–58).

The general principle should be clear enough. It goes back to the formulation I offered just above: I wanted to understand what each writer made of this portion of his or her existence, but my understanding of that will clearly depend upon my sense of contrast, of what each has *not* made of it. And for that I needed the other writers.

Relating New Interpretation to Existing Interpretations: The Communal Dialectic

As with other Scholarly inquiries, Hermeneutical investigations don't end with individual interpretation, but shift into a communal mode. And it follows, given the situation I've described, that even more than in the other two communities, there has been very little Hermeneutical dialectic yet—outposts don't attract that much attention. Still, there has been some, and it has been revealing. Here, then, by way of illustrating what Hermeneutical dialectic might look like, I want to present one fairly full response to Kinneavy; and then, turning to some pre-publication responses to my own case studies, to suggest not only how such responses can go wrong, but what sort of knowledge-making climate Hermeneutical investigations in Composition appear to face.

Perhaps the best response in print to *A Theory of Discourse* is Richard P. Fulkerson's "Kinneavy on Referential and Persuasive Discourse." Although he admits the attractiveness of what he calls Kinneavy's "paradigm"—his four types of discourse—Fulkerson's interest lies elsewhere:

> The more significant claim in the book, the one on which entire programs in composition can be built, is that "The aim of a discourse determines everything else," specifically the discourse's structure, its logic, and its style. The idea that aim controls these three features of a discourse is Kinneavy's *theory*, as distinct from his four-part paradigm. To the extent that the theory is sound, Kinneavy has given us a powerful taxonomical, pedagogical, and interpretive tool (p. 43, Fulkerson's emphasis).

The problem, naturally, is that the theory is, in Fulkerson's judgment, *not* sound: "I maintain . . . that Kinneavy fails to provide compelling support for the theory and that a number of this [sic] specific assertions fail to hold up under examination." Fulkerson raises four "general criticisms" to Kinneavy's theory. Two point out violations of what I have called Empirical Stage rules—objections to the adequacy of Kinneavy's canonical base:

> Kinneavy's assertion that a given discourse aim leads to certain traits is an empirical statement, one that should be settled by examination of discourse, not merely deduced from the work of other theorists. In four hundred pages, however, Kinneavy treats in detail only about six examples of discourse. Usually, for each discourse type, he analyzes one text in some depth. That simply is not adequate evidence to substantiate the causal

connections Kinneavy asserts. These texts constitute "illustration" rather than "demonstration," a distinction Kinneavy regards as crucial.

Furthermore, the key examples Kinneavy analyzes seem quite atypical of the discourse types they supposedly represent. The major instance of the scientific division of reference discourse is an argument by Camus that murder and suicide are ethically equivalent. Even when one overcomes the normal associations of *scientific*, realizing that Kinneavy means (roughly) "academic discourse," it is difficult to see Camus's piece as representative. A *Saturday Evening Post* column by Stewart Alsop represents the informative division of reference discourse. Kinneavy criticizes it as inadequate informative discourse (p. 95), but later admits it to be persuasion (p. 135). The key instance of expressive discourse is the American Declaration of Independence. None of the three seems typical of the discourse group it supposedly represents (p. 44).

The third and fourth criticisms point to violations of the Interpretive Stage rules. In one, Fulkerson points out that Kinneavy is led into a formal error—that is, an error in moving from premises to conclusion—by his tendency to slide from description to prescription, and from there into circular reasoning:

> The tendency toward prescriptivism also shows up in comments like, "The introduction to a scientific paper *should* announce very clearly the topic under consideration, *should* indicate the self-appointed limitations of the analysis, and *should* outline the general method of procedure" (p. 158, emphasis added). Probably it is easier to make prescriptive judgments than accurate analytic ones, but prescriptive comments do not carry out Kinneavy's argument that aim in discourse controls everything else. Instead the argument shifts to "aim should control everything else." Whenever it does not seem to, the discourse can easily be judged defective. Such reasoning is irrefutable because circular (p. 45).

And in the other, Fulkerson raises what I labeled in the last chapter a substantive objection—an objection to one of Kinneavy's premises. In sound dialectical form, he demonstrates that Kinneavy's assertion about aim—which he regards as "implausible"—would force Kinneavy (and us) "to accept the notion that all works of literature, for example—including the poetry of Yeats, the fiction of Richardson and Robbins, *The Dukes of Hazzard* and *My Last Duchess*, Gerard Manley Hopkins and Hopalong Cassidy, not to mention jokes, limericks, fairy tales and *Saturday Night Live*—have similar structures, similar styles, and similar logics" (p. 44).

Fulkerson goes on to deal with Kinneavy's treatments of referential and persuasive discourse in more detail, but these general criticisms are enough to illustrate what responsible communal response might look like. Fulkerson clearly knows the rules of this game—recognizes Kinneavy's theoretical, Hermeneutical purpose, and the kind of response it requires if the dialectic is to continue. Indeed, in this passage near the end of his essay, he tries to reassess the value of Kinneavy's work, and in doing so characterizes the nature of that dialectic pretty clearly:

> We need not accept Kinneavy's assertions about the relationships between aim and form, but they nevertheless provide useful hypotheses for works of rhetorical explication. When a given discourse fits Kinneavy's claims, as Didion's essay does, then his work provides one useful causal framework for explaining why the discourse might function as it does. And when a discourse fails to fit, as I believe is more often the case, the Kinneavian perspective still leads us to ask useful questions about how the discourse actually achieves its aims. Used with caution, Kinneavy's study thus can provide rhetorical critics with deductive expectational norms, norms that help to highlight, in individual works, the frequent variations from those norms. Instead of a finished taxonomy upon which we build curricula and syllabuses, Kinneavy has provided a complex set of hypotheses to be tested, used, and modified through rhetorical criticism (p. 54).

However, it is my sense that in terms of his methodological awareness here, Fulkerson represents the exception, not the rule. However strong the tradition of rhetorical criticism might be elsewhere, Hermeneutical inquiry would still seem to be pretty exotic stuff in Composition. That claim is based in part on what I have already pointed out has *not* happened: that at the level of theory, Kinneavy's book, for example, seems to have provoked little in the way of either extended response or following; nor, in more applied terms, has there been any more than a trickle of text-based, interpretive studies. I want to support it further here, and at least begin to account for the phenomenon, by considering briefly two sets of responses to my own investigation.

The first set, by a publications review committee to an earlier draft, raised two objections: first, that three students were too few for such a study; and, second, that two of the three students should not have been included on the grounds that they weren't, somehow, very good students (though both were members of the class, and both passed the course): "The course content was beyond the grasp of one student (Yvette), and another [Mark] remained aloof to it." The objection, in short, seems to be that my "sample" was improperly assembled. You can see the difficulty here. If we grant my study Hermeneutical status, these objections become roughly equivalent to the argument that a study of the work of three Nineteenth Century British poets was flawed because it only looked at three poets, and thus could not hope to say anything significant (about either the three poets, the Nineteenth Century British poetry scene, or whatever); and because it included as one of the three Christina Rosetti, who is not, in the objector's opinion, sufficiently Nineteenth Century British in some way, or was a woman, or a second-rate poet, or whatever. It would be quite proper, of course, to argue, as a point of Hermeneutical dialectic, about the "representativeness" of some text in the sense of its relative importance in some framework, even to the extent of arguing that it is in or out of the canon; or that looking closely at a small number of texts from some time and place can only distort our vision of the larger whole, and is thus not worthwhile. After all, it is by these kinds of disputes as much as any other that the various world views engaged in the dialectic are better articulated. But these objections to my study do not seem to be invoking those standards.

Still, I couldn't be sure to what extent these confusions were the fault of my explanation of method. In the version that was reviewed and accepted for publication, therefore, I addressed them as directly as I could. With the letter of acceptance came copies of the reports of the two primary reviewers. They were diametrically opposed, one voting to accept the essay essentially unchanged, the other to flat out reject it. It is the latter reviewer—for whose candor I am grateful—that I want to quote here in full:

> I must confess that it was difficult for me to get beyond the abstract before my prejudices blinded me to whatever virtues this work might have. And as I read further in the materials, I found those prejudices reenforced rather than disarmed. For example, one prejudice the work affronted was that it didn't have any particular hypothesis or hypotheses it was testing out. It seemed to lack the idea of any sort of control—control of influences on the students, and control in the sense of a similar case which is different in a systematic way. It affronted my prejudice against the fuzzy use of the term "hermeneutics." On the other hand, if this material were put forward as a narrative, and were well done in that mode, were interesting & profound, I'd be for it. But as *research*? (Reviewer's emphasis.)

Obviously, my study stands guilty as charged (although I might take exception to the "fuzzy" count): it simply was not designed to conform to these kinds of expectations, these "prejudices." And they are powerful prejudices indeed. They help explain, I think, the earlier reviewer complaints about sampling; however much my explanations may have contributed to any confusion, I was clearly writing for an audience predisposed to misconstrue my purpose in just the way they did. But as this reviewer makes plain, such prejudices are more than a cause of superficial confusion. They represent convictions that run very deep—deep enough so that even recognizing them as prejudices does not disarm them. Hence, what I offer by way of interpretation might be revealing in some narrative—i.e., aesthetic/pathetic—way; but what is offensive is that I should masquerade it here as knowledge, as "*research.*" That is simply going too far.

Conclusions and Implications:
Dissemination to a Wider Audience

Given this sort of skeptical reception to the study of student writing, and the mostly indifferent one given Scholars like Kinneavy, Fulkerson, and Halloran, who deal with more traditionally canonical texts, what can we say *is* the significance of Hermeneutical inquiry for other Composition audiences, and what kind of future might it have? Kinneavy, as we have seen, tends to let ambition narrow his vision—that is, he tends to think, despite his book's title, that what he offers will become *the* theory of discourse, and that the "norms" it offers will transform English as a whole: "Teachers for freshman composition and high schools can be trained more efficiently. Literature itself can emerge more intelligible in its own right" (p. 2). And while people have, in fact, taken him at his word, and tried to impose the theory for those purposes, Fulkerson does a pretty good job of explaining why these claims are too ambitious, and of suggesting more cogent arguments for its value: as an interpretive tool, it can help to give us better access to individual works.

And it is in this direction, finally, that I think the value of Hermeneutical inquiry for Composition must lie. Like the other two Scholarly modes of inquiry, it cannot be instrumental; in neither its theoretical nor applied form can it tell anyone what to do. If Historical inquiry gives us some access to who and what has come before; and Philosophical inquiry to the preconditions that lie behind the reasons we might use in deciding what to do; then what Hermeneutical inquiry provides is access to voices, our own and others: access to the nature of consciousness, in effect, and the way it makes the world in words. In "Writing in a Philosophy Class: Three Case Studies" I frame the issue this way: "Granted that it is possible to read student writing very closely, to apply some of the same sorts of interpretive strategies we use in literary studies, the question remains: Why bother? What do we learn?" My answer makes me the closest thing there is to an apologist for a Hermeneutical method in Composition. Let it stand here as a conclusion:

> By way of answer, let me return one last time to my comparison with a study of Whitman. After all, what does a hermeneutical method win us there? In its earliest applications, of course, the method's reason for being was more obvious: it gave us access to sacred texts, texts believed to be the revealed word of God. But when the same methods are applied to secular texts, the matter of purpose becomes much less clear. Indeed, that question, in one form or another, hovers over all debate in literary studies. For the purposes of this study, it seems safe to say that we study such secular texts because we value the perspective of the world we find "revealed" there in much the same way that we valued what we found in sacred texts. That is, using the term in its broadest sense, we value any understanding of the *genius* that informs it (p. 64, original emphasis).

IV

The Researchers
(Experimentalists,
Clinicians,
Formalists,
and Ethnographers)

IV

The Researchers

Influential as the Scholarly modes of inquiry have been in Composition, they have for the most part not been conceived—even, as we have seen, by many of their users—as representing its central line of development. If *Research in Written Composition* was indeed the new field's charter, then it designated as first citizens not the Scholars, but those who adopted modes of inquiry geared to lead them to more "scientific" knowledge; and their special status—one they have assumed, but one which has also been granted to them by the rest of the society's members—seems to me to be reflected in the title under which I have gathered them in this section: the Researchers.

Even with the deference accorded them, though, the rise to power of Researcher modes of inquiry has been a very gradual affair. As I suggested in Chapter 2, it's a lot easier to call for new or more careful inquiry than it is to get it—to generate methodological momentum, as it were. A handful of landmarks in particular stand out. One of the most important was the initiation of NCTE's *Research in the Teaching of English* in 1967. It has never been devoted exclusively to research in Composition, but a very substantial portion of its space has been, and its annual bibliographies have played an important part in legitimizing the Researcher enterprise. I think it can safely be called the leading Researcher journal in Composition. Of roughly equal significance, though of shorter duration, was NCTE's Research Report series. Here again, not all of the publications deal with Composition, but many do; and its thirteenth publication, Janet Emig's *The Composing Processes of Twelfth Graders* (1971), is arguably the most influential piece of Researcher work ever published.

By the mid-1970s, the pace of development, and the emergence of a more specialized Composition focus, had quickened, so that important markers are more closely spaced. Though its contributors take a much more eclectic perspective on what constitutes knowledge in the field, Gary Tate's 1976 *Teaching Composition: 10 Bibliographical Essays* extends the work of *Research in Written Composition* by framing possible inquiry in terms of what has been done. Even more directly in line with Researcher methodologies is Charles R. Cooper and Lee Odell's 1978 *Research on Composing: Points of Departure.* Its editors, who explicitly draw comparisons between their volume and *Research in Written Composition*, argue that inquiry must shift from asking "What materials and procedures will improve students' work in written composition?" (p. xi) to wondering what composing is, how it is done, and so on—in short, "to examine, test, and modify our basic assumptions about written composition" (p. xiv). By the early 1980s, there were a number of other collections with similar emphases: Lee Gregg and Erwin Steinberg's *Cognitive Processes in Writing* (1980), for example; the two volume *Writing: The Nature, Development, and Teaching of Written Communication* (1981), edited by Carl H. Frederiksen and Joseph F. Dominic; Richard Beach and Lillian Bridwell's *New Directions in Composition Research* (1984). Most recently, two substantial review/bibliographies have been published: Michael Moran and Ronald Lunsford's *Research in Composition and Rhetoric*, and George Hillocks' *Research on Written Composition: New Directions for Teaching.* And finally, *College Composition and Communication*, especially under the editorship of Richard Larson, has taken on a noticeably more Researcher bent, while new journals like *Visible Language* and *Written Communication* so far seem to have a dominantly Researcher orientation.

These are, you will notice, essentially generic landmarks. Methodological differentiation—indeed, even methodological self-consciousness—has come to Composition in general only very slowly, and these modes of inquiry have been no exception. The notion of "research" has tended to lump together any and all modes of inquiry grounded in empirical phenomena, however conceived, as opposed to the textual phenomena/dialectical grounding of the Scholars; and which purport to be descriptive, as opposed to the prescriptiveness of the otherwise empirical Practitioners. I will trace the emergence of the particular modes of Researcher inquiry, and any concomitant methodological self-awareness, in the chapters that follow. Here it will be enough to point out that this general naiveté—the notion that research is research is research—turns out to be something of a theme in this Section, coming up again and again.

For now, in any case, I have identified four major modes of

inquiry in Composition. The first, in both size and longevity, I call
the Experimental, and its users the Experimentalists: in broad terms,
those who seek to discover generalizable "laws" which can account
for—and, ideally, predict—the ways in which people do, teach, and
learn writing. The second I have dubbed Clinical, and its practitioners the Clinicians, borrowing the name from its uses in fields like
psychology and reading. Here, the focus is on individual "cases":
most commonly, the ways in which a particular subject does, learns,
or teaches writing. The third mode will be called Formal inquiry.
What Formalists do, to put it simply, is build models or simulations
by means of which they attempt to examine the *formal* properties of
the phenomena under study. In Composition, they have focused almost exclusively on the composing process so far—Linda Flower and
John Hayes are the most prominent—but in theory a Formalist could
propose a model for anything: teacher behavior, reading, talk about
writing, etc. Finally, I will call the fourth mode Ethnography, and its
practitioners Ethnographers. And if the Formalists can be said to
make models, then what the Ethnographers make are stories, fictions.
Their peculiar concern is with people as members of communities,
and their mode of inquiry equips them to produce knowledge in the
form of narrative accounts of what happens in those communities.

The first three of these constitute a methodological cluster quite
as neat as the three Scholarly modes, sharing as they do the positivist
tradition's fundamental faith in the describable orderliness of the
universe: that is, the belief that things-in-the-world, including in this
case people, operate according to determinable or "lawful" patterns,
general tendencies, which exist quite apart from our experience of
them, and which are, in addition, accessible to the right kinds of inquiry. Where they differ, as my sketches of them might suggest, is in
the kind of access to those patterns they provide. The Experimental
method proposes what amounts to a direct assault on them. In keeping with its natural science heritage, it attempts to systematically
control and manipulate the phenomena it studies—in short, to
experiment with it—in order to uncover those lawful patterns. The
emphasis in Experimental inquiry has been what Gordon Allport
calls nomothetic: the overall goals of inquiry are framed in terms of
generalization, not particularization. Data collected is valuable not
for what it reveals about any particular individual, but as evidence
concerning the sought-after broader patterns.

The Clinical method can be understood as the Experimental's
idiographic or holistic complement. Its concern *is* particularization;
data collected is valuable precisely for what it reveals about individuals. Clinicians may thus claim an access to the phenomena they
study not merely as direct as, but in many ways richer than, the

Experimentalists. For while they can (and usually do) manipulate their subjects—giving them tests, say, or asking them to compose aloud—they are not bound by the restrictions that establishing Experimental control imposes. The standard for Clinical inquiry is Janet Emig's case studies of eight twelfth graders, and it is typical in its efforts to examine a very small number of subjects in considerable depth. What Clinicians sacrifice to gain this depth, of course, is their access to the larger patterns. To make it epigrammatic: What they gain in particularization they lose in generalization.

Formalist inquiry, by contrast, might be described as an extension of the human power to understand things by analogy. If the Clinical method trades off its generalizing power to gain greater access to particulars, we might say that the Formal method goes the other way, swapping direct access to particulars for enhanced powers of general explanation. Rather than dealing directly with the phenomenon they wish to study, then, Formalists attempt to create an analogue for it—a model, a simulation. What they gain is great freedom to construct operative, tautological, convincing wholes: self-contained systems which *by definition* work perfectly. What they give up is their grounding in any particular phenomenon; so while the model may work perfectly, its correspondence to any of the empirical systems for which it might claim to be an analogue—even when there is only one such system—must be demonstrated Experimentally. In practice, as we shall see, such demonstrations present incredible, perhaps insurmountable, difficulties, but that need not seriously diminish Formal inquiry's worth; simply building the models themselves can be valuable. So while we might say, again epigrammatically, that Formalist inquiry produces generalizations in search of particulars to account for, it is the producing and the searching, more than any finding, that matters most.

The Ethnographic method doesn't fit with these other three very well at all. It is "research" in the general sense, of course, or it wouldn't be in this Section: as a "human science," it claims a grounding in empirical phenomena. But if both Clinical and Formalist inquiries represent compromises on the positivist faith in our ability to observe and describe human activities as part of what is "out there" in the world, a faith most fully manifested in the Experimental method, then Ethnographic inquiry is a flat-out rejection of it. From a positivist perspective, then, it may be said to represent a profound skepticism about our power to observe or describe any human phenomenon at all as if we were "separate" from it, as if the inquirer could be "objective," and so discount her presence as either participant or observer. But it derives, in fact, from the very different phenomenological tradition. From that perspective, Ethnography is anything but a kind of negation—is, rather, a methodological celebration of the individual consciousness as the source of meaning—of "lawful" order—in human experience. And its authority lies not in its objectivity—the "pure" use of language by observer-as-lens—but of a kind of collaboration whereby the life of the community finds articulation via the phenomenal experience, and the words, of a single individual.

The communities to which these modes of inquiry give rise need less by way of preparatory remarks than did their Scholarly counterparts. I have already accounted in general terms for both their size and their perhaps disproportionate influence, and will elaborate on both as we proceed. And, as will become clear enough in each chapter, a Researcher can be as polemical—for much the same reasons and to the same effect—as any Scholar. However, I would like to offer one reminder. In the Introduction to this book, I was careful to borrow Diesing's warning to the effect that neither he nor I could claim to be covering all of the modes of inquiry, he in the social sciences, I in Composition; that both of us had chosen, in his phrase, "prominent locations." That caution applies especially in this Section, where it can be hard to say at what point methodological variations go from producing differences in degree to differences in kind. In the Experimentalist chapter, then, I have included not only true Experimental studies, but so-called pre- and quasi-Experimental studies as well. At the same time, I have for the most part disregarded a mode of inquiry that essentially has grown out of Experimental inquiry, the statistical survey. By my rough count, there have been well over 200 survey studies of one kind or another since 1963. They have varied widely in topic and scope: surveys of classroom practices on a single campus, or a collection of junior colleges, or a particular state; surveys of administrative practices, such as how much of what kind of writing instruction is required, again on everything from a local to a national scale; surveys designed to find out things about how writers work—the kinds of outlines technical writers use, say, or the influences on children who write successful poetry.[1]

No doubt many of these surveys have had some influence: attempts were made to change teaching practices, new writing requirements were created, textbook dicta were adjusted. A handful that are based in whole or in part on survey work might even be familiar: Joseph Mersand's *Attitudes Toward English Teaching*; Richard Braddock's "The Frequency and Placement of Topic Sentences in Expository Prose"; Stephen Witte and Lester Faigley's *Evaluating College Writing Programs*; even George Hillocks' efforts at meta-analysis in *Research on Written Composition*, where the results of large numbers of experimental studies are, in effect, "surveyed" to generate a kind of profile. My sense, though, is that no community of inquirers, united by their loyalty to this methodology, has emerged. Instead, what might have become a method in that sense has been regarded merely as a tool, a technique—and one to be used, most often, not to make a contribution to a knowledge-making community, but to gain political leverage in a school or district or state. So it's no great surprise, either, that only a very few of these studies demonstrate any particular sophistication with the method.

The upshot, in any case, is that while a method for what might be called Survey research has been around in Composition, its use to date does not warrant full treatment here. And it seems safe to assume that there are other modes of inquiry at work that I have not accounted for—combinations of the methods I have described, or variations, or even methods of which I am simply unaware. All of which is by way of reiterating that opening caution: While I present these as the major modes of Researcher inquiry, they are still only *some*, not *the*, modes of Researcher inquiry in Composition.

6

The Experimentalists

It should surprise no one that the Experimental method has provided the basis for the oldest and, in terms of numbers of investigations, largest of Composition's Researcher communities. After all, it has been the dominant mode of formal educational research in this country over the past 75 years or so. And while it has always had its share of vehement critics—who delight in pointing out, for example, the origins of many of its techniques in agricultural research, in formulations designed to deal with corn yield per acre—it is not a dominance that it will surrender easily. Its roots in Composition run very deep. When Braddock, Lloyd-Jones and Schoer assembled their *Research in Written Composition*, the bulk of the 504 studies they listed were, in one form or another, Experimental. More importantly, all five of the studies they chose as models for their "Summaries of Selected Research" section—"five distinctly superior investigations" (p. 55)—fall under the Experimental rubric. Their faith in this kind of inquiry and, by implication, the faith of most of the nascent Composition, seems really quite complete—so complete, in fact, that they appear unable to entertain doubts about it. They begin their chapter on "Suggested Methods of Research" by quoting a protest lodged by a colleague:

> Hearing about the project of which this report is the result, a colleague wrote, "What is the sense of attempting an elaborate empirical study if there is no chance of controlling the major elements in it? I think . . . that the further we get away from the particularities of the sentence, the less stable our 'research' becomes. I do not for that reason think there should be no

study and speculation about conditions for teaching composition and about articulation, grading, and the like, but I do think
that it is something close to a mockery to organize these structures as though we were conducting a controlled experiment"
(p. 5, their ellipsis).

What I hear in this objection, albeit with ears made sensitive by
the intervening twenty-odd years, is a question about the appropriate-
ness of the Experimental model for significant inquiry in Composition. But Braddock et al.'s response suggests that they hear in it not
questions about either the method or its applicability, but about
Composition's historical mishandling of it:

> Certainly there is much truth in that statement, especially if one
> takes it as a comment on the bulk of the research which has
> been conducted thus far on the teaching of written composition.
> But research in this area, complex though it may be (especially
> when it deals with the "larger elements" of composition, not
> merely with grammar and mechanics), has not frequently been
> conducted with the knowledge and care that one associates with
> the physical sciences (p. 5).

In other words, they see the problem not as one of methodological
fit, but of investigator fitness. They are clearly convinced that Composition research can make progress using this method, but to do so
the field must reform its handling of Experimental designs and techniques, bringing to them a "knowledge and care" believed to characterize the physical sciences, from whence the method has been
adapted, and where its success is what made it seem so attractive in
the first place.

And it is presumably this sort of reform-minded optimism,
along with a sizable head start, that has sustained the Experimental
community's steady production since. Despite continued criticism of
the method and its usefulness for Composition concerns, then, and
despite considerable competition from other methods, it remains the
most prolific of the Researcher communities. In compiling the background for this chapter, for example, I assembled a list of well over
1000 Experimental studies conducted between 1963 and 1985.
Adding to that the Experimental studies cited in *Research and Written Composition*, and assuming that at least a few others have
escaped both lists, one can figure on upwards of 1500 Experimental
studies—more than that produced by all the other Researcher
methods *combined*.

The territory covered by a body of research this size is obviously
considerable, and not easily summarized. The investigations most
automatically associated with the method are the teaching studies,

those designed to test the efficacy of some whole "experimental"
pedagogy, usually by comparison to some "standard" or "traditional"
approach. Of these, far and away the most visible has been the series
on sentence combining, stretching pretty coherently from Kellogg
Hunt's exploratory work through John Mellon and later Frank
O'Hare's NCTE Research monographs, on to Max Morenberg, Donald
Daiker, and Andrew Kerek's "Sentence Combining at the College
Level: An Experimental Study," with a bundle of studies in between
and since. But all sorts of other pedagogies have been the subject of
Experimental inquiry, as well. To name just a few: the "stylistic approach"; the "Normal" vs. "Bibliographic" vs. "Kinescope" methods;
the "workshop" approach; the "small group, personal growth method"; the literary models approach; the "Garrison" method (mini-
conferences) vs. the traditional method; a "focused and sequenced
free writing approach." No telling how long such a list might be.[1]

As many such whole-approach studies as there have been,
though, they are not the most common sort of Experimental study,
in part because they present some fairly daunting logistical problems,
but also because their results are so difficult to interpret. For even
when students in an experimental curriculum are judged to have
learned to write better—by whatever measures—it is obviously very
difficult to say which features (or combinations of features) of such
complex, relatively long-term "treatments" have been responsible.
As Braddock et al.'s colleague suggested in the passage quoted above,
there is always considerable risk of making a mockery of the method
by pretending that such inquiry has been fully controlled. The more
common tactic, then, has been to identify some more manageable
feature of a pedagogy as the treatment, and attempt to measure its
impact on student writing. The long-term, high visibility leader here
is probably the study of grammar instruction. Braddock et al. single
out Roland Harris's 1962 dissertation, "An Experimental Inquiry into
the Functions and Value of Formal Grammar in the Teaching of English, with Special Reference to the Teaching of Correct Written English to Children Aged Twelve to Fourteen," but it represents neither
the first nor the last word in that debate. Their bibliography, for
instance, lists a 1933 study called "Individual vs. Group Instruction
in Grammatical Usage" (Warner and Guiler); and while Patrick
Hartwell, in a 1985 *College English* article called "Grammar, Grammars, and the Teaching of Grammar" tries gamely to lay the matter
to rest as a research issue, it seems unlikely that it will die out any
time soon.

But grammar instruction has been only one concern of these
more narrowly defined classroom studies. There has been a relatively
coherent series of studies on ways of teaching invention, from the

mid-1960s work of D. Gordon Rohman and A. O. Wlecke on what they called pre-writing, to Lee Odell's study of the tagmemic heuristic reported in "Measuring the Effect of Instruction in Pre-writing" (1974), on through Thomas Hilgers' "Training College Composition Students in the Use of Freewriting and Problem-Solving Heuristics for Rhetorical Invention" (1980). Another has concerned itself with teacher responses to student writing. In a review of this literature in a 1981 *Freshman English News* article, "Teacher Commentary on Student Writing: The State of the Art," C. H. Knoblauch and Lil Brannon list 15 studies, most of them Experimental, the best known of which is probably Dennis Searle and David Dillon's "The Message of Marking: Teacher Written Responses to Student Writing at Intermediate Grade Levels." There have been studies on the impact of peer feedback; of parental involvement; of class size; of teaching shorthand or typing or dictation at various stages in students' development; of different paper sizes; kind or ink color of writing implements; lined vs. unlined paper, and on and on and on.[2]

And this represents only part of the Experimentalist agenda. There is an almost independent literature on writing anxiety, much of it framed in Experimental terms. Testing and assessment in writing—the institutional, "licensing" side of the educational system, as it were—has mostly been controlled by Experimentalists, with the writings of such people as Paul Diederich, Charles Cooper and Lee Odell, Sarah Warshauer Freedman, Ellen Nold, and Karen Greenberg probably most widely known. There has been work, too, on development, efforts to explore the ways in which children acquire—or fail to acquire—facility in writing. Many of these have not been true experiments, but so-called descriptive studies, which usually rely on correlation: investigations which in effect posit age, gender, school year or other factors as the "treatment" or independent variable, and then examine their relationship to changes in writing products or processes. The best known is almost certainly James Britton et al.'s *The Development of Writing Abilities (11–18)*, but many readers will also recognize Lillian Bridwell's "Revising Strategies in Twelfth Grade Students' Transactional Writing," and perhaps Sharon Pianko's "A Description of the Composing Processes of College Freshman Writers."

For all its size, though, the Experimental community has not exercised anything like a proportionate influence on the field. Of the dozen or so studies named above that readers might recognize, none seems to me to have had the impact of a Practitioner work like Peter Elbow's *Writing Without Teachers*, Scholarly work like Berthoff's *The Making of Meaning*, or of other Researcher work—Janet Emig's

Clinical study of twelfth graders, say, or Linda Flower and John Hayes' Formalist work on the composing process. The sentence-combining studies probably come closest to that level of influence, but more via the resulting textbooks than specific Experimental investigations. And while *The Development of Writing Abilities (11-18)* has been influential, it would seem to have been so far more for its philosophical underpinnings than for any findings.

I don't mean to suggest that this relatively low profile is entirely an indication of Experimentalist failure. Two of the method's dominant features, both of which we will consider in more detail later, work against individual visibility. First, it is equipped for certification, not discovery, bad news in a field like Composition, where celebrity has so far tended to accrue to "discoverers"—inquirers whose perspectives depart fairly radically from convention, pretty much regardless of the kinds of evidence supporting their claims. Second, Experimental inquiry spends its energy *disconfirming* possible explanations, and so accumulates more "positive" findings rather slowly. What these features amount to in practice is that individual initiative in most ways comes second to communal goals. Investigators are expected to do what needs to be done as the community sees it, contributing carefully tested bits of knowledge toward the construction of some larger whole. And, in fact, a large percentage of Composition's Experimental studies—as is the case in most fields—are dissertations, the work of graduate students making their way into the community. In this sense, Experimental inquiry represents a cooperative, interdependent enterprise, and one that tends to produce neither stars nor star studies.

And yet not all of the community's relative anonymity is simply a function of the mode of inquiry. Given the nature of the method, the best way for any particular Experimental study to gain wide recognition is for it to (a) be part of a relatively long and well defined line of inquiry; (b) build carefully upon, and contribute to, the work of the other investigators in that line; and then (c) be associated with that line of inquiry if and when its cumulative findings finally have an impact outside the Experimental community. The first is a matter of communal loyalty; the second of methodological integrity and hard work; and the third a combination of good timing and plain old luck. We might be able to compile a list of what—fifty? perhaps a hundred?—well-known or influential Experimental studies that could meet these qualifications, but what about the other 1400 or more? Is that an acceptable ratio for this kind of work, or are too many of the low-profile studies the unacceptably sloppy work that Braddock et al. cited? Or is their colleague more on the mark with the suggestion that maybe the method just won't fit the problems? Or are there other factors at work?

Reform-minded optimism notwithstanding, the Experimental community in Composition must be considered a deeply troubled one. This judgment is hardly new. Braddock, Lloyd-Jones and Schoer make it; so does Dwight Burton, a decade later, in "Research in the Teaching of English: The Troubled Dream"; a decade later still, Carl Bereiter and Marlene Scardamalia reiterate it in "Levels of Inquiry in Composition Research."[3] Nor, of course, are Composition's Experimentalists alone; their counterparts in the human sciences generally are under duress, too. For all the apparent promise of the Experimental method as a way of making knowledge about people—in this case about how people do, learn, and teach writing— things just haven't added up the way it seemed they might or should.

As we proceed through this account of Experimental inquiry in Composition, therefore, it will be important to keep its troubled condition in mind. For a long time, the method and its practitioners have been regarded by the rest of the field—with a sense of comfort, I think—as something of a sleeping giant, upon whose eventual waking Composition might pin its "scientific" hopes. Investigators have invoked it almost ritually, concluding their reports by looking ahead to the day when their tentative conclusions would be "subject to more rigorous and carefully controlled research," or words to that effect. And both that ritual and the optimism it represents remain very much alive; volume after volume of *DAI*, issue after issue of *Research in the Teaching of English*, present new evidence of their durability. But well into a third decade now, the giant has barely stirred. The time may have come to begin wondering whether we haven't misread its quiescence all along—to wonder, in short, whether the giant is sleeping, or dying. Or maybe not a giant after all.

The Nature of Experimental Knowledge

Holding the Experimental community together—its core, if you will—is its membership's allegiance to the fundamental positivist assumptions I outlined earlier: that the world is an orderly place, a place of non-random causes and effects; that that order exists quite apart from our experience of it; and that the principles of that order are accessible to human inquiry. Specifically, it seeks these principles as they are manifested among the relationships of what it calls variables: "any natural occurrences," as Diesing puts it, "that exhibit measurable variations in incidence, or rate of occurrence, or rate of change of occurrence" (p. 2). Its communal ambition follows from these assumptions: to sort out all these principled cause and effect relationships—in this case, those which account for human behaviors concerning writing—from the apparent chaos of experience.

Both assumptions and ambition are reflected in the structure and logic of the knowledge Experimentalists produce. Its structure is what I will call, albeit with some reservations, paradigmatic. My hesitation, of course, derives from the widespread confusion over this term generated by Thomas Kuhn's *The Structure of Scientific Revolutions*, and by all the borrowings of it since—some of which, as they relate to Composition, I will return to deal with in Chapter 11. But I want to use it here in a fairly narrow sense, invoking at least to some extent its Greek origins in *paradeigma* (a pattern, a model, a plan), and so dampening, though not eliminating, the resonances of its more recent uses. Experimental knowledge, then, is paradigmatic in that its form corresponds to—is patterned after or, perhaps more precisely, *is assumed to constitute the pattern of*—that portion of the orderly and accessible world under study: here, that portion defined by an interest in the phenomenon called writing. A fully formed paradigm would thus consist of the complete set of principles necessary to account for the relationships among all the variables of that portion of the world to which the community's powers of observation and measurement provided access. In its earlier stages—and, to be sure, Composition's Experimental paradigm fits that description— there are only a relatively small number of accounted-for variables tentatively connected by an even smaller, and very loose, set of principles, posited relationships which nevertheless provide the basis for speculation about the larger paradigmatic whole (theorizing), and for framing further inquiry.

What makes this paradigmatic structure workable—that is, what drives this movement from a loose collection of variables and tentative guesses about their cause/effect relationships toward articulated general principles—is an inferential logic. More specifically, it is what was once called, and is probably still called in common usage, inductive logic, a logic for moving from specific facts to general conclusions; as opposed to deductive, where the movement is from general premises to specific conclusions. It is more accurately understood, though, as probable inference (with deduction as necessary inference). In other words, if the world under study, insofar as it is accessible by measurement and observation, is assumed to represent a closed, non-random system, it should ultimately be possible to work back from its specific "facts"—in Experimental terms, variables and the relationships among them—toward that system's general principles by a process of trial and error which discounts relationships that seem random and pursues those that seem to exhibit regular, and so potentially lawful, patterns.

An illustration should help here. Suppose, for example, that a potentially interesting variable turns up quite unbidden in my teaching—say, to keep this simple, that my students' in-class essays are, on average, twice as long on Tuesdays as Thursdays. I am, of course, puzzled. Why should this variation be? I think of possible reasons. My students have gym on Thursdays just before my class, which means that they exercise for an hour before they write. I now have a primitive correlation—in this case, a negative one: a decrease in my first variable (average essay length) runs parallel to an increase in my second (duration of exercise). There are obviously all sorts of other correlations I could make—an infinite number, in fact: that the Thursday essay is always their second of the week; that, for the semester in question, it has rained every Tuesday, but never on Thursday; that Thursday is the second-to-last day of the school week, and so on. But this one has a certain intuitive appeal, and will serve as a starting point.

The next problem is to figure out whether there might be some causal connection between these two variables—whether (as common sense might suggest) the Thursday essays are on average 50% shorter *because* the students exercise for an hour before they write them. To find out, I decide to proceed experimentally, treating the exercise hour as my independent variable (meaning, essentially, that I will act as though it were the cause), and average essay length as the dependent one (so it gets treated as the effect). I begin with a simple design: I cancel the Thursday gym class, and then check on how long the essays run. Let's say, again in the interest of simplicity, that this experiment goes just as I might have predicted: the Thursday/no gym essays turn out to be, on average, exactly the same length as the Tuesday/no gym essays.

I might now be said to have a contribution, albeit a modest one, to make to the fund of Experimental knowledge. My little experiment makes it possible to infer that it is a little less likely that the correlation between my two variables, exercise duration and essay length, is strictly random, a matter of pure chance; I have tinkered with one, and my tinkering seems to have registered on the other. Naturally, I am not absolutely certain—despite, in this instance, what common sense might say—that the exercise hour was *the* cause of reduced essay length. There are all those other possibilities I haven't explored. For instance, I tried this experiment on only one Thursday. Was it a typical one? What was the weather pattern for this week? And were the Tuesday essays for this week typical? If they were shorter, it may be that the 50% decrease I thought I had been observing was a red herring—that, in fact, the students were only capable of producing a certain number of words per week, and they'd simply been in the habit of using two-thirds of them on Tuesdays, but this week, for reasons I have not accounted for, they decided to split them 50%-50%. Moreover, I haven't even begun to look past *average* essay length. Suppose that, writing after the canceled gym class, some students wrote twice as much as they had on Tuesday, while a corresponding number of others wrote only one-fourth as much. The average gain would still be there, but my notions about the causal connection between writing and exercise would obviously have to be complicated: some people might write more after exercise, and others less. Or maybe attendance (in Experimental terms, mortality) does more to account for the experimental effect than the hour of exercise—perhaps the "jocks" weren't in school because they only come for gym, and they were responsible for the ordinarily lower average length. And on top of all these other problems, why should I assume that the entire exercise hour, and not just the last five or ten minutes of it, is the prime cause here? Or showering? Changing?

Obviously, this business of probable inference gets very complicated very quickly, even in the conveniently neat world of my imaginary experiment. Variables proliferate, and their interrelationships become enormously complicated. Just as obviously, my seat-of-the-pants, intuitive judgments about probability won't suffice for anything more than this rudimentary sort of experiment. I will clearly need help figuring out ways to determine whether in fact it was my wholesale manipulation of the exercise hour, and not other factors, that accounted for the longer Thursday essays—need help, in other words, to gain what Experimentalists call *internal validity*. And suppose I want to decide how to work next term's schedule to account for what I've learned—to claim some level of *external validity* for my findings. How can I tell if my class this term is somehow representative of other such classes?

The Experimental community's response to both these needs has been to harness the logic of probability statistics to govern its inferential paradigm building. Clearly, there is some risk in doing so. It means using a formal system to validate claims about an empirical one; and this, in turn, involves accepting the formal system's fundamental assumptions without any way to determine their empirical validity. So, for example, a frequent prerequisite for bringing statistical calculations to bear on a set of data is that the data represent a "random" sample. In formal statistical terms, this means that they must all be taken from the same "universe" (so that the same laws of probability operate on them all); and that they must be taken independently (so that my first data-collecting observation does not impinge probabilistically on my second, and so on). You can see how this creates a problem. My observations are obviously a part of the world I am studying; they represent a variable, too. In order to employ statistical methods, though, I must guarantee that these observations are not themselves governed by the basic principles I seek to uncover. To do that, I would have to know the principles that govern the phenomenon called "my observations," and I don't. I could make *them* the object of my investigation, of course, but that would mean looking at a random sample of them, and I'd have to know the principles governing my observations of those observations, and so on in infinite regress. There's no way out: Harnessing the power of probability statistics requires the acceptance of its presuppositions more or less on faith.

Nevertheless, statistical theory vastly increases the Experimentalists' investigative powers. The gains are perhaps greater in terms of internal validity because it helps the investigator foresee and control the kinds of confounding effects I ignored in the design of my simple experiment: things that may have happened between Tuesday and Thursday (history); shifts in attendance (mortality); the possibility that Thursday just comes later in the week (maturation), and so on. Its usefulness is somewhat more limited in terms of external validity; extending findings drawn from one situation to other situations is more difficult, inferentially, than controlling the one situation. But it could help me design future experiments in which I selected and characterized my subjects with greater care, and so decrease the risk that my findings were wholly idiosyncratic to this one group—that these students, say, were peculiarly touchy on Thursdays, or highly sensitive to exercise.

All of this—the assumptions and ambition, the structure and the logic—should make it clear that Experimental inquiry is not geared to produce discoveries. Discoveries, in the sense of insights or understandings, can be made by any (and maybe even no) method, and under all sorts of circumstances—via philosophical debate or common sense conjecture, for instance, and while boarding buses or dreaming, and so on—and the literature on the subject is full of anecdotes documenting that variety. So while I suppose we associate many discoveries with their claimants' experimental habits—one thinks of Mendel and his peas, or Edison and the light bulb, for example—the method itself cannot take credit for the discovery. Rather, the Experimental agenda directs an enterprise that might be called certification:[4] Whatever pattern of cause and effect an investigator thinks she discerns in some phenomenon, by whatever means, it can only gain status in the Experimental community by being subjected to the kind of testing I sketched for my essay length/gym class study; and that testing, in essence, is what constitutes the Experimental method.

This distinction is important enough to belabor a little. Human beings posit and operate on guesses about cause/effect relationships all the time. We do so in our physical world. The stone I drop will fall to the ground because it possesses, at least according to Aristotle, impetuosity, a need to be at rest; the sun will "rise" tomorrow morning because the earth is rotating on its axis at a predictable rate; my "incurable" disease went away because of prayers to St. Jude. And, more to the point here, we make and rely on them in our social world, too: I don't spank my children because my parents didn't spank me, and look how nicely I turned out; when I am offended, I turn the other cheek, because it will save my soul; my students get to be better writers because of the voluminous comments I make in the margins of their essays. As these examples suggest, the bases for such guesses, the views of the world from which they derive and within which they make sense, vary widely. Nevertheless, the need to make them would appear to be an invariable human one, essential for living in the world.

What the Experimental method aims to do is to change the status of such guesses, to organize them according to Experimental criteria. Probably the simplest way to describe the Experimental community's conception of its own role in the society of Composition— and one in which it is presumably supported by many members of other communities—is that of final arbiter. The Experimental community sorts through the knowledge produced by other communities, the various conjectures about cause and effect in the teaching and learning of writing offered by Practitioners, Scholars, and other Researchers, and tests them against Experimental standards. The testing of each such appropriated guess, transformed for Experimental purposes into an appropriately framed "hypothesis," results in it being assigned some Experimental community truth value: an expression of the degree to which the posited cause/effect relationship has held true under certain conditions. In theory, this process would be continuous, each relationship being tested and re-tested, each test potentially leading to a higher level of Experimental certification, until it is either disqualified or, as sometimes happens, the community's powers of observation and measurement increase, throwing the whole paradigm open to re-evaluation.

No matter how long this process is carried on, though, it never establishes an absolute certainty; all Experimental knowledge, no matter how carefully or rigorously tested, remains relative, a probability. Probably the better way to think of it, though it may seem counter-intuitive, is as a method that seeks to approach certainty by reducing uncertainty. In test after test, it looks to determine whether what seems to be a relationship between two variables is anything more than coincidence; and, if it is, to gauge the relative probability of competing ways of accounting for that relationship. But no number of proofs that some apparent relationship between variables is not the result of chance adds up to final proof that it is, in fact, the result of any particular posited connection. As the uses of Experimentally-derived knowledge in the physical sciences over the past few hundred years would seem to demonstrate, of course, the predictive value of these justified guesses, what might be called their operative certainty, can be pretty good—witness the word processor on which I am composing, the microwave oven in which I cooked breakfast, and so on. And a guess about the effectiveness of a particular technique for teaching writing—the notion I suggested above, say, that my voluminous marginal comments make my students better writers—has the same Experimental potential for certification as observations about falling objects and planetary motion have had to reach the "lawful" status that a conjecture like gravitation has gained in the physical sciences. The point here, though, is that whatever operative or pragmatic power hypotheses which gain this status may seem to wield, it is nevertheless a status with real limitations. The next time I drop a stone, the "law" of gravity notwithstanding, there is some chance, however infinitesimal, that it will fall up, or just hover. The designation "law" in Experimental knowledge is thus only a way of expressing the cumulative tendency of a variety of inquiries which, in the context of a particular paradigm, have made it seem less and less likely that some relationship between variables was random: that the behavior of falling stones was not a matter of chance, but explicable, instead, in terms of this "relationship" between stones and the earth.

Finally, though, whatever its limitations, and however awkward the philosophical implications of assuming that human behavior can be accounted for by principles on the order of those that account for the behavior of falling stones, it isn't hard to understand the appeal Experimental knowledge holds for people involved in teaching writing. Human beings dislike uncertainty, stress: not knowing what will happen next, not knowing what to do. The practice of any art, on the other hand—teaching included—is by its very nature fraught with such uncertainties. There are ways in which that stress can be made manageable. Indeed, that may be one way to define art; when properly directed, such stress becomes the seed for inspiration: artists handle it, and the ways in which they do so is what makes us admire their work—hence lore, as we have seen in Chapter 2, can be conceived as a body of knowledge designed to provide such direction. But when an art is to be practiced in settings like our schools, where a Composition teacher might well have as many as 150 students to "teach," the stresses, at least if the students are regarded as discrete, unique, idiosyncratic individuals, are obviously considerable, even intolerable. The natural urge is to move toward system, toward a vision of students not as discrete individuals, but as in some ways comparable units acting according to articulable general principles.

Experimental knowledge responds to this urge very, very well. In it, the intuitions and guesses of lore are assumed to have been transformed into a more powerful kind of truth, one by which the uncertainty, and so the stress, of what otherwise seems such a chaotic world might be brought under control. To the beleaguered classroom teachers, this can be magical stuff: a way, as Erwin Steinberg put it, to buttress their art with a science or, as Braddock et al. hint, to supplant that art with science altogether. Either way, the fundamental motive is survival. If the conditions under which writing is taught cannot be changed—and surely they have not changed all that much in the decades since 1963—then there may be no better way to go. This is the promise of Experimental knowledge, and it goes a long way toward accounting for the durability of Experimental inquiry in Composition.

Experimental Inquiry

In keeping with the format I have been following, we can outline the Experimental mode of inquiry as follows:

1. Identifying the Problem
2. Designing the Experiment
3. Conducting the Experiment: Collecting and Analyzing the Data
4. Interpreting the Data
5. Drawing Conclusions: Dissemination to a Wider Audience

And to some extent, my usual caution for such sketches holds here: this is a suggestive outline for Experimental inquiry, not a definitive one. It fits my imaginary study of the essay length/exercise duration problem, for example, pretty well. I identified and framed my problem in a paradigmatically acceptable way; figured out a plan by which to examine it; then put the plan into action, collected and analyzed the relevant data, and tried to interpret the results. But not every study will fit so neatly. Investigations like those I have already mentioned by Britton et al., Pianko, and Bridwell don't actually involve the conducting of an experiment in the sense of manipulating some treatment variable, and so alter step 3. And replication studies—studies, that is, designed to reproduce exactly some previous investigation—in effect skip over step 1, accepting a problem as already framed.

The most important and striking feature of this method, though, is one that doesn't show up in this outline. For while there is some room for variation, this is far and away the most closely supervised of the modes of inquiry in Composition. To invoke the distinction I made with regard to Philosophical inquiry: Experimental investigators are afforded the smallest private phase of inquiry. So whereas the pre-publication movements of Philosophers are pretty much beyond the community's purview, in theory every movement of an Experimentalist *as Experimentalist* is public, and subject to community review. The emphasis on "as Experimentalist" is important, obviously, because people doing Experimental investigations are going to talk and read and think and write just as other kinds of investigators do; there is a whole literature devoted to debunking the myth of the "objective" scientist. Nevertheless, if the practice of the method is to mean anything—is to lead to the construction of a communal paradigm governed by an inferential logic—it must be conceived, finally, as a public performance.

Like so much else about the method, the reasons for this public-ness derive from its positivist bases. The community's ambition, remember, is to account for the principles governing a single, accessible world. In terms of communal progress, then, agreement is everything. It is not possible, as it is, say, for Critics, that two opposing positions can be equally tenable, equally "right"; permanent, dialectical opposition is a luxury a paradigmatic knowledge cannot afford. There can be opposition, yes; an attempt at replication that fails is bound to provoke argument, with a careful examination of both original and replicate studies and, very possibly, the initiation of a third. In the sense that opposition of this sort leads to further investigation, it can be construed as a good thing. But for the purposes of the inexorable movement toward an operative certainty, this kind of backtracking is counter-productive; and one or the other or both of the first two studies must, in the end, be judged "wrong." It only makes sense. If the world is an orderly place, and if the principles of that order operate with reasonable consistency everywhere in it, then any Experimenter ought to be able to conduct the same experiment in any time or place and get the same result. When this turns out not to be the case, there are only two possible explanations: either the world is somehow not an orderly place, in which case the whole Experimental enterprise, at least as conceived here, is jeopardized; or else somebody (or everybody) has made an investigative error.

For communal purposes, then, it's crucial to guarantee that, ultimately, this investigative unanimity is possible. And the best way to do that is to insist that as much as possible of every inquiry be public: that both the variables under scrutiny and the means by which they will be observed are clear; that there are no hidden features in the design; that data collection and analysis are not confused or fudged, and so on. We will see how this concern is manifested in each of the sections below. Here we can simply capsulize it as the truism that outsiders—and Experimentalists, too—seem to forget so easily: An Experimental study is no better than its replicability.

Identifying Problems

As is the case with so many other modes of inquiry, the Experimental method is of little help in determining what kinds of inquiry are worth pursuing. Indeed, if anything it complicates matters, creating a tension between the demands of its inferential logic, on the one hand, and of its paradigmatic structure, on the other—between the competing demands of depth and breadth, if you will. In one direction, then, lies the drive for that tantalizing, just-one-more degree of certainty (or, to make the point one last time, of decreased uncertainty) that might come with one more experiment, one more replication. Followed to its logical end, it would leave each investigator conducting the same experiment over and over and over again. We would, in effect, still be dropping stones to establish that they do fall.

But the demands of breadth are strong, too; they come with being finite and human: the need to know about the larger picture, to reach some passable understanding about how any one phenomenon relates to others; the need to produce, in terms acceptable beyond the Experimental community, "results." In this direction—again, at its most extreme—lies the corruption and abandonment of method, a retreat to "common sense," and the collapse of the Experimental community. Thus, when I say that the Experimentalists are guided in their identification of problems by what I earlier called a paradigmatic agenda, I recognize that the process by which that agenda gets established and communicated is very complex. And although problems for investigation are identified partly in terms of the community's existing knowledge, the process by which that identification takes place is equally complex, and far more a matter of social, political, and economic forces than methodological ones.

In theory, perhaps, this isn't a serious problem. So long as one assumes that filling out the paradigm is both a widely shared and long-term (i.e., multi-generational) project, on the order of Philosophical inquiry; and so long as the full community is clear enough on what the paradigmatic whole is; then any contribution, however seemingly remote or tangential, should be a help. Presumably all cause and effect relationships will be sorted out eventually. In practice, though, determining the pace and direction of community effort has been a chronic concern. In the passage from *Research in Written Composition* I've referred to so often, Braddock et al.'s impatience with the prevailing, less-than-methodical approach to identifying problems (among other things) is very plain. Here again is the passage quoted in Chapter 1:

> Not enough investigators are really informing themselves about the procedures and results of previous research before embarking on their own. Too few of them conduct pilot experiments and validate their measuring instruments before undertaking an investigation. Too many seem to be bent more on obtaining an advanced degree or another publication than on making a genuine contribution to knowledge, and a fair measure of the blame goes to the faculty adviser or journal editor who permits or publishes such irresponsible work. And far too few of those who have conducted an initial piece of research follow it with further exploration or replicate the investigations of others (p. 5).

This assessment is maybe a little harsh; such uncoordinated efforts are probably neither quite as fruitless nor as inexplicably irresponsible as the authors suggest. From a long-term perspective, anyway, if the method is carefully applied, the results of even underinformed inquiries may be of some potential use, helping to point out directions for disconfirmation, although that potential will no doubt take longer to fulfill. Moreover, these scattered efforts may well serve a strategic purpose, offering up all kinds of hints, suggestions, insights—in short, discoveries. If that is the case, it may also be that for some Experimental communities, a stage or cycle of such Experimental discovery-generating is a good or necessary thing; that rather than relying on other communities to generate testable assertions, the community likes the sense of commitment it holds towards those it generates itself.

Still, whatever the advantages of this more or less scattered or exploratory work, this open-ended agenda, Braddock et al. are certainly representative of Experimentalist sentiment in their objections to it. Theirs is an apt reminder: the central business of Experimental communities is certification, not discovery, and in those terms these widely scattered, uncoordinated efforts are not very productive. It follows, too, that the long-term view, and its concomitant patience with an array of studies whose coherence will have to be established by future generations, is finally unacceptable. And this attitude shows up again and again, not only in major programmatic statements like Burton's "Troubled Dream" or Cooper and Odell's *Research on Composing: Points of Departure*, but in the work of the rank and file, if you will—in the monographs and journal articles, the dissertations, the conference papers—embodied especially in the same ritual calls for further research that I mentioned earlier. Whatever its sources, then—and, as always, the prospect of imitating the physical sciences' storied rise to power is an obvious choice—the urge for tangible, coherent progress, study building upon study in methodical paradigmatic increments, is very strong.

The hard part, however, has come with translating such a general urge into a workable paradigmatic agenda: figuring out just what direction ought to be taken, and then finding ways to bring investigators into line with it. As I have already suggested, Composition's Experimental community has so far been unequal to the task—so that, rather surprisingly, community influence has actually been weaker here than at any other stage of the inquiry. No Experimentalist I know of, for example, has offered an actual timetable for any projected program of inquiry. Nor have two-and-a-half decades of programmatic proposals and calls for research coalesced into even a broadly coherent guide. For while it is possible to arrange studies in clusters according to certain emphases, or to trace a few lines of inquiry that seem to claim their own kind of progress—both of which I did by way of introducing this chapter—the former is possible only in retrospect, while the latter represent isolated, special cases. Neither seems to me to have been driven by any community-wide agenda.

And in the absence of a reasonably clear agenda, of course, it's very hard to say what investigators ought to be brought into line *with*. The major communal mechanism for exercising control in this area is what shows up in final reports as the "review of the literature." Its intent is to exert paradigmatic control: to guarantee that the problem to be studied has been formulated in Experimental form in the first place, framed in terms of existing contributions to the paradigm. Braddock et al. seemed to think—with some justification, no doubt—that this requirement was being flouted, that not "enough investigators are really informing themselves about the procedures and results of other investigations before embarking on their own." But surely not all the blame should fall on the investigators, nor on the faculty advisers and editors who are expected to represent the community's interests here. Such reviews are tricky things in even a more coherent research community, where the relationship between paradigm-as-shared-construct and its invocation to give meaning to any particular investigation is fuzzy enough. Here, where the shape of the community's knowledge is so difficult to discern, the review often amounts to little more than a strategic fiction: Rather than being impelled by the paradigm as an existing body of knowledge, the investigator selects and arranges studies to create the paradigmatic context within which she wants her study to gain its meaning. Such a procedure doesn't automatically render Experimental studies paradigmatically meaningless; indeed, it may be only a relatively extreme instance of the way paradigmatically-driven inquiry works. But it does raise questions about *how* they mean, and especially about what the community has to do with saying so.

The point, in any case, is that while the Experimental community in Composition can be said to have both the desire and the potential to govern its own investigative agenda, in fact that agenda has been and continues to be controlled mostly by external forces. The community always exercises a kind of local control, to be sure; dissertation advisers, especially, and to a lesser extent the handful of journal editors who deal with Experimental work, have some say in what gets investigated and how. But in the absence of any wider communal agenda, they can have no clear orientation themselves. All they can offer is their own reading of what will sell—so that, in effect, they end up serving as a medium through which extra-communal forces operate. And these forces are essentially the same ones that impinge on all the modes of inquiry: pressures brought to bear by the other communities in Composition, on the one hand; and those that come from outside the field—from schools, parents, legislatures, and so on—on the other. So the community's ties with Practitioners, for example, account for much of its traditional emphasis on pedagogy; and its more recent ventures into developmental studies reflects its sense of responsibility to whole schools as opposed to single classrooms.

Two of these externally-generated pressures in particular have affected the ways Experimentalists identify problems. The first is essentially political, and I touched on it earlier when I suggested that Composition as a field has tended to reward discoverers, not certifiers or replicators. What this tendency mostly reflects is the institutional system of academic promotion, within which publication is the preeminent measure of success for academic researchers. Quite simply, the best research positions go to those who publish and seem to be leaders in their particular research community. Decisions about what problems to take on for Experimental inquiry, then, will first reflect estimates about the likely importance, visibility, and publish-ability of the research, with loyalty to the community a distant second. For the same kinds of reasons, a researcher may not pursue any single line of inquiry at great length. Importance, visibility, and publish-ability may all peak after one or two well-placed reports. So even though the subject may, in terms of the paradigm, warrant further investigation, that need may not be enough to offset the possible professional liabilities of appearing to stand still. The same holds true for replication studies: even when they can be published, they are less likely to be held in very high esteem. Tenure and promotion committees in the Humanities, especially, where many Composition Experimentalists are likely to work, are accustomed to more Scholarly methods. Where dialectic is honored as the primary means of advancing knowledge, replication is bound to seem at the very least foreign and perhaps even worse—unoriginal, or useless. (And, in fact, my reading has not turned up a single published replication study in Composition; there may be some, but they are clearly not common.)

The second kind of pressure is more directly economic: Experimental inquiry tends to be the most expensive mode of inquiry in Composition. Any mode of inquiry can run up expenses. Historians may have to travel to study the texts they need; Ethnographers, as we shall see ahead, put in enormous amounts of time in both data collection and analysis. And Experimental inquiry doesn't have to be expensive; modest designs—like, say, Lee Odell's "Measuring the Effect of Instruction in Pre-writing," which we'll be looking at shortly— are not all that costly. But the high standards for control that the community demands over both research environment and investigator variability, combined with the peculiar logistics created by school research on a phenomenon like writing, make it very easy to run up costs at a rate and to levels that easily outstrip the other methods.

Consider the following typical and really rather modest experiment. This study (by a colleague of mine for a doctoral dissertation) proposed to examine an approach to teaching revision over a fifteen-week semester. As is currently fairly standard practice, one of the dependent variables was overall quality of student writing, to be measured by holistic rating of pre- and post-treatment essays. There were eight classes of 20 students involved in the study, or some 320 essays. Setting aside questions about the design's value, let's look simply at the logistics of scoring the essays.

To begin with, the grades assigned by the instructors in the actual classes were not acceptable measures of quality, since unknown or uncontrolled factors may have entered into them. Nor could the essays be rated by the researcher himself; his scores would have reflected his knowledge of the experiment. Therefore, the investigator needed a separate set of raters, preferably one without knowledge of the experiment. Next, since independent ratings—ratings, that is, made by raters working in isolation from one another—are regarded as likely to be less reliable (that is, to diverge more widely and more often) than group ratings, the rating sessions were group affairs, conducted by head raters (again, not the investigator) who trained or "calibrated" the other raters before and during the session. Moreover, since raters could be influenced by handwriting, names, class year, and other unaccounted-for features of the original scripts, all the essays had to be typed and coded. Finally, in order to further guarantee uniform rating, each essay was given at least two ratings, and in the event of wide divergence, three.

The costs for the various features of this procedure can obviously vary, and some of them, like the typing and coding, might be done by the investigator. Still, in this instance this really quite elemental step in the study worked out something like this:

Typing and coding ($1.00/essay)	$ 320.00
Rating: 320 essays × 2.5 readings at 8 readings/hour (including training and breaks) × $9.00/hour (includes higher wages for head raters)	900.00
Total	$1220.00

For a graduate student, $1220.00 is not only a good deal of money, but it represents only a small portion of the possible expense involved in the full study, which also included an even more expensive, detailed analysis of textual changes and computer analyses of some of the data —all in addition to the investigator's time for which there was neither direct nor indirect compensation. Imagine the time and costs involved in projects like Britton et al.'s *The Development of Writing Abilities (11–18)*, with its 2122 essays rated on two separate scales. Or the Morenberg, Daiker, and Kerek sentence-combining study, where

(a) 580 essays were "segmented into clauses and T-units by a team of six graduate assistants," each essay being segmented twice independently (average essay length: 649 words pre-, 605 post-);

(b) the same 580 rated four times each on two different scales (holistic and analytic, each with a different set of raters to prevent bias; total: 2320 ratings); and

(c) 134 post-tests (pairs from the experimental and control groups) were rated by forced choice.

The investigators don't offer a figure, but the rating alone took a team of 28 people five consecutive seven-hour days. Costs must have run at a minimum of $10,000.

I trust that the point here is not lost midst all the figuring: compared to the other kinds of inquiry in Composition, Experimental research tends to be expensive. It is by no means essential to take on expensive investigations, but it isn't difficult to work one up, either. And with the promise of prestige likely to be greater for ambitious investigations, the notion of a more modest, apprentice-like first run is surely not very attractive by comparison. In terms of identifying problems, this means that to some extent the choice of studies undertaken by both new and veteran Experimentalists will be a function of cost. In very lean times, certain kinds of designs may have to be set aside. And when money is available, the holders of the purse strings, from the very large (e.g., the National Institute for Education, the Fund for the Improvement of Post-Secondary Education, the Mellon Foundation) to the very small (local foundations, campus or district grantors), will exert a considerable influence on the direction of Experimental inquiry, and even on who can afford to choose the Experimental method at all.

Designing the Experiment

Of all the stages represented as parts of the various methods described in this book, none plays so crucial a role within its method as Experimental design. Other kinds of inquiry require planning, to be sure; we have seen how important assembling texts can be for Historians and Critics, and we will see ahead that other Researchers, too, need to prepare carefully to get the best results—conduct background research, run pilot studies, and so on. But the certificatory function of Experimental inquiry makes preparation all-important: if a study is no better than its replicability, then its replicability is no better than its design. In effect, design represents an investigator's contract with the rest of the community: a formal, public agreement about what a given investigation will entail, and about the authority it hopes to claim.

For all its importance, though, the basic elements of design are— as my imaginary study will have made clear—very simple. One needs only a variable to observe (dependent); a second to manipulate (independent); some means of observing (and, usually, keeping track of) their interaction (an instrument); and some setting within which this manipulating and observing can take place without obstruction. Of course, as that imaginary study also showed, this basic simplicity is belied by the incredible complexity of real world settings. The ideal of Experimental inquiry is to set up investigations so that the interaction of the key variables can be accounted for unconfounded by other influences—to eventually be able to say, in the case of my study, that the relationship between variable A, exercise duration, and my measure of variable B, essay length, is such that, all other things being equal, the presence of A decreases B by 50%.

Of course the catch is that all other things are in practice very hard to *hold* equal. What is always at issue in this matter of design, then, is control: the greater the investigator's control over the variables present in a given situation, the greater his paradigmatic powers of inference regarding those relationships actually under study. This doesn't mean that the object in Experimental design is to guarantee perfect control or, failing that, to abandon the inquiry. Not at all. Even in the traditionally ideal laboratory setting, the investigator is always discounting all sorts of influences as a matter of paradigmatic course: the position of the moon, say, or the number of novenas being offered for a happy outcome to the experiment. And in any case, the kind of phenomena that have so far interested Composition's Experimental community are not generally amenable to laboratory treatment. Thus, whether it is generated logistically, so that things are physically held equal; or statistically, so that confounding effects can be calculated; the notion of control is always a relative one, and the object of design is to establish the best controls possible under any given set of circumstances.

One useful and fairly traditional way to think about the range of control-by-design is as a sort of continuum, a line which moves in one direction—say, to the left—towards no control, and to the right towards perfect control.

No Control	← Pre-Experimental Quasi- "True" →	Full Control

Arranging the studies of a given Experimental community along this continuum, then, those further left might be called pre-experimental designs; those furthest right, "true" experimental designs; while in between would be all those designs which, while they exercise greater control than the pre-experimental designs, are for one reason or another unable to control enough features of a given setting to gain "true" design status. These might be called, collectively, quasi-experimental designs. It's important to remember that these are only relative, not absolute, designations, *comparative* assessments of the inferential power a given study's controls afford it. Even my naive gym class/essay length design, which I would place so far left on this continuum as to have it hanging off the very edge of pre-experimental territory, generates some inferential power; and the very best true experimental designs are compromised in all sorts of ways. The level of control required for any study, then, and the inferential power it is granted, are finally a function of community standards. We will return to how these standards are established ahead under Interpreting the Data. Here I simply want to sketch out what this range looks like in Composition by examining three studies, one each from the left, middle, and right of this continuum. I have mentioned each one

before: Lee Odell's "Measuring the Effect of Instruction in Pre-
writing"; Sharon Pianko's "A Description of the Composing Processes
of College Freshman Writers"; and Max Morenberg, Donald Daiker,
and Andrew Kerek's "Sentence Combining at the College Level: An
Experimental Study."

Let's begin with the furthest "left" of these, the least controlled,
Odell's "Measuring the Effect of Instruction in Pre-writing." As is so
often the case in this community, Odell's article is a report based on
a dissertation. It is a modest, neat piece of work, with what can be
described as a one-group, pre-test, post-test design. Specifically, Odell
set out to teach two sections of freshman English—46 students in all
—with a curriculum based on the pre-writing procedures developed
by Kenneth Pike, procedures which were the basis for what has since
come to be known as the tagmemic heuristic. All 46 students followed
the same syllabus for the term, and all wrote six out-of-class essays,
the first and the last of which served as pre- and post-tests. Arguing
that it was "not practicable" for him to follow the conventional pattern of having a control group—a class or classes not exposed to the
experimental curriculum—Odell explains that instead he will "1) predict the changes that should take place in students' writing after the
semester's work; 2) determine the number of students whose writings
showed these changes; 3) determine how likely it was that these
changes could be attributed to chance" (p. 230). From the 46 pairs
of essays he collects, 20 were selected by a randomizing procedure
and, after various kinds of analysis, used as the basis for testing three
predictions about the effects of this curriculum:[5]

> The first was that by the end of the semester students would
> examine data more thoroughly. That is, they would perform a
> greater variety of intellectual operations, not only contrasting a
> given unit with other units, but pointing out its variant forms,
> classifying it, locating it in a physical context, etc. Also, they
> would perform each operation a greater number of times. The
> second prediction was that students' essays would be better
> organized in that they would contain fewer conceptual gaps,
> fewer instances in which the essayist appeared to have omitted
> an explanation, transition, or generalization. The final predic-
> tion was that students would solve problems more adequately.
> That is: 1) they would support hypotheses with a greater
> amount of specific evidence; 2) there would be fewer instances
> in which a reader might question their arguments because the
> writers a) did not present their hypotheses, b) overlooked evi-
> dence which might contradict or weaken their arguments,
> c) ignored alternative ways of interpreting data; 3) if they did

disregard certain evidence or hypotheses, they would more frequently acknowledge and attempt to justify their having done
so (pp. 230–231).

The control problems here should be pretty obvious. Putting off
until the next section the problem of how he plans to tell whether
students have changed in the ways he predicts, let's assume that he
can make such judgments, and that students perform just as he predicts: they use a greater variety of, and more, intellectual operations;
they leave fewer conceptual gaps; and they solve problems more adequately. Given his design, how would he be able to interpret such
changes? With no control group, of course, he has no way to know
whether a comparable set of students would show similar patterns of
change without this treatment. As an alternative, he might have increased the number of observations before the treatment—i.e., the
number and variety of writing tasks—to get a better idea of what the
students' untreated performances looked like, but he doesn't. As it
stands, then, he will be virtually unable to differentiate treatment
effects from any other influences; and with only this single pre-test
as a way of observing what is surely a very complex phenomenon,
won't even be able to say with any real authority what these students
were like as problem solvers/intellectual operators prior to instruction.
And then, of course, there is the problem of having only one instructor involved, so that it will be difficult to infer whether it was the
what or the how of the treatment curriculum that mattered; com-
pounded by the fact that this single instructor is also the investigator
who, we can reasonably expect, has a considerable stake in how this
experiment works out.

In essence, then, Odell would seem to be aiming to move just
slightly beyond the common sense notion that a teacher who works
for twelve weeks with a class of 23 students has some effect on how
they write. To do so, he will specify particular features in their
writing that he thinks his curriculum ought to affect; examine two
pieces of the students' writing to see to what extent such changes do
in fact occur; and then determine what the chances are, not that the
Experimental curriculum *caused* those changes, but that they could
have been simply accidental. As such, it may produce a gain in inferential power, but, even at best, it will be a very modest one indeed.

I found it somewhat more difficult to choose a design with
which to illustrate the wide middle expanse of the control continuum. The myriad circumstances under which Experimentalists work,
and the schemes they devise to compensate for control problems,
make "representativeness" in any narrow sense quite impossible. And
because, as I suggested above, Sharon Pianko's "A Description of the

Composing Processes of College Freshman Writers" is a correlational study, it might not be the ideal choice. Pianko treats three factors — age, gender, and what she calls "class status" (remedial or traditional) — as though they were independent variables, and then tries to trace their "effects" on how students compose. This kind of design is not always held in high regard precisely because the investigator has no control over the treatment variables. Nevertheless, I have chosen it for three reasons. First, it focuses on composing, not classroom practice, and so balances my other two choices in that sense. Second, as my mention of the Britton et al. and Bridwell studies indicated, the field has been markedly influenced by studies of this kind. And third, I chose it because it is a well-known, apparently widely respected study.[6]

What Pianko does in this investigation, then, is to randomly select, from the 400 students enrolled in a community college's freshman composition course, 24 who could be sub-grouped into six pre-determined categories: age (under 21 - over 21); gender (male - female); and class status (traditional - remedial). In other words, the students were selected in such a way as to guarantee that 12 were traditional and 12 remedial, 12 under 21 and 12 over, 12 male and 12 female.[7] These students were asked to do one writing "episode" each week for five weeks, during each of which they were to produce a 400-word essay in whatever part of an afternoon they needed. They were offered an assignment at every one but the last (in which topic was open). Episode 1, for example, offered "Describe a single incident which involves not more than three characters taken from an experience observed" (p. 6); but students were also free to write "on anything, in any mode of expression" at all episodes. Pianko then video-taped and observed at least one episode for each student, noting both frequency and duration of behaviors assumed to be associated with seven "dimensions" of the composing process: Pre-writing, Planning, Composing (Writing/Pausing/Rescanning), Rereading, Stopping, Contemplating the finished product, and Handing in the product. At the end of the observation period, the students were interviewed about "the behaviors exhibited during that composing experience to elicit the students' views on the causes and meaning of certain behaviors," and about their general feeling regarding the whole session. In addition, each subject was "interviewed in-depth concerning past and present experiences with writing" (p. 7).

The object of all this data collection, as her title suggests, was to generate a profile of these writers as they composed under the circumstances provided for the study — i.e., in a setting which, according to Pianko, represented "fairly usual classroom conditions," except that the writers knew their work would not be graded. Part of that profile is simply a quantitative accounting of the group as a whole in terms of 22 variables framed within the seven dimensions: the group's mean prewriting time was 1.26 minutes; planning for 14 of 17 (seven of the original 24 dropped out) was "mental" as opposed to written; their mean composing time was "38.85 minutes for an average length of 361 words per essay," or 9.3 words per minute, and so on.

The Experimental component of the design, though, comes into play when Pianko tries to find correlations between the six student categories and these 22 variables. In examining the relationship between class status and prewriting time, for example, Pianko finds that the remedial students' mean prewriting time, 1.00 minutes, seems to be a good deal shorter than the traditional students' 1.64 minutes—a difference she will calculate to be significant at the .05 level, meaning that there are fewer than 5 chances in 100 that such a difference would have been measured if there were not some real difference in the prewriting times of the two groups. Like Odell, then, Pianko is concerned with establishing the factors that might account for variations in students' writing processes, albeit by examining their behaviors, not their texts. But she is obviously not working to establish a causal connection in the way he is—that is, by introducing these factors into a setting to see what effects they have.

Such a design has at least one obvious advantage over Odell's. By controlling her sample selection—that is, by establishing the representativeness of her 24 subjects in a way that Odell does not—she gains some external validity: assuming that her six categories can be established in Experimentally acceptable ways, she will be able to infer with some confidence that, when grouped under the same rubrics and observed under similar conditions, other students from the base population of 400 will chalk up similar distributions and frequencies on these variables. As we shall see, there turn out to be substantial problems in store here. For example, her criterion for establishing remedial-ness—student scores on an objective entrance test, "supported" by a diagnostic essay—is pretty shaky, her sample by the end of the study is down to 17, and so on; so that the net gain in inferential power is rather small. Still, the design idea, by itself, isn't a bad one.

The chief disadvantage of her design, of course, is that, Experimentally speaking, correlational studies have no disconfirmatory power. Relatively sophisticated though it surely is, Pianko's investigation will give her no more inferential leverage than my offhand observation that the length of my students' essays seemed to vary with the amount of exercise they did before class. From a common sense perspective, the kind of apparent connections between variables thus generated can be very appealing. To return to the one example I've given, it might make intuitive sense that Pianko should find her "remedial" students' mean prewriting time to be significantly shorter than that of her "traditional" students. However, even if the means by which she arrived at those figures were beyond reproach (and they are far from it), she would still have shown them to be only co-, not causally, related: when one changes, the other changes. Without manipulation, Experimental inference can go no further. It's a sticky point of procedure; and, as we shall see, one that ends up getting Pianko in trouble.

The furthest to the right of these three on the control continuum, my example of a "true" experimental design, is "Sentence Combining at the College Level: An Experimental Study," and it follows a very traditional pre-test, post-test, control group design. Six sections of Freshman English (151 students), the experimental group, followed a special sentence-combining curriculum; while another six sections (139 students), the control or reference group, followed "methods of instruction traditional at Miami [of Ohio] and many other colleges . . . (1) the study of rhetoric, (2) the reading and analysis of essays written by professional writers and (3) the assignment and discussion of student compositions" (p. 247). The study had three hypotheses:

> It was hypothesized that the experimental group, trained in S[entence] C[ombining], would score significantly higher than a reference group on (1) syntactic maturity factors as measured by standard quantitative criteria; (2) overall writing quality as judged by a panel of experienced college teachers of college composition; and (3) reading ability as measured by a standard reading test (p. 245).

Like Odell, then, these investigators want to test the efficacy of a specific curriculum, but they want to do so in a way that will give them both a greater and a more directed inferential power. That is, they not only want to move further along the path of certification-by-disconfirmation, toward establishing a causal connection between an SC curriculum and certain desired textual features and patterns; but they want to do so in a way that establishes its superiority as an explanation for the appearance of those features over another specific curriculum. To do so, they need to establish many controls he does not. Thus, as in Pianko's study, their student subjects are "randomly assigned by computer to the 12 sections," all of which are the same size; and a sampling backup check of SAT and ACT scores "indicated no significant differences between groups." But they do much more than this. The experimental and control sections, for example, are "matched" so that "equivalent sections would meet on the same days of the week and at comparable times during the day" (p. 246).

In addition, the teachers for all twelve sections—no teacher taught more than one—were "carefully selected"; three graduate assistants and three faculty members were assigned to each group. They were also "paired according to age, academic rank, years of experience, commitment, and assessed teaching effectiveness," so that one person from each such pair could be assigned to a control and one to an experimental class. And, finally, the students in all sections "wrote eight compositions at exactly the same points during the term," with the first and last (from week 1 and final exam), on a reversible pair of "comparable expository topics . . . that would invite descriptive or narrative supporting details" serving as pre- and post-tests.

You can see the paradigmatic advantages of this design. By controlling the sample size and selection, the study gains a substantial external validity for at least Miami's student body. By establishing a control or reference group, they are in a better position to rule out confounding variables like maturation or history than Odell—that is, to rule out the possibility that pre- and post-test differences might be explained by influences on the students other than the experimental treatment. By involving twelve teachers instead of just one (although they don't say whether the twelve included any of the investigators) and by trying to match them across the two groups, they are better able to attribute any observed changes to the treatment, the SC curriculum itself, as opposed to something idiosyncratic in the way it was presented. And finally, by framing the investigation in comparative terms, they gain in both Experimental and political power. The Experimental gain—much the smaller of the two—will be that they stand not only to reduce the odds that chance, maturation, history and other such possibilities account for any treatment effects, but also that those same effects could be produced by at least one competing treatment. What makes this a relatively small Experimental gain, of course, is not only that there is a fairly wide range of other possible treatments—workshop classes, say, or a conference approach —but that this design provides no way of determining even broadly what features of these two very complex treatments account for any changes in what are, in any case, a pretty narrowly defined set of dependent variables (i.e., students' ability to produce expository prose on assigned topics in two hours under examination conditions). The political gain is obviously more substantial: This sort of race-horse design, pitting the "traditional" against the "experimental," generates an appealing dramatic tension; for readers willing to accept the idea that the competing curricula represent two replicable wholes, the emergence of a clearcut winner can be viewed as a mandate for action.

Conducting the Study: Collecting and Analyzing the Data

But there is more to design than the general sorts of outlines we've considered so far. Indeed, to some extent, I have created an artificial boundary in saving for this section the means by which these various designs actually come to be carried out—what Experimentalists often call operationalizing: strictly speaking, a given design is only possible in operational terms. Each investigator has to determine not only what kinds of data to collect, and how; but also, assuming that the "raw" data will not be in a form amenable to interpretation, how it will have to be transformed—analyzed—before it is interpretable. This shift to an operational design is obviously crucial for any Experimental inquiry, and just as obviously fraught with difficulties. The key issues, expressed in a pair of terms that anyone with even a cursory exposure to the method will recognize, are the aforementioned validity, the concern that these ways of observing and measuring, these instruments for collecting and analyzing data, actually do provide access to the phenomena under investigation; and reliability, the concern that they do so consistently, and without regard to time or place or investigator. In theory, anyway, no Experimentalist can afford to take either of these for granted. At the same time, it's worth recalling once again here Braddock et al.'s complaints about the paucity of pilot studies, and the use of untested instruments—complaints that might well still be made. The kinds of pressures—political, academic, economic—that promote "discovery" investigations over replications play a role here, too. It can take a good deal of energy, expertise and (very often) money to develop and test Experimental instruments thoroughly—when, indeed, fully satisfactory testing is possible at all. None of these are commodities very many investigators have had, or been willing to expend, in any abundance.

The sort of prose statements that have served as predictions, questions, and hypotheses in the three studies we have looked at, then, are not yet Experimentally workable. Again, we can begin by looking at how Odell handles the difficult transition to an operational design. Taking it as a given that students can "chunk" their experience, he expects his experimental course will teach them to (1) contrast a given chunked unit with other units; (2) specify its range of variation; (3) locate it in a larger class of things; (4) locate it in a temporal sequence; (5) locate it in a physical context and (6) locate it in a class system. If the curriculum works, students will, in the words of his predictions, "examine data more thoroughly," "be better organized in that [their essays] would contain fewer intellectual gaps," and "solve problems more adequately." The operational problem, obviously, is to figure out how to tell whether or not these predictions have come true: What kinds of data must he collect, and how will it have to be analyzed?

First, then, the data. Working from the assumption that all three predictions can be tested by directly examining student writing—as opposed, say, to making observations or conducting interviews the way Pianko does—he decides to use two writing assignments done as part of the term's ordinary coursework. The writing task he uses calls for students to "write an out-of-class essay in which they were to formulate and solve what seemed to them an interesting problem regarding a designated literary work"—a short story, as it turns out. Insofar as we are willing to accept his decision to look only at texts (the difficulties with which I'll explore shortly), validity is not much of a problem here. The writing is done out-of-class, just like the other assignments in the course; and it asks students to write about literature they're reading, also in keeping with the course's general pattern. In short, if the validity of this collection procedure depends upon its being likely to collect writing of the kind done in the course, this approach is pretty good.

Its reliability is another matter. On the plus side, he reports that the students were not told until after the course ended that they were subjects in an experiment (a practice probably not possible at most universities now), so their writing won't have been affected by any knowledge of that kind. But there are some fair-sized minuses, too. First, precisely because the students do work on this writing on their own time, under uncontrolled conditions, he loses reliability. He can't know where, or for how long, or with what sorts of help the essays were written. Suppose there is plagiarism? Help from roommates? How will evidence appearing as a result of such influences be handled, or is it assumed to balance out in a population of 46 students? A variety of correctives were possible; minimally, the sample might have included a set of in-class papers as a way of checking on student abilities. In fact, though, none are used.

The second minus is probably more serious, and not a little puzzling. Although the assignment itself is the same for both pre- and post-test, Odell takes the precaution of using two different short stories, having one class write on one and one on the other for pre- and post-tests. His object in doing so is to make the raters more reliable: to ensure that "the content of an essay would not let a scorer distinguish pre-test from post-test" (p. 231). This is a good move. In making it, however, he obviously takes for granted the comparability of the short stories as writing prompts—assumes, that is, that for the purposes of eliciting the intellectual operations the course purports to teach, one story is the same as the other. In fact, though, it seems perfectly possible that the stories (Ted Hughes' "Snow" and Isaac

Rosenfeld's "The Brigadier") are not comparable—so that, for example, writing about short story #2 might demand a greater number
and variety of intellectual operations, a difference that might be
further enhanced by a semester of instruction. If that were the case,
just reversing the topics by class as he does wouldn't cancel the effect
out. Hence, pilot testing of the topics would have been a good idea.
So would a statistical check of scores by class and/or by student,
looking for a pattern related to the sequence of assignments. In the
absence of either check, though, the reliability of the data as collected
can't be considered all that high.

As tricky as this collecting of data is here, though, analyzing the
essays turns out to be even more complex. Odell has three analytical
schemes, one for each prediction. For the first, he needs some way to
check on the number and variety of intellectual operations students
have used in writing their essays. To do so, he establishes a list of
what it calls "linguistic cues"—words and phrases he claims allow him
to determine which intellectual operations have taken place. To make
this analysis easier, he programs a computer to identify such cues
once the essays have been typed into it. Some percentage of the total
number of cues (he doesn't say how many) the computer can't score
reliably because they are context-dependent. These the program
prints out separately, including whatever falls 40 spaces on either
side of each cue, to be scored separately by Odell and an assistant.

Reliability presents no major problems here. That is, it seems
reasonable to assume that the essays can be typed into the computer
accurately; and, given a set list, the fairly simple sorting program
should identify most of the relevant cues. As for the context-dependent cues that are printed out separately, Odell claims that he and
his assistant agreed 88% of the time on which operation was represented; and in any case, only those cues on which they agreed were
used in the study. Some checks wouldn't have hurt—on the computer
program's accuracy, say, or on which cues gave Odell and his assistant
the most trouble—but given the scope of the study, they were not
essential.

The pivotal issue of validity, obviously, is how or even whether
these textual cues are related to the intellectual operations Odell
claims to want to study. He has a theoretical basis for making this
connection, although he doesn't spell it out in this article, nor offer a
list of the specific cues used. But his dissertation and, later, his
"Measuring Changes in Intellectual Processes as One Dimension of
Growth in Writing" both explain its origins, pointing especially to
the work of Kenneth Pike. And I think he would get little argument
on the general notion that there is interaction between thought—
however defined—and written language. The question here is how he

knows enough about that interaction to analyze these texts as he does. To raise an obvious objection: Suppose as a student I do, in fact, increase the variety of my intellectual operations in much the way Odell has predicted I should. Why assume that what I have learned will turn up in some single piece of writing—or in any writing at all? Or turn up as these cues and not some others? Or that the number of cues in the draft I submit will reflect the number or variety of operations I actually used in writing it? None of this is to directly question whether such operations exist, or that they can be taught, although these are surely legitimate issues, too. Rather, this is to ask whether, assuming that they *do* exist, they will manifest themselves, and be measurable, in this way. And that claim must be, I think, very much in doubt.

His second analytical scheme faces similar difficulties. Aiming to identify what he calls "conceptual gaps" in these essays, Odell gives xerox copies to four raters who are deliberately misled into believing that a secretary has removed "at random one or more sentences from each essay" (p. 233). The raters' job was simply to keep track of the number, but *not* the kind or location, of such gaps they came across as they read. Here again, reliability won't be hard to gauge. He will be able to tell fairly easily how often the four raters, working independently, agree on the total number of such gaps per essay. But he has little hope of validating such findings. What kind of reading is it that these people are being asked to do when thus falsely forewarned about missing sentences? And even if we should accept the mode of reading as valid, and be further willing to accept its relevance to writing (another matter entirely); without knowing which gaps the readers agree on, or what kinds they are, he will be able to make very little of the information they provide. And as it turned out, this procedure was as ill-fated as it promised to be. The judges not only couldn't agree on the number of gaps per essay, but the spread between their scores was very high. Odell does, as we shall see shortly, follow through on his findings here, applying them to the relevant prediction, but the question of validity never really comes up. Reliability was simply too low to warrant serious further consideration.

And his third scheme is equally problematic. Again, it involves raters—two, in this case—and asks them to score the 40 essays in three categories: use of evidence, use of questionable statements, and use of statements justifying omissions. In other words, as these raters read through an essay, they were to mark each instance of what they took to be evidence ("direct quotations, paraphrases of passages from a text, or references to observable phenomena"); each *failure* to present such evidence; and also any instances in which they thought the "essayist had attempted to justify his leaving out contradictory evidence or alternative hypotheses." As even Odell admits, of course, the relationship between these textual features and the intellectual operations that are the object of study is not all that direct to begin with. The idea is that if, as a result of improved intellectual operations, "a student thoroughly investigates data, he should come to a clearer understanding of that data, and the improved understanding of the material should allow him to present his ideas more coherently and to solve problems more adequately" (p. 231). To assume such a connection is to imply a rather simple model of the relationship between language and knowledge. Surely a thorough investigation of data can as often breed confusion as coherence; and clearer understandings, whatever those might be, can't automatically be expected to turn up in better written prose. Here again, though, questions about validity are rendered irrelevant by troubled reliability, the inter-rater agreement on the presence (or absence) of the features being counted: only 58% on the use of evidence, 39% on questionable items, and a dismal 12% on justified omissions.

But I don't want to give the impression that Odell's investigation is somehow alone in having these difficulties. Making an Experimental design operational always entails some degree of difficulty, and Pianko has at least as much trouble doing so as Odell. Her investigation is intended, surely, to produce a major improvement in validity over what can be called product-only studies; writing is characterized far more fully, both in the measures reported in this article, and in the even wider array described in the dissertation from which it is taken. And at least in terms of data collection, we can say it represents improvement in that sense. No Composition researcher had ever looked at college freshman writers writing in this kind of detail before, let alone under conditions so like those in schools.

At the same time, though, one has to wonder about the way this data gets collected and, for the most part simultaneously, analyzed. How reliable can even a descriptive study of composing be when the bulk of its data and data analysis (as presented in the article) are the result of single, naked eye observer records of one composing episode of approximately 39 minutes for each of 17 writers, albeit supplemented by two interviews? There were actually two researchers on the project—Louisa Rogers, the other one, is credited in Pianko's dissertation, but rather curiously mentioned nowhere in the article. Working from guides (the "Writing Behavior Question Guide," e.g.) to help ensure uniformity, they were sorting out—analyzing— the behaviors they observed as they observed them. However, these two observers not only observed and interviewed separately, but the guides themselves do not seem to have been field tested (and the one for behaviors, at least, was modified as the observations proceeded).

Worse, the videotapes were used only to "double-check" their observations—and not, as one might expect, for even so simple a procedure as having the observers cross-check one another. Without these kinds of precautions, the reliability of the data on composing behaviors as collected and analyzed has to be considered questionable.

And what about the validity of her analysis of this data? Pianko's title claims that she will provide a description of these writers' composing *processes* but, except for the interviews, she has access only to composing *behaviors*, a distinction she is pretty careful to maintain herself. As a result, her interpretations of what happens (or where or why or by what means) during, say, what she calls the prewriting period, even with the recall interviews to help, must be seen as consisting of a good deal more speculation than observation. Her leap from the behaviors and interview-prompted recollections of these admittedly indifferent subjects to a 7-dimensional, 22-dependent and 3-independent variable portrait of how college freshman writers write, therefore, is at least as problematic as Odell's effort to derive a profile of intellectual operations exclusively from textual evidence.

Even true experimental designs, though, never escape these kinds of problems in becoming operational. Given the overall quality of their design, of course, the Morenberg, Daiker and Kerek investigation fares the best of the three under this kind of scrutiny. In terms of collection, then, their student-essay data—like Odell's—was collected as part of the regular coursework, consisting of the first and last (eighth) compositions written during the course, so they have an equal validity in that sense. At the same time, they claim a greater reliability because both pre- and post-tests were written under "equivalent and rigorously controlled conditions"—they know more about when, where, and how the essays get written (p. 246). In addition, they are much more careful to establish the comparability of the pre- and post-test essay topics; a note points out that both were adapted from Educational Testing Service questions, with the implication that they had already been carefully researched and field-tested on a wide scale.

They were equally careful in terms of data analysis. Back in the section on Identifying Problems, where I dealt with the economics of Experimental inquiry, I mentioned that their pre- and post-test essays were analyzed in four ways: holistically, with each essay getting an "impressionistic" rating of from 1–6; analytically, with each essay getting a score of 1–6 on each of six criteria; by forced choice, where a pair of post-test essays (one control, one experimental) from students whose pre-tests were very close in score were given to a rater who had to decide which was best; and in terms of "syntactic maturity," so that each essay was analyzed in terms of words-per-clause, words-per-T-unit, and clauses-per-T-unit. For all of these except the forced choice (where a subset of papers with closely matched pre-test scores were assembled), all 580 papers were analyzed, so there was no waste or chance skewing of data. The syntactic maturity ratings (the essays were deemed long enough for "meaningful" analysis) were done by a team of six trained graduate students, with each paper receiving two independent ratings which the two raters then cross-verified, leaving any unresolvable differences to be settled by the investigators. As I noted earlier, all the other ratings were done by a team of 28 teachers of college composition working seven hour days for five consecutive days under what seemed to have been comfortable conditions. For holistic and analytic scorings, each essay got four ratings; care was taken that no rater scored the same essay under both scales, so that rereadings could have no effect. The interrater reliabilities here were in the 80% agreement range or better.

For all the rigorous attention to detail, though, this was by no means a perfect study. Admittedly, reliability is under pretty remarkable control. I see only one possible difficulty, and it is not major. They don't say whether or not the students knew they were participating in an experiment, so it is possible that a general enthusiasm for the experimental course's novelty—easily enough communicated by the instructors, who did know—could account for some effects. But the recurrent criticism of sentence combining studies has never focused on their reliability. On the contrary, the obvious advantage of accepting the kinds of prose features that are here presented as constituting "syntactic maturity" is that they do indeed provide a fairly reliable set of indices for measuring what purports to be growth in writing. Most criticisms, then, have been directed at the validity of such measures: Is the tendency to produce sentences with a greater number of words-per-clause, words-per-T-unit, and clauses-per-T-unit really a consistent feature of development in writing? And if it is, do the kinds of gains in those features achieved by experimental students via training in sentence combining represent authentic development, or a sort of forced precocity, a willingness to perform syntactic feats because the teacher wants them performed?

Morenberg et al. clearly hope to address both these concerns by making student essays their primary source of data, and by choosing the range of analyses they do. Rather than testing for syntactic maturity more directly, then, by having students rework the kind of kernel-sentence passages through which they were mostly taught—

passages in which content is a given, so that writing from them is, if not a-rhetorical, then not rhetorical in any usual sense—they look for the effects of such practice in more typical school writing. They put it this way: "Experimental gains in syntactic maturity without a corresponding improvement in writing quality . . . could be rejected by critics as irrelevant to the basic concerns of the composition class." In addition, they recognize that "scores showing that SC practice positively affects only certain analytic components of writing like sentence structure or supporting details could be dismissed as simply a function of what the experimental students were most intensively taught, and therefore as an insufficient measure of overall qualitative gains" (p. 253); hence the holistic and forced choice ratings to complement the analytic.

And yet there is still, perhaps inevitably, a shadow over the validity of these measures. The whole notion of "syntactic maturity" as a tendency measurable without regard for rhetorical context is very troubling. The ability to exercise some kind of syntactic freedom in these ways might serve as the basis for one definition of maturity. But there is no compelling reason to believe that the effects of such freedom would consistently turn up as longer units—more words-per-clause, etc.—either in whole populations, or in the writing of individuals, across tasks. And even if, for some particular sampling of prose, this did seem to be the case—as it was for Kellogg Hunt, whose work these authors cite—one would be hard-pressed to demonstrate that this tendency was a matter of growth or maturation and not simply socialization: i.e., learning to use certain language structures in some milieu because they seem to work there.[8]

Another, more specific criticism might be leveled here as well. With the exception of pre- and post-test, the report doesn't make it clear under what circumstances either the experimental or control students wrote their regular class essays. But *all* students were expected to write the pre- and post-test essays in-class. Is this a valid way to measure what students in the control classes learned? In "Perhaps Test Essays Can Reflect Significant Improvement in Freshman Composition: Report on a Successful Attempt," Sara Sanders and John Littlefield tried to determine whether this kind of essay writing was a valid measure. Their findings, while tentative, suggest that quite possibly it is not: "that the lack of improvement evidenced in many other research studies can at least sometimes be attributed to the nature of the impromptu test essay and test conditions rather than to the failure of composition students to improve in composition" (p. 152). Some of the differences between experimental and control groups in this SC study, then, might have been attributable to this way of measuring. Maybe the SC students simply developed a superior version of the kind of first draft fluency that works well under these conditions. Maybe if they had had to write under more normal conditions—with time to think and revise, say—the control students would have scored higher or, just as likely, the experimental students scored lower, editing out some of the features they were rated highly on. And suppose students had had to write more than one essay, not only under different conditions, but with different rhetorical constraints? If the concern is for validity, then these other measures would clearly have helped.

☐

    I want to close out this section with a reminder about my purpose here. Contrary to possible appearances, it has not been to denigrate the value of these three studies, each of which has, at least in its time, been recognized for some kind of excellence; nor to demonstrate the general futility of Experimental design for research on writing. As I have pointed out so often in this chapter, the object of Experimental inquiry is to make paradigmatic inference possible. The role of design, then, including this business of collecting and analyzing data, is to set things up in a way that maximizes that inferential power for any given study. There will *always* be limits on that power, but from an Experimental perspective any contribution that can make paradigmatic sense is welcome—those from very modest, low-cost, low-power designs like Odell's, as well as those from the ambitious, high-cost, higher-powered undertakings like Morenberg et al.'s. What I said earlier bears repeating: The Experimentalist's goal is to put together the best design possible under the circumstances. The community asks, and the investigator can deliver, no more. The next step—determining just what any such contribution will finally mean, how that inferential power will be brought to bear in terms of the paradigm—is another matter, and the subject of the next section.

Interpreting the Data

    Probably the most important thing to note about the interpretation of Experimental data is that it *looks* deceptively easy. The tendency, perhaps especially for novices and outsiders, is to be fooled here, as with design in general, by the conceptual simplicity of the process. In the idealized scenario, the dependent and independent variables have now been unobstructedly observed interacting in the chosen setting some appropriate number of times; the investigator has a body of data that will serve as a record of those interactions;

and this "raw" data has been analyzed—put into a form amenable to determining whether the hypothesized cause/effect relationship that prompted the design in the first place can still be plausibly considered or not. In the very simplest form of cause/effect prediction upon which such designs can be based—the so-called null hypothesis—the investigator adopts the extreme position that the treatment will have *no* effect whatever, so that interpretation requires only that the data support a single, very basic yes/no decision: Either something happened, or it didn't, and anyone looking at the data ought to be able to tell which it is.

But of course neither design nor, as a result, interpretation, are ever so simple in practice. Observations are rarely unobstructed, the body of data is necessarily only a partial record of the interaction, the analyses distort or reduce those data, and so on. And yet at the same time, the paradigmatic context within which the outcomes of these inevitably imperfect designs must be interpreted, expressed as it is in terms of the formal universe of probability statistics, is very demanding. True, the paradigm places some limits on what portion of that universe the community will explicitly address, and so relieves the investigator of the obligation to account for all possible variables —the phases of the moon, number of novenas, and the like. Nevertheless, the bottom-line investigative assumption will be that any observed effects are a function of chance until proven otherwise. Even if, on average, the paradigm demands an accounting for, say, 10 variables—which for non-laboratory research on so complex a human activity as writing doesn't seem like very many—establishing sufficient controls to generate such proof with any substantial authority is a pretty tall order.

I don't want to be misleading here. As I argued earlier, the shape of Composition's Experimental paradigm is not very clear, and certainly not so clear that anyone could really set such a standard for the average number of variables to be accounted for per study; Pianko, after all, claims to account for 25. Nor is its connection with probability statistics an absolutely necessary one. Data can be interpreted in contexts provided by paradigms framed in other ways. Recall once more my imaginary experiment. Despite the obvious weaknesses of my design, the data were pretty dramatic: When the Thursday essays written after the treatment were compared to the Tuesday essays, they were proportionately twice as long as usual. It would have been perfectly plausible had I cancelled all gym classes held before my writing classes. Sure, other explanations might have accounted for the effects I observed. But for my purposes, and given the circumstances—in other words, *given the demands set by my short-lived, one-person paradigmatic community*—I could have reasonably

decided that the hour of exercise was the factor that had hampered
my writers on Thursdays, and changed the schedule accordingly.
Subsequent events may well have lead me to second-guess that decision, but that's another issue. The point is, I could easily have accepted that interpretation of my data for my particular purposes,
despite its obvious element of inferential risk.

Clearly, though, the "local" interpretation that might satisfy
me under such circumstances would not so easily satisfy the larger
Experimental community—the one in which Odell, Pianko, and
Morenberg et al. presumably want to claim their authority. Whereas I
could afford to regard this little test as the end of an inferential process, that community would surely regard it as the most elementary of
beginnings: a first, very tentative identification of a possible cause/
effect relationship which, because of its poor overall design, contributed little by way of disconfirming competing hypotheses. The paradigmatic context in which they "read" these data would be very
different from my own; consequently, their interpretation would
differ, too. To make my study more meaningful in this larger context,
I would have to (a) account one way or another for more variables
than I do; and (b) test the ones I eventually did focus on far more
rigorously. It's hard to say how much re-designing would be required,
how many more variables I'd have to look after, or what levels of
statistical significance I would have to set. But I think the general
direction of reform is clear enough.

The key to interpreting Experimental data, then, lies in operating between two sets of constraints: satisfying the positivist ambitions of the paradigm, on the one hand; but without exceeding the
limits of the particular design, on the other. In the rest of this section,
we will look at how Odell, Pianko, and Morenberg et al. negotiate this
interpretive space. In doing so, we will also see just how very difficult
it can be.

We have so far seen that Odell's study, prompted by his curiosity
about whether students could be taught prewriting procedures, and
whether it would be possible to identify any effects of such teaching
in their writing, was designed to test three predictions about what
those changes would be. And we have seen, too, how he moved from
that curiosity to a design, how he collected the essays that were his
data, and how he analyzed them to make interpretation possible.
What he has at this point is a set of numbers—specifically, the results
from ten different "measurements" taken on the essays, pre- and
post-. He makes no bones about how he plans to decide what these
measurements might mean:

> To determine whether results for each measurement were pro-
> duced by chance alone, these results were subjected to the

Wilcoxon Matched-Pairs Signed Ranks test (Siegel, 1956). When this test, chosen because it took into account the magnitude of changes as well as their direction, showed a probability of .025 (one-tailed value) or better, results were considered significant. That is, it was assumed that results could be attributed to students' experiences in the experimental course, rather than to chance alone (p. 235).

In other words, he plans to use the Wilcoxon—a non-parametric statistical test, appropriate here because he is making no claims about the population from which the 46 students were drawn (and hence no assumptions about that population's "parameters")—to compare the differences between pre- and post-test measurements. The test will be one-tailed (and so more powerful) because he is predicting that the post-test scores will be higher; and he sets significance at .025, meaning that if via this test he finds that these differences could have happened by accident only 2.5 times out of 100, he will be satisfied that they were, as he says, attributable to the experimental course.

Obviously this is not an auspicious interpretive beginning. The statistical explanation is sound enough, even though nonparametric measures are not widely favored. Given the modesty of the design, the level of significance is high enough, with the custom for such research being to regard .05 as a minimum. But the bit of reasoning in the paragraph's last sentence is not sound: that is, given the rudimentary nature of his design, to demonstrate that "chance alone" will not account for differences between measurements is to demonstrate little else, and certainly not that such differences can be attributed to the experimental course. Any number of factors, many of which we have considered in this chapter, could very plausibly account for any such differences. In some sense, then, all of his interpretations will be made under the onus of this misconception.

But that marks only the beginning of this study's interpretive troubles. Let's track the procedure he proposes through a specific prediction. Prediction I, in two parts, stated that (1) all students would perform a greater number of what he ends up treating as five intellectual operations and that (2) they would perform each one a greater number of times. Part (1), says Odell, "received little support: only three post-test essays out of twenty showed students performing a greater number of the intellectual operations; sixteen showed no change" (p. 235). That is, in subtracting the number (0–5, presumably) of such operations used on each pre-test from those on the subsequent post-test, in only three cases was there a positive difference, and in one, a negative difference. The Wilcoxon would require him to discard the 16 no-change pairs, giving him a sample size of 4—a value for which the Wilcoxon table for determining significance makes no provision. Thus, his interpretation—that the prediction receives little support—is true enough; it might be even truer, though, to say that given his data, the Wilcoxon was unable to tell him much about it.

His interpretation of (2) is somewhat more interesting:

> In each of the post-tests there was an increase in the number of times the students performed at least some of the operations suggested by the heuristic model. For four of the operations, the proportion of essays in which the predicted increase occurred was statistically significant. For one operation, the proportion of essays showing this increase was more modest and could be attributed to chance (p. 235).

Something very puzzling is going on here. What one would expect would be a detailed account of just what these increases were—a table, say, which gives the pre- and post-test totals for each student, so that we could see the differences. Then the Wilcoxon would require that these differences be ranked, so that the smallest (regardless of sign—i.e., negative or positive) would be given a value of 1, the next smallest 2, and so on, with ties being given a value that was the average of the consecutive ranks they would otherwise occupy. (So, for example, three differences of 10 which tied for rank 5 would each be given a value of 6, the average of 5 + 6 + 7; and the next difference—say 15—would be given a value of 8.) Next, these ranks would be assigned the appropriate sign (the one from the difference); and then the positive ranks and negative ranks would be summed separately. Odell would then take the smaller of these numbers and, turning to the appropriate table, see if such a T, as it is called, for a sample of that size (20 minus any no-difference pairs) was significant at the .025 level.

But this isn't what he appears to be doing. Instead, he takes as the basis for his difference the number of post-tests in which there was any increase—apparently regardless of size—and then subtracts from them the number in which there was a decrease, again (presumably) discarding those (only one, as it happens) in which there was no change. But these are the wrong numbers to work from! Look at it this way: the fact that four students scored lower on the post-test on a given operation, while 16 scored higher, doesn't matter as much as how much higher and how much lower—that's the whole point of using a test that accounts for magnitude. If the four lower post-test scores were ranked highest on the Wilcoxon—say 16, 17, 18, and 19 —their sum would be 70, and the sum of the positive ranks 120. Checking the smaller number against the table at the .025 level for a one-tailed test, we would find that it is too high a value to conclude that the null hypothesis can be rejected; 46 is the maximum. It doesn't have to work out that way, of course. If the negative differences are in fact relatively smaller, the T value could easily enough fall below 46. The point here, though, is that we will never find out. Unless both the table he presents and his prose explanation are simply misleading, Odell has performed his Wilcoxon calculations on the wrong data, and in doing so lost the very interpretive advantage he had hoped to gain by choosing that test in the first place.[9]

And there are other interpretive puzzles in this study, regarding not only this first prediction but the other two as well. Still on this first one, for example: What is the relationship between the results for (1) and (2) here? According to (1), 16 students used the same variety of operations on both pre- and post-test. At the same time, according to (2), at least 11, and on average more than 14, used any given operation more often in the post- than the pre-test. If so few of the students added any operation to their repertoire over the term, and yet if so many used each one more often on the post-test, then isn't the implication that many of them used all of the operations to begin with? Surely this is somehow relevant to the experiment, so why not just say so, one way or the other?

Or on Prediction II, which hypothesized that post-tests would contain fewer conceptual gaps than pre-tests. As we have seen, the rating process here was of questionable validity and poor reliability. Nevertheless, Odell concludes that this "prediction was not confirmed. Only fifty percent of the post-tests showed the predicted change, while eight showed an increase in conceptual gaps" (p. 235). Setting aside the question of whether he has grounds for any interpretation at all—and that is pretty unlikely—it seems that here again, he has misused the Wilcoxon. For whatever reason, he seems to have looked only at the raw number of post-tests that had more or fewer gaps, without considering the *magnitude* of the differences between pre- and post-tests. A small increase in the eight post-tests that showed more gaps could easily have been offset by larger gains in the ten that had, as predicted, fewer gaps.

Pianko's investigation is equally troubled. For while there are no instances of her actually plugging the wrong numbers into formulas, the kind of interpretations she makes, with and without statistical support, are no less problematic. The essentially arithmetic calculations by which she generates her quantitative profile of the group's composing process go along smoothly enough, although her penchant for two decimal place accuracy (three places in the dissertation)—a mean prewriting time of 1.26 minutes, for example, or a pausing rate of 16.35 times per composition—seems odd. Surely two naked-eye observers couldn't be that accurate. Presumably, these numbers are artifacts of her averaging, in which case all they lend here is a false sense of precision. She does much the same thing with the results of her interviews which, as we saw above, she translates into what are essentially questionnaire answers: "52.9% had a positive attitude toward the writing they turned in; 47.1% did not consider any elements of style when writing," and so on (p. 11). In fact, 52.9% represents nine subjects, 47.1% eight, and so on. Again, the only apparent gain in offering such numbers is a pseudo-precision.

Her interpretation of these numbers begins to be more substantively troubling, though, near the end of her prose account of this profile and the initial interviews. She has been pretty careful about how much she infers to this point, and careful, too, to restrict any claims to the 17 students she and her co-investigator have watched compose once. Now, though, she wants to explain what these findings mean:

> Close scrutiny of the behaviors during composing and analysis of the data revealed that what causes the writing process to be of shorter duration with little commitment and little critical concern is the nature of what Emig (1971) refers to as the "context for the writing." If the writing is school-sponsored and must be written within limits set by the teacher, the composing process is inhibited. There is just so much energy that a person is willing to give to please others, and there is just so much energy a person can expend at any one time for composing. Some persons can only compose for a certain length of time, after which they must seek out diversions in order to replenish their creative and intellectual energies. A certain amount of time must elapse during which the writing is placed in the "distal," Polanyi's term to indicate that it is not being attended to. Later, the writer can return to the composition with new energy and perhaps new insights (p. 11).

What kind of analysis is this "close scrutiny" that it can account for such claims? They make a certain amount of sense, of course, and grow in large part out of the literature on writing, thinking, and so on she has reviewed for her dissertation—reviews obviously not readily available to a reader of her article. But what grounds has she for thinking her subjects' composing was "inhibited"? How would they uninhibitedly write, and how does she claim to know? Indeed, most of them seem to say in interviews that writing is not that big a part of their lives. Maybe what they do for her is, in fact, all there is—or maybe even extended, enhanced by her demands. Or again, in what observations are these assertions about energy founded? What are these limits? How does one measure them? Whatever is this "distal" doing here? Does it have an operational definition?

Her interpretation may be most misleading, though, when she moves to statistical inference, treating age, sex, and class status as independent variables, and testing them for correlations against her 22 dependent variables. When she groups her subjects in terms of the first two, she finds no significant differences at the .05 level between the groups thus created. Differences created when they are grouped by age, then, get dismissed quickly, although not without complications: "For the age groups," she writes, "the results . . . showed no evidence of differences between the two groups. It appears that once adulthood is reached, age (within the range observed in this study) is no longer a factor in determining the writing process" (p. 16). Even with that obviously crucial parenthetical qualification, her interpretation would seem to outstrip her data by a considerable margin. Having watched 10 people over 21—an arbitrary age to pick, to begin with—and 7 under 21 each write once is hardly grounds for claims about "adulthood" and writing, one way or another. Faced with similarly non-significant results when she groups them by sex, she resorts to arguing that "there are some noticeable trends for the two groups," and so tries to salvage an interpretation where, by the statistical limits she has set herself, she has no grounds to do so.

But her failure to find significant correlations in these two areas prevents her from giving her interpretive energies full play, and so getting into full trouble—a restraint that is removed when she groups her students by class status. On three of her variables here—prewriting time, pauses, and rescannings—she finds significant differences, at the .05 level for the first, and the .01 level for the other two. Combining these differences, some "trends" in script length and composing time, and the breakout of the students' interview answers, Pianko eventually reaches the following, really quite remarkable, conclusion:

> It seems clear at this point that traditional college writers have a more fully developed understanding of what contributes to good writing. They are more conscious of the elements necessary for a well-developed composition: style, purpose, getting ideas across. Therefore, they spend more time prewriting, pausing, and rescanning to make certain these elements are being properly considered for the particular writing being done. The difference between the two groups of writers with respect to pauses and rescannings has significance beyond merely the number of these behaviors. The pauses are also quite noteworthy: traditional students were pausing to plan what to write next, rescanning to see if their plans fit, and then pausing again to reformulate. Remedial students, during their pauses, were glancing around the room or staring into mid-air, sometimes as a diversion

and at other times hoping the correct spelling, correct word, or
something else to say next would suddenly appear to them.
They usually did not look to their own text for the answers by
rescanning what they had just written; perhaps they did not
feel they could find the answers there (p. 14).

There are as least four problems with this interpretation:

(1) Recall that her means of discriminating remedial and traditional students—the objective placement test, somehow buttressed
by a school-scored essay—was not demonstrably valid or reliable, so
that the basis upon which these people have been clustered is not
that clear. Any interpretations she makes should be very carefully
qualified by that factor, but none of them seem to be.

(2) She seems to forget the difference between correlation and
causation. That is, because she conducted no experiment, her comparison is only capable of showing that, when these people are
grouped in various ways, there are or are not interesting parallels (as
statistically defined) between the values of certain variables. This is a
long way from moving toward causation—from saying, for instance,
that students spend 1.00 rather than 1.64 minutes prewriting because
they are remedial, which is the assumption upon which she seems to
be operating. In fact, the most she could really claim would be something like this: As the entrance examination scores of these students
decrease, so does their mean prewriting time. And even then, because
she doesn't really look at individual writers, and treats "remedial-ness"
as a simply binary distinction, she knows only about a group average.
It may have been only one or two students—who didn't prewrite at
all—who accounted for this difference. But she says nothing about
range, either of times, or of placement test scores. (So, e.g., 3 of her
7 traditional writers also pre-write for 1.00 minutes. See her dissertation, Appendix B.)

(3) In what might better be understood as a design problem,
Pianko makes no effort to account for the interaction among the
three variables she treats as independent. For instance, the mean pre-
writing time for females is 1.50, and for males 1.06—very close,
obviously, to the 1.00 and 1.64 for the remedial and traditional students, respectively, even though the male/female difference is not
deemed significant. How many of the remedial students are also
males? Isn't it likely that the differences she does (and does not) find
statistically significant are a function of some combinations of all
three factors? Wouldn't it be safer to check?

(4) The numbers involved in this study are very small to begin
with, and made about a third smaller by attrition. When she begins to
use statistical analyses, this small sample size—and her single observa-

tion design—begins to undermine those analyses' usefulness. One way to describe what happens is to say that she has a shortage of statistical power—"the ability of a statistical procedure," to quote John A. Daly and Anne Hexamer, authors of "Statistical Power in Research in English Education" (1983), "to detect the presence of an effect if that effect is truly present" (p. 157). Power is essentially a function of three parameters: the level of signifiance, or the significance criterion; the reliability of the sample results, with sample size the most consistent concern; and effect size—or, as Jacob Cohen, whose *Statistical Power Analysis for the Behavior Sciences* is the standard authority puts it, "the *degree* to which the phenomenon exists" (p. 4).

When Pianko sets out to compare the students as grouped according to class status, then, she uses an analysis of variance. As is common enough in Composition studies, she fails to specify an effect size, but Cohen's power tables allow us to estimate power at three standardized effect sizes: small = .10, medium = .25, and large = .40. For Pianko's analysis of variance, then, her statistical power at the .05 level would work out to approximately .08, .30, and .63, respectively; or, at the .01 level, .02, .11, and .36. To put these numbers in perspective, compare them to Daly and Hexamer's average statistical power for 57 articles in *Research in the Teaching of English* (1978-1980) at the .05 level, based on the same range for effect size estimates: .22, .63, and .86. This puts Pianko's analysis of variance considerably below average for the field. Just how low is that? Well, Cohen himself favors a standard value of .80 for optimum power, a level Pianko doesn't reach even at the .05 level with a large effect size. Daly and Hexamer offer the second option of comparing English Education research to that in other fields. In that kind of ranking— one they admit is difficult to assemble accurately—English Education "ranks consistently in the top half" (p. 162). But Pianko's power (which is, by the way, the same or lower in the two other analyses she offers in the article) would still be lower than the lowest field listed—Education, at .14, .58, and .78. And that is very low indeed.

In spite of the range of dangers exemplified by these two studies, of course, it is finally possible to interpret Experimental data without such serious difficulties. In determining what their substantial body of data means, Morenberg et al. demonstrate pretty well how it can be done. Their first paragraph under "Results" makes it clear that they plan to stay within the limits of their design, and restrict their interpretations to the three hypotheses they offered at the outset:

> Both hypotheses related to writing skills were accepted. College freshmen trained in SC scored significantly higher than control

students on factors of syntactic maturity and wrote compositions judged superior in quality. The hypothesis that SC practice enhances reading ability was rejected (p. 251).

And their first step, a kind of pre-interpretive check, is typical of the caution they exercise throughout. Before actually testing each hypothesis, they run a t-test that compares the mean pretest scores of the experimental and control classes on three of the four measures under consideration—the factors for gauging syntactic maturity, the holistic scores, and the analytic scores. The object is to make sure (in addition, remember, to their original sampling procedure, and their check on SAT/ACT scores) that there was no significant inherent difference between the groups on this task before instruction. They find no differences significant at the .05 level.

With that assurance of the groups' pre-treatment equivalence on each measure, they move to the actual comparisons of post-test data. First, there is an analysis of covariance of the mean group scores for the three syntactic factors under study: words/clause, clauses/T-unit, and words/T unit. On two of the three, they find significant differences: in words/clause (at the .001 level); and words/T-unit (at the .01 level). There are only two peculiarities here. One is that they simply make no mention of differences in clauses/T-unit, which were not significant. Later, in their "Discussion" section, they argue that such a result is "consistent with Hunt's (1965b) prediction that little growth in subordination ratio occurs beyond the twelfth grade"; and, "furthermore, the SC classes emphasized the use of nonclausal free modifiers, virtually to the exclusion of subordinate clauses" (p. 255). But is this rationalization? And if not, why not frame the hypothesis in its null form in the first place—i.e., predict that there would be no significant difference? The original hypothesis was offered as a package: the experimental group was to score higher on "syntactic maturity factors as measured by standard quantitative criteria" (p. 245). Is it thus only two-thirds confirmed, or to be rejected? To be sure, this is a relatively minor problem, but the omission seems odd.

The other peculiarity is also an omission. As it turned out, the control groups actually had marginally lower mean scores on two of the three measures—a .13 drop in words/clause, and .05 in words/T-unit (p. 250). These are tiny changes, to be sure, and almost certainly not statistically significant, but they do exaggerate the size of the experimental gains, and they make one wonder: Why should the best efforts of six teachers—equal in ability to those in the experimental classes—have such bad luck? Or are these the wrong measures? I would have liked to see these questions addressed more fully.

In any case, Morenberg and his colleagues follow the same procedure for both the holistic and analytic scores with even clearer results. A comparison of the two groups' mean post-test holistic scores—3.73 (SD 1.02) for the experimental, 3.37 (SD .87) for the control—yields a difference of .36; the F-ratio (13.31) is significant beyond the .001 level. On the analytic measures, the post-test mean scores for the experimental group are higher in all six categories, and significantly different at the .05 level or better in five: Ideas, Supporting details, Voice, Sentence Structure, and Diction/usage. (The only non-significant difference was in Organization/coherence; in this case, no explanation is offered, under either "Results" or "Discussion.") In addition, on the forced-choice ratings described earlier, the Experimental essay in each of the 134 pairs was "picked as better by six or more of the ten raters almost twice as often as the post-test control papers—79 times to 42 times," with 13 ties (p. 251). This difference, subjected to a chi-square test of independence, was found to be significant at the .05 level, as well.

This is as good as Experimental interpretation gets in Composition, I think. There are no errors in the application of the three statistical tests they use, nor (insofar as I can determine from what's given) in any of their calculations. The reliability of their various measures, as we saw earlier, was always above .80, plenty high, by conventional standards, to make full use of them. There is no attempt to interpret data patterns that render no significant results. So when, for instance, they find that "the experimental students achieved a slightly higher post-test composite score (40.36) than the control students (39.45)" on the standard reading test they use to test their third hypothesis, they don't look for "trends," as Pianko does; they simply note that "the difference between the scores was not significant, and the third hypothesis was rejected" (p. 253). And while one might quibble that they don't compute the statistical power of these various operations themselves, nor offer an effect size estimate, in their defense I would have to point out that almost no one in Composition had (or does, even now). Moreover, if we estimate its range following Daly and Hexamer's pattern again, it comes in very high: Even if the effect size is small—highly unlikely given the kinds of differences they found—they come in at .45 at the .01 level; and with the far more likely medium or large effects, at .87 and .99 (or .70, .96, and $>$.995 at .05). Even by Cohen's standards, this is satisfactory power.

By this point, no doubt, it may seem I have been stacking the deck against the Experimental method, choosing in Odell's and Pianko's investigations examples for extended analysis designed to show the method at its worst. This isn't the case, of course. I chose these studies to illustrate the range of possible designs. As it turned out, they also happened to illustrate just how hard it can be to interpret the data produced by those designs, but that was essentially accidental, albeit usefully so. Obviously, I make no claims about the representativeness of any of the three interpretations, for better or worse, in terms of the rest of the Experimental community. In addition, I am especially anxious that neither Odell nor Pianko be judged too harshly regarding their work in these particular studies. Both were dissertations, presumably the first research undertaking of this kind for each investigator. Both were also fairly intricate first outings, and pretty clearly designed to extend the work of mentors—Richard Young, in Odell's case, and Janet Emig in Pianko's. Dissertations are as good a place to take chances—and make mistakes—as any.

So, for the most part, I am willing to explain the dramatic contrast in interpretive quality between these two studies and Morenberg et al.'s as a function of experience; this sort of thing gets easier with practice. However, what is a good deal more important about that contrast here, and more telling in terms of the Experimental community as a whole, is the way in which the Odell and Pianko studies were *received*. As I noted earlier, both were singled out for excellence at the time of their publication. When Odell's article appeared in *Research in the Teaching of English* (1974), it was introduced by the following assessment:

> The sort of small-scale experiment described in this article can and should be a part of each instructor's self-education. Although the study uses unscientific sampling procedures and perhaps involves the investigator too deeply for optimal objectivity, the basic strategy of predicting what will happen to the experimental subjects is actually a more sophisticated approach than the typical experiment conceived of as a horserace between experimental and control groups. Comparison of results of large numbers of such small and inexpensive studies can yield knowledge as reliable as that yielded by a single, expensive, impeccably designed experiment (p. 228).

Given what we have seen of the study in the past few pages, this seems rather an odd declaration. The compelling self-educational value of such an undertaking is far from self-evident. Odell must have put in a fair amount of time and energy, along with the secretary and raters, in working out this "small and inexpensive" design. What did he actually get out of it that could justify the effort? Of the six subpredictions tested, only two were supported even by his figuring—and that, as we have seen, was faulty. What did he learn, then? That his teaching was largely ineffectual? Even more disturbing, though, is the notion that lots of other people—"each instructor," if we take this commentator literally—should undertake a similar study, partly for this self-education, and partly because such work will have a cumulative value. Of course it is true, as I pointed out earlier, that even a study that produces a very modest disconfirmatory power can be of paradigmatic use. By means of meta-analysis, it may be possible to make sense of the results of large numbers of experimental studies—to find a pattern in the pattern finding. But surely each such study would first have to generate a genuine and accessible disconfirmatory power, a condition that has obviously not been met here. So unless they were all taken absolutely at face value, I find it hard to see how a hundred studies like this one could be made to yield, by *any* kind of analysis, a knowledge that could be construed as reliable, let alone valid, in any ordinary Experimental sense of those terms.

And one must raise the same sorts of questions about Pianko's project, which won her recognition as an NCTE Promising Researcher in 1978. That program "recognizes several beginning researchers for outstanding dissertations or initial independent studies after the dissertation."[10] Does this mean, in effect, that it is considered "outstanding" to characterize whole classes of people as "remedial" by a single test score? To confuse causation and correlation? To ignore Experimental concerns as rudimentary as variable interactions? To work with statistics at power levels below average not only for English Education, but for even the lowest of rated research fields? Almost certainly not, of course. What it means in Pianko's case, and what the reviewer's high praise of Odell's study means, presumably, is that these interpretive flaws were simply not noticed by adviser or reviewer, editor or awards committee; or that, if they were, they didn't constitute enough of a problem to merit serious objection.

I don't want to get carried away with these two bits of evidence. This all happened, as no doubt someone will object, a fairly long time ago—back in the 1970s—and perhaps Composition research has come a long way since then. And, too, one never knows what the politics of such situations were, or what the competition was like for either publication or award. And yet there can be no disputing these studies' visibility. However cautiously we consider them, they recall my opening claim that the Experimental community has been a deeply troubled one. That the work of novice investigators, and work so seriously troubled at that, should be held up as work to be emulated, is surely evidence in support of that claim.

Drawing Conclusions: Dissemination to a Wider Audience

So far as I can tell, Experimental investigations never end simply by interpreting their data, confirming or disconfirming (in a probabilistic sense) their hypotheses. Instead, they follow a very powerful convention that requires moving from those findings to some discussion of them. The primary purpose of this discussion, presumably, is to explicitly account for whatever inferential power the study has generated in terms of the paradigm: in effect, to recap what the findings mean in terms of the problem as originally identified for study. This will often include, sometimes under a specific heading, implications for further research. Most of the time in Composition, though, there is also the secondary purpose of moving from that paradigmatic inference to what that contribution might mean in non-paradigmatic terms—nearly always expressed, as might be expected, in terms of what teachers ought to do.

Even though the first of these purposes might be said, strictly speaking, to fall outside Experimental boundaries—the method, as we have seen, functions within, but does not much control, the paradigm—it is understandable enough as intra-communal discourse. Odell's handling of it (under the heading "Conclusions") may be the most interesting of the three we've been treating. After the debacle of analysis and interpretation, he very gamely pulls back and points out some of the design flaws we have dealt with here. It is brief enough to quote in full:

> Conclusions based on this study must be tentative, if only because the study cannot answer such important questions as the following: How much were the results of the study influenced by the teaching methods of the instructor? Could similar results be achieved by different methods or by teachers with different classroom personalities? Why did students fail to make statistically significant increases in their use of all the operations presented in the course? Could it be that for examining certain materials, some operations are simply more useful than others? Or could it be that the scoring procedures described above were not adequate to identify certain operations? Would other prewriting procedures have an even greater influence upon students' writing? Can pre-writing operations profitably be taught to students at other academic levels?
>
> Despite these and other unanswered questions, the study does provide some support for the belief that the teaching of prewriting procedures can affect student writing. Results of the study show that all essays studied revealed an increased use of

at least some of the operations taught in the experimental course, and several of these increases can be attributed to students' experiences in that course rather than simply to chance (p. 239).

This isn't a perfect ending, to be sure. One might wish that some of these questions had been raised earlier. Also, his misconception that a Wilcoxon-based demonstration of non-random relationship between pre- and post-test scores is evidence for the causal powers of the experimental curriculum still lurks here. And, finally, his presentation of this one statistically significant increase, especially since we know it to be mistakenly figured, looks like pretty desperate salvaging. Still, at least the questions have been raised, and pretty well, at that. So if it isn't quite the model the reviewer makes it out to be, it can still serve as a guidepost—not to say warning—especially for other novices. Just as important, Odell makes no attempt to extend the findings, to squeeze from them any more in the way of implications for research or for teaching than they will give.

Pretty much the same things can be said for Morenberg et al.'s much longer (just over two pages) concluding section (headed "Discussion"):

> The results of this study support and extend the claims made for SC by previous research. Both in standard factors of syntactic maturity and in measures of overall writing quality, first-year college students trained in sentence combining achieved significantly higher scores than students following a conventional curriculum (p. 253).

Note the careful limits to these claims: not "the SC students matured syntactically," but "in standard factors of syntactic maturity"; not "became better writers overall," but "in measures of overall writing quality." As we saw earlier, it is the combination of the higher scores in both these measures that they considered most important. They spend most of their discussion exploring this connection: why it was important; how the syntactic measures here compared with those in other research; what the connections might be between gains in the two measures, and so on. I find it a little curious that they offer even less direction for possible future research than Odell, not offering even so much as a question. Given the sophistication of their design, perhaps they think the subject to be closed, or at least that exhortations to extend or replicate the inquiry are out of place. Whatever their reasons, it would still be most interesting to see what results a replication turned up.

And finally, they go just a little farther than Odell in drawing implications for teaching. Having noted in passing that the study's evidence that SC "leads to more effective writing" is especially important from the standpoint of a college composition program, they nevertheless conclude with the same kind of caution that characterizes the study from the start. After a paragraph of speculation on just what sentence combining is that it should have such results, they offer the following summation:

> It is generally believed that writing skills can only be acquired slowly and painfully. As Kitzhaber (1963) remarks, "It is preposterous to claim or to expect that any single course in either school or college, no matter how well taught, or how intensively studied can assure [such skills] " (p. 7). While an intensive, rhetorically based course in SC is surely not the panacea for the accumulated ills of freshman composition, this experiment offers strong evidence that it is superior to a traditional course in improving student writing. Indeed, while SC students were more than keeping pace in reading ability, after just 15 weeks they outscored their control counterparts in the factors of syntactic maturity and in the holistic, forced-choice, and analytic measures of writing quality (pp. 255–256).

Allowing for just a touch of self-congratulatory enthusiasm (marked by the "indeed," I think), and aware of all the quibbles raised in this chapter, especially about validity, this still seems to me a conclusion very much in keeping with the investigation whose report it ends.

I have saved Pianko's study for last, as you may have guessed, because her discussion, in a section titled "Implications," is different from the other two. It runs about the same length as Morenberg et al.'s, a little over two pages. But whereas the rhetoric in both the other studies could be termed dominantly intra-communal, Pianko operates almost exclusively from an inter-communal stance. She adopts it, unmistakably, from the beginning:

> The findings of this inquiry suggest a number of interesting paradoxes in the methods currently used for teaching writing. In the first instance, students do not view writing which has the context specifically set by the teacher and which must be completed within the constraints of a class meeting as an activity that is worth committing themselves to. The limitations placed by the typical school writing activity negate the possibility for greater elaboration, commitment, and concern. Yet many instructors insist that the most effective way to evaluate students' writing abilities is to have the writing controlled for topic, place, and time. According to the students in this study, such a writing

activity does not permit sufficient time for them to regroup their energies and thoughts; therefore, they merely attempt to complete the assignment in some expedient fashion and "give the teachers what they want." So, in fact, what writing teachers are actually evaluating is how well students follow instructions, not how well they write (pp. 17–18).

These are obviously claims in need of serious qualification. In the first place, she has no grounds whatever—given her study, any-way—to make generalizations about how writing is currently taught: not in terms of what "typical" classroom limitations are, nor what "many" instructors "insist." Second, even if she did have such grounds, or if we were willing to grant them, her study of seventeen writers composing once would hardly seem to warrant claims as sweeping as these as a corrective to such pedagogical tendencies. Surely there are other students who do manage to commit them-selves to in-class writing, and like it? And third, however much one might agree with the sentiments, the reasoning here doesn't have much logical appeal. In some sense or other, students are *always* going to be giving the teachers what they want, no? Isn't authority a given in student-teacher relationships? So no matter how or where teachers lead (compel? cajole? encourage?) students to write, they will be trying to get what they want. That dilemma seems inescapable.

And her stance only becomes more and more aggressive through-out the discussion that follows: "Perhaps it is paranoia," she suggests, "which stops teachers from allowing students to do the major portion of their writing at home within a context set by themselves" (p. 18). Paranoia? Or how about this assertion: "Teachers must change their focus from providing writing experiences which are solely class-oriented and include writing experiences which evolve from within students, from their needs to communicate through writing to them-selves and others" (p. 18). These are claims made by plenty of people in Composition, and again, the sentiments may appeal. But what have they to do with the seventeen student-writers studied? How do we know what teachers' focus was? Did any of the students observed provide evidence that this writing-from-within ever happened? I don't recall any. Or, as a final example from what could be a much longer list, consider this recapitulation of her findings on class status:

> What characterizes "poor" writers in addition to the low quality products they produce are their underdeveloped composing processes, a factor which is rarely taken into account in teaching composition, but which significantly influences the outcome of the product. Although the processes are the same for traditional writers and remedial writers, for remedial writers they are of

much shorter duration, and of poorer quality. For example, remedial writers do not pause as often during the writing for additional planning or rescan as often to take stock of what they have written to aid in the next formulations as do traditional writers. These types of behaviors during composing assist students in developing a clearer conception of the content of their essays, in being more critical about what has just been written and what should be written next, and in making stylistic decisions along the way. What basically separates the two groups of writers is *the ability to reflect on what is being written* (p. 20, her emphasis).

The questionably reliable observation of one composing episode each for ten students whose scores on a placement test were below a certain cutoff point has come a long, long way. No one would deny that this characterization makes a certain *a priori* sense. The question is, how much of what kind of evidence has this study developed in support of it? Pianko has already argued pretty strongly that these students just didn't care about this kind of writing. How can she then hope that her analysis of composing behaviors *during* such writing has any validity? To invoke her own, however illogical, complaint, she isn't examining how or how well they write, but only how well they follow an investigator's instructions.

Having already excused much of Pianko's interpretive excess on the basis of her inexperience, I see little to be gained by belaboring that inexperience any further here. Given the investment in time and energy necessary for a dissertation that runs over 450 pages, her urge to inflate the power of its findings is understandable, if not commendable. But her handling of these "Implications" will serve to close out this chapter, for her situation presents a pretty good emblem for the predicament faced by the Experimental community as a whole. Here she has gone to such great lengths, so painstakingly collected so much data, and pored over it so long and so carefully. By virtue of its sheer size and weight, she seems to think it ought to somehow add up, to generate the kind of authority she attempts to wield. As we have seen, of course, it doesn't work out that way. Despite her investment in putting this study together, its inferential power is finally very, very small. We are not willing to grant—or at least I am not—the kinds of assumptions she demands; unwilling to grant, to recall what is probably her most demanding assumption, that there are two kinds of writers in the world, "traditional" and "remedial," and that they can be differentiated by what amounts to a linguistic litmus test. Simple dichotomies like this might work if we wanted to figure out how best to market hamburgers, but Pianko wants to claim knowledge about how people do, learn, and teach writing, and such simplicity will not do. Her attempts to force these data to operate with an authority far beyond their capacity, therefore, produce only a kind of reformist propaganda, with little or no basis in the inquiry itself.

And this is essentially the dilemma faced by the larger Experimental community. After 75 years, as the result of a tremendous collective investment in time and energy and money, it too has generated an enormous body of data, and developed from that data great numbers of analyses, interpretations, and conclusions—created, in other words, what looks to be the sleeping giant of my opening image. And surely the urge, as for Pianko, is to somehow awaken, to animate that giant, so that the community will at long last be able to wield an authority in proportion to its size, and to the size of its investigative investment. But it faces the same sort of problem. One way to characterize it, in a kind of social science shorthand, is as a combinatorial explosion. The phenomenon under study—in this case, people writing—is a complex of so many variables, and so many variable interactions (or *combinat* -ions), that Experimental inference beyond a certain rudimentary level is effectively stymied. It isn't entirely clear whether this explosion is a function of the phenomenon, so that accounting for people writing is inherently more complex than accounting for, say, cellular or molecular or atomic activity;[11] or an essentially ethical matter, so that neither the means by which Experimentalists in other fields work toward an operative certainty, nor the levels at which their communities are willing to grant that it has been achieved, are acceptable; or some combination of the two.

The point, in any case, is that community efforts to awaken the giant—to animate these mountains of data and findings as a cumulative, coherent whole—face considerable, if not impossible, odds. As in Pianko's study, of course, they can be forced to speak, but the results are likely to be just as far off the mark. Imagine the Orwellian consequences of an Experimental community committed to a notion as ethically and politically reductive as her traditional/remedial distinction, and the argument she constructs to explain her findings thereon. Nor is this possibility so far-fetched. The danger of this kind of reductivism is ever-present in a paradigm-based community. Even at its best—assuming the Morenberg, Daiker, and Kerek study represents that standard—we must have serious reservations about validity. And if that's the risk, if the giant upon which so many hopes have been pinned may in fact only be a monster, maybe it's finally a good thing if it never does awaken. The better course for such a community, if not silence, is surely a very deliberate and cautious reassessment, both of the kind of knowledge it can generate, and the nature of the authority it can—or even wants to—claim.

7

The Clinicians

My need to consider what will here be called a Clinical method arises, more than anything, from a single study: Janet Emig's *The Composing Processes of Twelfth Graders.* As I suggested earlier, it arguably stands as the single most influential piece of Researcher inquiry—and maybe *any* kind of inquiry—in Composition's short history. Presumably it appeared in print at a time (1971) when the field was ready for a Researcher's articulation of the shift in perspective that has since made a cliché of the way Earl Buxton described it in his brief foreword to Emig's monograph: After fifty or so years of "attention upon the *written product*," Emig's work represented "an expedition into new territory, an investigation of the writing *process*" (p. v, Buxton's emphases). Though it has since come under some criticism, Emig's study was not only technically innovative, but rewarding enough to make further investigation of this process seem worthwhile.[1] And while it might be too much to claim direct descendance, it is surely possible to trace a strong line of influence for the burgeoning assault on this mystery of the writing process in all the other modes of inquiry back to this single study—an influence so strong, in fact, that were it the only study of its kind, the Clinical method might deserve treatment as a mode of inquiry simply on that basis.

But Emig's pioneering investigation was not one of a kind. It has been followed by a fairly steady stream of studies similar in methodology. The vast majority of them have also focused on the writing process, variously conceived, albeit over a really quite striking variety of subjects. Two in particular, both completed in 1979, also by dissertation writers, have had an influence nearly as great as

Emig's: Sondra Perl's *Five Writers Writing: Case Studies of the Composing Processes of Unskilled College Writers*; and Nancy Sommers' *Revision in the Composing Process: A Case Study of College Freshmen and Experienced Adult Writers*. And there have been many others; here are some that suggest their range: Charles K. Stallard's "An Analysis of the Writing Behavior of Good Student Writers" (senior high school students); Terry Mischel's "A Case Study of a Twelfth-Grade Writer"; Elizabeth Metzger's *Causes of Failure to Learn to Write: Exploratory Case Studies at Grade Seven, Grade Ten, and College Level*; Ann Seaman's "Exploring Early Stages of Writing Development: A Fourth Grader Writes"; Betsy Morgan's "A Case Study of a Seventh Grade Writer"; Linda Leonard Lamme and Nancye M. Childers' "The Composing Processes of Three Young Children" (ages 2–4); John Sweeder's *A Descriptive Study of Six Adult Remedial Writers: Their Composing Processes and Heuristic Strategies*; Cynthia Selfe's "The Predrafting Processes of Four High- and Four Low-Apprehensive Writers." Nor has all the focus been on school writing. Bonnie Jean Stalnaker, for example, reports on *A Study of the Influences of Audience and Purpose on the Composing Processes of Professionals*; while in still another dissertation, James Hobbs looks at *The Poetry-Composing Processes of Proficient Twelfth Grade Writers*. Skilled adult writers, variously defined, have come under scrutiny, too: Charles Cooper and Lee Odell examined "Considerations of Sound in the Composing Process of Published Writers"; Carol Berkenkotter studied Donald Murray at work, reporting on what she found in "Decisions and Revisions: The Planning Strategies of a Publishing Writer"; Jack Selzer offers "The Composing Processes of an Engineer"; and Deena Linett, in a 1983 dissertation, reports on the examination of a writer and an architect in *Studies in Process: Writing and Architectural Design*.

Occasionally, though, the Clinical method has been brought to bear on other phenomena. Nina Ziv's dissertation study, for example, *The Effect of Teacher Comments on the Writing of Four College Freshmen*, deals with written commentary. And the following all deal with talk about writing: Sarah Warshauer Freedman's "Student-Teacher Conversations about Writing: Shifting Topics in the Writing Conference"; Suzanne Jacobs and Adela Karliner's "Helping Writers to Think: The Effect of Speech Roles in Individual Conferences on the Quality of Thought in Student Writing"; Jerry Herman's *The Tutor and the Student: A Case Study*; Tom Reigstad's *Conferencing Practices of Professional Writers: Ten Case Studies*. Hence, while the tradition for Clinicians in Composition has been to concentrate on the act of writing *per se*, the method is in fact potentially quite flexible in its applications.

Despite the apparent continuity of this line of inquiry, however, and despite its really remarkable influence on the field, this, too, is a community beset by fairly serious difficulties. Not those of the Experimental community; Clinicians have not had to worry that they are toiling in obscurity toward amorphous, maybe unreachable goals. Rather, their central problem can be characterized as a problem with self-image. For all their influence, the Clinicians have so far been reluctant to fully recognize the power of their method for what it is, and so have not claimed any substantial methodological authority of their own.

As with so much else concerning this method, we can begin to understand this self-image problem by looking at Emig's inaugural study. In the published monograph itself, I should point out, she does not use the term "clinical" to describe her approach. In fact, she offers no explicit methodological identification at all, except to refer, in what has since become something of a ritual, to the argument in Braddock et al.'s *Research in Written Composition* that case studies have been used successfully in a variety of fields and disciplines, and so make sense for Composition. However, the design of her study—indeed, the fact that she describes it as having a "design" at all—and much of her terminology suggests that she sees it as rising out of an Experimental tradition. So, for instance, she frames it in terms of four hypotheses, her first being that her subjects will "engage in two modes of composing—reflexive and extensive—characterized by processes of different lengths with different clusterings of components" (p. 3). She eventually implies, by repeating this assertion verbatim under "Findings," that the study has somehow confirmed it. What is never very clear, of course, is why she should have "found" only two such modes in the first place—and not three or eight or ten—except that she wasn't looking for them. In other words, she doesn't really regard their existence as hypothetical, but simply groups the various activities she does observe under these two headings. This seems a sensible enough strategy for observational purposes, but the fact that it can be done hardly constitutes confirmation in any Experimental sense.

So why state these hypotheses in the first place? Presumably, they indicate her uneasiness with her method: are an effort, despite the Experimentally dubious nature of her undertaking, to maintain her ties—or at least keep the peace—with the Experimental community proper. And she carries this campaign even further, gauging the relative potency of the study by invoking Experimental criteria: sample size and makeup (hers is "far too small and skewed," she cautions); validity of her primary investigative tool (composing aloud is "an understandably difficult, artificial, and at times distracting procedure"); and the correlation of her findings with other measures of writing ability or creativity (she checked none) (pps. 4–5). And she follows through on these criteria in her "Implications for Research" (p. 95), calling for larger samples, more sophisticated means of assuring the validity of her data-collecting techniques, and a range of correlational searches.

Her motives here are understandable. As I suggested in my general discussion of the Researchers, the Clinical method can be said to represent the nomothetic Experimental method's idiographic complement. The Experimentalists seek generalizable laws, patterns that hold for whole populations. Clinicians, on the other hand, are concerned with what is unique and particular in some unit within a population (a writer, a teacher, a writing tutorial, etc.), but they also bring to bear on their investigations all that they know about the larger population of which that unit is a part; in short, they are concerned with the manifestation of those general laws in particular instances. As a result, they naturally tend to think of their idiographic investigations, as Emig clearly does, as a subsidiary, second-class kind of inquiry, a feeder system for the Experimentalists' nomothetic agenda —a way of discerning, usually in conveniently operationalizable terms, tentative cause/effect relationships, the value of which can later be determined by genuinely Experimental designs.

Her impressive show of loyalty notwithstanding, though, Emig's is obviously *not* an Experimental inquiry. She asked eight students to write three pieces of work for her; two were written in her presence, and the students were asked to compose those aloud. She also interviewed the students at some length about their writing experiences in general, and about specific pieces of writing they had done, including one she assigned. These seem useful ways to come to understand these student-writers, but there is no treatment, no really tested or even testable hypotheses, no framing of a problem in paradigmatic terms. So while it does operate on essentially positivist assumptions, in the absence of any such treatment it won't qualify as quasi- or even pre-Experimental.

Interestingly enough, Emig eventually reaches a similar conclusion herself. In "Inquiry Paradigms and Writing," an article published some eight years after *The Composing Processes of Twelfth Graders*, Emig wants to label her early study's assumptions "phenomenological" (p. 163) as opposed to positivist, claiming for it and for all versions of the "case-study"—which she treats as a generic term—a concern for "context" that is not characteristic of positivist inquiry. Granting that Emig's study was in fact guided by such assumptions— and it should be clear that I am willing to do so only for the sake of argument—would be to place it, in my scheme, in the Ethnographers' community. This would be more or less in keeping with Paul Diesing's classification of the Clinical method in psychology, which he treats, with a reservation that will prove important below, as "similar to participant observation":

> . . . it deals with a whole, unique, self-maintaining system—in this case a person—and aims at construction of a system model; it involves the intimate participation of the therapist in the functioning of his subject matter, so as to develop an intuitive understanding of it; it involves the development of specific hypotheses out of recurring themes and the testing of them against several kinds of data, including the clinician's own reactions and the responses to his probing actions; and it involves the continuous reconstruction of the system model in terms of internal coherence and of agreement with the continuing supply of data. It falls short of participant observation at its best in that the clinician cannot, in principle, get as complete an inside understanding of his subject as can a group of field workers. If the personality is, in part, a system of roles and role expectations, the clinician participates in it by taking one or two roles that are offered him. He can then participate in and observe the activity of his subject in those roles. But the subject's activity in other roles, as husband, father, employee, and the like, is not accessible to direct observation and must be reconstructed intuitively from the subject's reports (pp. 6-7).

As much as I sympathize with this position—I have, after all, kept Diesing's label—I have to disagree with both him and Emig here. In trying to establish an authority for the Clinical method independent of any Experimental ties, they go too far left, as it were, and end up making it a satellite of Ethnography instead. At the heart of my objection is their apparent assumption that something called the "case study" is a generic method, such that any manifestation of it is by definition very like Ethnography (or participant observation, as Diesing calls it) in its assumptions. The fact is that any of the modes of inquiry treated in this book can provide the basis for its own version of a case study. The historical study of a single figure is a kind of case study; so was my Hermeneutical examination of three student writers; so would be an intensive Experimental study, where an N of useful size is generated by increasing the number of observations of one or a very few subjects (in contrast with the more common *extensive* study, where the N is mainly a function of the number of subjects). And we shall see, in the next two chapters, the kinds and uses of case studies recognized by the Formalist and Ethnographic communities—studies exemplified, for instance, in the work of Linda

Flower and John Hayes or Mike Rose, for the former, or Susan
Florio and Christopher Clark, for the latter. All these studies can be
considered similar insofar as they focus on some "unit" or phenomenon intensively. But the nature of that focus—how the scrutinized
unit is conceived, how findings are tested and validated, what happens
to the knowledge generated by the inquiry, and so on—these will all
be a function of the sponsoring mode of inquiry.

Not all case studies, therefore, are created equal. And the mode
of inquiry Emig follows in *The Composing Processes of Twelfth
Graders* is, among other distinguishing features, simply too intrusive,
too context-irreverent, to be considered Ethnographic, or to be paired
with it under the heading of phenomenological. The demand for activities like composing at the investigator's convenience (for Emig, in
fact, during summer vacation, when for many twelfth graders it seems
unlikely that any writing at all would naturally occur); aloud, for a
tape recorder, with the investigator not merely present but even questioning and prompting the writer; in a setting (unnamed by Emig) of
the investigator's choosing; and, indeed, her efforts to make sure that
these conditions were the same for all subjects—these seem, on the
contrary, quite without regard for context in any Ethnographic sense
of that term.

Moreover, there is the difference Diesing cites regarding the investigative limitations imposed by the clinic or laboratory setting as
opposed to the field. However the investigator is construed by the
subjects in a study like Emig's—as an extension of "teacher," or as a
friend, or as someone to try to please because she pays you and flat-
ters you about how bright you are—and however intimate subject
and investigator may come to be, the investigator will have only indirect access (i.e., through the subject) to the other sorts of relationships that characterize the activity of writing as it is usually performed
in the subject's life. This is not a bad thing, any more than it is bad
that clients in psychiatric relationships can't take their therapist home
with them to solve their problems. It is, however, a distinctive and
noteworthy feature of the method, and one which separates it,
finally, from what I will be calling Ethnographic inquiry.

Emig's methodological waffling is, I think, symptomatic of the
entire Clinical community's difficulties in coming to terms with its
own authority, and the long term effects of this image problem have
been pretty severe. Perhaps the most notable consequence (and it
may be a cause, too) is that nobody stays very long. So far as I know,
Emig never did another such study, nor have any more than a handful
of the other writers cited above. In some ways, the Clinical mode has
been to Researcher inquiry what the Philosophical has been for the
Scholars: the easiest place to break in. It tends to be simpler and

cheaper, requires little in the way of specialized knowledge, and has proven to be quite marketable, in the sense that it will satisfy dissertation requirements or generate publishable articles. But the transience of the Clinical community has been extreme. At least among the Philosophers, a core group has stayed on, so that the community has gradually increased its self-awareness. Here, even the most advanced and/or celebrated practitioners have departed. As a result, no core group has formed to provide direction. Methodological self-consciousness has remained very low; no apologist has come forth to explain or defend this way of making knowledge. So while Clinical investigators have been able to produce some interesting work, they have been nearly silent about *how*, and the method itself has been refined very little.

Assembling them in this chapter, then, I am rather forcing the issue, doing what none of the investigators I will discuss has been willing or able to do. I want to argue what I think is true: that treating this mode of inquiry as simply a subset of Experimental work, on the one hand, or of the Ethnographic method, on the other, is to make faults out of what might well be considered its strengths, and to ignore the rather special role it has played in Composition. Nor are its users best understood as the poor cousins of the better established communities founded on those methods. They constitute an independent community whose members I will call, since they have no name for themselves, the Clinicians. In making this argument, though, I don't want to create a false coherence. It makes sense to treat these investigators as a community, yes. But—and this might well be the chapter's major theme—it is a community whose growth as a community has been severely stunted.

The Nature of Clinical Knowledge

As befits the product of a method that lies, however uneasily, between Experimental and Ethnographic inquiry, Clinical knowledge can be characterized in hybrid terms. It has what I will call a canonical structure, in the sense that it is built around an identifiable, if not universally agreed-upon, set of texts; but it is a canon held together not by a dialectical, but a paradigmatic logic. Let me explain what this means. Other modes of inquiry have canons. We have seen how Hermeneutical inquiry works, and will see, in Chapter 9, how the "fictions" produced by Ethnographers can be said to accumulate canonically, as well. The obvious difference between these Researcher canons and the Hermeneutical one is that, at least traditionally, the Critics themselves have no hand in producing canonical texts—they only operate from or on them; whereas both Clinicians and Ethnographers are themselves in one sense or another primary text makers, producing accounts of some observed and/or experienced phenomena which eventually serve as part of the community's object of study.

But if its canonical structure connects Clinical knowledge with Ethnographers and Critics, its paradigmatic logic keeps it tied to the Experimentalists and Formalists. I described the Experimental paradigm by saying that it was assumed to constitute the pattern of that portion of the world under study. A paradigmatic logic, then, is one that regards any contributed piece of knowledge as a portion of this larger pattern. A mode of inquiry guided by it will assemble, through a gradual process of accumulation, a composite image—a sort of multi-dimensional jigsaw puzzle, the final shape of which the investigators cannot know. As positivists, Clinicians assume that there is, in fact, only one possible "correct" solution to this puzzle; but for a very long time they can only put pieces together by guesswork, looking for congruencies that make sense in terms of the ones they do have. The dynamics of such a process should be familiar enough: each new piece is fitted in according to some tentative solution. If it won't fit, there are three options: (a) set it aside for later, in the hope that its place will become clearer; (b) rearrange all the existing pieces in a new pattern that includes it; or (c) reject it, claiming that it is a piece of some other puzzle, or simply random. Matters are complicated, of course, by the puzzle's multi-dimensionality, and by the fact that no single piece will necessarily account for all dimensions. To complicate them further, there is a good chance that the full image can never be completed. So while attempted solutions can create insights, they may well never be confirmed.

For Clinical inquiry, these "pieces" consist of the individual studies contributed by the community's investigators; these are the results of what I will call first-level inquiry. Attempts to assemble these pieces, then—either within or across investigations—can be called second-level inquiry: as soon as there are two or more pieces, Clinicians are free to try putting them together. Since the community's dominant line of inquiry has focused on subjects in the act of writing—twelfth graders, basic writers, a fourth grader, an engineer, and so on—the larger "puzzle" for this dominant line can be called "People Writing." The assumption is that if we watch people do writing, measure them and their activities in various ways, test them and probe them and talk to them about it, we can not only produce coherent accounts of these individual subjects but, because the phenomenon itself is assumed to operate according to nomothetic laws, we can also move toward a coherent account of the whole, as well. So even though the puzzle may never be completed, we count on there being a discernible commonality running through all of the phenomenon's various manifestations. And if our investigations are careful enough, they will all provide some access to that commonality, making it possible to tie otherwise independent inquiries together.

In effect, then, Clinical knowledge accumulates by accretion. In contrast to its Experimental counterpart, it approaches the world it studies by examining phenomena again and again, looking at them from different angles, probing them in different ways, aiming to render a composite—or, to make its ties to Ethnography clearer, holistic—image. If I may be excused a second analogy: Experimental inquiry works like sculpting in marble; it aims to cut away the random bits and pieces of experience in order to reveal the "real" form beneath. Hence it proceeds cautiously, always with careful control, through disconfirmation after disconfirmation, looking for the "true" lines. Clinical inquiry, on the other hand, is more like painting (or perhaps collage-making). It builds its image of what is "real" layer by layer, so there is less need for the same kinds of caution or control: the true lines are expected to emerge from the layering on, not the stripping away.

The advantages of working within the framework of this kind of knowledge, at least for first-level inquiry, are pretty obvious, and go a long way toward explaining my claim that the Clinical method provides the easiest entree for would-be Researchers. The combinatorial explosion that so inhibits Experimental progress is not a major concern here. An investigator doesn't have to control variables, just account for them. And she needn't even worry about the ones she will inevitably miss, because she—or other investigators—can pick them up later. In the same way, replicability is not important. Investigators want to be as clear about how they conduct their studies as they can; credibility depends on it. But comprehensiveness, not replicability or the need for investigative unanimity that drives it, is where the power of Clinical knowledge resides. Clinicians setting out to study twelfth-grade writers in precisely the same way Emig did could not expect to get exactly the same results. Would that be a problem for Clinical knowledge? No. Different findings would simply serve to make the emerging portrait that much fuller.

But probably the greatest advantage of Clinical knowledge is what I called its marketability. Whereas Experimentalists usually end up reporting on the relationships among relatively isolated variables, and Formalists offer models—in both methods, information rather detached from the human beings from which it was derived—first-level Clinical inquiry can result in satisfyingly full portraits. That is part of why it has had such an extraordinary, almost instant impact on the field, especially among Practitioners. Such individual portraits reflect the kind of complexity Practitioners face in their own work, and are very easily translated into lore. Emig, for example, devotes 28 pages of actual text, plus another 33 in two appendices, *exclusively* to one student, Lynn: 61 pages in a 151-page monograph. And though she serves an illustrative function, so that her story is framed in terms of Emig's "Dimensions of the Composing Process among Twelfth Grade Writers," Lynn is not reduced to some set of variables —is not, as she might have been for Pianko, merely traditional, under 21, and female—but is as fully realized a person as Emig can make her in the space allowed.

The advantages that might accrue for second-level inquiry have not yet had much chance to come clear. It would not be quite true to say that there has not been any. From Emig onward, most Clinical studies have involved several subjects; some have even been explicitly comparative, contrasting subjects of different "types" with one another. In that sense, then, there has been a good deal of intra-investigation second-level work, as these investigators try to make sense of their subjects in some collective way. If anything, though, these efforts are another symptom of the community's self-image problem. As we shall see in the sections that follow, such efforts have had a mostly negative effect on first-level inquiry, diverting the investigator's energies away from discovering what is unique in particular subjects, and so short-circuiting the inquiry's holistic drive. And the absence of any full-fledged, second-level inquiry is perhaps the most notable outward sign of the community's stunted growth. No writer has made it his or her primary business to pull together this line of Clinical studies to see what sense might be made of them; nor has any single investigator stayed with the method long enough to do what, say, Piaget has done in psychology, and generate a theory from his or her own canon.[2]

In discussing its uneasy position between the Experimental and Ethnographic methods, I have already suggested what the disadvantages of accumulating this kind of knowledge can be. To this point in its history, other inquirers have been quite tolerant of Clinical studies, even welcomed them. They have been considered appropriate because the field itself was rather new. But for all its pleasing properties, Clinical knowledge finally tends to be regarded by other communities as the result of a bad compromise: an impure method birthing a bastard knowledge. From an Experimental perspective, then, Clinical knowledge—whatever its validity—is bound to be unreliable, creating a gap which, if the longstanding enmity between the same two camps in psychology is any indicator, will not easily be closed. Formalists would want to steer Clinicians away from their paradigmatic logic toward a model-making ana-logic; the full, complicated portraits of

Clinical work are too messy for Formalist taste. Ethnographers can be pleased that Clinicians should concern themselves with real people, but will find Clinical tactics laughably obtrusive in terms of the phenomena they purport to examine. And it seems reasonable to assume that this collective disapproval accounts for some of the Clinical community's instability. Succumbing to this pressure, its members have abdicated, moving on to other methods.

So why go to the trouble of explaining—and, to some extent, defending—Clinical knowledge? Why devote a whole chapter to it? To some extent I have already explained why: Emig's monograph, like only a handful of other publications in the field, demands treatment in a book of this kind, and this is where it belongs. And that sort of reasoning extends to the other investigations I have cited. They have to go somewhere, and this is the place. I also think, however, that Clinical knowledge has gotten short shrift in Composition, been badly misunderstood—made far too much of in a few cases, mistakenly ignored in too many others. In fields like psychology, psychoanalysis, medicine, reading, and so on, Clinical knowledge has not only been tolerated but, in many instances, been a mainstay, celebrated, seminal. In most instances, it is true, the method has had what it has only very rarely had in Composition—a treatment dimension. But with or without that dimension, the method has too much potential value for Composition to simply let it fade away.

Clinical Inquiry

It's simple enough to represent Clinical inquiry in stripped-down, outline form, where it is almost identical to the Experimental mode it complements:

1. Identifying Problems
2. Designing the Study
3. Collecting and Analyzing Data
4. Interpreting the Data: Contributions to the Canon
5. Drawing Conclusions: Implications for Research and Teaching

And, as I have suggested since the beginning of this chapter, there are some good reasons for such a resemblance. Although most investigators since Emig have opted for research *questions* over hypotheses, they still most often follow the format of Experimental inquiry in their reports: Review of the Literature, Design of the Study, Results, Discussion, Implications and Conclusions. Moreover, they almost universally adopt a "scientific" or "objective" rhetorical stance: no first person, lots of passive constructions. Often the investigator will not be mentioned at all, even when she is present: "Students were shown certain segments of their composing-aloud videotapes and asked to try to recall the mental processes they employed in the featured situations" (Selfe, p. 47). In other cases, following Emig, the persona of the research report is some third person, so that "the investigator" is represented as one of the players: "At the end of this session, the investigator asked that the subject bring with him to the fourth session a piece of imaginative writing . . ." (Emig, p. 30).

What the outline doesn't convey, though, and what both format and persona help to disguise, are those features of Clinical inquiry which distinguish it from Experimental inquiry, and move it more toward Ethnography. To a far greater extent than in most Experimental studies, the Clinical investigator depends on her relationship with the subjects to get the information she wants. Asking people to compose aloud while you and a tape recorder sit with them; stimulated recall, where you go over such tapes or other materials, asking them to remember how they thought and felt at the time; background interviews, where you ask them to tell you their habits, fears, fantasies—all these and other typical Clinical techniques demand not only that subjects trust you as investigator, but that they be willing to work very hard, as well, and to concentrate in unusual ways.

During all of this contact, a Clinician's relationship with her subjects is bound to change—to become, as Diesing suggests, increasingly intimate; with the result, too, that her understanding of the phenomenon she studies becomes increasingly intuitive, a product of that relationship. It also means that while, in deference to Experimental practice, Clinicians usually call their research plan a "design," it is necessarily far more flexible, and probably better characterized as simply a plan. When the investigator is a major instrument in the study, and talk its primary medium, too, too much must happen that cannot be orchestrated or controlled in any Experimental sense. Beyond a certain point, improvisation must be the order of the day.

Identifying Problems

We have already seen that the bulk of Clinical inquiry, taking its cue from Emig, has been concerned with the act of writing. Such studies are usually defined within some combination of the following four boundaries:

1. Some portion of the act of writing, or writing-related activities. Most often, studies have focused on the whole activity—i.e., Emig's "composing processes"—but sometimes one or more

constituent subprocesses, like planning or revising, have gotten discrete attention.

2. Some set of subjects, identified along lines established by the investigator. Emig characterizes hers by year-in-school; age (sixteen and seventeen); sex (5 girls, 3 boys); race (one Black, six White, one Chinese-American). She also describes the six "types" of schools they attend, both in prose and table form, in terms of size, racial distribution, percentage attending college, and drop-out rate (e.g., "an almost all-black ghetto school in Chicago" vs. "a private, university-affiliated laboratory school," p. 29). Year-in-school seems to have been most popular in studies since. Some other dimensions: occupation, level of experience (variously defined), level of writing apprehension (as measured by standardized test), academic ability ("gifted" vs. "average," "basic"). As noted earlier, some designs are explicitly contrastive: experienced vs. inexperienced, high- vs. low-apprehensive.

3. The kind of discourse being produced. As we saw, Emig launches this trend by giving her subjects "three stimuli" (writing assignments) that were supposed to lead them to write in what she calls "the two major modes," reflexive and extensive. This plan didn't work for her; responses, "with one exception, were not engaged, nor even very personalized"—in short, she got little reflexive writing (p. 31). Still, later Clinicians, trying to qualify the phenomenon under study, have offered similar delimiters: Perl also used extensive and reflexive; Sommers opted for expressive, explanatory, and persuasive.

4. The setting for the writing. This can be conceived in either a physical or rhetorical sense: writing on a word processor, for example, for the former, or to different audiences, for the latter. Of the four boundaries, this one has been invoked least often, in either sense. My guess is that most investigators assume that specifications for (3) cover rhetorical context, while the laboratory-like conditions for most studies leads to physical context being treated as a non-variable, as controlled-for. However, there have been exceptions. In her study of Donald Murray, for example, Carol Berkenkotter goes to considerable trouble to account for the context of his writing in both senses: the where, when, and how of it, as well as the to whom and why.

Studies of writing-related phenomena, like talk about writing, have been framed along similar lines—often, in fact, in terms of writing conceived as a "process" in much the same way. In Karliner and Jacobs' work on tutorial conferences, for example, they take

note of who is involved, roughly equivalent to (2); what their relationship is—(4); what kind of writing they talk about—(3); and
where the writer is in writing it—(1).

To some extent, of course, that Clinicians should come to frame
problems in these ways was inevitable, a function of the subject matter; but there can be no mistaking the influence of what I have been
calling the canon of Clinical work, either. Emig's study stands like
the first piece in the puzzle, all others taking their place in relation
to it. A check of the literature reviews finds the same Clinical studies
named over and over again: Emig, Stallard, Mischel, Beach, Sommers,
Perl. As I suggested above, there has been no inter-investigation
second-level inquiry, no attempt to generate a coherent Clinical
theory. So far then, the object has been to extend the explored territory, to mark out new space: Emig explored twelfth grade writers, so
Perl takes on unskilled writers; Emig provided no contrast with adult
writers, so Sommers includes them and focuses on revision; Selzer
sees the claims of Emig and others affecting the way students are
trained to write in schools, ultimately for the world of work, so he
studies an engineer. And so the Clinical canon grows, each investigator framing out his or her work in terms of what has come before.

Designing the Study

However, this canonical influence has affected more than just
the kinds of problems Clinicians have identified and the parameters
within which they have framed them; it has also carried over into the
investigations they design to study them. Here again, Emig sets the
standard, and we can trace the legacy of *The Composing Processes of
Twelfth Graders* in the size and scope of Clinical investigations, which
we'll cover in this section; and in their technical eclecticism, which
we'll cover in the next, Collecting and Analyzing Data.

In terms of size and scope, then: for reasons she never makes
explicit, Emig examines the composing processes of eight students
over what appears to be a period of about 6–8 weeks—the school
year's summer vacation. One major feature of her design is to get a
good deal of background on each of these eight. To the information
about the students and their schools described under (2) above, then,
she adds the following: for five, she is able to get school records;
these indicate, she says, that "three have above-average intelligence
and two, average" (p. 29). The three others report College Entrance
Board Examinations verbal and quantitative scores of 670 or higher,
"suggesting that they should be considered to have above-average
intelligence." She also gets the opinions of the students' English department chairs or most recent English instructor.

Judging from her profile of Lynn, though, she also sought considerably more, and more personal, information on each of them, although most of it does not finally appear in the monograph. Among other things, then, we are told that Lynn lives in "Pine Hill," where "many Jewish doctors, dentists, and professors live." She is the "oldest of four children of a Jewish lawyer"; her mother "is a high school history teacher." She is academically in the top five percent in her class—a member of the "Century Club." She coedits the yearbook, is a study hall monitor, and her most important extracurricular activity seems to be the Midwest Jewish Youth Institute. And finally she is, Emig tells us, "very vivacious" as well "very perceptive," and proved "an exceptionally interesting subject" (pp. 45–46).

Each of the eight students meets with her four times for some 4–6 hours. All sessions are tape recorded. She asks each to do three pieces of writing for her. Two are composed aloud with Emig present as prompter/observer (taking notes on the writers' actions), one each in sessions #1 and #2. In #1, each subject was asked to write "a short piece in whatever mode and of whatever subject matter he wished." The "stimulus" for #2 was given at the end of #1, and was as follows: "Write about a person, event, or idea that particularly intrigues you" (p. 30). The third assignment, "a piece of imaginative writing," they were asked to compose in the week to ten days between sessions #3 and #4; six submit it, one turns in nothing, and one turns in "a piece of obscenity" (though exactly what that is, Emig doesn't say). In addition, as part of the autobiographical interview in session #3, she asks them to bring samples of writing produced at any age; six do, two don't.

In some ways, of course, this is a perfectly sensible plan. It certainly commits Emig to a substantial amount of work: between 50 and 70 hours of data collecting, during which she will amass more than 100 pieces of writing, audio-tapes of some 30 different occasions, 16 sets of observational notes, and 8 sets of background material. And yet it is a rather curious plan, too—one that manifests, once again, the symptoms of the community's methodological self-image troubles. Look at what happens: if Lynn's materials are to be taken as typical, then we are talking about a study of each person's composing processes based primarily on some 567 words of prose composed on two very unusual occasions over a period of about three hours, supplemented by an account of the composing of 86 words of poetry (her piece of "imaginative writing"), and an hour-long background interview that included questions about 10 or 15 pieces of other writing.

Or, if we want to take the larger perspective, the one Emig leads us to take with her monograph's rather sweeping title—she doesn't, after all, call it *The Composing Processes of Eight Twelfth*

Graders—then we are talking about the composing processes of millions of "twelfth grade" people on the basis of this very brief study of eight members of that loosely defined population: eight versions of what amounts to this snapshot study of Lynn.[3] And no matter which perspective we take, we get no longitudinal dimension at all. Emig's efforts at characterization notwithstanding, these are not people she has known over any reasonable length of time, nor with whom she has had any significant interaction. They may, as she suggests at one point, regard her as a teacher-like figure, but she doesn't try to teach them. For all the attention to detail, then, these are little more than bus station biographies—vignettes which, while interesting, are based on very limited, very artificial contact.

I don't want to get sidetracked on a full-fledged critique of Emig's study here. But surely the peculiarities, not to say liabilities, of her design in terms of size and scope are clear enough. Torn between the desire to develop authentic, idiographically sound portraits, on the one hand, and the perceived need, at least, and perhaps the ambition, to move toward nomothetic certainty, on the other, she ends up—rather unfortunately, I think—somewhere in between. Consider a couple of alternatives. Suppose Emig had devoted all 50–70 hours of data collecting to Lynn, spreading the study across a full school year, say, and even establishing some real relationship with her—as mentor, perhaps. She would no doubt have ended up with fewer total texts, but she would have been able to give both more depth and breadth to the individual portrait: more interview time, more occasions for and kinds of writing, a sense of how Lynn changed over time, and so on. Or, had she decided to go the more fully Experimental route, she might have had a design more like Sharon Pianko's: a larger sample of subjects chosen in ways that gave them greater representative power, more structured observations, fewer but more explicitly addressed variables. As it stands, the design teases us with writers who, though characterized to some extent both as individuals *and* representatives of a population, have no very strong claim to either status.

We will return to the problems this sort of design creates a little further on, especially in terms of interpreting data. What is more interesting for now, I think, is not so much that Emig should have used it—after all, she was very much the pioneer breaking new ground—but that subsequent studies should have followed her pattern so closely. Consider these three:

Investigator: Sondra Perl

Title: Most accessible is "The Composing Processes of Unskilled College Writers," but I will refer to both it and her dissertation, *Five Writers Writing: Case Studies of the Composing Processes of Unskilled College Writers.* (For reference purposes, the former will be "Art.," the latter "Diss.")

Subjects: Five "unskilled" but willing-to-participate students from an "introductory social science course" at Eugenio Maria de Hostos Community College of the City University of New York. For what it's worth, Perl explains that she chose five in order "to represent a range of educational background and experience and yet to remain within reasonable case study proportions" (Diss., p. 44). All are from a special interdisciplinary skills program ("Libra"); all scored below "the 10.0 grade level on a nationally standardized reading test," and all wrote placement essays which "exhibited the 'writing deficiencies' associated with unskilled writers" (Diss., p. 45). Beyond these general features, Perl restricts her background research to interviews with each subject, and includes in her chapters on them such sections as "Awareness of Writing Difficulties," "Experience with Writing: School" and "Experience with Writing: Home."

It is also important to note here, though, that Perl taught the class from which her subjects were drawn. According to her dissertation, the study was "introduced during class time and represented as a collaborative effort between the students and the teacher" (p. 47). All fifteen members of the class volunteered, and the chosen five did so without any "mention of remuneration," as she puts it. What is particularly interesting about all this is that while in the dissertation Perl explains her decision to use her own students, claiming that she opted for the deeper student-investigator relationship over the "objectivity" of a detached observer, in her article, she never mentions that the students were hers at all. There is "the researcher," and "the teacher" is mentioned as audience for the writing, but we are not told that the two are the same person.

Design: Students meet with "the researcher" in "a soundproof room in the college library" for five 90-minute sessions, twice each to compose aloud on assigned topics in the reflexive and extensive modes (sessions #1 and #2, #4 and #5); and once for an open-ended background interview (session #3). In #4 and #5, students were "directed to talk out their ideas, to plan their answers orally, before beginning to write" (Diss., p. 331). The topics were based on the class work in social science, so that both teacher/investigator and writers were familiar with the material. Perl assumes "that the teacher was always the audience" (Art., p. 318).

Investigator: Nancy Sommers

Title: Revision in the Composing Process: A Case Study of College Freshman and Experienced Adult Writers (1980) in her dissertation. She also has an article in *College Composition and Communication* under the more sweeping title of "Revision Strategies of Student Writers and Experienced Adult Writers" (1980). It would appear that the article includes the original dissertation case studies (done in Boston), then adds on an extra 25 subjects (from Oklahoma). For whatever reasons, Sommers herself never clarifies the connection, nor does she ever explicitly mention the dissertation in the later article. However, since it offers far more detail, I will work primarily from the dissertation here.

Subjects: Defined (in the dissertation) as "college freshman" with age, SAT Verbal scores and proposed major; and "experienced adult" writers (age, level of education, profession, publication types). She includes the two groups in order to represent "a contrasting range of writing abilities from inexperienced to experienced" (Diss., p. 30), but she doesn't say why she needs so many, nor why these two ends of a continuum should represent a range. And in fact, while she says that originally "the researcher intended to write individual case studies for each subject," she claims to have found such "consistent similarities within the groups that it was considered redundant and inefficient to present each individual case study," so that she ends up doing only two from each (Diss., p. 45).

Perhaps because of the relatively large number of subjects, Sommers seems to be a little bit less concerned with background than Emig or Perl, although she does do a little characterizing. Daniel, for example, one of her freshman, "feels very proud of the rigorous training he received" in a Jesuit high school (p. 48). As with Perl, the students were all from Sommers' own writing class. She notes only that they were "randomly selected" (p. 30). Just how this selection worked, or whether they volunteered or were paid, she doesn't say. The adults answered a notice posted in public libraries; it isn't clear if any such volunteers were turned down, although three of what seems to have been an original ten are reported to have dropped out.

Design: Sommers assigns three writing tasks, one each "expressive," "explanatory," "persuasive." Her choice of these "discourse types" was "guided," she claims, by the theories of Kinneavy and Britton et al. (p. 32)—a somewhat problematic claim, since Kinneavy and Britton are not really interchangeable. In any case, the "tasks" (compare to Emig's "stimulus," Perl's "topics") are all limited to two pages, a constraint neither Emig nor Perl imposes; and each one had to be completed over three one-hour sessions. Students did their writing in class as assignments, so presumably Sommers was present; the adults could do it pretty much where they pleased. Subjects were told to do "whatever is natural" over the three sessions, but to use provided paper and not to erase or X-out, instead drawing a "thin line" through any deleted material. In a fourth task, subjects were asked to "list on what basis" they thought a passage provided by the investigator should be revised. The idea of this last was to lead them to articulate some of their implicit notions about revision.

At the end of each writing task, Sommers interviewed the subjects (all but 3 of the students in her office)—for 90 minutes after task #1, and for 45 minutes after #2 and #3. The interviews were guided by specific questions in three areas: Background (information about the writer's general habits); Theory (based on the assumption that writers' habits would be based on an articulable, albeit implicit, theory of written language); and Revision Questions (which explored the subjects' habits and/or theory, both in general and regarding specific textual changes).

Investigator: Cynthia Selfe

Title: "The Predrafting Processes of Four High- and Four Low-Apprehensive Writers" in a 1984 article in *Research in the Teaching of English*. Her dissertation (University of Texas at Austin, 1981) would appear to cover some of the same territory, but she makes no reference to it in the article, so I have worked exclusively from the article here.

Subjects: Selfe is more deliberate than the other three in selecting her subjects. She begins by randomly selecting four sections of a first-semester freshman writing course to which she administers the Writing Apprehension Test, noting that a 1981 study using students in the same course had found that they did not differ significantly from section to section "in either ECT scores or verbal and mathematical scores on the Scholastic Aptitude Test" (p. 46). Then, from the 86 students who took the test, she randomly selects four who scored in the top 20% (high apprehensives) and four who scored in the bottom 20% (low apprehensives). Although we are later given their names, and while Selfe spends a fair amount of time quoting them to suggest how they are alike or different as writers, she tends to treat them more as groups than individuals—she does not, for example, single out one or more writers to profile in the way the other three researchers do.

Design: The subjects are asked to do three pieces of writing, composing aloud each time. All writings were videotaped. The first "assignment" (Session #1), done for practice, is not specified; the second (Session #2) was an "illustrative narrative"; and the third (Session #3), an "address" to a board of directors. There were also four other activities:

1. "A role-playing scenario" during session #1, in which they were "to detail . . . the processes they used when they wrote a freshman composition" (p. 47).
2. Some time at the end of #1 during which they were shown videotapes of themselves composing aloud.
3. In session #4, the subjects were again "shown certain segments of their composing-aloud videotapes, this time being asked to try to recall the mental processes they employed in the featured situations" (p. 47). Selfe chose for this stimulated recall segments of tapes that "included pauses," or featured "frequently repeated" or "unusual" composing activities.
4. At the end of session #4, Selfe asks the students about their "past composition instruction, and about their current attitudes toward composing" (p. 47).

There are, to be sure, some differences among these designs, and between them and Emig's original. Both Sommers and Selfe, for instance, have narrowed their interests down to something less than the full set of composing processes Emig and Perl examine—revision and predrafting, respectively. Sommers and Perl use students from their own classes. There are some differences in investigative technique, too. Of the four, only Emig invites "imaginative" writing; only Sommers doesn't have her subjects compose aloud; only Perl has her subjects do actual school writing; only Selfe uses videotape. And Selfe, as I noted, is the only one of the four who can claim that her subjects represent a "sample" in any Experimental sense, though it isn't precisely clear what she gains by such a definition in a Clinical study.

But in so many other respects—in most significant respects—these designs follow very much the same pattern. Sommers might seem anomalous in that she begins with about twice as many subjects as the others, but in the end she chooses to offer detailed accounts of only four. And while she and Selfe are most interested in some specific aspect of composing, they nevertheless have their subjects engage in, and so produce data concerning, the full set of processes. More to the point, look at the remarkable uniformity in kind and duration of investigator-subject contact. Devoting in the neighborhood of 50 hours to the business of data collection, each investigator puts in three or four sessions of between ¾ and 1½ hours per subject, involving 3 or 4 writing tasks, some time spent in recall sessions, and a background interview that seeks to probe the subjects' writing histories and attitudes.

The net result is that the essential peculiarities—or, as I suggested, liabilities—of Emig's original design are repeated over and over again across the 15 or so years between her dissertation and Selfe's study, published in 1984. Like Lynn and her fellows, the subjects in all these studies hover right on the edge of individuality. Even when, as in Sommers' study, the names assigned for the report ignore the actual subjects' gender, they are still names, not numbers or letters: Tony and Dee, Daniel and Diana, Kathy and Don, not #1 and #2, or Subjects A and B. We are given their backgrounds, their attitudes toward writing, and, as often as not, their very words: "Well, I like to write . . . just like I like to write home. If someone's going to read it I get really apprehensive about my writing, and it's got to be letter perfect . . ." (Bev, in Selfe's study, p. 57, Selfe's ellipses). And we know, too, that each subject has begun to form some kind of relationship with the investigator. It may not yet be very stable—4-6 hours isn't all that much time—but they must be 4-6 very intense, often almost intimate hours, full of real concentration and probing talk. And Perl and Sommers, as both teachers and investigators, have even more contact with their student subjects.

But in each case, the promise of nomothetic authority seems to tug the investigator back from any more intimate contact, any greater idiographic depth. Even Perl, who makes a point of insisting that she "worked with each of the five writers individually for many hours" (Diss., p. vii), never moves beyond the limits of Emig's design—sticks with the four composing aloud sessions, and reports nothing about her work to help these students become better writers.[4] In all four studies, *who* the subjects are finally tends to be treated as accidental: Emig's Lynn may be vivacious, Perl's Tony separated from his wife and child, and so on, but these properties of them as subjects end up not impinging on their composing processes. Rather, those processes are a function of *what* they are—"twelfth graders," "unskilled college writers," "experienced" or "inexperienced" writers, "high-" or "low-apprehensives." To put it at its most extreme, they are treated like organisms within which those processes, rather like amoebic osmosis or fetal cell differentiation, can be artificially stimulated and then observed. Certainly there is plenty of precedent for such an investigative posture in medical or psychological research, where the patient is very often seen simply as a body, an organism, within which the featured phenomenon can be observed. What makes it odd here, of course, is that it comes into conflict with the investigators' insistence on the subjects as individuals—the genuinely Clinical impulse toward a holistic, not analytic, perspective. For these three researchers, as for Emig, this unresolved conflict robs them of a fuller, clearer methodological authority.

Collecting and Analyzing the Data

Almost certainly, the most striking feature of the Clinical method is its technical eclecticism. We have gotten a fair glimpse of it in just the four designs we've considered here. Subjects are asked to write on assigned and free topics in classrooms, library conference rooms, and at other unnamed locations, sometimes with arbitrary constraints in terms of time and pages, sometimes with none at all. They are asked to compose aloud for observation, audio- and video-taping; and to list ways they might revise someone else's writing. They are asked to role play, and to watch or listen to tapes of themselves composing aloud, and then to try to explain what they were doing or thinking at the time. They are asked to explain features of the writing they have produced while composing aloud, or which they have written while away from the investigator. They are asked to find and submit their old writing. Their school records are examined, their former teachers interviewed. They are given writing apprehension tests, and interviewed themselves—about past instruction, about their feelings toward writing. They are asked about their personal lives, too—what they do for fun, who their parents are, where they live, and so on.

And while these techniques for gathering data—especially the composing aloud and the interview—have been the most popular among Clinicians, they by no means represent all that has been tried or is possible. All of the observation in these four illustrative studies, for example, was overt; obviously covert observation is an option. And writers have been or easily enough could be asked to keep daily logs; to fill out questionnaires; to submit, in the interest of treating their non-productive habits, to various behavioral rewards and punishments; to write while under hypnosis, or the effects of various drugs (e.g., caffeine or nicotine, those two standbys of so many writers); to write on NCR paper with inkless pens, or on word processors, or via dictaphone; to be wired to measure subvocalization, the tiny movements of speech-related muscles during writing. The list of possible techniques is probably endless.

Nor is it hard to figure out why this mode of inquiry should promote such eclecticism. Here again, what we are seeing is a natural byproduct of its peculiar combination of idiographic motives and positivist assumptions. The idiographic motives impel Clinicians toward what they call, in keeping with their Experimental ties, validity. To discover what writing is, and how it works, they need to be sure they study writing itself, real and whole, as it is manifested in particular, unique individuals. However, because they work from a fundamentally positivist perspective, they also assume that, within instrumental limits, this process of writing is measurable and recordable. It is "out there" to be studied, a complex phenomenon whose various layers, to re-invoke my earlier metaphor, can be peeled off by a variety of techniques for investigative purposes, and then re-layered to form a communal knowledge. Hence their freedom to poke and prod subjects, to make them compose when and where and how they want. Complex though writing may be, the essential uniformity of human beings—the lawfulness of the universe of which they are constituents—assures Clinicians that people writing are people writing. Thus, while these investigators may acknowledge, as Emig does, that their investigations are intrusive to some degree, they will also insist—again, like Emig—that the phenomenon they stimulate for study is the one they *want* to study, and one whose lineaments they can trace in whatever manifestations of it their techniques invoke.

In a way, then, this eclecticism represents both an obligation and a freedom. Cynthia Selfe does a pretty good job of explaining its obligatory side. Her study, she argues, rests on three assumptions "which can provide a theoretical basis for designing any study of composing processes":

> First, the richly complex nature of composing processes is not immediately and specifically accessible to direct observation because investigators cannot see the human psyche at work. Second, since they lack direct access, researchers who hope to study the intricate processes involved in composing must employ indirect methods of observation (e.g., making protocol transcripts of writers composing aloud; coding, timing, and videotaping composing-aloud activities; and interviewing writers about their own perceptions of how they compose). Finally, because each of the above mentioned methods of indirect observation provides only an incomplete reflection of the complex set of processes involved in composing, a combination of several such methods should be used to gather data in any one study. Cross checking data from multiple sources can then help provide a multidimensional profile of composing activities in a particular setting (p. 56).

But if their method thus binds Clinicians to use a range of techniques to collect and analyze data on the phenomena they study, it has the corollary property of considerably easing the constraints of reliability and validity for any *particular* technique, giving them a kind of technical freedom not really accessible to either Experimentalists, on the one hand, or Ethnographers, on the other. Yes, Clinicians are obliged to collect and analyze a wide variety of data in their effort to get at the problems they study; but no one technique—not interviewing, not textual analysis, not even composing aloud—needs to be especially reliable or valid by itself. As I suggested earlier, it is comprehensiveness, more than replicability, that matters in making Clinical knowledge.

And there is no better technique for demonstrating how this freedom has been exercised than the one which has brought the method such visibility, composing aloud. From the beginning, it has had clear limitations as a means of collecting data about how writers work. The most obvious have to do with validity. Very few people, if any, talk out loud when they write, let alone for a tape recorder while under orders from an observing researcher, who has also chosen the time and place and topic. As we have seen Emig admit, "even the most mature and introspective students in the sample found composing aloud, the chief means the study employed for externalizing behavior, an understandably difficult, artificial, and at times distracting procedure" (p. 5). What, then, is the relationship between this strange activity and what people actually do when they write?

Reliability presents a slightly less serious problem. It seems plausible to assume that a tape recorder will capture most of the audible utterances of the subjects. But the recorder doesn't solve all problems: How can one account for the observer's presence? What about the inaudible utterances? Gestures? And, on an issue that Emig herself raises in her "Implications for Research," how can the text produced be tied to the tape with any accuracy, so that the connection between what is spoken and what is written can be made precisely (p. 96)? How reliable can an observer's notes be—for this specific purpose, or for others—and how is that reliability to be checked?

And yet despite these substantial limitations, composing aloud has been the technique of choice in some of the most important Clinical studies—the cornerstone of Emig's work and, with some interesting alterations, of Perl's and Selfe's studies, too. Of the three, Emig is the most cautious with it for the purposes of collecting data. In addition to admitting its questionable validity and at least raising problems concerning the reliability of her simple tape recorder/

observer approach, she also tries to maintain the distinction between composing and composing aloud. In Chapter 3, for example, "The Composing Process: Mode of Analysis," she is explicit about her assumption that *"composing aloud,* a writer's effort to externalize his process of composing, somehow reflects, if not parallels, his actual inner process" (p. 40, her emphasis). To be sure, the "if not parallels" is ambiguous, and the notion that there is an "inner process" (the "real" composing process?) could use some clearing up. Still, she does try to make it clear that the composing aloud is simply one basis for making guesses about composing, and not the process itself.

Neither Perl nor, later, Selfe, turns out to be quite as cautious. Neither explicitly addresses the difficulty of composing aloud for their subjects, although it comes up in both studies: Perl indicates that Dee, for example, "often lapses into periods of silence" (Diss., p. 167); while Selfe gives her subjects both a practice session and the chance to watch replays of that session, implicit acknowledgment that it might be hard work. What makes their reluctance to say any more especially curious, of course, is that their subjects—Perl's unskilled writers, and, in particular, Selfe's high apprehensives—might, by definition, be expected to have a harder time composing generally, and so to find the added burden of composing aloud heavier than Emig's mostly "above average" subjects. In other words, the technique might be even less valid in these studies, and yet the issue is never even raised. More importantly, neither one seems even to make, never mind maintain, the subtle distinction between composing and composing aloud that Emig tries to establish. They are not aggressive about this collapse of categories; the matter never becomes overt. Composing aloud simply comes to equal composing by default.

They are a little more attentive to reliability. Perl notes that her tape recorder captures not only what the writer is saying, but also "the literal sound of the pen moving across the page" (Diss., p. 56). This gives her somewhat more reliable access to ties between words spoken and words written, though she still has no sure way to know just which words the pen is forming as it makes these recordable noises. And in any case, she does not clear up either the impact of her own presence, or the significance of the non- and in-audible. Selfe, of course, tackles nearly all these problems by opting for video-instead of audio-taping. Her "observer" is a constant (although she never says where the camera is, or whether she is present as well); gesture and the like are more reliably accessible, at least within the limits of camera angle; and the text/tape correspondence may be more readily trackable. Despite these advantages, though, the camera is no magic solution. Its intrusion raises further questions about validity; and, for the most part, it simply postpones questions about reliability until the data has to be analyzed.

But if composing aloud raises such problems as a means of *collecting* data, things get even more tangled when these investigators turn to *analyzing* the data thus gathered. Remember that, except for whatever time or reel-space increments the act of tape recording might generate, all of the data the technique produces will be in the form of words. Emig, for example, ends up with the 16 texts produced in sessions #1 and #2; the 16 tapes of those texts being composed aloud, supplemented in session #2 by the writer's investigator-prompted recall of "whatever prewriting and planning he did" since getting the "stimulus" in session #1 (p. 30); and her 16 sets of observational notes. What sorts of analyses can be done on these three rather different kinds of text that will make them amenable to interpretation? Their validity is shaky to begin with. If they are analyzed further—treated, as for example Perl treats them, as if they could be sorted into 31 behavioral categories—there is considerable danger that their already tenuous connections with the way people might write under more regular conditions will be stretched even further. And even if we settle or ignore the matter of validity, there is still reliability to consider: Can the investigator perform such analyses with any consistency? Could another investigator do so with anything like the same results?

As it turns out, Emig makes assessments of her data analyses nearly impossible: She never really describes them. True, her third chapter claims to account for "The Composing Process: Mode of Analysis," but in fact what she describes are more the results of some analysis than any procedures. She offers a set of categories which purport to be "dimensions" of the composing processes of twelfth-grade writers, five or six of which seem to relate more or less specifically to the composing-aloud data.[5] All she says about their origin is that they were arrived at inductively, "derived from an extensive analysis of the eight case studies" (p. 33). What she means, to judge from her presentation of Lynn's case, and from remarks she makes about the other writers, is that she read over the composing-aloud tapes and texts, along with her observer notes, until she felt she could identify significant patterns within them. The categories she offers do have a common sense appeal: "Starting," for example, with subdivisions like "Seeming Ease or Difficulty of Decision," or "Element Treated First Discursively"; or, under "Composing Aloud: A Characterization," "Selecting and Ordering Components," which she further sub-categorizes as "Anticipation/Abeyance," "Kinds of Transformational Operations," and "Style." And indeed, these may be perfectly valid categories, admixtures though they are of what she calls "elements, moments, and stages"; but she makes no effort to show why.

Let's grant, though, that demonstrating validity would be very difficult in a pioneering study—any scheme is bound to have problems. We still might hope that wherever the scheme came from, and whatever features of the phenomenon it emphasized or ignored, we could see how, and how successfully, it had been applied. But while Emig is reasonably eloquent in characterizing her categories—explaining, for example, that "anticipating shuttles between the present and the future; planning does not" (p. 41)—she doesn't say how she knew a particular passage in a tape was anticipation (i.e., whether it shuttled or not), and not planning or vocalized hesitation or anything else. Nor does she try to establish that someone else working from the same tape and the same scheme would make the same decision. Nor, for that matter, does she say what role either the texts or her observations might have played in analyzing the tapes. For instance, could something the writer did, but didn't say, have served as evidence of this shuttling? She never says. In short, we are left simply to take Emig's word for the whole analysis: that the categories she finds inductively are valid, and that she has applied them reliably.

Of the other two investigators, Perl in particular is openly critical of accounts like Emig's, describing them—albeit not by name—as having "taken the form of narratives with the observer choosing to highlight whatever seemed important at the time" (Diss., p. 54). Such narratives "detail, with relative precision and insight, observable composing behaviors," but they are still narrative, not analysis, and so "an inadequate tool for representing what behaviors occur during composing, for establishing what the relation is between discrete behaviors and the whole, and for detecting patterns among those behaviors" (Diss., p. 55).

Perl's solution is to develop a coding scheme for which she claims five virtues:

1. It is standardized, and so at least potentially reliable;
2. categorical, in that it "labels specific, observable behaviors";
3. concise, so that she manages to represent as much as 1½ hours of composing on one page;
4. structural, in that it makes it possible to relate parts to whole;
5. and diachronic, so that it "presents the sequences of movements that occur during composing as they unfold in time" (Diss., p. 55).

What this coding scheme boils down to is a set of 31 categories and sub-categories, each with its own symbol (e.g., W = writing silently, TW = writing aloud) for labeling what is happening at any given moment on a composing-aloud tape. By arranging these symbols along a time line, Perl is able to create a visual display of her subjects at work.

Standardized in this way, her symbol system obviously makes it easier to check on the reliability of her analysis of composing-aloud data. Two or more coders could independently apply this system to all or part of a tape, then compare their results to see how often they agree. For some reason, however, even though it is clear she recognizes the value of such a strategy, Perl in fact does not report having performed any such check in this investigation. Moreover, while she argues that this code is an important product of her study, with possible applications in diagnostic work, large groups, and longitudinal studies (Art., p. 334), so far as I know she has made no further use of it. In other words, while this system *might* be more reliable than Emig's, we never actually find out how reliable it is.

And what of its validity? Well, it comes from essentially the same source as Emig's: "It should be noted that although the coding system is presented before the analysis of the data, it was derived from the data and then used as the basis for generalizing about the patterns and behavior sequences found within each student's process" (Art., p. 322). Like Emig, then, Perl seems to have studied the tapes and texts until, by means of this unexplained "derived," she ascertained that between talking, reading, and writing, there were 31 different behaviors. She doesn't say why there should be 31 and not the 38 Selfe uses, or 10 or 50 or 100, nor does she offer any evidence that these 31 have any special validity. There is also some confusion—or at least a considerable looseness—in her designation of all the categories she lists as "behaviors." She does get rid of the ambiguity of Emig's "dimensions," with their constituent "elements, moments, and stages." But what people do when they compose aloud—their actual *behavior*—consists of moving jaw and tongue, eyes and hands, making sounds, and so on. In categories like "Global Planning" or "Talking leading to writing," Perl obviously has another definition of behavior in mind; these call less for the identification of a behavior than for an inference, an interpretation, based on an unspecified set of behaviors.

What most threatens the validity of this coding scheme, though, is that it tends to discount the individuality of the writers and the particularity of the contexts within which they worked. That is, a more fully valid scheme might have examined each composing session and characterized its constituent parts in terms of the specific writer, treating composing as one of many kinds of behavior that person engaged in, and so to be understood in the context of his or her life at that time. If a month's worth of work with Tony reveals him, at least tentatively, to be untalkative, a poor reader, a reluctant writer, deeply troubled by his failing marriage, hostile to women, and so on, then we would have to understand his attempts at composing aloud in light of these Tony-specific considerations. Instead, of course, Perl's coding scheme allows us to make sense of his composing aloud only in its quasi-behavioral terms. He spends a lot of time on what she calls "editizing" (editing during composing), mostly in the form of proofreading; has a lot of "miscues" (the reading in of textual features that aren't there); applies an inadequate set of rules to his work, and so on. In short, the scheme is constructed to tell us less about "Tony composing" than about "Tony-the-illustrative-unskilled-writer-composing." Thus, although Perl's scheme makes coding her composing-aloud tapes a potentially more reliable procedure, it does so at some cost to validity.

Selfe doesn't make any major changes to Perl's system. Her coding scheme has, as I mentioned, 38 symbols, and she constructs it mostly by borrowing from Perl, Ellen Nold, and Linda Flower and John Hayes. She makes curiously little explicit use of the video portion of her tapes; she mentions only one gesture (Bev "would bow her head in defeat" p. 57), and none of the categories in her scheme would seem to require visual cues. Moreover, if the scheme presents advantages in terms of reliability—and one might expect the video would help here—she never mentions them. And finally, her borrowings from these other researchers don't seem to improve the scheme's validity. For instance, from Flower and Hayes she borrows a category called "Translating Behaviors," one of which is "Retrieving words from long or short term memory" (p. 63). Since she offers no illustration of the coding scheme at work, it isn't clear how this item is made operational, but the problem is obvious enough: How can a videotape camera and microphone capture such a "behavior"? The writer doesn't say "I'm searching long term memory now," so the investigator must rely on some correspondence between an utterance (or a silence?) and a textual feature. But an inference about what the writer is "doing" at such an interval, especially one whose duration and textual connections are measured so loosely, seems very risky. Surely such a category lacks even the validity that Emig and Perl's inductive derivation provides.

I needn't carry this critique any further to make the message clear. Despite some alterations over its fifteen-year history in Composition, composing aloud still presents Clinical investigators with serious problems in terms of validity and reliability. Viewed in one way, this is further evidence of the Clinical community's retarded growth; it seems as though someone ought to have gotten a better handle on the technique by now. However, what is more interesting—and more germane to the major point of this section—is that, serious though these problems have been, they have not substantially impeded the technique's use. Indeed, if anything, composing aloud has gained momentum as a way of learning about writing. Whatever that tells us about the community's slow development, it also stands as a considerable tribute to the power of the technical license afforded Clinicians by their way of making knowledge.

Interpreting the Data: Contributions to the Canon

As you might expect, though, such license has its price—and for Clinicians, most of it gets exacted here, as a function of interpretation. Exciting as it can be to collect and analyze such seemingly fertile data, it can be very hard to interpret, to say with any real confidence what it might *mean*. Clinicians interpret their data in much the same general way as other kinds of investigators—i.e., by finding patterns in it, and then ascribing significance to them. But finding meaningful patterns in and across such disparate data is no easy task: How are coded interview results to be matched with data from composing aloud, or those two with the outcome of textual analyses, the results of standardized tests, and so on, especially when a fair portion of such data are likely to be of suspect validity, questionable reliability, or—as we have seen with composing aloud—both?

What is finally at stake here, of course, is community sanction. Each investigator offers the community individual portraits (first-level inquiry), group profiles (second-level inquiry), or some combination thereof, trying to make sense of the data in a way that wanders neither too far idiographically, claiming too much about any single subject; nor nomothetically, claiming too much about those subjects as a group, nor that group as representative of some larger population. No investigation can be rejected outright. Even a study of twelfth graders forced to write wrong-handed, in the dark, under hypnosis could claim its place in the Clinical canon. What does happen, however, is that contributions will eventually be qualified by that canon's paradigmatic logic, accorded a place in keeping with their relative importance as conceived by one or another canonical theory.

There has been little exercise of this sanction among Composition's Clinicians to date—no surprise, given what we have seen of the community's methodological self-consciousness—and I have found no intra-communal disagreement whatever over any specific interpretation of data. Still, it isn't hard to suggest what the grounds for such disagreement might be. The potential for interpretive problems among the four investigators we've been looking at—Emig, Perl, Sommers, Selfe—arises, as I suggested it would, from the basic design they share. All find themselves with data that seems at once too shallow to draw any very full individual portraits, and yet too narrow to justify any terribly useful broader claims. Of the four, Emig's portrait of her star subject, Lynn, wanders furthest into dangerous idiographic territory. Remember how little she has to go on: their four meetings, with the resulting two essays (289 and 279 words) and one poem (86 words); a folder of Lynn's earlier writings, mostly from one eleventh-grade English class; some portion of her academic records; and background on her school and family. From these various, often partial strands of information, Emig weaves a 28-page interpretation of Lynn as a writer that seems to me, at least, amazingly ambitious and freewheeling.

Consider, for instance, her discussion of Lynn's choice of a topic for session #3, during which she composes "Terpsichordean Greetings," a piece about a cardboard statue of Charles Schulz's Snoopy that stands in her livingroom. At the end of session #2, Emig gives her the assignment to think about for the next meeting: "Write about a person, idea, or event that especially intrigues you." Lynn "immediately" comes up with three possible topics, telling Emig about them even before she leaves: a bus ride downtown, two boys she's been dating, and two "old ladies" she saw on the bus. When she returns for session #3 two weeks later, she has come up with two more: Snoopy, and her grandmother who, on a recent visit, seemed to her "a lot older than she used to be" (p. 48). Emig tells us to "note that two of the possible four topics involve Lynn: her grandmother and the two boys," and so might lead to writing in the reflexive mode; while the other two—the old ladies on the bus and Snoopy—"could be handled at a greater distance. Lynn chooses Snoopy, the cardboard dog. Why" (p. 48)?[6]

The answer to this question turns out to be far more complex than one might expect. The girl herself offers what Emig terms the "ostensible reason" that the boys would appeal to too narrow an audience, and result in a trite essay, to boot; while her "ostensible reason" for not writing on her grandmother's visit is that it was "two weeks away and no longer fresh in her memory." Emig, obviously not satisfied with these reasons, asks if there are others. Lynn offers the following:

> To write about my grandmother one thing that really struck me was when she would sit down in a chair she would sort of almost fall into it and my mother would sort of watch her when she was going up the stairs because they don't have stairs at her house, and this had never occurred to me before that she was rather old. And it would be kind of hard to formulate an entire theme. If I would have perhaps seen her again this week or, I didn't see too many old people on the buses going downtown which would have given me some insight. No, this is the easiest thing to write about (p. 48).

On the basis of this evidence, Emig deduces what Lynn means by "easy" and "hard" subjects: "Clearly, an 'easy' one is a nonpersonal subject, one that does not demand interacting with her feelings, one that is *not* reflexive" (pp. 48–49, her emphasis). Even this much of a leap seems a little puzzling—"clearly" is rather strong for so sweeping a generalization founded on such little information. That is, there may be grounds for speculating about Lynn's emotional distance from her topics as one element in her choice among them—even *a priori* grounds—but she says nothing explicit about the connection here, and the implicit evidence seems pretty weak.

But Emig is actually just beginning to build her case. Switching to a passage from Lynn's taped writing autobiography, she quotes a passage in which Lynn says that she finds it easier to write "about a specific incident," that it "still is very hard for me to write about abstract things like feelings about something, I do a lot better when I have facts" (p. 49). In the same interview, Emig says that she asked Lynn "why she thinks she feels more comfortable writing about facts rather than feelings." This seems a troubling question—rather directive, and, worse, based on a distortion of what Lynn actually said, which was that she had trouble writing about "abstract things," of which feelings were only one example. Be that as it may, she answers the question as asked:

> I've always . . . I've always had trouble talking to people about, my feelings on something, I can quote from other people I can . . . talk about, ahm . . . I can talk about facts more easily than I can talk about abstract things . . . when . . . I was at this Institute, one of the kids kept saying, "Lynn, you know, you're a great kid but you know it doesn't come out in our discussion group because you seem to be talking in clichés, you never seem to be talking about yourself, about your own feelings, you seem to be giving examples all the time," I don't know why this is, I could, get some sort of explanation, rather I'm sure, but I don't know (p. 49, Emig's ellipses, presumably indicating pauses).

Emig now moves her line of interpretive reasoning ahead two more steps. Not only does Lynn avoid potentially reflexive topics because, as the just-quoted passage was intended to demonstrate, "she admits that she finds expressing her feelings painful," but the girl is troubled by this characteristic in herself: "Lynn is clearly discomfited," argues Emig, "by her difficulty in expressing feelings, both in speaking and in writing" (p. 49). Surely both these claims have to be made very, very cautiously. In answer to this question that subtly twists her words, Lynn does say that someone else has claimed that she doesn't seem to express her feelings in a certain public forum

—but she doesn't say that she is reticent because she finds such disclosure painful. Maybe she finds it foolish, or boring, or unbecoming. It is even less clear why Emig finds her "clearly discomfited" by this "difficulty": From what evidence has this discomfiture been deduced? Lynn does mention avoiding clichés in the two pieces she later composes aloud, a tendency Emig suggests might be explained "as a struggle to find feeling and express it in her writing" (p. 49)—but that isn't much to go on. Emig closes out this interpretation of how Lynn comes to choose her topic with this short paragraph:

> That her grandmother is moving toward death deeply distresses Lynn; she has difficulty examining her feelings about it, even at the distance of writing about the old ladies on the bus—clearly surrogates for her grandmother. In choosing Snoopy, the cardboard dog, she chooses the subject of the four least requiring emotions from her, although the decision makes her feel guilty (pp. 49-50).

This is pretty ingenious stuff. And let me say that I have no argument whatever either with Emig's intuitive sensitivity or her skill at textual analysis. All of what she says here about Lynn might well be true. What I do question, however, is the depth of the evidence on which these interpretations are based. When Emig asks Lynn that slightly distorted question on writing about feelings, they've known each other for some two hours. Two hours! And in response to it, Lynn does an admirable job of—well, of expressing her feelings about expressing her feelings. So how much stock can we put into Emig's reading of this answer to what is essentially an "are-you-still-beating-your-wife" question asked of an eager-to-cooperate teenager by an authoritative stranger? Or how sure can we be that Lynn is "deeply" distressed by her grandmother's mortality? Is she really having difficulties examining her feelings about it, or is she just typically confused? Are these two old women "clearly" (that word again) surrogates? Indeed, what would we have thought if this seemingly well-adjusted young woman *had* chosen to write about her grandmother, and had proceeded to turn her composing-aloud session into a kind of therapeutic encounter, baring her soul for this woman she hardly knows? In other words, given how very little we—or Emig—know about Lynn, how safe would any such far-reaching interpretation of her choice of topic in this one very unusual situation be?[7]

As it turns out, Emig herself backs off in the very next paragraph, admitting that to suggest "fear of feeling" as "the sole, or even the predominant, reason for Lynn's choice of topics is not just," and that time is more important (p. 50). But surely she has spent the previous three pages leading us to think in precisely such "not just" terms. The interpretive damage has been done. We will inevitably think of Lynn as having this "difficulty." And it simply isn't clear that we should.

None of the other three investigators goes anywhere near this far out on a limb for a given subject. Perl and Sommers, as I suggested above, might conceivably have done so—they were their student-subjects' teachers, and so had at least a longer term relationship with them—but they, like Selfe, mostly ignore the wider range of information Emig tries so hard to account for, and thus produce portraits that are idiographically much more conservative. Given the inherent limitations of their shared snapshot design, we should probably regard such restraint as an improvement over Emig's study. But I would also argue that it represents only a very minor improvement, and that it is the design itself, far more than any handling of interpretation, that is the real problem. Emig's holistic instincts, her desire to understand her subjects as fully as possible, seem to me perfectly sound; she was simply handicapped by her shortage of data. Thus, when Perl and Sommers and Selfe avoid the interpretive hazards of trying to make sense of their subjects as composers *and* people at the same time, they might claim a surer approach to their data, but it is likely a less fruitful one. By comparison with Emig's Lynn, the portraits they offer seem narrowly conceived, two-dimensional. For the idiographic refinement of the Clinical method, it is Emig's design, not her ambition, that needs the most work.

No one of the four studies stands out as so clearly challenging the nomothetic limits of its design. Oh, there are some interesting moves made. Emig, for example, trying to account for why two of her male subjects didn't write stories or poems while the third did, introduces race as a factor: "perhaps the white boys genuinely believe writing poems and stories is an unmanly activity. Bradford [who is black], in contrast, seems perfectly comfortable writing his poetry" (p. 82). The *white* boys? It is surely possible, of course, that race and/or gender have something to do with these boys' self-images as writers. Given more time and more writing, maybe Emig could have generated data to support such an interpretation of what they didn't do. As it stands, though, she must be out of bounds. After all, Lynn wrote a poem, and Emig makes it very clear that Lynn is a Jew. Are there racial or ethnic implications in that? Emig doesn't mention any. Are they somehow more warranted for the boys? It seems unlikely.

By and large, though, all four investigators seem pretty sensitive to the constraints imposed by their designs, and take pains to make them explicit. Sommers, for example, offers the following delimiters by way of introducing her "Conclusions" in the section on student writers, and repeats them almost *verbatim* in her section on the experienced writers:

> From an analysis of the student writers' three compositions, the transcripts of three interviews, and their suggested revisions of the "Ana" passage, the following set of conclusions can be drawn about the congruence between these eight student writers' theory and practice of the revision process (Diss., p. 90).

Statements of this kind strike me as very responsible, in effect serving as warnings for consumers: "Claims made here about this group are based on data drawn from these very specific, very limited, sources." The catch is that, in the four studies we're considering here, and to varying degrees in other Clinical studies, they can be expected to cover an awful lot of interpretive ground. Like warning labels on a package, they are clear enough as we read them, but tend to get lost once we become involved with content. The technical limitations of the data being interpreted can blur, for example; or we can forget how individual subjects—already reduced by observation and analysis—are stripped even further of any individuality in favor of a group coherence. So, for instance, a paragraph after her warning, Sommers gets to the second of her six points of congruence:

> (2) The student writers have over-generalized the principles of effective writing that they have been taught and their strategies are an amalgam of what they have inferred from their observations of written language (Diss., p. 90).

Now it isn't that this statement, this interpretation, can't be true; it makes a certain, albeit not terribly specific, sense. Seeing it framed in this way, though, removed in physical distance and phraseology from its supporting data, it might well be construed as more authoritative than it really is. We are forced to supply a good many qualifications for ourselves. Pointing up just the technical limitations of the design, and imposing a first-person investigator, it might read something like this:

> Given what I could tell from the 333 total changes these eight students made in the three assignments I had them write in my classroom, insisting that they do them in three one-hour sittings; combined with what they told me in three, tape-recorded post-writing interviews (of 90, 45, and 45 minutes) held in my office —during which, as I mentioned earlier, they tended to be very uncomfortable, so that the most frequent response to my questions was "I don't know" (Diss., p. 46); and supported by what I learned from having them write out for me a list of the things they might change in a passage I provided for them; it would

seem that they have taken advice from their teachers about the importance of the word in effective writing and made it of too much importance, and then picked up other notions about how to revise and put them together without thinking much about their practical coherence.

Obviously, though, neither Sommers nor any other Clinician can be expected to go on qualifying their interpretations in this cumbersome way. She does provide most of this information at various places in her report, and it is up to us to follow her line of reasoning. Still, my point should be clear: Despite their general caution, Clinicians remain vulnerable to questionable nomothetic interpretations as they move toward these summary claims. Swept up in the power of their own words, there is always the risk that they will lose sight of their investigative limits, much as we can. Do I think Sommers is guilty of that here? Not exactly. But let's be clear about just what has she done. Eight students wrote on topics of her choice at her times and in her setting. We are not shown what they produce, but we are given the information I include in my revision: that they make a total of 333 changes, 111 per essay, about 15 per student/ essay; and, when asked to explain these changes, are more often than not simply unable to do so. From these few changes, then, and from what they do manage to tell her, Sommers draws this conclusion about the congruence between their revising theories and practices.

Should she do so? Perhaps. But consider one of several possible alternatives: that, as for example Pianko might argue, students writing on assigned topics under these conditions for no real purpose or reward simply don't invest much time or energy in revising. Suppose she had let these students, or a group recruited in an open competition, write on a topic of their choice, for a first prize of—oh, say $1000. Would they have revised? Consulted other sources? Gotten one or more expert readings? I don't mean such speculation to invalidate Sommers' interpretation of her data. The behaviors she stimulated, observed, and probed obviously have some relevance for school writing; and, within the very narrow limits of her data, this interpretation seems a plausible one. At the same time, though, we need to remember—as *she* needs to remember—how thin a slice of the whole phenomenon of "students revising" that data represents in the first place. However well it matches with her or our experience, then, its *methodological* authority is a function of that data base. And given how little she has to go on, that authority must be pretty tentative here.

Drawing Conclusions: Implications for Research and Teaching

Throughout this chapter, we have traced the effects of what I
early on called the Clinical community's identity crisis, its problem
with self-image. Since Emig first took up Braddock et al.'s challenge
to apply a case study methodology in Composition research, the investigators who have opted for this method seem to have been uncertain both about what form their authority ought to take, and from
whence it ought to derive. Nowhere are the forces which foster this
uncertainty more evident than here, where Clinicians try to bring
that authority to bear: to draw conclusions about the significance
of their work for others, to argue its implications for further research
and for teaching.

In the four studies we've been following, easily the most pronounced symptom of this uncertainty is a kind of schizophrenia:
radical differences in the stances the investigators take toward other
Researchers, on the one hand, and Practitioners, on the other. In
spelling out their various implications for research, they tend to be
acutely aware of the limitations of their work. They are modest,
almost obsequious, casting their findings as tentative and exploratory,
far better suited to generating questions than answering them. Look
at Emig's opening sentence to Chapter 7, "Implications":

> So much remains unexamined about the composing process of
> children, youth, and adults that this chapter could well become
> the longest in this study if a full catalogue of such research
> questions were attempted (p. 95).

Sondra Perl, in her chapter of the same title, explains why she has
had to restrict her discussion to only two of "the many possible ways
this study can be concluded":

> One of the values of basic research lies in its generative capacity.
> It enters a relatively unexplored area and asks the kinds of ques-
> tions that open up that area to closer scrutiny. Paradoxically,
> the kinds of answers that emerge from close scrutiny often point
> to the need for more extended questioning in those areas. As a
> result, a discussion on the implications of basic research can
> often be longer and more detailed than the discussion of the
> research itself (Diss., p. 351).

And both Sommers and Selfe express similar sentiments, the former
almost apologetically offering only two of the "many possible ways
this study can be interpreted for future research" (Diss., p. 164), the
latter asserting that her investigation "has only begun to identify the

difficulties these [apprehensive] students experience as they struggle through academic writing situations" (p. 61).

Given this sort of modesty, no one could accuse these investigators of claiming too much for what they have found. See what happens, however, when they turn from research implications to address, instead, writing instruction. Here is Emig introducing the subsection labeled "Implications for Teaching":

> This inquiry strongly suggests that, for a number of reasons, school-sponsored writing experienced by older American secondary students is a limited, and limiting, experience. The teaching of composition at this level is essentially unimodal, with only extensive writing given sanction in many schools. Almost by definition, this mode is other-directed—in fact, it is other-centered. The concern is with sending a message, a communication out into the world for the edification, the enlightenment, and ultimately the evaluation of another. Too often, the other is a teacher, interested chiefly in a product he can criticize rather than a process he can help initiate through imagination and sustain through empathy and support (p. 97).

Let's take due note, right away, of the hedge in "strongly suggests": Emig does not claim to have demonstrated, or shown, or proven. Beyond that, though, where has all her caution gone? Is this a paragraph about the same modest study? How much can four sessions with eight twelfth graders over one summer vacation have told her about school-sponsored writing among "older American secondary students"? Where has she acquired the evaluative power implicit in "limited, and limiting," such that she knows what *ought* to happen for those students? Where did she get her information about these critical, unimaginative, unsupportive teachers? Half of her subjects had fairly full portfolios of writing from their eleventh-grade English classes; but even if those portfolios revealed some very consistent pattern of pedagogical abuse—something Emig does not demonstrate —what kind of "sample," as she persists in calling her group, would those four portfolios among eight writers represent? And she goes on and on in this vein: One cause of these problems is "teacher illiteracy" (p. 98); in part because high school teachers don't write themselves, they "underconceptualize and oversimplify the process of composing" (p. 98); they offer instruction that is probably "too abstract for the average and below-average students" (p. 99). How, we must ask, does she claim to *know* such things?

Fortunately for their collective credibility, the other three are not quite so extreme in drawing pedagogical implications. Still, some of their arguments, too, lead one to wonder where the modest, research-directed persona has gone. In her subsection "On Writing Instruction," Perl begins this way:

> Unskilled writers often hold themselves accountable for their lack of skill in writing. However, the failure, if there is one, is not theirs alone. It must be shared by the teachers, the schools, and the larger social system outside of the schools for conceiving of the problem in the wrong way. If one assumes that what goes "wrong" in student writing can be detected through an analysis of the finished product, then one comes up with solutions different from ones derived from an analysis of process. These product-based solutions tend to be simplistic, to provide a model of instruction based primarily on correction, and to implant upon students struggling with the deeper problems of composing a premature model of perfection (Diss., p. 352).

The line of reasoning seems to represent fairly standard 1970s liberal thinking on such issues: teachers (and the social institutions they represent) are as responsible for the unskilled-ness of unskilled writers as those writers are, apparently because they mistakenly base their teaching on the analysis of the writing process's outcome, rather than of the process itself. But has Perl's study put her in a position to make this claim? Let's suppose that Perl's five subjects did thus hold themselves responsible—even though her Beverly, for example, doesn't see herself as a poor writer at all (Diss., pp. 262–263). Would that actually be sufficient grounds for her opening generalization? Would the study of five such subjects support any generalization of this breadth? It wouldn't seem so. But let's suppose further, and grant that this handful of students, plus Perl's experience, do provide such grounds. Can she take her next step? That is, has this study actually gotten at the more broadly conceived sources Perl invokes for their unskilled-ness? When? How? Surely each subject's composing aloud, supplemented by a single interview, has not revealed how "the teachers, the schools, and the larger social system" conceive of the problem, let alone why. As neat as it would be if all this were true, then—for it would give Perl a problem perfectly suited to her solution—the fact is that her research *per se* gives her no special authority in such matters. Even readers sympathetic to her position would be hard-pressed to find support for it in her sketches of these five students.

And the other two investigators take very similar approaches. Sommers asserts that the "strongest implication from this study for the teaching of composition is that teachers should recognize that although students lack a synthesized theory of revision they do have a well developed set of assumptions about the revision process"—a claim upon which she proceeds to base four rather sweeping pedagogical proposals (Diss., pp. 168–170). Even Selfe, the only one of the four who does not offer fairly pointed teaching advice, moves in the same direction, concocting a real-world problem—one that smacks a little of reification, perhaps, but for which her findings provide the beginnings of a solution:

> The construct of "writing apprehension" is an intuitively cred-ible one to most teachers of composition. They know that a class seldom goes by without yielding one or more students who dread every writing task assigned and who allow their dread to come between them and effective written expression. Before we can help these individuals, however, we must examine the nature of the apprehension that affects them and determine in which ways their apprehension acts upon the composing processes they employ (p. 60).

There is nothing inherently remarkable about this Clinical ambi-tion to direct Practitioners, of course; we have seen the same urge in all four of the non-Practitioner methods we have looked at so far, and will see it again in the next two. Clinicians only want what the users of those other methods want: recognition for the authority of their way of making knowledge. Unfortunately, the pattern of this method's development in Composition—and, in particular, its rela-tionship with Experimental inquiry—has led its users too often to misunderstand the nature of that authority themselves. Hence the schizophrenia: Despite the extent to which they let what are essen-tially Experimental rather than Clinical concerns affect their designs, neither Emig nor Perl, Sommers or Selfe believes that they have generated any substantial nomothetic authority, and they say so; and yet, having thus admitted that their work will not really support such an effort, all four try to go ahead and present Practitioners with generalized implications.

The tragedy—a strong word, perhaps, but I think accurate here—is that this misdirected ambition has both subverted and ob-scured much of what is potentially most valuable in Clinical inquiry. Consider, for instance, what Composition might have had had Janet Emig originally framed her investigation not as a sort of preliminary or second-class Experimental undertaking, but as genuinely, defen-sibly Clinical—so that, to choose an emblematic difference, rather than ending with a call for larger samples or more reliable analyses, she had argued that such inquiry needed greater and greater depth along the lines I have been suggesting: more time and kinds of writing per subject, a broader exploration of context, a more substan-tive writer-investigator relationship, and so on. Suppose she had then conducted one such study every year since 1971. What a remarkable corpus that would have produced! Fifteen portraits of writers at work, each drawn with the acute sensitivity Emig shows in her portrait of Lynn, but with steadily improving sources of data, and within a gradually richer canonical framework. Those would be writers we could begin to understand—not as members of the dubious category of "twelfth-graders," but as whole, complex people. And if those who later emulated her—like Perl and Sommers and Selfe—had followed her lead, we would have a far more powerful image of "People Writing" than we have now, along with a method that would have evolved in ways which, as things stand, we can only imagine.

I don't want to be melodramatic about this. Clinical inquiry obviously has had a powerful impact on Composition—even if it has often been for the wrong reasons. I invoke this image of a "tragic" past in the hope of affecting its future. Carol Berkenkotter, whose study of Donald Murray I mentioned earlier, seems to recognize what is involved as well as any Clinician I've read. "This project," she writes of her study, "has been a first venture in what may be a new direction."

> Research on single subjects is new in our discipline; we need to bear in mind that each writer has his or her idiosyncracies. The researcher must make a trade-off, foregoing generalizability for the richness of the data and the qualitative insights to be gained from it. We need to replicate naturalistic studies of skilled and unskilled writers before we can begin to infer patterns that will allow us to understand the writing process in all of its complexity (p. 167).

Her language still suggests a certain methodological confusion—replication, for instance, seems an unlikely possibility—and her ultimate goal is obviously very ambitious. Still, the general idea is close enough. The Clinicians' primary concern must be the individual writer, whole and in-depth, not the type—Lynn and Tony and Donald Murray, not twelfth graders or unskilled writers or professional writers. The larger image, the canonical theories, will emerge in due course. Let me try to make it axiomatic: To claim the authority that is rightfully and most usefully theirs, Clinicians need to recognize—and indeed, to revel in—the power of idiographic inquiry.

8

The Formalists

I have borrowed the term Formalist from Paul Diesing's *Patterns of Discovery in the Social Sciences*, where he uses it to describe a method that "is characterized first by the use of formal languages, and second by the development of an axiomatic, deductive structure" (p. 29). Now in fact, no Formalist research in Composition fully meets this description; none of them have yet dealt in a formal language (e.g., mathematics, computer language, symbolic logic). They do, however, attempt to develop an "axiomatic, deductive structure," and their object is, as in fully developed formal theory, the building of models and their interpretation—that is, determining the relationship between the model and some portion of the real world. Thus, they are best understood as what Diesing categorizes as "implicit formal theories": would-be formal theories which use little or no formal language or formal deductive technique, so that their structures are "incompletely developed owing to the inadequate language used." The implicit nature of Composition's Formal theories can and has, as we shall see, caused some confusion, especially about the nature and authority of Formalist knowledge. Nevertheless, the best way to avoid such confusions, and to clarify the boundaries of Formalist knowledge, is to consider Composition's implicit Formal theories in the larger context of full-fledged formal theorizing.

Euclid's geometry is probably the formal system with which most people have the fullest acquaintance. Every high school sophomore is made to understand its axiomatic and deductive structure, and to wonder about its interpretation, the correspondence between its neat axiom and postulate system and the real world: to test, with compass and triangle, its relevance for the two-dimensional world of circles, rectangles, rhombuses and the like. What that sophomore might also learn, though, are the limits of the system's relevance. As the presence of other geometries makes clear, no Formal system applies equally well to every situation; Euclid, for example, seems awfully limited in Einstein's universe. Formal inquiry in other areas may also be familiar. The economic projections we hear and read so constantly are most often the product of some economist's use of an economic model. There is a substantial body of learning theory that is mostly formal in character; Diesing spends a good deal of time discussing game theory; and computer simulation, in any field, is likely to be the articulation of a formal theory.

The object in all these kinds of Formalist inquiry is model building. An Experimentalist sets out to sort through competing theories by attempting to isolate the features of some portion of the empirical world and working to correlate the relationships among them. A Formalist, by contrast, investigates by what amounts to analogy. The basic idea is to construct, usually in a formal language, a model whose internal logic in some specifiable ways resembles that of the phenomenon under study. A fully realized Formal theory, argues Diesing, will have both an explicit, clearly articulated model or calculus; and one or more sets of what are variously called bridge principles or rules of interpretation outlining its correspondence to one or more empirical domains:

> First, there is the model or calculus (or theory in some versions of terminology), a set of interrelated propositions stated in a formal language. The propositions of a calculus are nothing more than a network of relations that allow one to move from one term to another in a certain sequence. By itself a calculus is neither true nor false, since it says nothing about the empirical world.
>
> Second, there are one or more sets of rules that relate the calculus to the empirical world. These are called rules of correspondence or rules of interpretation, and each set provides an interpretation of the calculus. That is, it gives a verbal translation of the terms of a calculus and thus tells us what the calculus means empirically. However, unlike ordinary translation, a rule of interpretation never gives a definitive set of possible empirical meanings, since any calculus can have an indefinite number of interpretations (p. 35).

In English, we are probably most familiar with Formal theories from linguistics. In transformational-generative grammar, for instance, the phenomenon under study is language-making. In simple terms, the Formalist's problem is this: Language (speech) is the production of, the output data from, some system. The question is, what can be the nature of such a system that it produces this phenomenon, this set of data? Denied direct access to the operations of that system itself, the Formalist can turn to examining the output data, to whatever indirect methods of observation are available (the utterances of children, say) to imagining, and so on, as means by which to devise a model system that might be made to produce the relevant data—in this case, language. The claims that might be made for the resulting model are not empirical; it is not a *description* of the way that humans make language, but a model whose internal logic is such that, given the right input, it can turn out a product, "language," which is at least in some ways equivalent to that produced by humans.

For all the popularity of linguistics in the 1950s and '60s, though, Formalist inquiry has come to Composition *per se* only quite recently. It may be that that earlier contact with a Formalist-based inquiry in some fashion prepared the way, but when it finally appears its heritage seems to lie as much with cognitive psychology as with linguistics. As a result, while the "output data" is similar—both linguistic and Composition research deal with language, although Composition has dealt almost exclusively with written language—the system or process to be modeled is conceived rather differently.

What is particularly interesting about Composition's Formalist inquiry is its tremendous appeal. For while the Formalist community has neither the age nor anything near the size of the Experimental community, its influence has been remarkable—far out of proportion, by any measure, to either the number or sophistication of the investigations. Moreover, it seems to me that, along with Ethnography, it is the fastest growing Researcher method in Composition.

And, while one might point out various important predecessors —James Ney's 1974 "Notes Towards a Psycholinguistic Model of the Composing Process," for example—the central figures in its rise to prominence are Linda Flower and John Hayes. Their first widely accessible formulation was a *College English* essay, "Problem-Solving Strategies and the Writing Process." Since then, in dozens of articles, chapters in various collections, and a textbook, they have extended and refined the implications of their cognitive-based model of writing. During roughly the same period, a number of other investigators have espoused some version of the Formal method. Robert de Beaugrande, for example, whose work does derive more directly from linguistics— in particular, text linguistics—explores in a series of articles beginning about 1977, and in *Text, Discourse, and Process: Toward a Multidisciplinary Science of Texts*, models for reading and writing, or what he terms the "processing" ("reception" and "production") of texts.

Ann Matsuhashi, in "Pausing and Planning: The Tempo of Written Discourse Production," citing as her background "nearly three decades of psycholinguistic studies of pauses during the production of spontaneous speech" (p. 114), does some preliminary work on a writing-process model by correlating the pauses of writers composing with textual junctures, and then making inferences about the nature of the process that might account for the correlations she finds. In his *Writer's Block: The Cognitive Dimension*, Mike Rose attempts to refine a portion of an essentially Flower and Hayes-based model of composing by exploring the dimensions of what he calls "blocking," defined as a cognitive dysfunction that prevents writing in people otherwise sufficiently skilled and motivated. On the basis of questionnaires, interviews, and composing-aloud protocols, he tries to account for such writers' non-production in terms of his model.

There is no reason, of course, that Formal inquiry could not be extended to other phenomena of interest in Composition. So, for example, in "Holistic Assessment of Writing: Experimental Design and Cognitive Theory" Sarah Warshauer Freedman and Robert C. Calfee develop "An Information Processing Model of the Rater" of holistic essays (p. 91ff.). Writing in the same collection (*Research on Writing*), Peter Mosenthal works toward what he calls an "ideologically unbiased model of classroom writing competence" (p. 53ff.). And one can easily enough imagine a model of writing classroom interaction, say, or of the dynamics of the writing conference. So far, however, Formalist inquiry in Composition has focused almost exclusively on modeling writing.

The Nature of Formalist Knowledge

Formalist inquiry is almost certainly the most difficult of Composition's Researcher methods for outsiders to understand. The source of the difficulty lies in the difference between models and descriptions. Formalist knowledge may be said, like Experimental knowledge, to have a paradigmatic structure: community activity is directed by reference to one or another models. The difference lies in the assumed relationship between the paradigm and the empirical world. As I tried to stress in Chapter 6, an Experimental paradigm is assumed to constitute the pattern of some portion of the real, empirical world. That's partly why it has come together so slowly in Composition; it is assembled piece by piece, from the bottom up, and it has been very hard to hold the pieces together. That is not the case for a Formal paradigm. Instead of following an inductive logic (or probable inference), the Formal paradigm or model has two other logics: a tautologic, in the sense that as a model it is internally complete; and an analogic, by which it can be tested against, interpreted in terms of, one or more empirical, real-world systems.

Now the obvious advantage of the Formal over the other positivist methods for studying complex phenomena like the writing process is that it evades, although it cannot entirely escape, what I referred to earlier as the combinatorial explosion: the proliferation of variables to be accounted for in Experimental work, especially in the study of human activities. There is, however, a price to be paid for this freedom. Experimentalist knowledge, hard as it can be to come by, will finally be, according to its own rules, knowledge directly about the world. Formalist knowledge is not so simple. Each model will be, in and of itself, perfect, a tautological whole; but its correspondence to any empirical domain can never be perfect or complete. We might summarize the trade-off this way: While Experimental inquiry holds out the potential for a full and paradigmatically stable explication of the order of things, any progress that is made is made very slowly. Formalist inquiry gives up that paradigmatic fullness and stability in exchange for the broader-ranging, more quickly accessible explanatory power of its models, but the knowledge they can generate is far less stable. And in fact, it is worth pointing out from the beginning that Formal models may well be valuable less for what they can tell us about any system or process than for the heuristic power of the discrepancies between a model and any empirical domain. Especially in the study of human activities, they highlight for us what we do not understand.

What makes all this difficult for outsiders is that it can be hard not to mistake the elements of a Formal model for the "real" things to which they correspond in some way. This has been especially troublesome with Composition's implicit Formal theories, where the pattern has been to label model elements with terms which, in ordinary language, we would probably use to refer to the phenomena themselves. For instance, Flower and Hayes, whose work we'll be considering at some length, create a model in which there seem to be three major elements: "the task environment," "the writer's long term memory," and "the writing process." These labels illustrate the problem clearly enough. They sound like they ought to be empirical entities, but in fact they are essentially place holders, nouns which represent some set of formal properties assumed to be traceable also in the "system" by which humans produce written texts. However, an outsider reading them or seeing them depicted in an illustration is very likely to mistake the model for a description, and so think that the model "shows" or "demonstrates" that writers "have" long term memory, a task environment, and a writing process. Indeed, it is easy enough for even the researcher who invokes such terms to confuse their empirical and Formal significances.

But if a Formalist model is not a description, how does it work? One way to put it is to say that, while an Experimentalist wants to *quantify* phenomena, the Formalist wants to *qualify* them. That is, both methods are positivist in their orientation, assuming that despite surface appearances of chaos, the world is fundamentally an orderly place and that humans have access to that order. The Experimental method seeks to find that causal order in the interaction of the particulars of the chaos themselves. The object is to identify and then count (quantify) sufficient instances of such interaction to be able to draw statistical inferences about them.

The Formalist goes about understanding the phenomena under study in a different way. If the Experimentalist wants to record enough instances of x happening after y happening after z to be able to link this sequence causally—to be able to say, in other words, that 99% of the time, when x then y then z—the Formalist wants to know how or why or by what mechanism. Re-conceiving these events as the x/y/z system or process, the Formalist will set out to discover its underlying logic. He will do this by choosing, from among the many possible logics or logical sequences that might explain the system, one that seems plausible, construct from it a model, and then work at testing the correspondence between the model and the system in question, refining the model to account more and more fully for the empirical system. This last process, usually referred to as successive approximation, is at the heart of Formalist work.

Formalist Inquiry

Driven by this demand for successive approximation, then, the general pattern of Formalist inquiry might be outlined like this:

1. Identification of Problem/Constructing a Model
2. Formalization
3. Testing and Refining the Model: Successive Approximation
4. Dissemination to a Wider Audience: The Uses of Formalist Knowledge

Identifying the Problem/Constructing a Model

It isn't difficult to understand the attraction the Formalist method holds for investigators interested in studying how people do, learn, and teach writing. In addition to avoiding the combinatorial explosion that plagues Experimental inquiry, it seems far better suited to studying a phenomenon the bulk of which is assumed to be unobservable—what might be called a black box phenomenon, in this case the operations of the human mind. That is, while we might, in Experimental inquiry, measure various sorts of activities—eye or hand movements, say, or even neurological events of different kinds —we would be on very shaky ground trying to say what such activities represented in terms of some underlying but unobservable "composing process." Rather, we would be restricted to saying that these activities, taken collectively, *were* the composing process, operationally defined; and then perhaps set about finding ways to observe, measure, and eventually relate other features of it. Under Experimental rules, then, we would be constrained to develop our theory of the composing process from the bottom up.

In Formalist inquiry, in part because claims about the authority of our knowledge will not be limited to any particular empirical domain, we are free to build from the top down; rather than having to work toward a full explication by painstakingly accounting for innumerable component correlations, we get to make some sort of educated guess right away, and then go back to see if or how the details will or will not support our guess, gradually altering it in the direction of greater accuracy. On the basis of even just casual observation, then, or experience, or the findings of other kinds of inquiry—in short, on the basis of whatever sources we want—we get to construct a first version of a model of the composing process. We will know in advance, of course, that while our model will be internally complete, it will both simplify and distort the phenomenon we are trying to model, but that is not a problem.

However, we will need to meet a two-part minimum requirement. First, even though we are deliberately constructing a model of limited relevance, so that it seems to come with a single, built-in interpretation, we must nevertheless articulate a set of bridge principles, or rules for interpretation. In other words, even though we derive our model from what we know about how people write, and plan to restrict our testing and refining of it to that particular empirical domain (not extending it to, say, the production of discourse in other media), we still need to stipulate the nature of the correspondence between the features of our model and the properties of the process it models. *How* does it simplify and distort what it tries to depict?

Second, because we are modeling a phenomenon to which we expect to have limited direct access, we need to be particularly careful about the extent to which our model accounts for the process's observable output data. The testing and refining of a model for such a process—successive approximation—will necessarily depend to some extent on corroborative evidence of varying reliability and validity—interviews, protocols, questionnaires, and so on. That is one reason for choosing the Formal method in the first place: the process is just plain hard to get at. But for the model to have any claims to explanatory power, it must be grounded in whatever hard empirical evidence is available. In the case of the writing process, the most accessible output data is presumably writing, texts, words on a page. Thus, the eventual potency of any model we construct—its ability to compete against other models—would depend heavily on the degree of correspondence between its output data and the output data of the writing process, texts. No model could ever account for all features of texts, and different models will necessarily emphasize different textual features, so it doesn't follow absolutely that the best model will be the one that accounts most fully for texts—"most fully" turns out to be very hard to define. Still, models which do account for text more fully than others are likely to have a considerable edge.

Part of the point here, of course, is that how various investigators decide to conceive of the black box of writing is to some extent arbitrary. Although, as positivists, Formalists do assume that systems and processes exist in the world waiting to be modeled, a process like writing is complex enough that, at least at this early stage of investigation, no single model can come anywhere near to accounting for it fully. As it turns out, all the Formalist work in Composition I can find has treated writing as a cognitive process: the operation of the mind conceived as a system working to gather information from outside of itself, sift, store and retrieve it in some way, sort and arrange it meet various criteria, and eventually transform it into words on a page that accomplish some set of goals. Flower and Hayes are almost certainly the most articulate about this approach, and particularly so in an essay called "Identifying the Organization of Writing Processes" (Hayes and Flower, 1980). We can consider their model as articulated in that essay to illustrate how a model gets constructed.

I need to note, by way of introduction, that Flower and Hayes rely very heavily on a technique called the verbal or "thinking aloud" protocol to both develop and test their model—a decision guided, presumably, by procedures in the cognitive psychological work that influences them so heavily.[1] Essentially, the technique involves asking research subjects "to say aloud everything they think and everything that occurs to them" while performing a given task (p. 4) —in this case, writing. We will return to consider the technique itself, and their handling of it, later in the chapter. For the moment, it's enough to know that the model they propose derives in large part from what a series of protocol-making subjects have said. Flower and

Hayes' first move in constructing their model is to divide the "writer's world" into the three parts mentioned above—"the task environment," "the writer's long term memory," and "the writing process." Next, after restricting the scope of their investigation by declaring that their "model describes the writing process," they offer the following (double-spaced for easier reading):

We propose that writing consists of three major processes: PLANNING, TRANSLATING, and REVIEWING. The PLANNING process consists of GENERATING, ORGANIZING, and GOAL-SETTING subprocesses. The function of the PLANNING process is to take information from the task environment and from long-term memory and to use it to set goals and to establish a writing plan to guide the production of a text that will meet those goals. The plan may be drawn in part from long-term memory or may be formed anew within the PLANNING process. The TRANSLATING process acts under the guidance of the writing plan to produce language corresponding to information in the writer's memory. The function of the REVIEWING process, which consists of READING and EDITING subprocesses, is to improve the quality of the text produced by the TRANSLATING process. It does this by detecting and correcting weaknesses in the text with respect to language conventions and accuracy of meaning, and by evaluating the extent to which the text accomplishes the writer's goals (p. 12).

And the schematic they use to represent this model is on the top of page 247.

We can begin our analysis by testing this model against the minimum two-part requirement I sketched out. Obviously, on the first requirement—the matter of interpretive or bridge principles—we can't get far. Like all of Composition's Formal models, this one is as yet only implicitly Formal. As such, it operates under something of a handicap: because the line between model and description in implicit Formal theories is often fuzzy, it is not always clear that the investigators recognize the need for rules of interpretation at all, let alone

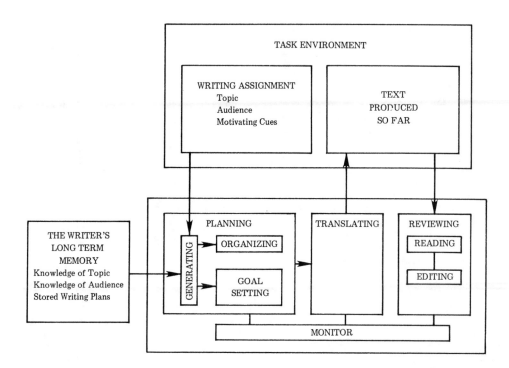

the need to make them explicit. So while in this instance Flower and Hayes indicate with their choice of "propose" that they do recognize the model's Formal nature, they also write that it "describes," as opposed to, say, "accounts for" the writing process. We will return to the nature—and dangers—of this ambiguity more fully below, under Formalization. For here it is enough to say that, while Flower and Hayes are clearly aware of the limitations on the correspondence between their model and how people write, they for the most part do not make those limits clear, and they definitely do not offer an explicitly stated set of rules for interpretation.

The other criterion, though, can be more usefully applied: To what extent do they account for the process's output data? The chart on page 248 capsulizes the output data for each of the model's major processes and subprocesses. The middle column describes the cognitive output data, while the right-hand one gives the specifications for textual output, where there is any.

As you can see, the textual specifications are pretty rudimentary. For example, the model ignores almost entirely the sheer logistics of a text: the shape of letters, their spacing, their left to right, top to bottom arrangement, etc. Are these to be handled by

PROCESS	COGNITIVE OUTPUT	TEXTUAL OUTPUT
PLANNING		
GENERATING	Information "items" in "associative chains"	Notes: single words, sentence fragments, complete sentences
ORGANIZING	"Writing plan": selected and ordered (temporal, hierarchical) information	Organizational form for notes: systematically indented, numbered, or alphabetized
GOAL SETTING	Goals: criteria for editing	None
TRANSLATING	Propositions (taken from memory)	Acceptable written English sentences
REVIEWING		
READING	Information (now derived from text) re-represented*	None
EDITING	Judgments (about any produced words, read, spoken, written): Yes/No/Change	Text altered to meet standard language conventions, accuracy of meaning, reader understanding, or reader acceptance**

*This is my speculation; Flower and Hayes actually say nothing about this subprocess. So it isn't entirely clear, e.g., whether "read" text becomes "information" in memory, or is directly present as information in TRANSLATING, etc.

**It is not fully clear whether (or when) such alterations invoke TRANSLATING, or if EDITING produces text independently. The authors do indicate that the whole writing process might be invoked, but the example they use introduces fairly extreme circumstances (see pp. 17–18).

TRANSLATING? EDITING? How? And the text conceived as units of other kinds gets only the broadest attention. That is, the model will account for two general kinds of text (notes and non-notes); three forms of organization (actually only relevant to notes); and three grammatical structures (words, sentence fragments, and sentences). What about such features as parts of speech? Paragraphs? Clauses? The implication, perhaps, is that the model's text-analogue output will be governed by a grammar and a rhetoric—the EDITING function tries to cover most of this ground—but the model provides for the details of neither. If text is really the output data this model is designed to produce, it has a very long way to go towards specifying its formal properties.

Formalization

Even though, as I suggested earlier, none of Composition's Formalist models has been formalized—expressed in a formal language—I have included this discussion of the process in order to discuss the dangers and difficulties of model building when it is thus "trapped" in a non-formal language. The advantage of developing a model in a formal language, of course, is that it forces one to be clear and complete: about elements, about relationships, about assumptions, and so on. It also has the effect of making the model's status as model clear, reducing the chances that a Formal assertion will be mistaken for an empirical one. The principal danger of ordinary language models, then, is the potential for confusion they create in these areas for investigator and reader alike.

Flower and Hayes' model, which, despite some interesting refinements, has remained fundamentally unchanged over the past nine years, will continue to serve as a good illustration. We can begin with a reminder that it is, as far as ordinary language will permit, internally complete, tautological; there are no gaps or loose ends in it. As we have seen, though, this sort of completeness poses a considerable problem. Dressed out in everyday language, the model looks very much as though it's making empirical statements about observed phenomena. To make matters worse, Flower and Hayes' introductory phrasing tends to foster the empirical illusion. They write "We propose that writing consists of three major processes," rather than something more strictly accurate, like "In our model, writing consists of three major processes." Their use of "propose" suggests that they may recognize the propositional nature of such an assertion, but it is easily enough read as an empirical one. Despite the all-caps designation of the various processes (which I assume is intended to mitigate the effect), such a formulation of the model tends to lead us to fill our own experience into its terms, and so to see "empirical" evidence in support of its validity everywhere: "Yes, I plan, translate, and review, I generate, organize, and set goals," and so on. But as the definitions they offer later in the same paragraph at least try to make clear, the terms as used here actually have very special, much more restricted meanings. They do not correspond to observed psychological states or entities or processes. Rather, they indicate relations among the as-yet unspecified elements of the model system being proposed.

A second, more serious difficulty also appears to stem from the model's non-formalization. Specifically, while Flower and Hayes make it clear that they will be modeling a process—the dynamic of some system—they are not very clear on just what the components of that system are. In fact, one might well have expected them to take what they offer as the three parts of their "writer's world" as the system's basic elements. Two of them, the task environment and the writer's long term memory, are already offered in a suitable form, and some of their features are at least tentatively defined. Flower and Hayes don't actually name a third component—the third box in their diagram has no label, and elsewhere is simply referred to as the writing process—but one could imagine calling it "the writing processor." Writing could then be conceived as the dynamic of the system comprised of these elements.

As it stands, however, they designate task environment and the writer's long term memory as "the context in which the model operates," so that it isn't finally very clear what their status is; and then try to offer a model that accounts for three processes (PLANNING, TRANSLATING, REVIEWING) without fully specifying the characteristics of the element(s) involved in them. In other words, although they posit "things" in both the task environment and the writer's long term memory (e.g., the assignment and the text produced in the former, knowledge and stored writing plans in the latter), for the writing process the only such "thing" or entity specified is something called "The Monitor." Its function is to define the relationships among the three processes, and it consists simply of a sequence of ten of what are called "condition-action rules" that govern priorities during text production. So, for example, EDITING and GENERATING take precedence over all other processes, and will interrupt (take *action*) whenever the *conditions* for them are satisfied.

What remains unspecified is the nature of the entity that does these things: What "unit," parallel to the task environment and short term memory, does the REVIEWING, such that it can apportion its energies (if it can be said to have those) between its two subprocesses,

READING and EDITING—one of which (EDITING) can apparently be invoked independently? The REVIEWING unit? In what form does this unit handle the information it works with? How much can it hold at any one time, and how does it hold it? Is it the same unit that does, say, GENERATING, converted to another use, or something partly or entirely separate? Can REVIEWING and GENERATING go on at the same time? Are they restricted by some limits—consciousness or awareness, say—or could the retrieval of information from long term memory be going on while the text was being reread? In other words, are we talking here about three separate faculties operating from an energy source that can run only one at a time, or a single faculty that can only handle one process at a time, or three faculties that can run simultaneously? Flower and Hayes make it clear that these processes are not stages (i.e., that writing is not PLANNING, then TRANSLATING, then REVIEWING). They do seem to suggest, if only by their flowcharts, that the various subprocesses are operationally exclusive—that they occur one at a time only, albeit in no set sequence. What they never do, though, *is explain the characteristics of the figurative "box" where all this takes place.* I attribute that omission to the absence of formalization. My guess is that Flower and Hayes, and their readers, automatically fill in something like "the writer's mind" in that third box, attributing to it whatever properties allow them to make sense of these various processes. But, once again, there is an obvious and dangerous circularity in such thinking. The object of building the model is to contrast it with some empirical system. Any time an element of the model slips from its status as potentially analogous to become instead identical with an element of a particular system, the model loses potency.

The object of formalization, then, would be to force these problems and confusions into the light. Suppose, to attempt a crude renaming, we revise the model proposed by Flower and Hayes using a set of less loaded place-holders. We can call the task environment B(lack) B(ox) #3, long-term memory BB #2, and the writing process BB #1 (to indicate its focal status). What we want to assemble is a model of the process such that some "information" units in BB #2 and BB #3—call them $\langle I_n \rangle$s and $\langle \$_n \rangle$s, respectively, with a subscript letter to indicate their various forms and functions—can be processed in BB #1 in such a way as to produce some output data $\langle T_n \rangle$, with its various forms and functions designated by subscript numbers. All of what is in BB #2 and BB #3 will be in keeping with the original model. BB #2, then, contains three kinds of $\langle I_n \rangle$s, corresponding to the three kinds of knowledge in the original model. These $\langle I_n \rangle$s are stored "as propositions but not necessarily as language" in "memory

structures" like "concepts, relations, and attributes" (p. 15). In
BB #3, there are four kinds of $\langle\$_n\rangle$s, one of which is also the gradu-
ally accumulating output data of the process, $\langle T_n\rangle$. We will not
specify the nature of any of these $\langle\$_n\rangle$s, including those that are
features of $\langle T_n\rangle$, nor compare them to the $\langle I_n\rangle$s in BB #2 although,
as we shall see, they can have similar functions. Our model now
looks like this:

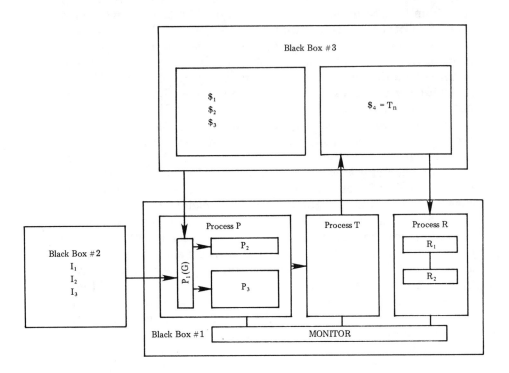

This is essentially the system for which Flower and Hayes offer
their model. They are particularly interested, of course, in developing
such a model as it relates to a specific empirical domain: that is, by
contrasting it against what they can learn when they observe adult
writers "thinking aloud" as they write on assigned tasks in a lab
setting, and so conceived as somehow operators of (or containers for?)
such a system. They want to know how the model serves to predict
what happens when the various $\langle I_n\rangle$s and $\langle\$_n\rangle$s are information con-
ceived as somehow "in" the task environment and in a writer's long
term memory, and when the $\langle T_n\rangle$s are in the form of a written
(English) text.

Even my crude bit of symbolizing should help make clear the

shift in perspective formalization requires. When we see BB #2 instead of "the writer's long term memory," we are far more likely to want to know what its characteristics are: What are the properties of the $\langle I_n \rangle$s stored there? We are told that they are stored as "propositions," but "not necessarily as language." Then what are they? How are they accessed, and by what agency? *Can* they be in language? How much energy does it take to store them? Retrieve them? Now, in fact, Flower and Hayes do address some of these issues. Here is their account of GENERATING:

> The function of the GENERATING process is to retrieve information relevant to the writing task from long-term memory. We assume that this process derives its first memory probe from information about the topic and the audience presented in the task environment. Because each retrieved item is used as the new memory probe, items are retrieved from memory in associative chains. In order to focus search on relevant material, the retrieval chain is broken whenever an item is retrieved that is not useful to the writing task. Search is then restarted with a new memory probe derived from the task environment or from useful material already retrieved (pp. 12–13).

This seems a very careful description, but because it's framed in English, it is hard to read it for what it is—the abstract account of what happens in a model—and not a description; and hard, too, to get a clear grip on what is being made explicit, what assumed, what not accounted for. I have sketched it out here according to my crude symbolization, indicating some of the missing information:

> The process (G) is characterized by the movement of certain $\langle I_n \rangle$s from BB #2 to BB #1. The first $\langle I_n \rangle$ is chosen (means unspecified) for some relationship (unspecified except as "relevance") to an $\langle \$_n \rangle$ that has moved from BB #3 to BB #1 (by means unspecified). The first and all subsequent $\langle I_n \rangle$s are then somehow tested (means unspecified) for "usefulness" (undefined) against criteria $\langle I_n \rangle$ that are also retrieved from BB #2, but that have different characteristics, and which are "stored" (means, location, and arrangement unspecified) for such use. Each subsequent $\langle I_n \rangle$ is connected to the next (in an arrangement defined only as an "associative chain") by some property (still unspecified except as "relevance") save when it fails to meet the established and stored criteria $\langle I_n \rangle$, after which it is (presumably) rejected (fate unspecified). When that happens, the next $\langle I_n \rangle$ is chosen for some relationship (unspecified) to $\langle \$_n \rangle$ from BB #3 (new or old not specified), or from previous $\langle I_n \rangle$s in current associative chain (manner of storage unspecified).

Obviously, there are a lot of questions to be answered here, but that is not the point. As Flower and Hayes are careful to indicate, this is simply a first, provisional model, the primary purpose of which is precisely to raise such questions. No: The point is that for the model to raise such questions with anything like maximum effectiveness—and minimum confusion—some kind of formalization would seem to be essential.

Testing and Refining the Model: Successive Approximation

Establishing a Formal model, with or without Formalization, is relatively easy. All it requires, as we have seen, is the ability to construct a workable tautology. Everything in the model must be accounted for, must come from somewhere, and go to somewhere. No such model can itself be tested; because it is a tautological construction, it is whole or "true" by definition. What can be tested, though, is the correspondence between the model and one or more particular empirical domains, one or more systems or processes in the real world that seem to have a similar logical structure. Strictly speaking, then, testing and refining a model refers to determining, via its bridge principles, what Diesing likes to call its "conditions of relevance"—the extent to which it has explanatory power in any given domain—and then trying to alter the model to make its explanatory power greater.

As the discussion of Flower and Hayes' model to this point will have illustrated, the relationship between a model and any particular empirical domain—even when, as has been the case here, there is only the one—is problematic. As I suggested above, the first and most crucial area of correspondence to be established, especially in the study of a black-box process like writing, is that between the accessible output data of the model and the output data of the process being modeled. For example, it is easy enough to accept, in a casual way, that people writing take what my simple symbolized model designates as $\langle I \rangle$s and $\langle \$ \rangle$s and transforms them, via the writing process, into $\langle T \rangle$s; that is, to think of it as meaning that people take information from their environment and their memories and turn it into written material. However, for Formal inquiry to proceed, the relationship between these symbols from the model and corresponding features of people writing needs to be specified. And first in order of importance among such relationships is the nature and limits of the correspondence between $\langle T \rangle$s and texts. In other words, given the assumption that written text was writing's output data, a fully successful model would be able to account for any textual feature produced by any system to which it claimed correspondence. This is not any simple matter; we have seen how few features Flower and Hayes account for.

Still, as difficult as it is to construct a model that fully accounts for text as output data, even one that did so would not therefore be automatically sufficient. Diesing goes to considerable trouble to point out that while the first model of a process like writing can come from almost anywhere, its maker needs to be very cautious with what happens to it next:

> He may base his initial postulates on hunches, tautologies, empathy, verbal theories, discarded physiological theories (Hebb, 1955), or what not, and should not have much confidence in them. Obviously, when discrepancies appear between deduced predictions and data, he will change his assumptions to conform to the data. However, it is a mistake to think of his aim as simply that of modifying his assumptions until he can deduce the data from them. This would be committing the fallacy of affirming the consequent. This fallacy is as follows:
>
> B. (A set of data to be explained)
> If A, then B. (Discovering a set of assumptions A from which B can be deduced)
>
> A. (Claiming that A has now been verified and is a valid explanation of B)
>
> The error here lies in forgetting that the same consequences B can be deduced from any number of different assumptions, not only from A (p. 56).

In terms of our concern here with writing, there are plenty of models which, deduced from the text itself as output data, might account for various textual features. The question is, which ones are most useful for the further study of this process as it occurs in people? Which are worth pursuing via successive approximations? What is called for, clearly, is further, corroborative evidence that can provide information about the nature of the process in question, so that there will be some way to choose from among potential competing accounts.

One Formalist study which handles the output data correspondence and the corroborative evidence pretty well is the one reported by Ann Matsuhashi in "Pausing and Planning: The Tempo of Written Discourse Production." Unlike Flower and Hayes, she does not specify even a tentative model of writing in this article. Still, she is concerned with writing conceived as a cognitive process, so that lying behind her investigation "is a model of the writing process as a cognitive activity best explained with concepts of planning and decision-making" (p. 114).

As is usual among Composition's Formalists, of course, we are dealing here with an implicit Formal theory, so that the model, not even fully articulated in the research report, can hardly be expected to have been formalized, either. As we have already seen, it can be difficult under such circumstances to tell when the investigator is making empirical claims and when she is making Formal ones. And it is not always clear in this study that the two are not confused, even though Matsuhashi explicitly states that she is engaged in model building. However, since clarity about this distinction is crucial for my purposes, I will again take the irregular liberty of explaining her study to some extent in terms of the symbolized model I developed above.

As her title suggests, Matsuhashi's study essentially consists of timing the pauses ("moments of physical inactivity during writing" p. 114) at various junctures during the production of texts by her subjects. Using two videocameras and a special-effects generator, she is able to videotape the writer and the text simultaneously, and to record on the tape elapsing time in minutes, seconds, and tenths of seconds. Given this record of the texts' production, she is then able to correlate the length of the recorded pauses with the nature of the juncture (defined in textual terms), looking for patterns among those correlations from which to draw inferences, which in turn will help her contribute to a model accounting for the cognitive processes assumed to be taking place during those pauses. Her exploratory questions are these:

> 1. Planning for the major discourse context: Does mean pause length differ in written discourse produced for the purpose of reporting, of persuading, and of generalizing?
> 2. Planning for specific units of language: Do mean pause lengths differ prior to the presence or absence of a specific unit of language? Do mean pause lengths differ when compared prior to several types of a specific unit of language? Do mean pause lengths differ when these units of language are embedded in discourse for the purpose of reporting, of persuading, and of generalizing (p. 115)?

What makes her study useful for illustration here is that, while we never actually see the model she's working toward, the investigation at least meets the basic requirement of accounting to a comparatively high degree for the accessible output data of the particular empirical domain of people writing—that is, their texts. In order to characterize the different textual junctures, Matsuhashi develops an analytic system that consists of three "discourse types" (reporting, persuading, generalizing [p. 116]) and eight of what she labels "units of language" (level of abstraction, sentence roles, paragraph, initial modifying structure, two kinds of lexical cohesion, syntax, and content words [p. 118]). There is a little terminological confusion here. Strictly speaking, only five textual "units" are represented: words, clauses, T-units, sentences, and paragraphs. The categories she spells out are better understood as the possible relationships among these units, and of these units within the discourse types. Drawn from a variety of sources, then, and defined in a range of ways, these are essentially a set of abstracted specifications for the ⟨T ⟩s in her model —in other words, a set of their *formal* characteristics. The nature of the correspondence between each such set and the features of the texts her subjects write is then articulated in the form of some kind of rating or coding scheme, so that these schemes constitute the requisite bridge principles, and govern the model's interpretation.

So, for example, one set of relationships among T-units (minimum *t*erminable units) is level of abstraction, identified here by using a system for representing text structures developed by Ellen Nold and Brent Davis (1980) called the "discourse matrix." The discourse matrix is based on the assumption that in a text conceived of as a sequence of connected T-units, there are "three possible hierarchical relationships between T-units: superordinate, coordinate, and subordinate" (p. 118). In Formal terms, this means that whatever processes her model includes, one or more of them must account for the production of an output data consisting of a sequence of ⟨T_n⟩s identifiable (somehow) for their minimum terminability, one further property of which must be that each such "unit" is related to the subsequent "unit" in one of these three ways. In order to move from the formal to the empirical—that is, in order to interpret this feature of the model in terms of her subjects' writing—she posits this relationship: ⟨T_1⟩ in the model corresponds to T-units in the texts. Given that correspondence, it is a relatively simple matter to identify each T-unit, and then classify it as either superordinate, coordinate, or subordinate. Insofar as the posited correspondence between the formal element ⟨T_1⟩ and the empirical T-unit is valid—insofar, in other words, as real texts are a sequence of T-units, and insofar as such T-units can only be related hierarchically in these three ways—the model corresponds to, is relevant for, this empirical domain.

She similarly establishes schemes with varying degrees of formality, rigor, and usefulness for each of the three "discourse types" and the other seven "language units." All of this is done implicitly, of course, without the perhaps tedious model-to-domain correspondences spelled out; that part of the explication is mine. Nevertheless, the net result is that she specifies, in these eleven categories, some twenty-five properties of her model's output data; and specifies, as well, the rules by which such properties are to be interpreted in empirical textual terms. There are, of course, other textual features for which the model has not accounted—for instance, it might be that certain letters, seldom used, require microseconds longer to prepare to write, with consequent fluctuations in overall pause times —but what is important is that these three types and eight categories establish the model's scope for the purposes of this investigation.

With the correspondence between model and subject matter thus defined, Matsuhashi can now turn to her corroborative evidence. Remember, the object here is to escape the fallacy of affirming the consequent. Regardless of how many or how plausible the Formal properties of texts for which a model accounts, there is still the danger of circularity:

> What can one conclude about Model A if it fits data B reasonably well? It is possible that Model A does explain the data, and that those data which do not fit are accidental or random disturbances to be ignored. Or it may be that A explains some aspect of the data, perhaps peripheral, while other as yet unknown models would explain other aspects. Or the connection between A and B could be entirely accidental, due to some special characteristics of the particular set of data. In the latter case any further work that treated A as already verified could only mislead and confuse. Without further information, knowing only that B can be deduced from A, one cannot decide among these possibilities (Diesing, p. 57).

No matter, then, that Matsuhashi can explain a comparatively substantial portion of her subjects' output data with a process model that specifies so many formal textual characteristics. So far it is still a model that has been developed from inferences based on the nature of texts. To articulate it more fully, then, and to test its general direction of development, she needs to move outside of text-based inference. This is why she turns to timing the pauses. If the formal textual properties in the model do indeed have analogues in real texts, then the differences among them ought to be reflected in the processes that produce them; and one way that such differences might be characterized is in terms of temporal duration. If the pauses vary in a way that accords with what the model posits about textual complexities— so that, say, superordinate junctures are consistently longer than subordinate ones—it would represent independent support for the relevance of such features in the model. And indeed, this is one of the conclusions Matsuhashi reaches. One of the "major findings of the study," she suggests, is this:

> Throughout discourse of any type, writers must decide on the abstraction level for any sentence—or T-unit—in the discourse. Highly abstract sentences (superordinate) require more planning time than sentences which add detail to support the abstraction (subordinate). In addition, as a result of the pervasive influence of purpose, the writer uses more time to plan highly abstract sentences in pieces of generalizing than in reporting. This occurs because generalization, as a discourse type, requires the writer to make a critical decision prior to a highly abstract sentence which will provide an organizing concept for the entire text or for a section of the text (pp. 129–130).

Despite her phrasing here—Matsuhashi seems to get rhetorically rather carried away in drawing what sound suspiciously like generalizations from what purports to be an exploratory study—this is a reasonable tentative conclusion in formal terms. The model can now specify a temporal relationship among its various processes that corresponds in some roughly proportionate way to the context, location, and complexity of the textual unit produced, and do so with a greater confidence that such a relationship will correspond to the temporal relationship among processes in people writing.

Other kinds of corroborative evidence about the nature of composing are also available. Matsuhashi mentions body language "as clues to patterns of attention and focus" (p. 131); there has been at least one study (by J. D. Williams) of what his title calls "Covert Language Behavior During Composing"; studies of textual changes, either in handwritten or computer-composed texts, might be revealing; so might the study of eye movements during composing along the lines of those used to study information processing in reading, and so on. The leading form of corroborative evidence about the nature of the writing process in Formalist studies, however, has been the one Flower and Hayes rely upon so heavily, the "thinking aloud" protocol. The technique presents problems in terms of testing and refining Formal models that are worth explaining here.

You will recall that the basic idea of a "thinking aloud" protocol, to return once more to Flower and Hayes' "Identifying the Organization of Writing Processes," is to ask the subjects performing some task—in this case, writing—"to say aloud everything they think and everything that occurs to them while performing the task, no matter how trivial it may seem:

> Even with such explicit instructions, however, subjects may forget and fall silent—completely absorbed in the task. At such

times the experimenter will say "Remember, tell me everything you are thinking" (p. 4).

All of this talking during writing is audio-taped and then transcribed, and the text that results is called a protocol.

The technique itself is plainly not terribly complicated. There are some predictable problems—getting adequate recording equipment, learning as investigator how and when to prompt, getting subjects used to the rather foreign activity of speaking while writing, deciding on a set of transcribing conventions, and so on—but nothing that a little instruction and practice can't overcome. Where the problems arise, rather, are in assessing the status of the data collected: Just exactly what do the words transcribed in a protocol represent? No one seems ready to argue that the words the subject speaks are themselves mental processes; they are, rather, some sort of a record or output thereof. But what sort of record or output? And of what processes?

Flower and Hayes seem satisfied that the protocols are a reasonably reliable form of evidence about the otherwise unobservable mental processes "behind" or "beneath" the observable act of writing. They are not identical with those processes—for protocols to yield information about mental processes, they must be analyzed—but they are nevertheless "an incomplete record" of the mental processes which occurred during the performance of the task, and from which an investigator armed with "knowledge of the nature of the task and of human capabilities" is able "to infer . . . a model of the underlying psychological processes by which the subject performs the task" (p. 9). Their metaphor for the analysis itself—it has gained, I think, a certain notoriety—suggests that it "is like following the tracks of a porpoise, which occasionally reveals itself by breaking the surface of the sea. Its brief surfacings are like the glimpses that the protocol affords us of the underlying mental process. Between surfacings, the mental process, like the porpoise, runs deep and silent. Our task is to infer the course of the process from these brief traces" (p. 10).

Not surprisingly, objections have been raised to granting protocols this sort of status. Probably the clearest and certainly the most pointed have been offered by Marilyn Cooper and Michael Holzman in "Talking About Protocols." They make a number of telling arguments about Flower and Hayes' handling of the Formal method in this essay, but their concerns over protocols boil down to two major issues. First, they wonder about reliability: What kind of fictions do people create when they are asked to talk while they write? In a series of questions, they wonder about the relatively narrow focus of

Flower and Hayes' subjects, at least in the protocol portions that have been published:

> Their introspectors notice virtually nothing other than that which is to the point. Do these people never fantasize about, say, lunch? Or were they instructed never to mention such things? Or were the transcriptions of the protocols edited? Do protocols "capture a detailed record," [a reference to a Flower and Hayes phrasing] or invent one, one as literary in its own way as those of [Virginia] Woolf [from whom they have just quoted a passage about her thinking] and other writers (p. 290)?

They are even more concerned, however, about validity. The matter of the reliability of such reports aside, they are not certain about what sets the protocol-talk in motion:

> What stimulus are the writers of the Flower/Hayes protocols responding to? Is it only that of the writing process, or is there something special about the conditions of the writing task set them in this instance? How are we to know that even the same writers would produce similar protocols in a different environment? For, as [Michael] Cole points out, "In so far as we are unable to specify formal equivalence of tasks across settings, we cannot generalize about the behavior of individuals from one setting to another" (p. 291).

In other words, they wonder about what they call the "ecological validity" of protocols. How could it ever be established that the processes inferred on the basis of protocol-based writing would be consistent across individuals, or even across settings for the same individual? In short, what is the relationship between the processes that produce the notes, text, and talk that Flower and Hayes collect, and the writing that people ordinarily do?

As it turns out, though, neither Flower and Hayes' explanations of their use of protocols nor Cooper and Holzman's objections really quite get to the heart of the matter. It is true, of course, that the reliability of protocols is far from perfect—but, as Flower and Hayes are at pains to point out a number of times, no indirect method of getting at what is a largely unobservable phenomenon will be. For the purposes of further refining or testing a model of such a phenomenon, reliability in that sense isn't crucial. So long as the unreliable data is just one form of corroboration, used to help choose among models that can already be demonstrated to account for more reliably accessible data, the dangers are small.

The matter of ecological validity is somewhat more complicated.

Whereas Cooper and Holzman may be right in arguing that the ecological validity of much Researcher inquiry in Composition is open
to question, it is obviously far more vulnerable from a phenomenological than a positivist perspective, and Formalists like Flower and
Hayes are clearly playing by the latter rules. Thus, while the phenomenological assumption is that any describable "reality" will necessarily
include investigations of it, so that intrusions like protocol collecting
will create, in effect, a new reality; the positivist assumption is that
the underlying formal logic of such phenomena exists independent of
our experience of it. For Formalist purposes, then, the question of
whether evidence about the process under study is valid is a matter
of establishing a model's relevance for the various manifestations of
the process under study, including those induced by the investigators.
So while it is true that, for the moment, Flower and Hayes neither
offer nor test much in the way of bridge principles for applying their
model to settings other than the one in which they actually collect
the protocols, that situation could easily enough be changed. They
may be somewhat lax in establishing the breadth of their model's
relevance, but that is not grounds for discarding the technique most
responsible for their development of it.

What is methodologically questionable about Flower and Hayes'
use of protocols, then? The answer lies not in the nature of protocols
themselves, but in the *use* to which they are put. If, as I have already
suggested, they had posited a model of the writing process that accounted quite fully for the nature of texts, and then, in an effort to
further test and develop that model, turned to protocols as one of a
number of kinds of corroborative evidence, there could be little substantive objection; protocols have a fairly solid track record in cognitive psychological research. That is not, however, what they do; and
what they do instead has a curious effect both on what their model
represents and on what it means to test and refine it. Look once
more at the chart (on the opposite page) breaking down the model's
processes and the output data specified for each.

Even a cursory comparison with Matsuhashi will suggest that
these are pretty weak specifications. They are weakened even further
when, for the purposes of testing their model by interpreting these
characteristics of it in terms of a set of real data (protocol and text
from one of their subjects), those data undergo a curious kind of
transformation. First, then, the verbal transcript—the thinking-aloud
talk—itself is divided, without explanation, into units called "segments, each containing a simple comment or statement" (p. 20).
These segments are placed in one of three general categories: "Metacomments—comments that writers make about the writing process
itself"; "Task-oriented or 'content' statements—statements that

PROCESS	COGNITIVE OUTPUT	TEXTUAL OUTPUT
PLANNING		
GENERATING	Information "items" in "associative chains"	Notes: single words, sentence fragments, complete sentences
ORGANIZING	"Writing plan": selected and ordered (temporal, hierarchical) information	Organizational form for notes: systematically indented, numbered, or alphabetized
GOAL SETTING	Goals: criteria for editing	None
TRANSLATING	Propositions (taken from memory)	Acceptable written English sentences
REVIEWING		
READING	Information (now derived from text) re-represented*	None
EDITING	Judgments (about any produced words, read, spoken, written): Yes/No/Change	Text altered to meet standard language conventions, accuracy of meaning, reader understanding, or reader acceptance**

*This is my speculation; Flower and Hayes actually say nothing about this subprocess. So it isn't entirely clear, e.g., whether "read" text becomes "information" in memory, or is directly present as information in TRANSLATING, etc.

**It is not fully clear whether (or when) such alterations invoke TRANSLATING, or if EDITING produces text independently. The authors do indicate that the whole writing process might be invoked, but the example they use introduces fairly extreme circumstances (see pp. 17–18).

reflect the application of writing processes to the current task"; or "Interjections—such as 'OK,' 'Well, let's see,' . . . etc." (p. 21). Again, the origin of these categories is not offered. Third and last, about half of the now-segmented protocol is further divided into three "sections." Examining the segments classified as "metacomments," Flower and Hayes looked for marked changes in the writer's goals, and they claim to find them:

> The writer's metacomments suggest that the protocol can be divided quite cleanly into three sections. In the first section, including segments 1 through 116, the writer's goal is to generate; in the second, including segments 117 through 270, it is to organize; and in the third, including segments 271 through 458, it is to translate (p. 21).

These section designations are not absolute, but relative. So in the first section, for instance, "the most frequent process . . . will be GENERATING interrupted occasionally by EDITING," and so on (p. 22).

With the protocol in this new form, they set out to test the model. Here is their first hypothesis:

> 1. The form of the written material should vary from section to section corresponding to changes in process from section to section. Thus, in the first section, we expect the generating process to produce many single words, detached phrases, and incomplete sentences. In the second section, we expect the organizing process to produce material that is systematically indented, alphabetized, or numbered. In the third section, we expect the translating process to produce many complete sentences and some material associated in the verbal protocol with interrogatives suggesting search for sentence continuation (p. 22).

In order to test this prediction, of course—to check the connection between process and text—they need a way to match the subject's writing with the thinking-aloud transcript. They come up with a pretty simple solution. They divide all corresponding text—text produced, that is, during the protocol segments identified—into sections called "items": "a word, phrase, or sentence that was identifiable in the verbal protocol as being written during a single segment or several contiguous segments. It was, in effect, a short burst of writing" (p. 22). The text produced during the 458 segments in question turns out to consist of 62 such items: 26 in the first, 116-segment section; 24 in the second, 154-segment section; and 12 in the third, 188-segment section.

This package of segments and items is next given to three raters to work on independently. They are asked to answer three questions:

1. Does it have good form, i.e., is it a complete, grammatical sentence?
2. Is it part of a systematically indented, alphabetized, or numbered structure?
3. Is it associated in the verbal protocol with an interrogative suggesting search for sentence completion (p. 23)?

You see how this works. Each of these questions embodies a rule for interpreting the model's posited formal properties. So, for example, if the answer to all three questions for a particular item was "No," and it corresponded with a segment from the first section of the protocol, that was evidence for the model's soundness. Text produced during GENERATING should get a "No" on all three. And, in fact, the overall results of this test tended to confirm the first hypothesis. Most of the items from section 1 got all "Nos"; those from section 2 got a "Yes" for question #2, but "No" on the others; and those from section 3 got a "Yes" for #1 and #3, but not #2.

However, I don't want these seemingly happy results to obscure what has happened to the protocol data Flower and Hayes began with. Our purpose here, remember, is to figure out what the status of the protocol talk is, especially vis à vis text. Consider where things stand. The net result of all this transforming is that Flower and Hayes' model can be said to correspond to their chosen empirical domain ("normal composition") *insofar as a text is a sequence of "items" which either are or are not complete grammatical sentences, and which may or may not be "systematically indented, alphabetized, or numbered."*

It is fairly obvious what has happened here. Instead of designing a model that treats texts as its primary output data, and whose "black box" operations can be somewhat illuminated by protocol analysis, Flower and Hayes have given the *protocols* primary status. The model they posit—inferred, as they put it, from the protocols and their knowledge, as investigators, "of the nature of the task and of human capabilities" (p. 9)—is designed so as to offer a far better account of how protocols, rather than texts, are produced. Indeed, by making the basic textual unit the segment-dependent "item," the model effectively denies text any independent status as output data at all. For interpretive purposes, if a textual feature does not correspond to a protocol segment, it does not exist.

This is not to suggest that Flower and Hayes are not aware of what they are doing. Their explanation of the basis on which they have inferred the model, as well as the way they set about testing it, makes it clear enough that their reliance on protocols is deliberate. Still, two matters seem to me unresolved. First, why claim to be constructing a model of the writing process that almost deliberately does not account for that process's primary output data? Second, and in some ways even more puzzling, is the Formal invisibility of the protocols themselves. Having made the decision to rely so heavily on protocols as the output data from which to infer a model, one might well expect them to show up somewhere in that model. "Text Produced So Far," for example, is a cumulative feature of the "Task Environment"; why isn't there a parallel "Protocol Produced So Far"? In their "Counterstatement" reply to Cooper and Holzman's charges of ecological invalidity, Flower and Hayes argue that while "reporting methods which direct subjects in how they should attend or what they should attend to are likely to modify the processes being observed," reporting methods which do *not*—like theirs—"may slow processes but not change their course or structure" (pp. 95–96). Whether or not that is true, they have already admitted that protocols, like the text, need to be analyzed to get at the processes that underlie them. This in turn means that if their model is to be relevant for the empirical domain they seek to investigate, it must account more clearly for the Formal properties of some output data $\langle P \rangle$, *and* provide a set of rules for interpretation that would articulate the nature of the correspondence between those $\langle P \rangle$s and the protocols that their subjects generate. If and when they should seek to expand the relevance of that model to other empirical domains—to establish its explanatory power, that is, in situations where writers are not required to "think aloud" when they write—they would have to adjust the model accordingly, and seek other forms of corroborative evidence to determine whether its power still holds.

Dissemination: The Uses of Formalist Knowledge

For all the difficulties that Formalist models can obviously present, they also hold out the promise of considerable utility. They can be used in a number of ways, at least three of which have been tried in Composition. Before I explain those uses, however, a reminder is probably in order. Diesing begins his discussion of the uses of models—he identifies nine—by assuming that "an adequate, well-interpreted, and well-analyzed model" (p. 108) has been developed. As I have suggested throughout this chapter, Composition's Formal models do not fit that description very well. Given Diesing's criteria, then, any use of Composition's models as other than first approximations would probably be ill-advised.

To some extent, the Formalists featured in the discussion so far here would seem to recognize the necessarily tentative status of their models and findings. Flower and Hayes, for instance, give as their first and apparently primary ambition that their model ought to serve as " 'a target to shoot at,' and hence a guide to further research on writing" ("Identifying," p. 29). And although they never do show signs of moving to formalize it, in later essays they do work to further elaborate on it, concentrating on such things as writing's episodic movement; and, in "Images, Plans, and Prose: The Representation of Meaning in Writing," the nature of what I have been calling ⟨I ⟩s and ⟨$ ⟩s—or, as they put it, the various forms in which writers "represent what they know at any given point" (p. 122).

The same is true for Matsuhashi, who is adamant about the exploratory status of her inquiry:

> At present, this research is basic and exploratory. Basic research asks questions about how the mind works to compose written discourse even when the results may have no immediate peda-gogical implications. This research is exploratory in that it is a study in search of a theory, not a test of one. Current research on the composing process is pre-theoretical; that is, it lacks a coherent, process-oriented theory from which to generate and test hypotheses. Clearly, the goal of much writing process re-search must be towards model-building: towards the construc-tion of an abstract system which characterizes the writing process and which directs us to regularities or patterns in ob-servational data (Diesing, 1971). Consequently, the search for a model of the writing process is part and parcel of a search for a method to improve or elaborate these hypothetical models (p. 131).

She obviously hopes that the model to which she is here contributing will eventually have greater explanatory power; in fact, she may see such Formal inquiry as in some sense preliminary to Experimental inquiry, with some model providing the "coherent, process-oriented theory from which to generate and test hypotheses." Nevertheless, the spirit of the remarks is consistent with the investigation's de-clared status as a first or even pre-approximation.

But while these investigators acknowledge the limits of their inquiries, they don't always seem to operate within them. In pre-senting Matsuhashi's study of pause lengths in the last section in a way that highlighted its essentially Formal character, I de-emphasized much that is potentially confusing (and possibly confused) in it, con-fusions of the sort I described earlier with regard to Flower and Hayes' model. Consider, for example, this portion of her "Discussion" section, an account of the production of a paragraph from one of her subjects' reporting task:

> Guided by a years-long familiarity with a script for narratives of personal experience, John moves confidently ahead to report an event from his own experience. The opening orientation or generalization signals his intent to tell us how the event was coordinated, and he then proceeds to give us the major sequence of events involved in that coordination. John chooses, from episodic memory, a narrative sequence of salient, easily-codable happenings from the event and presents them briskly, using very little pause time even before T-units as he presents the event. In fact, this paragraph is written so quickly, with so little pausing to plan, that John appears to be writing using automatic, integrated movement sequences in subsidiary awareness while simultaneously using his focal awareness to make propositional and lexical decisions about the next T-unit (p. 129).

This passage is representative, I think, of the kind of difficulty Formalist inquiry presents when it moves prematurely to use a model to explain a set of data. We know, to begin with, that all Matsuhashi has to work from is a videotape of John writing, with the capacity to time his pausings. Readers unfamiliar with Formalist conventions are likely to be somewhat skeptical about basing inferences on pauses in the first place. It smacks of a kind of mind reading. After all, a pause might indicate dead air time, as it were, or hunger, or an itch or a fantasy—any number of phenomena that a model of writing as a task-directed cognitive process won't account for, and which no statistical manipulation of pause times can factor out. And then to be offered, in the face of such skepticism, a narrative like this one, that reads for all the world as if these "events" were observed, that this is what happened . . . it's too much.

Clearly, then, if this passage is to make any sense at all, it must be understood as a Formal account of what happened as John wrote, not the empirical one it reads like: a loose interpretation of the unarticulated model in terms of this videotape of John writing that ranges far, far beyond the careful identification of textual features and their correlation with measured pause times that constitutes the actual study. It suggests, too, that the implicit Formal mode that provides the study's investigative context is more fully developed than Matsuhashi seems to indicate with her protestations that the work is pre-theoretical. It may be pre-theoretical in an Experimental sense, in that it does not test hypotheses; but there is certainly an implicit Formal theory at work. Various features of it, neither mentioned earlier nor explained here, crop up: episodic memory, movement sequences, subsidiary and focal awareness. As with Flower and Hayes' use of long term memory and task environment, we are left wondering: What are these entities? Where did they come from? If they are features of a model, what are their properties, and what is the nature of their correspondence to something in John?

To some extent, of course, one's understanding of the passage depends on a familiarity with the body of literature drawn upon, and the account of the investigation in Matsuhashi's dissertation helps provide that fuller context. It is even conceivable that readers used to thinking in Formalist terms might read this passage, and the other results of the study, in the proper—i.e., Formal—way. But it isn't easy, and the rhetoric of the report, so very empirical in its way of asserting things, makes understanding that much harder, and misunderstanding that much more likely.

There is, as we have already seen, a similar potential for confusion between empirical and formal in Flower and Hayes, although the instances of it are not so pronounced as they are in Matsuhashi. On the other hand, whereas Matsuhashi holds strictly to her investigation's "basic" status—hers is one of the rare reports on an inquiry of any kind in Composition that does not include some sort of "Implications for Teaching" section—Flower and Hayes seem to see no problems with suggesting other applications for their model. At one point, for example, they give it a normative function:

> . . . we should note that we do not intend to imply that all writers use all of the processes we have described. Our model is a model of competent writers. Some writers, though, perhaps to their disadvantage, may fail to use some of the processes. We have, for example, observed a writer who failed to organize. This writer, however, could not be viewed as competent ("Identifying," p. 29).

This would seem to explicitly claim for their model, much as Matsuhashi does implicitly, an area of relevance that extends far beyond what any inquiry they have reported would warrant. Having only sketchily explained their model in Formal terms, they seem to be offering it as a kind of, well, diagnostic tool: "We believe that our model, if it is approximately correct, can serve as a guide to the diagnosis of writing difficulties" ("Identifying," p. 29). The model as it stands might be used as a kind of metaphor, a way of thinking about how someone writes, comparable, say, to the Elbow freewriting/cooking/growing metaphor, but that's all. It would have little or no Formal power. A Formal model could indeed serve such a function, but it seems a heady task for what even its makers admit is a new and underdeveloped one.

One doesn't have to look very far for an explanation for these extensions of the use of Formal inquiry beyond safe boundaries. The pressure for some practical application, however premature, that we have seen at work in every other kind of inquiry is at work here, too, and maybe even more strongly. Indeed, even in a study as carefully framed as Mike Rose's *Writer's Block: The Cognitive Dimension*, where he modestly characterizes what he presents as "a hypothesis preliminary to model-building, a metaphorical representation that highlights several key dimensions and functions of the composing process relevant to the present study" (p. 10), there is a fifteen-page section (pp. 84–99) on "Implications for Instruction" that covers everything from "diagnosis" of composing problems—an explanatory/normative use, again—to teaching invention and even grammatical rules. This is not to say that exploring such implications is wrong; given the audience for the book, they are almost certainly necessary. Nevertheless, whatever the usefulness of the suggestions offered there, and however much the effort of working toward a model has influenced them, their power can only marginally be a function of their Formalist origins.

In fact, probably the best way to characterize the uses of Formalist models in Composition to date is to invoke the term that has cropped up in the other chapters, too: propaganda. Consider Diesing's observations on such uses of implicit formal models in some of the social sciences:

> In general, implicit formal theories in economics and political philosophy are well suited for propaganda purposes. The abstract formal model implicit in such theories is an idealization of one facet of a complex reality, while the verbal language of the theory disguises the abstractness of the model and makes it look like a simple empirical description. Thus the theory can readily perform the essential function of all propaganda, which is to pass off an idealized picture as a true account of reality (p. 121).

At its most effective, of course, such propaganda also has the effect of obscuring those features of the empirical domain that the model doesn't account for—and especially those troublesome ones which the propagandists and/or their audiences would prefer to forget.

Nor has the potential for such abuse gone unnoticed. We have already considered some of Cooper and Holzman's criticisms of Flower and Hayes; it is worth noting in this context that the way they frame them is consonant with Diesing's account of the power of propaganda: "Our acceptance of such [Flower and Hayes'] work, if we accord it, will lead us away from, rather than toward, valid understanding of how writers write" (p. 284). And such criticism becomes even more pointed, and perhaps even better justified, when a Formalist moves out of model-building and into offering pedagogy, as Linda Flower does in her textbook, *Problem-Solving Strategies for Writing*. In a really quite blistering review, Anthony Petrosky, too, formulates his concerns on precisely the grounds we have been considering. Arguing that what sets this textbook apart from any number of others is that "it claims to be based on a cognitive model of how the mind works," he explains his reservations:

> Within the contexts of these claims, this book minimizes, I think, the mind and writing and reading in an oversimplified model of human communications, and then it makes matters worse by patching and covering up the limitations of the model, rather than admitting them. Throughout the book Flower paints a one-dimensional picture of the mind by continually asserting that thinking is problem-solving, and communication is the encoding and decoding of meaning into messages. She ignores reflective, associative, metaphoric, intuitive, and imaginative thinking because, I guess, they are not easily represented as aspects of conscious, goal-directed problem solving (p. 233).

Whether or not these criticisms of the textbook are justified,[2] Petrosky's reaction is clearly to what he regards as its propagandistic properties. And indeed, to the extent to which the approaches espoused in the book are to derive their credibility from Flower's Formalist research, the interpretation of what must be considered a very tentative account of writing as a generalizable pedagogy is problematic. As Petrosky puts it, "this book is deeply disturbing not for its suggestions for writing, all of which have been around for a long time, but for its assertions about the mind and how people communicate" (p. 234)—in short, for the way it threatens to confuse Formal and empirical realities.

None of this is to say that Composition's Formalist Researchers are deliberate propagandists in some particularly malevolent sense. But it is to reiterate the argument I offered early on in this chapter: that Formalist knowledge is the most easily misunderstood of the brands produced by Composition's Researcher methods. Some of the responsibility for the misunderstanding belongs to the Formalists for their tendency to confuse Formal and empirical; just as much probably goes to the field's knowledge consumers for their naïveté. Questions of intent and culpability aside, the fact remains that the nature of implicit Formalist models, their familiar form and seeming comprehensiveness, makes control over their public uses—and abuses— nearly impossible.

9

The Ethnographers

This last of the major mode-of-inquiry based communities in Composition presents at least two very interesting problems. It is, first of all, the most recently "founded" of these communities. While investigators will sometimes point to Donald Graves' 1973 dissertation, *Children's Writing: Research Directions and Hypotheses Based Upon an Examination of the Writing Processes of Seven-Year-Old Children*, or Carol Talbert's 1974 "Anthropological Research Models," as early examples of the method's presence, its emergence as a more or less official entity is more accurately marked by the 1981 publication in *Research in the Teaching of English* of Kenneth Kantor, Dan Kirby, and Judith Goetz's "Research in Context: Ethnographic Studies in English Education." As the title suggests, of course, this really quite unusual manifesto—so far as I know, there is no parallel document for any other method—covers all of English education, not just Composition. Still, for our purposes here, it serves as a useful starting point: a sort of rallying cry aimed at mustering what it can from past investigations under the banner of "ethnographic studies," hoping both to promote a greater understanding of extant work and, perhaps more important, to foster more of it.

Despite such a visible launching, though—lead article status in what must be considered Composition's leading Researcher forum—Ethnographic studies can hardly be said to have taken Composition by storm. Kantor, Kirby and Goetz list some thirty-three titles in the "Composition Studies" section of their article, but the status of all thirty-three is not entirely clear. Seventeen are mentioned as "basic research" which looked closely "at the conditions under which

272

students wrote," and includes investigations as methodologically diverse as Kellogg Hunt's work establishing T-units as a developmental index, Lillian Bridwell's pre-Experimental work on revision, and Flower and Hayes' Formalist studies of the writing process. The implication is that these were necessary precursors of Ethnographic inquiry proper, examinations of "basic processes involved in producing written discourse," after which "it became logical to ask how these phenomena occurred within school, classroom, and even non-school settings" (p. 300).

Of the remaining sixteen titles, five are conference papers (Daly, Florio and Clark, Freedman, Kinney et al., Kirby and Kantor); two are dissertations (Worsham, Nelson); three more (Graves, Calkins, Sowers) stem from the same research project; while still another (Whiteman) is a research review. The net result is that, counting the Graves/Calkins/Sowers work as a single source (the articles cited were published as a series in *Language Arts*, and are based on the same three-year study), we are left with perhaps six genuinely accessible reports on Ethnographic inquiry. There has been a good deal of interest in the method in the years since 1981, with more published articles, dissertations, conference papers, and a general groundswell of moral support, especially from Practitioners and Scholars tired or suspicious of other Researcher methods. Still, as of 1986, the entire corpus of published Ethnographic work in Composition remains well under 2000 pages.[1]

The second of the problems posed by this community, or community-in-the-making, in part a function of its novelty and small size, lies with the matter of definition. In practical terms, it takes the form of deciding what to *call* the method. Any number of terms have been or might be used in addition to the one I have chosen. Consider this list of eight of the more familiar: naturalistic, holistic, descriptive, qualitative, phenomenological, hypothesis generating (as opposed to hypothesis testing), participant-observation, micro-ethnographic. But difficulties in naming are only symptomatic of the far more fundamental problem. To put it quite simply, it is hard to locate this community's methodological heart or center. The methodological boundaries of any community, of course, can blur at the edges, especially within clusters of communities: Experimental work can edge into Formal can edge into Clinical and so on. Still, it is possible with these other communities to locate, at their respective centers, a set of at least implicit tenets about knowledge-making that give them fairly clear and separate identities. In Composition's fledgling Ethnographic community, however, this is not yet the case. For historical and political reasons, it is so far a community better defined at its borders, by its *contrasts* with other methodological communities,

than by reference to any internal coherence: to say what Ethnographic inquiry is not than to say what it is. While its members and
proponents embrace a range of methodological principles which have
in common their divergence from positivist-based, and especially Experimental, principles and procedures, they do not mutually accept
all of one another's principles and procedures. So although some portions of its borders are pretty emphatically marked, its interior remains ambiguous, full of potentially significant differences, many of
which have yet to be encountered, let alone recognized or resolved.

This is not to say that the tenets of an Ethnographic position
are not articulable. On the contrary, as Kantor, Kirby and Goetz,
for instance, are only too aware, such a position can be framed in
militant—and, in the context of educational research, radical—terms.
By way of explaining the rise of Ethnographic studies in English
Education, they cite a growing uneasiness and dissatisfaction with
the results of "conventional experimental design" among English
educators. In doing so, they acknowledge the attractiveness of
"descriptive, qualitative, naturalistic, and holistic approaches" as
alternatives that stand for everything their positivist-based, experimental counterpart is not:

> Researchers with humanistic biases may therefore be attracted
> to arguments that draw sharp distinctions between qualitative
> and quantitative, naturalistic and manipulative, or inductive
> and deductive programs. . . . Theorists like Guba (1980) and
> Mishler (1979) have argued that experimental inquiry empha-
> sizes hypothesis testing, control of variables, "stripping" of
> contexts, educational outcomes, generalizability, reductionism,
> and researcher detachment from objects of study; while natural-
> istic inquiry is concerned with hypothesis generating, grounded
> theory, educational processes, unique and multidimensional
> features of contexts, and the involvement of researcher with
> subject required by participant-observation. These theorists
> argue that since experimental design derives from the natural
> and agricultural sciences, it is less appropriate to the study of
> educational phenomena than methodology developed from the
> investigation of human behavior in social settings (p. 294).

But while they seem disinclined to quarrel with either the soundness
or the appeal of such extreme positions as theoretical constructs,
they balk at consolidating them into any more coherent methodological whole, or accepting them as core principles that might govern
the making of Ethnographic knowledge. However much these arguments may represent Ethnographic inquiry's ties to the patterns of
phenomenological thought from which it was derived, to insist on

them as essential principles, at least for Kantor et al., is unnecessarily divisive, at least partly untrue in practice and, they would seem to argue, somewhat beside the point for research design:

> Unfortunately, dichotomies like those above tend to create rifts within the research community, to obscure some important practical issues, and to misrepresent actual research practices. Cook and Reichardt (1979) have cautioned against confusing heuristic research paradigms with alternative methods and designs. Quantitative strategies can be associated with investigation of processes, grounded theory, and close examination of contexts, while qualitative approaches can serve the study of outcomes, hypothesis testing, and generalizable conclusions. What is important, argue Cook and Reichardt, is that researchers choose methods appropriate to the purposes of their studies, rather than arbitrarily restricting themselves to methods that seem to be required by a particular paradigm (p. 295).

There can be no mistaking the conciliatory posture here. By minimizing the differences between Ethnographic and more traditional kinds of Researcher inquiry, and by introducing this concept of appropriate-ness as a replacement for the various methodo-logics of different modes of inquiry, Kantor et al. attempt to gain a wider acceptance for what is necessarily a minority position, and at the same time to make that position stronger by increasing the number of studies they can include under the Ethnographic banner. And the strategy may well have had the desired short-term effect, threatening —and thereby alienating—fewer of the readers otherwise pre-disposed to dismiss such inquiry as unscientific.

But the price for such conciliation runs pretty high. For one thing, it tends to confuse the distinction between method and technique. It is true, as Kantor et al. suggest, that it makes little sense to tie either particular kinds of research problems or specific techniques (assuming that is what they mean by "strategies") too closely to particular methods. Any mode of inquiry can be adapted to investigate a range of problems in writing; each would require, in some form, access to writers, their texts, their situations, their readers, and so on; and the interview, the questionnaire, the writing prompt—all the means by which information about such things might be gathered— might as easily be harnessed by one sort of Researcher as another. Restrictions in terms of investigative problems or the use of techniques, in this sense, are likely to be arbitrary.

That is not the same thing, however, as arguing that allegiance to particular ways of conceiving of those problems, or of understanding how or what the various kinds of data mean, is arbitrary in the same way. Indeed, such a claim would run counter to the central argument of this book: An inquiry produces knowledge to the extent to which it is sanctioned by some community of inquirers. In their effort to defuse the potential tension between Ethnographic and other Researcher modes of inquiry, Kantor et al. come rather too close to wishing method—including the one they are promoting—out of existence. For while discovering the grounds for some sort of rapprochement among competing modes of inquiry seems a desirable goal—and reducing the hostility of inter-methodological rhetoric, as Kantor et al. do, is certainly a step in the right direction—such grounds cannot be manufactured by collapsing or denying the very real distinctions among the methods. Obviously, anyone can label herself an investigator, mix and match techniques and interpretive rules as she sees fit, and produce, for example, what she wants to call an ethnographic study of statistically chosen episodes of composing aloud as the basis for philosophical dialectic and syllabus design—but no one, finally, is likely to take it seriously. Individual investigators are free to do what they want, but the sanctioning of knowledge offered for communal consumption has less to do with the investigator's declarations about its status—that will only get it a hearing— than a judgment on the part of the other community members that the proffered inquiry meets, within whatever are deemed acceptable limits, the required forms and levels of communal decorum. To the extent that deference to this decorum represents a compromise of individual autonomy in deference to group power, its rules can be regarded as restrictions; and in the sense that the group's members have imposed these on themselves and one another for reasons no more compelling than a shared desire for group coherence—i.e., to make sense to one another—they can be seen as arbitrary. Nevertheless, these are the facts of life for a Researcher. Insofar as the making of knowledge is a public, communal enterprise, the performance of individual investigators is subject to the review of those whose sanction they seek.

To their credit, Kantor et al. do try to hold to their position, whatever its flaws, as they outline the major features of the Ethnographic method and argue its "suitability" for studies in English Education. They eschew the hard-sell, and do not insist that Ethnographic inquiry is suitable for research in English Education because it provides us with the knowledge we want in the form we want it: that the kind of knowledge it produces is different from and more appropriate for the purposes of English educators, their students, and their constituencies than that produced by other kinds of inquiry. But again, the conciliatory posture comes dear. In avoiding the confrontational, hard line position, they subvert the power of the very method they set out to support. By implying that Ethnographic inquiry is not a "heuristic research paradigm," but one of many "alternative methods and designs," they deny its status as a method or mode of inquiry, reducing it instead to a set of technical emphases. That is, they argue that Ethnographic studies tend (1) to be hypotheses generating; (2) to have a reverence for context; (3) to be characterized by what is known as thick description; (4) to rely often on participant observation; and (5) to essentially focus on meaning-making, "the ways in which individuals construct their realities and shared meanings" (p. 298). But they want these to be regarded only as emphases or "aspects," a set of strategic tendencies, and not as the hallmarks of a mode of inquiry whose epistemological and ontological assumptions are distinct from, even diametrically opposed to, those of other modes.

The Nature of Ethnographic Knowledge

Obviously, whatever authority a phenomenologically-based knowledge has must derive from sources different from that of the positivist-based Researcher modes. It may help again here to characterize this brand of knowledge in fairly extreme terms, and assert that Ethnographic inquiry produces stories, fictions. Ethnographic investigators go into a community, observe (by whatever variety of means) what happens there, and then produce an account—which they will try to verify or ground in a variety of ways—of what happened. The phenomena observed are gone, will not occur again, and therefore cannot be investigated again. What remains, then, is whatever the investigators have managed to turn into words. Clifford Geertz perhaps puts it best in Chapter 1 of his *The Interpretation of Cultures*, "Thick Description: Toward an Interpretive Theory of Culture": "The ethnographer 'inscribes' social discourse, *he writes it down*. In so doing, he turns it from a passing event, which exists only in its own moment of occurrence, into an account, which exists in its inscription and can be reconsulted" (p. 19, his emphasis). This is not to say, as Geertz is careful to explain, that the Ethnographer *transcribes*, literally, all of what a community's members say. Rather, the inscribing is an effort to capture what he calls, borrowing from Paul Ricouer, the "said": " 'the *noema* ["thought," "content," "gist"] of the speaking. It is the meaning of the speech event, not the event as event' " (p. 19).

The stories constructed from such inscription are useful because they help us to understand what happened, and to some extent what happens, in the places the Ethnographer studies. That is, as Geertz puts it elsewhere in the same essay, they "reduce the puzzlement— what manner of men are these?—to which unfamiliar acts emerging out of unknown backgrounds naturally give rise" (p. 16). And, presumably, this value holds even when, as is mostly the case in Composition, the settings seem less than exotic—when they are communities, schools, homes in our own culture—because the unfamiliarity of acts and the unknown-ness of backgrounds are a relative matter, so that the behavior of a classroom of American elementary school children dealing with writing can be as puzzling as that of a group of Maori tribesmen preparing for some initiatory rite.

However much they may reduce our puzzlement about the people and places studied, though, these fictions have their limits as knowledge. One such limit lies in the insularity of investigations: the difficulty of somehow extending the findings of an investigation in any one community to any other. Ethnographic findings are made in the context of, and thus tied to, the specific phenomena accounted for. So, for example, reporting on a two-year study in "The Functions of Writing in an Elementary Classroom," Susan Florio and Christopher Clark can generalize sufficiently to say that "Writing was a part of the lives of the children in room 12" (p. 128)—a claim that they qualify and expand upon in various ways during the course of their report. But they cannot safely extend that generalization to classrooms they have not seen; the statistical "bridge" by which positivists connect the various portions of the single, underlying order they investigate is of no use to a phenomenologist. It doesn't matter, then, in what ways what happened in the community that constituted room 12 can be shown to be somehow "typical." Other classrooms, to be sure, will have children and teacher, books and desks, paper and pencils and writing; other classrooms could even be shown to have the same mean IQ score, the same socio-economic mix, or whatever. What matters to an Ethnographer, though, are not these ingredients, common or otherwise, but their peculiar mix in this one instance: how, in the unique interaction of this community's members in this place and time, they came to *mean*. To borrow from Geertz once more, the Ethnographer seeks to understand the "imaginative universe" within which the acts of its inhabitants "are signs" (p. 13). For Florio and Clark, as for all Ethnographers, then, that imaginative universe, that particular mix, is a one-time, one-place occurrence. What writing is or was for children in other elementary classes, they simply cannot say.

It follows, too, that Ethnographic knowledge cannot *accumulate* in the same way as other Researcher knowledge. The pattern is closest, in Researcher terms, to what I characterized as canonical accumulation in the Clinical community. Knowledge-making is essentially a two-stage process. Over time, the community develops a collection, a

canon, of first-level knowledge in the form of what I have been
calling stories, accounts of individual cases or communities. When the
collection is deemed large enough to warrant the effort—and that can
happen as soon as there are two studies—it is possible to make a
second-level kind of knowledge by trying to connect one study with
another, to see what individual studies do or do not share. And even
further levels are conceivable—it is possible to make generalizations
about the generalizations about the original studies, for example—
but for reasons to be explained shortly, these "higher" levels, further
and further abstracted from the particular contexts in which the constituent accounts are grounded, present risks of their own.

Even in this matter of a canon, of course, the phenomenological
versus positivist orientation creates differences. While Clinical inquiry
is, insofar as it accumulates and concerns itself with what is unique in
individual cases, canonical, the grounds for coherence within the
canon derive from its positivist assumptions—are, as we saw in
Chapter 7, paradigmatically driven. In Ethnographic inquiry, individual studies simply don't add up in the same way. With no single,
paradigmatic reality to close in on, the phenomenologically-based
Ethnographers are essentially in the business of collecting multiple
versions of what is *held* to be real by the people they investigate. The
canon, then, might be said to hold together in part because the studies
that make it up share a common concern with what the community
of inquirers has agreed to call writing; but rather than working to
close in on what is essential or fundamental about it, investigators are
better understood as looking to unseat their own taken-for-granted
notions of what it is—what it means, how it comes to mean—by investigating and then presenting accounts of alternate meanings. This
is, I think, the fundamental reason why so many commentators see
connections between Ethnographic inquiry and humanistic, or what I
have called here Scholarly, inquiry: Ethnographers try to make themselves the spokespeople, the media, for what amounts to an inter-
cultural, inter-communal, dialectic. Serving as a kind of alternate
reality brokers, they deliberately juxtapose one imaginative universe
with another, struggling, in the effort, to make both more intelligible
—to themselves, to us, to the inhabitants of those alternate universes.
The result is a canonical knowledge which operates more like
Scholarly, and perhaps especially Hermeneutical, knowledge, than
any other Researcher knowledge.

But even here there are significant differences. Thus, although
we can start by saying that new Ethnographic investigations stand
with respect to old ones in the way that previous critical interpretations stand to new readings, we will need to add the crucial proviso
that no two investigations can ever be of the same "text," the same

reality. This is the essence of its phenomeno-logic. To make the Hermeneutical analogy explicit: Whatever I know of other Ethnographic studies of classroom communities will affect me in my study of a classroom community in much the same way that what I know of Herman Melville's fiction from reading the criticism of *Typee*, *Omoo*, and *Redburn* will affect my reading of *Moby-Dick*—and that's assuming that what these classroom communities have in common as institutional entities is roughly equivalent to the common authorship of the novels. This may seem a pretty remote sort of influence, and an odd way to accumulate knowledge; still, short of somehow bringing the two communities under study into direct contact, the connection can never really get closer: I have no direct access to the communities my predecessors have studied, and they have no access to mine. In this sense, then, the Ethnographic canon is not founded, as is the case in literary study, on a set of original "texts." The counterpart to those originals here is the unique but evanescent social discourse in the time and place originally investigated, and that is irretrievable. Instead, the canon consists of a set of commentaries on those "texts"—that is, the Ethnographers' inscriptions and, subsequently, interpretive accounts of them.

This sort of canon constitutes a peculiar heritage. It is not possible, obviously, for Ethnographers investigating different communities, or even the same community at different times, to work toward some sort of interpretive consensus; there can be no consensus where there is no common text. (They can do so, of course, working in the same community at the same time, and in fact team investigation is pretty common among ethnographers generally.) Insofar as Ethnographic inquiry is driven by dialectical forces, though—by the articulation and opposition of contrasting world views—such a canon has its uses. Knowing what other interpreters have said about how meaning is or has been made in other communities can and should affect how an investigator goes about accounting for how it is made in the one presently under study. For example, previous inquiry can serve as a guide to early observation. Diesing explains it this way:

> The newcomer to a strange culture or organization or personality is overwhelmed by movements and sounds that make no sense and therefore cannot be described. The idiosyncratic cannot be distinguished from the typical for that culture, and the meaning, the connections, of an event are not apparent. . . .
> Many meanings can eventually be sorted out and clarified by long observation and participation, but this is a slow and uncertain process. The process can be speeded up if the observer has a set of reliable guides that suggest things to look for and possible interpretations of what is found (p. 184).

Actually, though, the more likely problem in studies within one's own culture, especially in settings like classrooms, where the investigator, having usually been educated in the same sort of system, is bound to enter with a fairly full and strong set of preconceptions, would be that the newcomer will feel too easily at home, feel that she can, in fact, distinguish the idiosyncratic from the typical, practically without looking. In that situation, the canon serves as a source for disorientation. In either case, the canon functions as a kind of counterbalance: a fixed starting place for the disoriented, or, for the too-familiar, a source of disorientation, a set of readings that can help make the ordinary seem more exotic.

The advantages such a canon offers in this respect, however, can easily enough become liabilities. Since no two communities, no two imaginative universes, can ever be identical, anything borrowed from the interpretation of one and applied to another must be the object of considerable skepticism. A simple illustration will serve. In Florio and Clark's study, they identified four of what they call "functions" of writing in room 12:

1. writing to participate in community,
2. writing to know oneself and others,
3. writing to occupy free time, and
4. writing to demonstrate academic competence (p. 120).

These seem perfectly plausible functions, and an investigator who decided to study writing in another elementary classroom would be bound to be influenced by them, just as Florio and Clark may have been influenced by the functions proposed by James Britton et al., or the discourse aims offered by James Kinneavy. But they could not, indeed *must not*, be accepted as is. Early observations that confirmed their validity would have to be subjected to serious questioning—not because, in and of themselves, they are flawed, but because of the danger that they were preventing the investigator from seeing what functions writing actually did serve in the new classroom community.

Consider, to begin with just a formal consideration, that this quartet does not seem to be composed of parallel elements. Three (writing to participate in community, to know oneself and others, and to demonstrate academic competence) are defined in terms of other people, while the fourth (writing to occupy free time) is defined in terms of scheduling. Why is that? As even Florio and Clark explain it, "writing to occupy free time," during which the children "produced stories, letters, and cards that were colorful and illustrated" (p. 127), was "typically realized as 'keeping in touch' or 'making contact' with others—often expressing in writing what would be hard to express face-to-face" (p. 128). Isn't this the same as "writing to know oneself and others"? Or, perhaps, "writing to participate in community"? It would seem that these categories might have used some refinement even in the original study. It would make little sense to import their flaws, unquestioned, into a new investigation.

Or, to offer a different sort of problem, suppose the new classroom under study were in a Catholic school where the children were required to copy out, write from memory, or put into their own words the teachings in their catechism. This could be characterized as "writing to participate in (religious) community," but is that how the community members would view it? What are the lineaments of "community," and to what extent do they need to be distinguished? Would writing in this sense be a form of prayer? If so, could it be subsumed under any of these four functions without pretty severely reducing it? Do any of them account for what its users would argue were the writing's liturgical or supernatural powers?

The point, again, is not that the four functions Florio and Clark attribute to writing in room 12 are somehow wrong, but that such functions—which may look to be perfectly equivalent in two or more classrooms—may in fact be very different depending on the context in which they appear. So long as such borrowings serve an essentially heuristic function, then, helping an investigator make sense of what she sees, they work to her advantage; as soon as they begin to rigidify, to hinder the investigator's ability to see things in context, they become a liability.

The difficulty of establishing grounds for inter-investigation comparison, let alone accumulation, may be the most difficult feature of Ethnographic knowledge for outsiders—and perhaps insiders, too—to accept. For better or worse, the Ethnographic canon is most influential in this pretty strictly sequential (Diesing uses the term "piecemeal") way: one study informing the next, one at a time, and not as some sort of aggregate. Its phenomenological coherence operates primarily via these juxtapositions, and since each study represents, by definition, an account of a different imaginative universe, that logic will obviously be at its most effective—and so the canon at its most coherent—when one study directly confronts one other study.

Still, the urge to make broader generalizations, to combine individual investigations in some more powerfully cumulative way, is very strong, and perhaps that is not surprising. If in Composition, for instance, we were to gather studies of 100 first-grade classrooms, wouldn't it seem only sensible to try to make assertions about first-grade classrooms in general, drawing strength from that large number of observations? And, in fact, it would be possible to do so—to examine the 100 studies, searching for common themes and patterns.

Keep in mind, however, the status the results of such a search would have. Assuming again, for the sake of illustration, that the institutional homogeneity of first grades was approximately parallel to common authorship, such a study would at best be roughly equivalent to a literary investigation which examined the studies of 100 commentators, each of whom had read one story by Melville, some of whom had read one another's commentaries, but none of whom had read the same story. Such an investigation might lead us to some fairly plausible guesses about the work on which these commentators wrote, but to which we no longer had access, some sense of what Melville stories were like: that they tended to focus on the sea; that they tended to be in the first person; maybe, from quoted passages, a sense of what his style was like.

The same would hold true for an examination of those 100 first-grade studies. We would inevitably come away with a sense of what American first-grades were like: what kinds of authority were exercised, by whom, and in what ways; what the range of interaction patterns tended to be; what first-graders talked like. But in both cases, the process of reaching such a sense would take us further and further away from, on the one hand, what the commentators founded their inquiry on—the stories and first-grades; and, on the other, what we presumably want to know—the relationship between those individual imaginative universes, the stories and first-grades, and our own. In order to make sense of 100 such universes, some features of two would have to be compared, and then either opposed, or joined by compromise. Then that feature from a third would have to be compared, and either grouped with one of the other two, or opposed, or made into a third category. Then a fourth study would be introduced, compared, and so on. From a purist's perspective, the end result ought to be 100 categories for any compared feature, 100 points arranged on whatever continuum we chose to construct. Strictly speaking, no feature could be—*mean*—the same as any other in its unique context. Every compromise, then, would represent a dilution of the fundamental, phenomenal power of the original inquiries.

And, in fact, the further we reduced these accounts, the more we would learn, not about the things we purportedly were trying to understand—the stories and the first-graders—but about the commentators as a kind of community, whose "social discourse" is contained within this collection of their commentaries. In other words, we would come to create an account of *their* imaginative universe as a community of investigators/commentators, trying to account for how they dealt with the phenomena they studied: the features they tended to focus on, the kinds of critical stances they adopted, the rules for evidence they seemed to follow. Our strongest generalizations, then, would not be about Melville stories or first-grade class-rooms, but about the people who studied such things.

From some perspectives—a positivist perspective in particular—this pattern of accumulation may seem a disheartening, not to say crippling, weakness in Ethnographic knowledge. And, indeed, not every member of Composition's loose-knit Ethnographic community seems willing to accept or recognize it. Nevertheless, it represents the logical outcome of the mode of inquiry's premises; to deny or evade it is to deny or evade, as well, the kind of authority Ethnographic knowledge does have, and so to undermine the integrity of the inquiry as a whole. The aim of Ethnographic inquiry, as I argued earlier, is to enlarge "the universe of human discourse," in Geertz' phrase—not to describe it, or to account for it, or to codify it, but to *enlarge* it, make it bigger. Its power as a mode of inquiry, and hence the authority of the knowledge it produces, derives from its ability to keep one imaginative universe bumping into another.

Ethnographic Inquiry

The relatively small number of accessible Ethnographic studies in Composition, coupled with the communal identity problems already outlined, makes the discussion in this section necessarily tentative. The general outline below fits the corpus of work completed to date well enough, so that I will use the subsections to illustrate the form, range, and where possible the rationale for the kinds of methodological variations that characterize the community's work.

In outline form, then, Ethnographic inquiry follows a pattern like this:

1. Identifying Problems: Finding a Setting
2. Entering the Setting
3. Collecting Data: Inscription
4. Interpretation: Identifying Themes
5. Verification
6. Dissemination

Identifying Problems: Finding a Setting

One of the distinguishing characteristics of Ethnographic inquiry is the process by which problems for investigation are formulated. You will recall that Kantor et al., pointing to this process as an issue on which theorists base polarizing distinctions, called it hypothesis-generating. In light of what I have said so far about the nature of

Ethnographic knowledge, it should be fairly easy to understand what such a term means. If the Ethnographer's object is to investigate an "imaginative universe" other than his own, it makes little sense for him to formulate, in advance of such investigation, hypotheses about how things mean in that universe, at least in anything like an Experimental sense. What purpose would it serve? The hypotheses would necessarily reflect either the investigator's sense of how things meant in his own imaginative universe; or, possibly, a guess about how they might work in another such universe, but framed nevertheless in terms derived from the investigator's. The result would be a built-in distortion: the investigator, testing the hypotheses, would have to deliberately bring to bear ways of making meaning that were foreign to the very context he was trying to understand.

It is not the case, however, that Ethnographers enter the communities they study with empty heads, with no preconceptions or assumptions. Quite the opposite, in fact: Ethnographers must enter the new context equipped with the meaning-making rules that operate in their own contexts; and, even, with a heightened awareness of or self-consciousness about them, a sense that they are now foreign, and so suspect. Nor is this somehow a matter of choice. It is an article of phenomenological conviction that we will make sense of what we see and hear and feel, and in our own, customary, ways, whether we want to or not. What the Ethnographer tries to do—and what the notion of hypothesis-generating, then, refers to—is understand what is happening in this new context *in terms of the rules for meaning-making that operate there.* The term itself is rather heavy with Experimental connotations. It isn't clear to what extent it even makes sense for Ethnographers to use it, and it suggests, for me at least, the Experimentalist's perspective: that Ethnographic inquiry is a preliminary sort of work that can *only* generate and not test hypotheses, and is consequently not a distinct mode of inquiry. As we shall see, this is simply not the case. Nevertheless, insofar as Ethnographers can be said to deal in hypotheses, their inquiries will be designed to generate them as an integral part of the investigation, and not as a prior condition for it.

Whenever or however they might be said to develop hypotheses, though, Ethnographers can be said to identify their problems whenever they (a) decide upon some general topic of interest to study: the acquisition of literacy, teachers as a collective agency for change, the functions of writing, the nature of talk about writing; and then (b) choose a community or context in which to investigate it: a town, a school, a first grade, a writing conference. Strictly speaking, I think, it would be safest for the choice of community, of setting, to be primary here. Even the most general topical interest would have to be subject to change after the investigation began, and might even have to be discarded altogether. Suppose, for instance, that I set out to study talk about writing in a college classroom, only to discover that, in the classroom I chose, there was none, or very, very little. This would not invalidate the investigation—my expectations about what ought to happen are irrelevant—but it would alter my focus. Again, strictly speaking, Ethnographers ought to enter a community prepared to explore and account for it as a whole, and not simply along lines predetermined by their own interests. In that sense, Ethnographers cannot identify their investigative problems until they see them. And even then, formulated problems—questions and answers about what happens in that community, and what it means—must be regarded as tentative, subject to partial or total revision either as the investigator's understanding of them grows clearer, or as things in the community change.

As I say, however, this extreme holist stance, this deliberate and really perpetual tentativeness, represents an ideal. The constraints imposed by time, money, professional expectations, and so on force investigators to make choices. Composition's Ethnographers are not immune. Not every investigation can afford to focus on an entire town or village as a whole, or a school, or even a single classroom; some can afford to cover a year, some six months, some only a matter of hours. So, for example, the Ethnographic corpus includes multi-investigator, externally funded work like the Florio and Clark study described above, or Donald Graves' long term study of elementary school children; but also the more modest dissertation studies of a basic writing class, or a writing class small group, or of a single college writer, over the span of 12–15 weeks.

But while resources obviously affect the size and scope of Composition's Ethnographic investigations, they do not present quite the same methodological difficulty that professional expectations, disciplinary ties, do. It may seem self-evident, but consider: one way or another, all of these investigations focus specifically on writing and writing-related activities. That is, so far as I can tell, all of these investigators entered the communities they studied (however construed) predisposed—indeed, determined—to understand, in some sense, what writing was there, how it came to mean. What makes this a difficulty, of course, is that such a predisposition is bound to act as a focal point of sorts, so that at least initially the activities of the studied community are bound to seem to revolve around writing. This doesn't make such an interest any more "wrong" than any other of the ways of framing what is "real" the investigator inevitably operates by, but it does mean that the investigator's effectiveness depends to some extent on how well she can deal with this tendency in herself, this baggage from her own imaginative universe. And it is baggage with a somewhat different status. Her peers are expecting her to report on writing, and her professional status depends on how well she is judged to do so. It boils down to a question of fidelity, of dealing with two loyalties: How much will the investigator's interpretation represent a compromise between what she has come to see and what happens?

Consider, as an example in which the focus is not as narrow as usual, Shirley Brice Heath's *Ways with Words.* This is not specifically a study of writing, although Kantor et al. mention it as focusing on "writing in community contexts" (p. 301), but it does deal with writing to some extent. It is the account of a study, conducted over roughly a ten year period, of two communities in the Carolina Piedmonts (Roadville and Trackton) that deals, as its subtitle puts it, with "Language, life and work in communities and classrooms." The book deals, then, with a wide range of language acquisition and use in these communities. Chapters are titled "Learning how to talk in Trackton," "Teaching how to talk in Roadville," "Oral traditions," "Literate traditions," and so on. In a 421-page book, writing is mentioned on perhaps 50 pages. In Roadville, for instance, "Writing is not a high priority among the 'shoulds' of community members, and there is little interest in extending their writing habits or improving their children's except insofar as writing relates to specific school tasks" (p. 219). In Trackton, writing plays, if anything, even less of a role in people's lives: ". . . the uses of writing and reading in the community are multiple [for writing, in order of frequency: memory aids, substitutes for oral messages, recording finances, public records], though there are few occasions for reading of extended discourse and almost no occasions for writing such material, except by those school children who diligently try to complete their homework assignments" (p. 198). The point here, in any event, is that we end up with a sense of writing's relatively small role in these communities because we see it framed by the other kinds of activities people there engaged in.

Look, by contrast, at the Florio and Clark investigation of writing we have dealt with before. It is the account of a "descriptive study of writing in an elementary classroom" aimed at answering the following questions:

> What opportunities for writing do students find in school? How is writing used by students to meet those opportunities? How do students come to differentiate among the functions of writing and the forms appropriate to them? What role does the teacher play in this process? What other contextual forces are operant (p. 116)?

Now, in fact, these investigators were clearly conscious of the dangers inherent in too narrow a predetermined focus. And, as the following passage indicates, they were careful to try to keep control over it:

> Since the study of Ms. Donovan's class was ethnographic in nature, fieldworkers did not limit their sights to activities explicitly involving writing and its instruction. Instead, pains were taken to spend considerable time in the school and classroom, observing and sharing in the round of daily activities and gradually noting patterns in the use of writing by teacher and students. Similarly, when teacher and students were asked questions about writing in both formal and informal interviews, the questions came at first in terms of the larger context of their classroom life. Finally, in the same spirit, student writings and drawings were collected widely and in large quantity. Gradually, the documents were classified, but with an eye toward how they related to classroom activity and with the help of students and teacher.
>
> The researchers framed and tested working hypotheses about the types of functions writing was performing in the classroom. As the researchers generated these hypotheses about how the teacher and students might be using writing, they tested them against subsequent instances of classroom activity. In this enterprise the researchers sought meaningful contrasts in the use of writing, and indications of those aspects of writing activities that appeared to make a difference to participants (p. 121).

For all their caution in moving toward an account of the functions of writing, though, one nevertheless comes away from their accounts of life in room 12 either without a clear sense of proportion or, more likely, with a sense that writing was enormously important: The other observed events, the larger picture of the community which balances Heath's account, are for the most part not recounted. Moreover, even when, in a section of another article ("Understanding Writing Instruction: Issues of Theory and Method" [Clark and Florio, 1983]), they are able to present larger portions of a day in room 12, one cannot help sensing that their interest in writing shapes not only their account but even the investigation more than they know. In this particular segment, the class is described as "writing" when the students are asked to contribute safety rules they remember from an assembly held earlier in the day. The teacher, acting as "scribe" ("Understanding," p. 254) writes these on the board, with the list finally reaching eleven items. Students are then told to select any one of these eleven and make it the subject of a safety poster, with the option of actually writing (copying) the rule themselves, or of having the teacher write it. The whole episode takes about 45 minutes. (On subsequent days, the students will present their posters to the kindergarten class, and eventually hang them in the hall.)

It isn't that this activity should not or cannot be construed as writing; the authors make it clear that it was deemed writing because at least some members of the community—and in particular the teacher—considered it to be so. Thus, the discussion of the assembly and the group recall of safety rules is a kind of pre-writing and group composing; while the actual copying of a rule (for those who chose to do so) and the poster-making constitute individual writing. Still, some students may have spent no time actually *writing*—i.e., contemplating or making symbols themselves on a page. One has to wonder how the same activity would have been accounted for by investigators concerned with, say, the visual arts (and so for whom the poster drawings, which are more the children's individual productions than the safety rules, might be primary), or curriculum design (who might want to know what "facts" the students learned). The shape of the events as recounted represents their arrangement in time, space, and significance around the class-composed list and the posters. Suppose some other event in the day—recess, lunch, going home— were used as the focal point? In short, while the articles do provide us with a sense of what happened with writing in room 12, it is hard to get a fix on scale, to see writing as part of some larger whole.

Of course, every ethnographer faces this same difficulty in some form. In trying to account for how things come to mean in a particular imaginative universe, some phenomena will inevitably be emphasized over others—and in Composition, the phenomenon of choice is writing. Nevertheless, I think that the narrower the focus provided by a disciplinary-based predisposition, the greater the danger of unaccounted investigator bias, on the one hand, and of under-framed accounts leading to distorted perspective for outsiders, on the other. It is a matter that requires considerable caution by all parties.

Entering the Setting

If there is any principle on which all of Composition's Ethnographic community can be said to reach something like agreement, it is on what Kantor et al. call "the importance of context": the phenomena to be investigated must be examined where and when it exists. In light, again, of what I have already said about the principles of a phenomenologically-based Ethnography, the principle involved is simple enough. In order to explore another imaginative universe, you need to move out of your own and enter, infiltrate, the new one. For operational purposes, this universe is assumed to be a fairly fragile entity, so that entry needs to be made carefully. No matter how careful that infiltration, though, the investigator's presence in the investigated community inevitably changes it; the imaginative universe must deal with the presence of a new person, a new consciousness. What the Ethnographer counts on is that the rules for making meaning that operate there will be tough enough, resilient enough, to accept a foreign presence without substantially changing. The object, at least ideally, is to (1) keep the degree of disturbance as low as possible and (2) try to account for whatever effects there are.

But while the principle is simple, the practical difficulties involved are not. With a very few exceptions—Heath's study, Odell and Goswami's naturalistic explorations of writing in the workplace, Cole and Scribner's study of literacy in the Vai culture—all of Composition's Ethnographic work has taken place in school settings. The problem this presents is obvious: except for teachers, adults simply don't hang around in instructional settings very often. If data collection will depend a good deal on the presence of the investigator as a "participant-observer"—and in most studies to date it has—then both children and teacher must accommodate that presence. And even when, as in Odell and Goswami's naturalistic study, the setting makes the investigators' presence less anomalous, or when techniques for gathering data require them to spend less time there (e.g., video- or audio-taping), the probing will still affect the group being studied, and so must be accounted for.

The most common entry strategies, not surprisingly, would seem to be those dealing with host teachers in classroom studies. Not all investigators explicitly report such strategies. In a study by Anne Haas Dyson that we will look at shortly, for instance, she reports in some detail on her way of approaching the children, but mentions nothing about how she dealt with the teacher—not even, rather surprisingly, to acknowledge her cooperation. (Mention of the teacher is so noticeably missing, in fact, that one is lead to wonder whether Dyson was not, as we saw Sondra Perl was in Chapter 7, both teacher and researcher, but for some reason unwilling to say so.) Florio and Clark report taking more aggressive measures. In addition to interviewing their teachers regularly, they report holding monthly dinner meetings throughout the year of actual field investigation; these meetings were audiotaped and transcribed. Thus, while the teachers were not full partners in the study—in fact, the investigators backed off on their original plan to hold weekly meetings because they imposed too great a burden on the teachers—they were made to feel included in some way ("Understanding," p. 249). In "Collaborative

Analysis of Writing Instruction," Joan Pettigrew, Robert Shaw, and A. D. Van Nostrand report having gone even further: eight researchers teamed with eight teachers to study the teachers' elementary classroom. All of the teachers, along with five of the researchers, served as what were called "non-participating observers" in the eight classrooms. By arranging these thirteen people in rotating teams, and moving from room to room according to "observation cycles," "every class was observed by every team member during the course of the year" (p. 333). The net result was that, on paper at least, the teachers were full and equal collaborators in the study of their own classrooms.

Other kinds of participants present different problems. When Odell and Goswami set out to gather information on the rhetorical sophistication, as it were, of workers in a social services agency, they took pains to establish what they considered an appropriate identity for themselves, thereby laying the groundwork for their relationship with the participants. In preparing interview materials for subjects based on the subjects' own writing, for instance, they "did not want participants to look upon us as English teachers and, therefore, as authorities on style. Consequently, we deliberately ignored variations (e.g. in syntax or level of diction) that we felt participants might associate with English classrooms" ("Writing in a Non-Academic Setting," p. 204). In addition, to "reduce anxiety that might arise from being interviewed about one's writing by an English teacher, we repeatedly assured participants:

1. that all the options listed on the interview sheet were equally "correct";
2. that we felt that the interviewee was the expert on making appropriate choices in writing for the agency where he or she worked;
3. that we were interested solely in the reasoning that led the writer to prefer one alternative to another" (p. 206).

The bulk of the participants the Ethnographers have dealt with, though, have obviously been students, of ages anywhere from two years on up—and they present their own special problems. It is clearly difficult, for one thing, to treat elementary school children as collaborators in the way that Pettigrew et al. treated the classroom teachers. And so far as I know, even in studies involving older students, no investigator has tried. We will consider the kinds of problems posed for adult investigators trying to enter the imaginative universes inhabited by children shortly, under Interpretation of Data. Here I want simply to consider the difficulties inherent in the mechanics of it: To consider how the presence of a new adult in a classroom, or a small group, or a writing conference affects that context. For that purpose I want to turn to the aforementioned study by Anne Haas Dyson, reported in "The Role of Oral Language in Early Writing Processes." Dyson's purpose, as the title suggests, was to investigate how children use talk in their early writing—that is, writing "which occurs before formal instruction within the school context begins" (p. 2). Her research site is a kindergarten in which the teacher, following the district's curriculum, "did not include formal instruction in reading and writing in the beginning of the school year." As I suggested above, she says little about her relationship to the teacher. Here is how she frames her introduction to the students:

> I established a writing center, asking the children simply to write; they wrote according to however they defined the writing task. Since my focus was on oral and written language use, I considered this provision for child- (as opposed to researcher-) initiated and structured writing critical. A child's intention in a particular situation "sustains and supports" the resulting utterances (Donaldson, 1978, p. 75). Thus, presenting children with a writing task which is isolated from a personal intention of their own might lead to inaccurate judgments of their writing abilities. It is each child's interpretation of the writing task (i.e., what the child intends to do) which shapes the resulting oral and graphic activity.
>
> While at the writing center, I both observed and interacted with the children to gain information on their perceptions of what "writing" entails and the reasoning behind particular writing behaviors (p. 4).

There is nothing intrinsically objectionable about the method described here; it seems carefully planned. But from an Ethnographic perspective, her handling of context is puzzling in two ways. First, if writing was not something that ordinarily occurred in this kindergarten—so that, in order to study it, Dyson needs to establish a writing center—then what does it mean for her to introduce it there? Once she is present, she gets the students to write (mostly during their "free-choice period," p. 5) by asking them individually to " 'come over and write with me' and, then, to 'tell me what you wrote' " (p. 6). She seems to regard this as non-intervention: ". . . I was a curious participant in a child-structured situation—not a teacher-figure who routinely requested the completion of particular tasks" (p. 8). But is this non-intervention? Would they have written otherwise (or at all) without the friendly lady who seemed to take such an interest in it? And would their writing—or their talk—have been the same?

Second, one would assume that, having deliberately chosen the school context for the inquiry, and even risking what would seem to be this considerable intrusion to keep it there, that somehow that context would play a major role in her interpretation of the children's behaviors. The promise is implicit, at any rate, in the way she seems to align herself with the Ethnographic community. She refers to her primary technique, several times, as participant-observation, and even refines it by terming it "reactive"—that is, as following the students' lead in her interactions with them. She describes her goal in studying them "as a phenomenological one," as one of entering their imaginative universe: to understand this early writing "from the point of view of the children—from within the framework of each child's understandings and intentions" (p. 2). She even points out, albeit parenthetically, that she observed the "case study children in situations other than the writing center" for nine of the twelve weeks she was there (p. 8).

For all that, though, her findings offer no reason—except maybe convenience—for her to have conducted this investigation in school, as opposed to a clinic or the children's homes or wherever. Her reports on individual writers take no account of where particular writing sessions fit into specific days—what preceded or followed them that might help explain what happened. The same is true for her analysis of the writing itself. Thus, while she delineates ten different kinds of writing events, they all begin with the child's arrival at the writing center, and end with either a change to another type of event or with the child leaving the center. What happens before they come and after they go—a missed breakfast, a fight with a playmate, a story read by the teacher—is not considered. Except for the essentially superficial explanations of references, then, the children's discourse is not seen in the larger context of the classroom, but treated as an isolated phenomenon, something that happens at, and is explained in terms of, the writing center.

I don't raise these points to discredit the study, or to split methodological hairs. After all, while it seems to me that Dyson aligns herself with the Ethnographic community, and that the study's parallels to Graves' work suggest that Kantor et al. would certainly place it there, Dyson herself makes no explicit methodological claims in that direction. Nevertheless, for all the agreement about the importance of studying phenomena in context, this matter of just how that importance is to be recognized seems to be one of the areas of as-yet unfaced, unresolved confusion within the Ethnographic community. Dyson's is a valuable inquiry, and we do learn from it something about how children use talk when they write at a writing center established by a researcher in their classroom. It is also true, though— and this holds for much of Graves' work as well, where children are observed closely only during "writing episodes"—that she is either willing to sacrifice much of the value of conducting an investigation in context, or has very different, unexplained reasons for doing so. For despite the Ethnographic elements in her investigative style—her sense of making a careful entry into the setting, and her phenomenologically-defined sense of purpose—her perspective remains essentially Clinical. Thus the intrusiveness of the writing center seems to pose no problem. And, while she views the children as "active constructors of knowledge" (p. 2), and is anxious to understand their use of oral language in this particular social context, she appears to narrow the boundaries of that context down to the edges of the table at which the children write.

The point is that simply moving investigations out of the laboratory or clinic and into the "field" does not automatically make them more powerful or authentic or, even, more "ethnographic." The pattern Dyson follows, I think, is the pattern we have already seen set by Kantor et al.: the investigator would like to claim the grounded-in-context power of a phenomenologically-based Ethnography; to say that what she reports is an interpretation of what the children felt and saw, of their "point of view." At the same time, she does not want to be bound by that specificity, to have her account of the role of oral language in early writing processes be restricted to the single imaginative universe she has actually investigated. The result is this rather mixed bag of technique, a sort of Clinical study conducted in a school setting, with children who are both real people in a specific place and time, and who write and draw and talk in and of that place and time; and yet also types, exemplars, who will or can be made to produce manifestations of a phenomenon called "oral language use in early writing" which transcends individuals and place and time. It is at best an uneasy compromise.

Collecting Data: Inscription

As the discussion of Dyson's writing center strategy would suggest, the chief constraint Ethnographers face in terms of their methods of data collection must be their concern for context. The central Ethnographic technique is participant-observation: the investigator tries to become, in some sense, an acceptable member of the community under investigation. At the risk of belaboring the matter, I'll put it in terms of the informing philosophical perspective once more: The object is to gain some understanding of an alternative imaginative universe by coming, through a kind of gradual immersion, to inhabit it. Obviously, though, the degree to which such habitation is possible varies considerably. An investigator who studies a religious sect within her own culture—a born-again Christian group, say—could quite conceivably become a full-fledged member, and so in a sense faces the risk of losing, via conversion, her observer status altogether. Full participation is genuinely possible. Participant-observation of adults in classrooms full of children is a different matter. Investigators can obviously inhabit such classrooms, but while there is some chance that they could gain full membership as teachers, they run little risk of losing themselves in the children's world—or, perhaps more to the point, of having the children lose sight of them. Even the friendliest of adults, however deft with children, cannot fully enter the world of the playground or the lunchroom, cannot participate fully in the social discourse she might be able to observe. As we consider here some of the means by which Ethnographers have tried to inscribe the discourse of their host communities, we'll need to recognize that this matter of gathering data is always a compromise between what the investigator might like to know and what, in terms of intrusiveness, it will cost her to find out.

The participant-observer's primary mode of inscription is usually called field notes, and they do in fact constitute the major form of data in most of Composition's Ethnographic studies. As with so many features of their method, Ethnographers seem to have relatively little to say about them. Donald Graves offers the fullest account of his field notes in his early study, "An Examination of the Writing Processes of Seven Year Old Children." His procedure was to watch selected students in the classroom until "the researcher noted that a child was structuring materials for a writing episode," and then to move "close to the child," usually seating himself "directly in front of his [the child's] desk or table" (p. 231). Watching the child work from this upside-down position, he would keep track of pre-composing behaviors—drawing, for example—by reproducing the drawing, and numbering the operations "to indicate the sequence in which the picture evolved. Notable behaviors that accompanied each step were also recorded" (p. 231). When the child appeared to begin what Graves calls "the composing phase," he would switch to a three-column notation system. Beginning and ending times would be recorded at the top and bottom, respectively, of the center column. The left column was used to record just what the child wrote; each word was given a number to indicate its place in the sequence. If he saw a behavior accompanying the writing of any of these words that he regarded as significant, Graves would circle the number, and then do two things: first, use a shorthand code to classify the behavior in the center column (e.g., RR = rereads); and, second, explain the behavior in a correspondingly numbered note in the right hand column (e.g, "36—rereads to 36. Lost starting point").

No other published account is anywhere near as explicit. Florio and Clark offer some fairly lengthy excerpts in which the frequent recording of time intervals indicate that some kind of note-taking was going on during the events observed, but there is no sign of the kind of coding Graves reports. In the Pettigrew, Shaw, and Van Nostrand study, the non-participating observers took notes (at least in the early observations), from which tentative categories were derived in the form of an observational grid, which was subsequently retested, refined, and so on. The general direction of the investigation is thus similar to Graves' in its movement toward a coding scheme, but while the finished grid is offered, neither the form nor the content of the early notes is specified.

This reticence about the details of field notes matters because, as should be obvious to even the untrained eye, there can be considerable variation in what constitutes field notes: they can be taken during events, in a sort of informal shorthand; they can be taken in some formal shorthand system; they can be in some code form, like Graves'; they can be taken as soon after events as is practicable. And in any of the rougher forms, the notes may well be rewritten and/or fleshed out when time allows. Moreover, *what* gets into the notes is as or more important than how: How does an investigator know what to note? The rule of thumb is that everything must initially be assumed to be of interest, but that doesn't solve the practical problem of where to begin. How does a participant-observer, working alone or in a team, keep a check on her note-taking and observational tendencies? What patterns does she fall into? Why? We will deal with the issue of verification below, but will focus for the most part on post-interpretive concerns. What's at issue here is that participant-observation would seem to require as deliberate a self-consciousness about the kind of notes that get taken as about their interpretation.

In any case, it is a rare study that restricts itself to field notes alone. Perhaps in an ideal Ethnography, the participant-observer's intrusions would be limited simply to his presence and participation, with time—the simple opportunity to participate in and observe more and more of the community's life—presenting all the chances for information-gathering the research required. But field conditions are never ideal, and Ethnographers can and do fall back on a wide range of other techniques: interviews, both formal and informal; audio- and video-taping; the obvious expedient of collecting or copying participants' writings; asking participants to keep journals or logs, which are then collected or reproduced; visits with participants outside the context of the investigation; reviews of written records (test scores, school grades, health records, etc.). The techniques themselves are neither very special nor intrinsically "Ethnographic." Training and practice no doubt make investigators more adept with them, but what matters most is their deployment in different settings, the when and where and how of their uses. To outsiders, for example, audio- and video-taping no doubt seem like an ideal replacement for field notes: the machine can record what happens. But in fact very few of the studies to date rely on such recordings in any very significant way. For one thing, taping can be obtrusive, making participants self-conscious. For another, it adds considerably to the hazards of field work. Broken tapes, stalled machines, inaudible recordings—in the absence of careful field notes, these can pretty well ruin a day's work. And more important, of course, machines do not record "what happens" in some neutral way, any more than an observer can. The participant-observer, remember, is trying to understand how things come to mean, and meaning in context derives from more than just some of the talk, or what can be seen from a single camera angle. It is the whole point of *participant*-observation that transcribing and inscribing are different activities: being there, consciously trying to participate in the community's social discourse, is crucial. Hence, tapes have been used for various purposes (as a supplement to field notes, e.g., as the focus for an interview, or to calibrate observers' use of some instrument) but they are no replacement for an investigator. And this is true for the other techniques. Each is limited in its own ways—carries with it a certain bias, increases the investigator's visibility, piques the curiosity or heightens the self-consciousness of the participants—and therefore needs to be used with appropriate caution.

The limitations of these techniques raise a question that brings us up against one of the boundaries of Ethnographic inquiry: Can there be an Ethnographic study, as I have defined it here, without participant-observation? That is, to what degree is it possible to understand another imaginative universe without direct and active participation in it? Kantor et al. list participant-observation as one of their five key "aspects" of ethnography, but on this point, as on so many others, it is hard to tell whether they see it as an option or a tendency or as *de rigueur.* Two of the studies they mention provide useful tests of this boundary. The first is the Pettigrew, Shaw, and Van Nostrand investigation we have looked at already, in which there were no participant-observers in the classrooms studied, but only participants and non-participant observers. The investigative trinary groups they worked from consisted, then, of the classroom teacher, a non-participating observer, and "a third member who had only the observer's notes," and so had no direct experience of the events in question at all.

The trinary groups' task early on in the study was to sort

"instances of behavior into categories, most of which were established during the first few observation cycles." Later, they tried to "fit what they had observed into the categories of the emerging descriptive system, noting instances in which this system was inadequate, wherein current categories needed to be modified or new categories added" (p. 333). The meetings of these trinary groups, say the authors, "provided an ideal forum for conducting these analyses":

> None of the three had an unbiased or fully informed view of the lesson, and they all had different perspectives on the teaching of writing. Thus, the trinary meetings met the criteria for triangulated inquiry set forth by Sevigny (1981): a comparison of more than one setting using a variety of perspectives. In these meetings the three members combined their various perspectives to derive a description of the teacher's intentions during the lesson (p. 333).

The end product of this analysis is an observational grid. The horizontal axis represents a set of nine "activity constructs," categories into which any writing lesson can be broken down (e.g., Presenting, Giving Instructions, Orienting, etc.). The vertical axis, then, consists of four groups of what might be called modifiers, via which observers could keep a coded record of some of the details of the activities observed. The four modifier headings were Participants (who was working with whom), Mode (via what interaction), Materials (paper, pencil, handouts, etc.), and Foci of Activities (concerning what textual or rhetorical features). The checklists under these headings range from four items for Mode (Telling, T[eacher] Q[uestions] /S[tudent] responds, T Q/no response, S Q/T responds) to eleven for Foci (e.g., Spelling, Capitalization, Punctuation, Purpose/ Audience, Form). In addition, the group identified four variables which they felt allowed them to differentiate among writing lessons: the duration of what they called "subscenes," their basic observational unit; the proportion of the lesson spent on each activity; the sequence of activities; and the characteristics that modify each activity (expressed in the modifier checklist).

All of this makes considerable sense. But the tendency of this study is much the same as in Dyson's. Basing it on the observation of 160 writing lessons, 20 per teacher, seems to ground it in a specific context, a single time and place. And yet when these observations are analyzed, the object is not to discover how or what writing instruction came to mean in each of those particular classrooms—the students' perspective, after all, is neither represented nor considered—but rather what sorts of general descriptive categories the observed activities will fit into; and then, as the investigation proceeds, how those categories can be modified to operate successfully across classrooms.

As useful and interesting as the process of constructing such a grid might be, then, it clearly moves the investigators farther and farther away from the ways in which meaning is made in any of the observed classrooms. Rather like Dyson's "writing event," the "writing lesson" in this study comes to be a phenomenon which, despite being observed in the context of the classroom, actually acquires its *meaning* elsewhere—that is, in the context of the trinary groups and, later, the full research group. As the nine activity constructs and their definitions are gradually defined more precisely, and as the team's ability to apply them to any classroom lesson, regardless of its contextual particularities (to a reported agreement high of 80% as measured by their coding of a video-taped lesson), the study's authority becomes grounded more and more strongly in the research group as a community, and less and less in the classrooms visited.

What is the significance of involving the teachers in observation and analysis in addition to teaching? That is no longer very clear. If the eight teachers had constituted an integral community to begin with, and if the researchers had then joined it as participant-observers, there would be better grounds for the authors' claim that these constructs "represent the teachers' perceptions of what they *intended* to happen from moment to moment in the lesson; these constructs were used by the teachers in directing ongoing writing lessons" (p. 335, their emphasis). As it stands, however, those constructs represent something rather different. The teachers were from different schools, were not a regular group, and were convened for the express purposes of this study. Therefore, the constructs cannot be simply the *teachers'* perceptions of their intentions. Rather, they must represent those of the research group, as construed in the observational notes. Hence, their having taught the lessons that prompted the writing of the notes under study can be said to supply the difference in perspective the sought-after triangulation requires (but so could the involvement of a student), and it is surely of political significance that they are included on the research team. But because the investigation does not aim to discover how the actions of each teacher acquired meaning in his or her particular classroom; and because, moreover, whatever the teachers might think about their actions as they come to mean in the classroom is necessarily altered by the interaction within the trinary groups (else why not let the teachers work alone?)—for these reasons, the teachers' role as participants in the original event lends no special authority to the findings, and indeed influences those findings probably less than the role of observer, who produces the text which is, after all, the object of the trinary groups' work.

The community under investigation in this study, then, existed in neither the classrooms nor in the schools, but in the research team itself. What we learn from the study is how, over the year of investigation, this small group constructed its version of a shared reality— one framed by the nine constructs, the four sets of modifiers, and the four differentiating variables. Does this reduce the value of the study? Not especially. But it seems to me an important qualification of its authority. As even the authors recognize, "the procedure used to develop the grid, and the separate concepts represented in it, are more useful than the grid itself" (p. 335). In other words, this study is better understood as a mirror for the research group than as a window on the classroom communities. In its findings the investigators come to see reflected their own habits of mind, their own rules for making meaning, their own ways of construing the kinds of texts they worked from. My question about the absence of participant-observers in the classrooms turns out to be something of a red herring. The study might be characterized, in its way, as phenomenological, an examination of experience; but the experience being examined, the *shared* one, is the experience of analyzing observational notes made by members of the research team. In that sense, and perhaps depending on their degree of self-consciousness, all sixteen people were participant-observers, participating in the collection and interpretation of the lesson notes, and observing in themselves and others the rules they invoked in doing so. If this is Ethnography, then, it is best understood as the Ethnographic self-study of a research group.

A rather different problem is presented in what Lee Odell and Dixie Goswami call, in "Writing in a Non-Academic Setting," their "naturalistic" study of writing. Citing a tradition in research on spoken language, they define a naturalistic study as one that examines the phenomenon in question (in this case, writing) "as it occurs spontaneously in the context of day-to-day activities" (p. 201). Basically, then, this study of a social services agency focuses on the writing of eleven individuals (administrators and two types of caseworkers) chosen from a larger group of thirty who were in turn identified by two "key informants" ("administrators who were thoroughly familiar with all aspects of the agency and with agency personnel," p. 203) who were simply asked to choose workers whose jobs were "likely to involve a good deal of writing" (p. 204). However, the investigation involved neither participant- nor non-participant-observers at all. Instead, all information was gathered via three other techniques: specially designed data-gathering interviews; collected writing samples; and a stylistic preference test.

Of the three, the data-gathering interviews seem most ingenious. These interviews were based on variations found in a collection of the writings of each subject—variations, for example, in how the writer addressed the reader, or signed her name. The interviewer would select one text actually written by the subject, and then at the appropriate junctures (the salutation, say, or the signature) generate one or more alternatives that reflected choices made in the subject's other work. In the interview, the researcher would ask the subject, for each such juncture, whether she could accept the alternative(s), and why or why not. By this means the investigators felt they could get the writers to articulate at least some of the rules that governed their writing in the context of their jobs.

The writing samples served two functions. One was that just described: providing information about the kinds of variations in a given subject's writing. They were also used, however, as a source from which to characterize differences in writing between different kinds of jobs: "Within a given institution," they wondered, "is the writing of workers in one job significantly different from that of workers who hold quite a different job" (p. 207)? To find out, the samples were analyzed and compared in terms of six textual features: mean number of T-units, mean T-unit length, mean clause length, mean number of clauses per T-unit, mean number of passive constructions per T-unit, and types of cohesive markers used and the mean number of each type per T-unit.

And finally, the stylistic preference test (my term—they call it "Judgments about Acceptability of Style," p. 207) presented participants with three versions each of nine short pieces of writing in which some stylistic feature had been varied according to what were characterized as a verbal, a passive, and a passive-nominal style. They were asked to read these, and then to rank the three pieces in each trio as most, less, and least acceptable. From these rankings, the investigators hoped to see whether the subjects "consistently prefer one style of writing," and whether those preferences varied according to the type of writing (e.g., "pink" memo vs. "white" memo).

The study's results are framed modestly enough (although the phrasing—which shifts to a very general level, qualified only by an introductory "at least for participants in our study"—is a little surprising). Two of the techniques, the data-gathering interviews and the analysis of the writing samples, "indicate that, at least for participants in our study:

1. Writing within a single organization does vary from one group of writers to another:
   - The two groups of caseworkers gave somewhat different justifications for the choices they made in their reports;
   - Texts written by the two groups of caseworkers differed significantly with respect to a number of linguistic features;

2. Writers in non-academic settings are sensitive to rhetorical context:
   - Administrators in our study varied several features of their writing according to the type of writing they were doing;
   - When giving reasons for preferring one alternative to another, both caseworkers and administrators showed a complex awareness of audience, self, and subject;
   - Caseworkers and administrators rarely justified choices by citing an a-rhetorical rule, and they never relied exclusively upon one type of reason in justifying a given type of choice" (pp. 220–221).

As it turned out, though, the results of the stylistic preference test did not support these conclusions. Insofar as its results were an indicator, job type "had little influence upon participants' judgments about what constituted 'acceptable' style," within or across types of writing (p. 221).

However, the question here, you will recall, is about where such an investigation falls with respect to the boundaries of the Ethnographic community. As I have indicated, Kantor et al. include it (albeit without citation) in their section on Composition. On the other hand, Odell and Goswami simply characterize it as "naturalistic." What kind of authority can their findings finally claim? The answer, I think, is that the study is best understood as Clinical, in the tradition of Emig's study of twelfth graders: a relatively in-depth examination of eleven writers who, by virtue of the process by which they are selected, are deemed in some sense "typical" of workers in this agency; while the agency, to judge by the broad wording of both research questions and findings (e.g., "To what extent are non-academic writers sensitive to rhetorical issues . . ." or "Writing within a single organization does vary from one group to another") is considered broadly representative of such organizations.

The only intersection between the Ethnographic and naturalistic method as exemplified in this study, then, is that in both investigators collect their data in the field. Odell and Goswami might be said, via their interviews, to get a glimpse of the workers' imaginative universe, but from an Ethnographic point of view they have no way to make sense of what they see. That is, while the writing may have been *produced* in context, the researchers have no access to how it comes to mean there—no apparent interest in when or where or why or for whom it was written, nor in how it was subsequently received, read, and acted upon. Interpreted in light of field notes, the data-gathering interviews could be useful in an Ethnographic study, but not by themselves: we have no way of knowing how the social discourse that they represent corresponds with the workers' regular patterns. And the other two techniques, which look for significant patterns in the handling of specific textual features identified *outside* of the community, are both clearly positivist in their assumptions. Once again, let me point out that this analysis is not intended as a criticism of the study. Odell and Goswami are generally quite careful about explaining its limitations. But Kantor et al., presumably on the grounds of its concern with writing in some non-laboratory setting, group it with studies like Heath's and Florio and Clark's, thus implying that some of its authority derives from the same Ethnographic roots. And that simply is not the case.

Can there, then, be a phenomenologically-based Ethnographic study without participant-observation? I don't think so. As the adjective suggests, the *phenomenological* Ethnographer's chief investigative tool must be his or her own consciousness.

Interpretation: Identifying Themes

Given their general reticence about data collection, it should be no surprise that Ethnographers have also had relatively little to say about how those notes, and to a lesser extent data collected via other techniques, are interpreted. Not that the general pattern is terribly complicated. As we have seen, the ongoing life of the investigated community serves as the central text, perpetually unfolding before the investigator. From this source, the investigator gathers her various kinds of data, working to create what I have been calling, following Geertz, an inscription of the original social discourse, a consultable record of the otherwise evanescent events. Early on in this process, there is likely to be a good deal of confusion; the threads that tie events into a coherent whole for the participants will not be clear to the newly arrived participant-observer. And besides, an Ethnographer is likely to land in this new setting out of time, as it were, in the middle of the story: the meaning of much of what happens will stem from a past to which she has no direct access.

As the inscribed data accumulates, though, the investigator begins to go back through it, to reflect on it, looking both for patterns— events which seem to recur in some sort of connected way—and for explanations of them, ways in which such patterns seem to make sense. The entire process, I daresay, is an automatic enough human activity; one way or another, we will make sense of what is happening around us. The difference here is that that normal activity is harnessed, made more deliberate and self-conscious, with emphasis given to finding patterns and explanations that will make sense not only to the investigator, but to the members of the community being studied as well.

These patterns and their explanations—*themes* is a useful term for them—are then tested against both new events and more inscribed data: Does the string of events connected as a possible pattern continue? Do the new pieces fit the old explanation? Do other events, previously only noted in passing, now seem more important?

As was evident in the discussion of Ethnography as hypothesis-generating, this process is a continuous one. One reason is logistical: data from most Ethnographic studies piles up at a really quite remarkable rate. Florio and Clark, for example, note that the "processes of reduction and analysis of the descriptive data would have been unwieldly, if not impossible, if we had waited until the completion of data collection to begin them" ("Understanding," p. 249). But there is more at stake here than logistical convenience. Far more than with the other Researcher modes, the division of Ethnographic inquiry under discrete subheadings—the collection of data, their interpretation, and the subsequent testing of those interpretations—is misleading. As I have already suggested, an Ethnographer is never a simple recorder in the investigated community, but always an improving, though perhaps fledgling, meaning-maker. Whether or not he deliberately works through this data before the study ends, positing and challenging, refining or discarding themes, he will necessarily interpret the experience he inscribes, and will begin to test—simply by acting on—interpretations he has made, even if they have not been articulated.

The cycle of inquiry, then, runs from experience to inscription to interpretation and back to experience again, with interpretation thus emerging as a series of attempts to ease the tension between event and inscription. Investigations that bypass the full cycle by waiting until after all data has been collected run the obvious risk of short-circuiting it, and thereby losing some or all of their Ethnographic authority. In Dyson's study of oral language use, for instance, she waits until the eleventh week to begin analyzing her data. Rather than refining and testing her interpretations against further experience, then, the work is all retrospective. She "initially based the analysis on the data collected during the first two weeks of the post-assessment observational period (phase 2)" (p. 9), and then reworked it in light of data from later weeks, which she has collected without benefit of any explicit experience-inscription confrontation. Every study, of course, is at some point closed—new data stop coming in. But the primary text in an Ethnographic study, and its primary source of power, must be the social discourse itself, and not the investigator's inscription thereof. Ethnographic interpretation derived solely from inscribed data, without recourse to actual events, is like literary criticism from reading notes, without recourse to the original text: it can be done, but at a price. The pattern Dyson follows, working only within the closed body of collected data, is far more in keeping with the Clinical tendencies of her study than with the tenets of a phenomenologically-based Ethnography.

Much more difficult to explain than interpretation's general outline, however, is its substance—saying by just what means such interpretations arise. If Ethnographers have done little explaining of it, there are good reasons. They sometimes discuss the mechanics involved. So, for instance, in the Pettigrew, Shaw, and Van Nostrand study, we are told that the trinary groups met after every four observations; the trinary minutes were then circulated to the full research team; and then every four weeks or so a plenary session of the full research team met, on Saturday mornings, for three to four hours. But what happens during these various meetings? The trinary groups "sorted instances of behavior into categories" (p. 333). In the plenary meetings, the task was to move from the trinary group minutes to "the synthesis of concepts into a descriptive system" (p. 333). But how did the sorters decide what behaviors to focus on, or what categories to put them into? How did "synthesis" come about? We can assume there was reading, talking, writing, and thinking involved; that patterns were discovered, explanations offered—but where did they come from?

Florio and Clark have perhaps the most to say on what is obviously a difficult subject. "For the most part," they write, "categories for analysis were arrived at inductively, as participants sifted the naturalistic data for patterns of meaningful activity in writing and writing instruction. In addition, insights from previous research literature on both the writing and teaching processes, and the experience of participating teachers provided potential 'conceptual levers' that we used to make sense of our data" (p. 249). As explicit as that description tries to be, however, the essence of the process is rendered only figuratively: the investigators "sifted" the data, worked "inductively." In some way, then, drawing upon their own direct and indirect experience, they discovered an order in—or imposed one upon—their data. Still, the hard questions remain unanswered: How did they know when a pattern of activity was "meaningful"? What marked the difference between meaningful and non-meaningful activities?

This is the sort of account—when, indeed, there is any account at all—that Ethnographers offer, and I think finally must offer, for the process by which they look for themes in their data. They sort, they sift, they work inductively, looking for patterns to "emerge" from the data. And this is so because the process they describe, finally, is the re-formation of their own consciousnesses: their emerging fluency in the ways of making meaning in this new imaginative universe. The in-

scribed social discourse is important, then, not so much as a stream
of events—streams of events are always available—but as the medium
in which the Ethnographer works to express her new vision, one that
she believes to be ever more closely aligned with those of her hosts.
The various constraints Ethnographers place on themselves—the insistence on self-consciousness, for example, or triangulation of data
collection or analysis—may to some degree enhance this process
(although I suspect they may hinder it, too), but they can neither
control nor account for it. It is essentially internal, finally accessible
only to the individual researcher and, for all its apparent vulnerability,
the key link between the investigator and the social discourse from
which Ethnographic inquiry derives its power.

The potential for error or abuse in this kind of interpretation
lies in two directions. The more obvious one, perhaps, is that it can
be done all too loosely. An investigator enters a setting, takes some
notes, and then produces an account of his experiences that has an
authority somewhere between a good newspaper story and romantic
anecdote. Looseness of this sort poses a threat to both researcher and
consumer. Even for experienced, well trained, highly scrupulous investigators, there are no clear rules that say how many times through
the experience-inscription-interpretation cycle will be enough. That
judgment, like the interpretations themselves, rests finally with the
investigator, who must not only learn to see things in a new way, but
gauge for himself the congruity of his vision with that of his hosts.
And for readers, it can obviously be hard to discern from a research
report the processes by which interpretations have emerged, and I see
no evidence of a convention for reporting the stages in their evolution.
Skillful writing can produce passages of so-called "thick description,"
("the concrete and careful account of particular events" Kantor et al.,
p. 296) that can make any reasonably plausible interpretation
acceptable.

Whatever the dangers of this sort of loose interpretation, though,
a greater danger still may well lie in the opposite direction, with the
urge for tightness, control: that is, investigators may succumb to
pressure they feel from the larger research establishment to make
this sort of interpretation be (or seem to be) something other than
what it is—to make it seem more controlled, more systematic, more
"scientific" in a positivist sense—and so to lend those attributes to
findings derived from it. We have seen this tendency at work, for
example, in the Pettigrew et al. study, where the concern is increasingly for an observational grid that can be used with demonstrable
reliability. Rather than fostering an interpretive dialectic, such an instrument attempts to quash it, indoctrinating the observers into the
meaning-making habits of the research group so strongly that they

are no longer sensitive to the nuances of the classrooms observed. As they gain system and control, then, they gradually lose their interpretive freedom, with the results I have already indicated: a study that reveals much more about the group that conducted it than about the communities nominally under study.

The search for greater control can thus lead to one or another kinds of reduction, where the role of the individual interpreter is diminished or eliminated in deference to other kinds of authority. Worse, it can prompt a kind of fraud, where interpretation is disguised in a jargon that suggests it is some other kind of analysis. Even in work as responsible as Florio and Clark's, the language tugs them in that direction: "descriptive data" undergoes the "processes of reduction and analysis," as though the material in question could as easily be the residue of some chemistry experiment as the words of participants and participant-observers. There is only one final source of authority in Ethnographic inquiry. So while the perspective of a single investigator might be buttressed in a dozen different ways, the final analysis, the determination of what any such data finally *means*, necessarily lies with interpretation.

Testing Themes: Verification

Given this continuous interpretive cycle, there can be only two places to test posited interpretations: further direct experience, or further data. That is, an investigator can devise ways to cross-check tentative themes in the field itself or, second-best but more common, against (a) existing data analyzed in a new way, (b) new data collected in an old way, or (c) new data collected and/or analyzed in a new way. The term most commonly associated with Ethnographic verification is triangulation, and it is applied to both data collection and analysis. While it gets defined in various ways—Composition's Ethnographers all seem to cite a different favorite authority—the general idea is fairly straightforward. If an Ethnographer's object is to come to terms with the collaboratively constructed reality of some community, then she will want access to it from as many vantage points as possible, and she will want to get maximum return in insight from the information she does collect. In other words, the wider and deeper her exploration of this imaginative universe, the more likely it is that her account of it will be attuned to that of its members. The word triangulation, of course, suggests that three perspectives are somehow optimal, but my sense is that it is borrowed from mathematics more figuratively than literally, no doubt with the hope that it will carry with it some of the aura of precision its origins in trigonometric functions provide. The point is that an Ethnographer's ability to verify an interpretation depends to a great extent on how effectively she can supplement her own direct experience with—and test it against—other kinds of information.

Verification can thus appear in Ethnographic investigations in different forms and to different degrees, with every effort at triangulation tending to add a layer of complexity. At one extreme is the solo investigator, working only from his own field notes, without recourse to any other data (including even informal interviews with participants), who develops interpretations from his own review of those notes, then tests them in the field, relying exclusively on time— the gradual unfolding of events—to provide his opportunities; or who might even, as we saw in Dyson's study, wait until all data are collected before attempting interpretation, and so in effect remove direct experience from the cycle altogether. At the other extreme would be a multi-investigator, multi-technique, multi-data analysis enterprise, in which interpretations from various investigators' field notes were regularly compared not only with one another, but with formal and informal interviews with participants, written records of various kinds, surveys, and whatever other kinds of data were collected; and in which, moreover, these various kinds of data were subjected to more than a single form of analysis—so that interviews and texts were not only read and reread, for example, but coded and/or analyzed after the manner of Odell and Goswami. Of the published studies, Florio and Clark's is probably most complex in this sense, employing five investigators, all of whom appear to have been involved in both collecting and interpreting data; and including, besides field notes, videotapes of classroom activities, teacher journals, tapes of interviews with teachers, and student work samples. They do not, however, report using different kinds of data analysis.

However, the sticking point for this process, and almost certainly the most crucial of the unresolved issues facing Composition's Ethnographic community, is the matter of how to *gauge* verification: How is an investigator to know how much or what combination of the available means for verification is enough? What sorts of standards apply in determining the relative authority of Ethnographic findings? Kantor, Kirby and Goetz—who, as we have already seen, are very sensitive to the position of Ethnographic vis à vis Experimental inquiry—deal with these questions in a way that exemplifies, I think, the community's confusion. If ethnographic inquiry is to be "defended to the educational research community," they argue, "there are difficult issues of reliability and validity to be addressed" (p. 302). They offer the following standards, along with suggestions for how Ethnography might satisfy them:

External reliability—whether individual researchers would discover the same phenomena or generate the same constructs in the same or similar settings—can be enhanced by thorough and accurate descriptions of research status position, informant choices, social situations and conditions, analytic constructs and premises, and methods of data collection and analysis. Internal reliability—the degree to which researchers will congruently match data with constructs—is strengthened by use of low-inference descriptors in both collection and presentation of data, participant research assistants, peer examination, and mechanically recorded data. Internal validity, the issue of whether researchers' constructs match the empirical world, is enhanced by use of long-term field residence, by a variety of researcher self-monitoring strategies, by triangulation of data sources and collection techniques, and by methodical sampling across categories of phenomena. The most difficult issue for ethnographic research has been external validity, the extent to which results are comparable across groups. In addition to the strategies that strengthen reliability and internal validity, similar results obtained from concurrent or sequential study of multiple sites further enhance external validity (pp. 302–303).

The problem with these standards is essentially the same one we have traced throughout Kantor et al.'s position. Borrowed directly from Experimental inquiry, they derive from a positivist, not a phenomenological, perspective. Of course they can be *made* to apply. Florio and Clark's four functions of writing in room 12, for instance, would be considered fully externally reliable if you or I or any other investigator, visiting room 12 or some "similar setting," came up with exactly the same functions based on the phenomena we observed there. They would be internally reliable to the degree to which Florio and Clark and their assistants could agree on how to sort new data into those categories. They would be internally valid insofar as the phenomena Florio and Clark observed in room 12 "really" constituted these four functions of writing. And, last, they would be externally valid insofar as the four functions, applied according to whatever criteria for comparability could be worked out, accounted for writing-related phenomena in other classrooms.

As reassuring as such unanimity and universality might seem, though, to invoke reliability and validity as criteria for judging a phenomenologically-based inquiry is to miss the point. As we saw in the Pettigrew et al. study, two or more investigators may certainly be made to "see"—or at least to talk about what they see—as though they were one person, and so achieve some measure of internal reliability . . . but then, why have more than one observer in the first place? The point of triangulation, of putting different kinds of collecting "instruments" at different places to collect different kinds of data, is not coverage—trying to get as many angles as possible on some single, unified "event" that happens in order to say, with increasing certainty, what it was. By now it's a refrain: what matters is not what happens—an infinite number of things, from tics and winks to screams and shouts might happen—but rather how what happens comes to mean, and that is assumed to be both a relative and a collaborative matter. It not only depends on who sees what from where, but its essence lies precisely in the interaction of those multiple perspectives. To perfectly calibrate all the participant-observers in a setting, then—to get them all to "see" in the same way—is to strip them of precisely the sensitivities that make them worth deploying in the first place.

The desire for both external reliability and external validity may be even more misguided. No doubt the dialectical energy of Ethnographic studies can be enhanced by the kinds of techniques Kantor et al. recommend; all of them could help clarify, in Geertz' phrase, "what manner of men" were being described. But their concerns over whether other investigators would "discover the same phenomena or generate the same constructs in the same or similar settings," and whether the "results" obtained in one setting can hold for other people in other places and times is just plain wrongheaded. In the first place, as we have just seen with internal reliability, the positivist ambition to render all investigators somehow uniform or interchangeable—which is basically what impels the drive for reliability—is inappropriate for a phenomenologically-based inquiry. More to the point, though, these concerns imply that Ethnographers need to be concerned with what amounts to replicability: that the phenomena they investigate can be studied again, in other times and other places—a notion which is, from a phenomenological perspective, simply absurd. All imaginative universes are, by definition, comparable, capable of being juxtaposed through the medium of Ethnographers' fictions; but they are, also by definition, never the same or similar in the positivist sense intended here. As I have argued so often, the social discourse that is the primary object of Ethnographic inquiry represents a one-time, unrecoverable phenomenon. The social discourses of other places, or of the same place at other times, represent not another manifestation of a constant, underlying order, but a whole new text—tied in some way, to be sure, to whatever has come before, but new just the same. Things can never come to mean in quite the same way twice. So Ethnographic studies cannot be verified by being "replicated," nor can their findings be tested against their power to account for other people in other places or times.

Internal validity is a somewhat different matter. The interpretive cycle I have described, from experience through inscription to interpretation, could be construed by an Experimentalist as an effort to gain internal validity—to verify that the patterns and explanations traced in the data can also be found in, and have explanatory value for, the life of the studied community. One danger here, then, is that the acceptance of this criterion, simply because Ethnographic inquiry seems able to meet it, implies an obligation for it to meet the others as well—is tantamount to an admission, in other words, that Ethnography is internally valid, but neither externally valid nor particularly reliable. More importantly, though, it obscures just what it is an Ethnographer is trying to validate his interpretations against. The issue is not, as Kantor et al. would have it, "whether researchers' constructs match the empirical world"—that is a positivist formulation—but whether the constructs match those held by the other members of the community. The distinction is crucial, and for the same reason I have given so often: it is not what happens that is at issue, but how what happens comes to mean.

The ideal goal of Ethnographic verification, then, and so the standard against which it needs to be measured, lies in this matching up: to make the final interpretation one that the participants, understanding the investigator's aim of carrying it back to her own imaginative universe, would approve. This is obviously an ideal not often within easy reach. Participants are seldom in a position to adopt such a stance; the students in room 12, for example, could not simply be given drafts of Florio and Clark's report-in-progress and asked for their feedback. Moreover, since verification is usually a continuous process, this testing can't really be only an end-point affair. Participants must somehow be consulted all along, but since such consultation is always potentially disruptive it must be handled with caution.

Nevertheless, techniques for verification are best understood as compromises on this ideal made necessary by investigative circumstances. As I suggested at the beginning of this section, they fall into two large groups: those that test interpretations in the field, and those that test them against other data. Interpretations can be most powerfully verified, then, when circumstances allow participants to be members of the research team, regularly engaged in both collecting and interpreting data. Next best, and more commonly possible, is to consult participants in the field (with formal and informal interviews the obvious approach), the investigator testing emerging interpretations as a regular feature of her relationship with them.

The "purest" form of verification, at least in terms of intrusiveness, is what Kantor et al. call "long-term field residence." If an investigator stays in the field long enough, it is thought, events themselves will either confirm or disconfirm his interpretations. Florio and Clark take this strategy to its logical limits, suggesting that its proper end is prediction: "In short, the goal was to render descriptions that were able to be 'based on an accumulation of data, [to] predict an event or state that people will behave in special ways under certain conditions'" ("Understanding," p. 250). What makes the ability to generate such predictions a good thing, of course, is that it may represent the sought-after matching up: if I can predict how you will behave under certain circumstances, it may mean that I have made entry into your imaginative universe. Despite its purity, however, a strict reliance on long-term field residence has a couple of drawbacks. The first is that a correct prediction of what people will do doesn't necessarily demonstrate an understanding of why as they understand it— as in the Dyson study, where claims about seeing things from the children's perspective are bound to be exaggerated. Second, prediction smacks of positivist influence, implying that the phenomenon under study is regular enough to be graphed, as it were, so that once the right variables have been isolated, the coordinates of the future can be plotted. It may be that, for an Experimentalist, some human systems are stable enough to make this kind of plotting possible, but it makes no phenomenological sense: the proper province of Ethnography is the inscribed present, as it were, not the future.

All other techniques fall into the testing-against-other-data category. We have covered almost all of them at some point in this chapter: those that involve different kinds, sources, and methods of collecting data (e.g., written records or standardized tests, multiple investigators, mechanical recording devices, and so on); and those that involve different methods of data analysis. What makes these less potent as sources of verification is that they are one or more steps removed from the social discourse that is the object of study. It's easy to see why there might be advantages to having two investigators collaborating in their efforts to make sense of an imaginative universe; but two or three or ten outsider perspectives can never accumulate the authenticity of that of a single insider.

Dissemination

The body of Ethnographic work in Composition is too small to warrant any lengthy discussion of dissemination. Kantor et al. point out the key potential logistical problem, report length: "Inherent in the use of such prolific data collection strategies is the problem of reducing the findings to journal length articles. How can this be done without sacrificing flavor, thick description, or a sense of the full context? How do researchers avoid getting bogged down by discussion of methodology? Which transcripts, field notes, illustrations are most important to include? . . . Book and monograph length reports may in many cases be necessary to reveal the full context of field studies" (p. 304).

What makes this problem even more pronounced is that the format and length of Researcher journal articles have been determined by the Experimental tradition. Knowledge has to be packaged, as it were, in paradigmatically acceptable units, a form to which Ethnography's fictions obviously don't lend themselves. This may be part of the explanation for why there are so few such studies; Researchers of any stripe are under pressure to publish, and conversion to an Ethnographic methodology certainly doesn't improve one's chances. And the studies that do get published, I suggest, are those most amenable to Experimentalist standards. That may be why the research reports examined here vary so widely with respect to the tenets of a phenomenologically-based Ethnography, forming this community with borders but no center.

For all its promise, then, the future of the embattled Ethnographic community cannot be all that bright. There still seems to be, among users and consumers alike, considerable confusion about what sort of authority it has. That situation will not be helped by the publication of methodologically-mixed research reports, where the right terminology—the mention of context, participant-observation, key informants, triangulation, and so on—is used rather indiscriminately as a reason for labeling an inquiry as Ethnographic. And confusion over the nature of that authority leads to further confusion about the kinds of relationships Ethnographic knowledge can have with that from other modes of inquiry. However diplomatic its users might wish or need to be in the face of a positivist culture's latent hostility, the method itself will inevitably be both threatening and radical. It will not mix and match. Only when its users come to terms with that fact can they move toward a stronger methodological integrity.

V

The
Dynamics of Inquiry

V

The Dynamics of Inquiry

The previous three sections of this book have offered an account of eight of Composition's most significant methodological communities, for which purpose it made sense to treat them as essentially independent entities. In truth, of course, they are far from isolated. As we saw in Chapter 1, the field has been driven by the need to replace practice as its primary mode of inquiry and lore as its dominant form of knowledge. That drive resulted in what I called a methodological land rush: a scramble to stake out territory, to claim power over what constitutes knowledge in Composition; and to claim, as well, whatever rewards that power might carry with it. That scramble is what I mean here by the dynamics of inquiry, and it is the subject of the next two chapters.

10

The "Revolution" in Composition

The most popular way for commentators in Composition to account for the radical internal changes of the past two-and-a-half decades has been to characterize them as the results of a "revolution." As might be expected, of course, just what that term means—who revolted against whom (or what), why, and to what effect—depends on who is telling the story. Probably the most widely accepted account might be called the paradigm shift theory, and two versions of it have been particularly influential: Richard Young's 1978 "Paradigms and Problems: Needed Research in Rhetorical Invention," and Maxine Hairston's "The Winds of Change: Thomas Kuhn and the Revolution in the Teaching of Writing." These are by no means the only versions. There has been a range of variations; indeed, it was even implicit in Braddock et al.'s alchemy/chemistry analogy, predating the 1964 publication of Thomas Kuhn's *The Structure of Scientific Revolutions*, from which the concept of paradigm gains most of its potency. And there have been some very articulate objections to the applicability of the whole idea of a paradigm shift to Composition. Both variations and objections will be dealt with as the discussion in these two chapters proceeds. What I want to do here is to treat Young's essay as an early, representative and, at least in its general outlines, widely accepted recounting of Composition's internal turmoil to serve as a starting point.

Young begins his argument, then, by claiming that "since the beginning of the century, the teaching and researching of composition have been guided by what Thomas Kuhn (1970) has called a 'paradigm,' a system of widely shared values, beliefs, and methods that determines the nature and conduct of the discipline" (p. 29). He is reasonably prudent in borrowing Kuhn's term, making it clear that he is aware that Kuhn's usage of it varied, and that Kuhn himself had restricted it to a description of scientific disciplines.[1] Still, he contends that "the similarities between scientific disciplines and other disciplines, including our own, are substantial enough to make its use here at least tenable" (p. 29).

With that equivalence established, Young is free to argue that Composition's "shared system" can be called the "current-traditional" paradigm. It is, he suggests, somewhat difficult to discuss, or even to recognize, because "so much of our theoretical knowledge about it is tacit" (pp. 30–31). Nevertheless, he thinks that its "overt features . . . are obvious enough":

> the emphasis on the composed product rather than the composing process; the analysis of discourse into words, sentences, and paragraphs; the classification of discourse into description, narration, exposition, and argument; the strong concern with usage (syntax, spelling, punctuation) and with style (economy, clarity, emphasis); the preoccupation with the informal essay and the research paper; and so on (p. 31).

From this starting point, Young proceeds to demonstrate how the revolution in the teaching of writing can be conceived of as parallel to Kuhn's description of a paradigm shift in the sciences, a shift Young sketches as follows:

> A paradigm acquires wide support by demonstrating its superior ability to solve problems generally acknowledged by those in the discipline to be acute and fundamental; once it is established, research is directed primarily toward its articulation and application. New problems arise, however, which those committed to the paradigm cannot solve adequately, and a crisis develops, accompanied by a sense of uncertainty and insecurity in the profession. The response to the crisis is typically the development of new theories which are able to provide more adequate solutions. A new paradigm emerges from the inquiries and controversies of the crisis state and with it another period of relative stability (p. 35).

For his purposes, the Composition crisis is fomented in particular by the current-traditional paradigm's "failure to provide effective instruction in what is often called the 'prewriting stage' of the composing process and in the analytical and synthetic skills necessary for good thinking" (p. 33)—a failure which, he claims, has been noted "repeatedly" over the previous fifteen years. The response to this crisis, he insists, has been a new perspective on composing as a process, and the emergence of four "substantial theories of invention," by which he refers in fact to four pedagogical techniques: classical invention, Burke's dramatistic method, Rohman's prewriting method, and Pike's tagmemic method.

In other words, Young's version of the paradigm shift explanation argues, first, that Composition is and has been a "discipline," bound together by this "shared system of beliefs, values, and methods"; and, second, that this "shared system" began, after about 60 years (by his count), to prove inadequate for solving certain "new problems"—in this case, the allegedly new problem of teaching writers how to generate material for writing. The result thus far has been the emergence of perspectives and "theories" inimical to that paradigm. The next step, he claims, must be "research that helps us make reasonable judgments about the adequacy of the theories of invention" (and, by extension, other of what he might deem critical matters). His research agenda is quite eclectic. It would seem to be dominated by Experimental work—which, given his insistence on a paradigmatic structure, makes sense—but he explicitly includes "philosophical responses" (p. 41); something he calls "metarhetorical research" (p. 42—and which sounds philosophical in method); "sociological and philosophical studies" (p. 43); and "historical research" (p. 46: "an invaluable supplement to metarhetorical research"). The eventual result of this multi-methodological assault, presumably, would be either a decision to maintain the old paradigm, perhaps in some revised form, or to reject it, and thereby simultaneously adopt some new one.

I do not want to completely discount the paradigm shift explanation, or at least the observations on which it is based. There has unquestionably been a shift in the internal order of the society of Composition, and one manifestation of it has been to give increased attention to all sorts of composition-related issues, including those that interest Young. What is wrong with the paradigm shift explanation, as Robert Connors and C. H. Knoblauch, among others, have pointed out, is its assumption that Composition—if it can even now be called a discipline at all—can really be assumed ever to have had this sort of a paradigmatic structure.[2] The *a priori* assumption that it had (and still has) such a structure is bound to lead, as it leads Young, to a misunderstanding of the methodological pluralism I have been at such pains to delineate in this study. Young seems quite content to lump all modes of inquiry—"teaching and researching," "teachers and scholars"—together, epistemological and ontological assumptions notwithstanding, arguing in effect that the dynamics of Composition as a whole are modeled on those of its Experimental community, so that all contributions gain significance paradigmatically.

But consider, as the most obviously contradictory case, Practitioners' lore. One can certainly trace in it trends and fashions; and in textbooks, especially, where it seems most accessible, and where its predominantly oral nature is obscured, someone looking, as Young is, "through the lens of Kuhn's theory" (p. 39) might feel he sees a consistency that can be read as paradigmatic. But lore is far too elastic, too ectoplasmic, to suffer crises. Adopting a new theory does not mean rejecting an old one. Indeed—to invoke Young's own sort of evidence—it is not at all uncommon for a contemporary textbook to include not only all four of the methods for invention that Young mentions, but others (e.g. brainstorming, freewriting) as well. This is not because the textbook's author wants to have competing theories battle it out in solid paradigmatic fashion, but so that, in keeping with lore's pragmatic base, a given Practitioner will have as many choices as possible.

However, if the paradigm-shift explanation for the revolution in Composition is not itself particularly valuable for what it *says*—as a way of accounting for the dynamics of inquiry—it does reveal a good deal by what it tries to *do*. That is, Young uses it in the context of *Research on Composing: Points of Departure* to provide a platform from which to launch his particular research agenda, a use which amounts to a kind of propaganda: an account of Composition's developmental dynamic articulated for some political purpose. In terms of this study, it might be described as a power play, an attempt by one methodological community or cluster of communities to assert its dominance over the others. And this is the sort of movement that has in fact been most characteristic of the emergent field of Composition. It is possible, of course, to describe such power plays as revolutionary; and for those, like Young, who fancy themselves as being on one or another version of the "revolutionary" side, the term has a certain fashionable appeal to it—carries with it a certain flair, a kind of daring and, not least, a sense of righteousness. So we can continue to use the term, without qualifying quotation marks, because it is so much in fashion, and because the alternatives—takeover, squabble, usurpation, wrangle—seem either too sinister or too petty. Keep in mind, though, that this revolution is not best understood, as Young would have it, as a more or less unified response to some shared paradigmatic crisis, but as an inter-methodological struggle for power.

□

As this inter-communal struggle for power over knowledge has played itself out in Composition, it has been dominated by two themes. The origins of both can be traced back directly to the chain of events recounted in Chapter 1: the academic reform movement, the quest for Federal dollars, and the emergence of Composition as a third leg in the English tripod. The first theme, then, is that there exists in the teaching of writing a knowledge and method crisis that justifies radical—i.e., revolutionary—action. It becomes a kind of slogan: The teaching of writing is in a sorry state. The second locates a target for that action, in effect sanctioning the divestiture of the Practitioners, and it goes like this: Most of the responsibility for the crisis lies with the Practitioners, the vast majority of whom, even the most well-intentioned and industrious, lack the knowledge or the methods to do anything about it on their own.

Of course, the crisis theme in the teaching of writing does not begin in 1963.[3] In a 1961 essay called "What Has Happened to Written Composition," Joseph Mersand takes note of the then-current crisis claims that fueled the academic reform movement's extension to Composition (and that would lead to *The National Interest and the Teaching of English*):

> Judging from the stories in the newspapers, not much has happened in written composition. The United Press carried a dispatch on October 14 [1960], with the headline "Students Stumble on English." "Specifically," reads the story, "they have trouble with English, the language they are supposed to use in communicating their ideas. To put it another way, Johnny can't read, write, or talk properly" (p. 231).

As Mersand points out, however, citing such works as Percival Chubb's *The Teaching of English* (1902) and Sterling Andrus Leonard's *English Composition as a Social Problem* (1917), this has all happened before:

> My files of newspaper clippings are bulging with similar com-plaints about the writing skills of students at all levels of our educational system, but I am sure that you are all aware of this attitude. My purpose is not to recite the charges against our in-struction and results in written composition, but to trace pat-terns with respect to aims, content, methodology, and evalua-tion during the past half-century. We shall discover that at the same time that our critics were denouncing our meager results, our forward-looking teachers had long before enunciated the principles which today are so widely proclaimed in such docu-ments as the Conant report and *The Pursuit of Excellence* (p. 232).

What made the crisis of 1963—and, in particular, the case of *The National Interest and the Teaching of English*—different, though, is that NCTE rather turned the tables: the crisis was declared from *within*. Given the goal of winning NDEA and Federal funding in general, its authors apparently deemed it rhetorically effective and politically expedient to muster as much of a sense of urgency as possible. The government could not be expected, after all, to fund what was already a fat and sassy endeavor.

The argument they end up presenting is thus, in some ways, a curious one. A good deal of space is spent arguing the importance of English in the curriculum, in educational, political, economic, and cultural terms—arguing so effective, in fact, that in places the document makes it hard to believe that there is a crisis at all. For instance, as evidence that English teaching has been effective heretofore, the authors point out that over the previous hundred or so years, the "goal of total literacy practically has been reached, and it is no accident that the achievement of literacy has resulted in valuable economic, cultural, and political by-products: the most productive economy in the world, leadership in the sciences and arts, and an increasing extension of democratic rights and responsibilities to most of our citizens" (p. 23).

But, the argument continues, now the profession that has played so prominent a role in this rise to power is in crisis. The world has changed, so that "total literacy", which had once seemed so admirable a goal, must now be considered "mere literacy," and it "is no longer enough" (p. 25). The system that has taken us to such incredible heights has crumbled badly and will no longer serve: "The drift into the present state of chaos has been subtle and complex; the causes run deep. We must now become aware of the critical problem and muster a national effort to solve it" (p. 23).

What never becomes quite clear in this document, though, is how "the present state of chaos" or the "critical problem" of which we must become aware is to be translated in terms of how Americans read, write, and speak. A couple of symptoms are offered: public perception of a systemic failure ("National concern about the deficiencies of English instruction has become almost commonplace." [p. 13]); and the costs of testing and remediation at the college level based on a survey that garnered 619 responses. (For instruction, the report offers the curiously precise figure of $10,114,736.62.) In addition, at least four causes are listed: (1) the inability of the training system to keep pace with the demand for teachers; (2) the increasingly complex nature of English teaching; (3) the lack of "articulation" across curriculum levels; and (4) the absence of coordinated national and state efforts. And, finally, a good number of recommendations are offered, most of them having to do with the professional preparation and working conditions of English teachers, but including a call for more basic research.

In the end, however, we never learn exactly what it is, in terms of what English teaching provides, that Americans can't do that they should be able to do, or how anyone claims to have found out. My sense is that it was basically a "keep-up" argument: math and science have been funded in response to both the promise of wartime advances and Cold War-generated fears; English needs, and maybe even has a right, to keep up. And, since English did, for a decade or so, get some of the funding it sought, the argument can be said to have worked. The obvious drawback, however, was the price English-teachers-as-Practitioners had to pay in self-abasement. As we saw Applebee suggest back in the first chapter, the prestige and busy-ness that go with Federal recognition—the infusion of research money, the summer institutes, the conferences, and so on—go a long way toward making members of a field feel professional. But it is a professionalism the material rewards of which accrue for a very few, a small elite: the funded researchers, the project directors, the conference keynoters. For most members of the field, it is a matter of basking in a reflected limelight. To generate the candle-power required for even that second-hand recognition, it was necessary to offer a self-portrait—or, perhaps, a portrait of the cast of thousands as concocted by the stars—of English teachers as overworked and undertrained semi-professionals operating according to outmoded knowledge and without coordination, and generally making a mess of their mission. Or, as the document puts it, "Poorly prepared teachers of English have created a serious national problem" (p. 13).

The obvious shortage of hard evidence of a gap between Americans' literacy and the demands of their lives or the national interest, or evidence that the blame for such a gap, should it exist, ought to be placed on English teachers, is finally irrelevant here. The pattern in modern Composition, to which this document certainly contributed, is that crises are invoked for political ends, and they are invoked in the form most convenient, and according to criteria most useful for, the invoker. Thus, for the authors of *The National Interest and the Teaching of English*, the crisis is professional and logistical, one that can best be addressed, as the expression goes, by throwing money at it; for Richard Young—armed, as he is, with a Researcher agenda—the crisis is paradigmatic, and so its solution demands a realignment of priorities in inquiry. What these and most other crisis invocations share, however, is the identification of crisis with Practitioner, the second of modern Composition's themes: If there is a knowledge and method crisis, somebody has to have it; and while the students may be, finally, its victims, it must be those charged with their care—the Practitioners—who are somehow its source, its location.

Assessments of the nature and degree of Practitioner culpability for these crises vary considerably. Perhaps most often, Practitioners are made out to be something like the simple, indigenous population of the newly discovered, mostly unexplored territory of Composition. For Braddock et al., remember, this meant that they could hardly be expected to know anything: if research was more like alchemy than chemistry, "laced with dreams, prejudices, and makeshift operations," then practice must be even fluffier, less substantial stuff—but Practitioners couldn't really be blamed for that. Worried over, perhaps, or pitied, but not blamed. Of course, this is interpolation; the fact of the matter is that Braddock et al. simply don't recognize practice as knowledge-making at all.

In any case, not all commentators let Practitioners off so lightly. Consider, for instance, Sidney P. Moss's appeal in "Logic: A Plea for a New Methodology in Freshman Composition" (1969). Moss invokes his version of the crisis in pedagogical terms, so that he can explain his own method (as laid out in his textbook, *Composition by Logic*):

> To say that teachers and directors of freshman composition constitute one of the most conservative bodies on our campuses is to speak gently. Not only as a group do they resist experiment, and innovation in their pedagogy, which would be understandable if they were achieving remarkable success, but they persist in their pedagogy in the face of failure remarkable only for its predictability. What is equally disturbing is their steadfast allegiance to this pedagogy. If one did not know better, he might assume it shared the sanctity of the Ten Commandments or the Sermon on the Mount" (p. 215).

Moss doesn't want to argue about the existence of a crisis. His evidence that there is one, he claims, comes from these people's own testimony. So despite their incredible conservatism, he is willing to believe teachers when they say that students don't write well in their classes. However, he wants to shift the blame for this illiteracy off the students and on to the teaching methods—and, of course, their teachers:

> It has been years since I heard a teacher question its [the pedagogy's] value. Instead, I only hear them complain that their students, with few exceptions, are recalcitrant, scatterbrained, lazy, or stupid; or that they come from linguistically and intellectually wretched backgrounds; or that their high-school instructors were obviously delinquent or inept; or that the McLuhan effect has taken its toll. The conscience-clearing goes on and on; the litany of complaints about students seems limited only by the complainants' ingenuity. And if one asks

them, What is the evidence for saying that students are so poor, the answer you get is that very few students learn to write well or think well by the time-tested pedagogy. It never seems to occur to these teachers that all that time has tested, in a kind of idiot repetition, is not that students are so weak as that their pedagogy is so poor (p. 215).

Not far removed in terms of harshness is Janet Emig's indictment of secondary school teaching in *The Composing Processes of Twelfth Graders*, some of which we sampled in Chapter 7: "Much of the teaching of composition in American high schools," she contends, ostensibly on the evidence of her eight case studies, "is essentially a neurotic activity" (p. 99). At the heart of the problem, she argues, is the disjunction between what writing is in the world (one senses she means what it "really" is), and what it is in school. Although she allows that this breakdown might be to some extent systemic, a failure in our teacher training system, the disjunction nevertheless ends up as a function of what we saw her label "teacher illiteracy":

> how many of the teachers described in this inquiry, would one guess, have read one or more of the writers [Norman Mailer, Truman Capote, Philip Roth, Saul Bellow, Gloria Steinem, Tom Wolfe] mentioned above? Yet without such reading of wholly contemporary writers, teachers have no viable sources of criteria for teaching writing in the seventies, even in the single mode they purport to teach. . . .
>
> More crucial, many teachers of composition, at least below the college level, themselves do not write. They have no recent, direct experience of a process they purport to present to others (p. 98).

Indeed, like Moss, Emig hints at a certain Practitioner malevolence, in this case with what seem to be political overtones: "One wonders at times if the shying away from reflexive writing is not an unconscious effort to keep the 'average' and 'less able' student from the kind of writing he can do best and, often, far better than the 'able,' since there is so marvelous a democracy in the distribution of feeling and of imagination" (p. 100).

Nor have all the harsher assessments come from those whose persona places them more or less outside of the Practitioner community. Some none too gentle arguments have come from those who address the Practitioner community from within, as it were, as "we." For instance, in "A Brand New World Every Morning" (1974), Paul Bryant offers a most unflattering comparison: that college teachers of composition seem to operate a lot like barnyard geese:

There is an old saying that a goose is a very stupid animal, because for a goose it is a brand new world every morning. Geese resolutely refuse to learn from experience. Instead they insist upon being constantly surprised, puzzled, and alarmed by everything that happens, even when it happens over and over again. Their consciousness can handle only the present, never the past or future.

I mention this bit of barnyard folklore because we as college teachers of composition too often seem to operate on the same basis. . . . As a group, we are the living proof of the adage that those who do not know history are condemned to repeat it (p. 30).

For Bryant, Erwin Steinberg's notion that an art could be buttressed by a science has shifted, so that now "teaching composition is both a science and an art" (p. 31). In neither sphere, he insists, have Practitioners been much better than those geese. They have been consistently unable or unwilling to accumulate knowledge, to make what he calls "linear progress" by building "systematically on past experience and knowledge already acquired by others" (p. 33). The problem? It would seem to be, rather as in Emig's assessment, a combination of goose-like simple-mindedness and malevolent self-interest. Practitioners are accused, on the one hand, of being simple or illiterate; and, on the other, of being somehow self-serving: clinging to a pattern of "erratic circles" and "unrelated solos in a wild blue historical limbo," discovering and re-discovering the same knowledge over and over again in order to perpetuate the thrill of discovery, and so keep aloft their "soaring egos" at the expense of their students and their "intellectual integrity" (p. 33).

A similar criticism, this time in direct response to an early- to mid-1970s version of a crisis, and with a much stronger element of professional self-flagellation, shows up in the essay I cited in my Preface, Carl Klaus's "Public Opinion and Professional Belief" (1976). His argument neatly enunciates both of the revolution's themes. First, there is the crisis:

My title is occasioned by the sound and fury of all the news I've been hearing lately about bad writing and all the remedies about how to make it better. No matter where I turn, whether to television or newspapers or weekly magazines or institutional newsletters or professional journals or academic colleagues, I hear the same feverish cry: "Johnny Can't Write" (and apparently Jenny can't write either). Walter Cronkite says so, and so does the *Iowa City Press Citizen*, and the *Des Moines Register*, and *The New York Times*, and *Time Magazine*, and *Newsweek*, and the

> *Reader's Digest* . . . Suddenly it seems as if the whole country is
> about to take arms against a sea of stylistic troubles and by
> opposing end them (p. 335).

Next, there is the problem: that "we have, in fact, only a handful of
professionally trained writing teachers in the whole country" (p. 335).
Experience at teaching is not enough; even with twenty-two years of
experience, Klaus claims not to count himself among that handful.
Truly professional training in Composition, he says, "demands an
interdisciplinary approach," including "the expertise of such disciplines as psycholinguistics, sociolinguistics, and linguistic anthropology"; "cognitive psychology, semiotics, and transformational
linguistics"; "rhetorical theory and communication research"; "literary criticism, rhetorical analysis, psychoanalysis, and statistics"
(p. 337):

> Clearly enough, one discipline or another can provide only one
> perspective on only one element or stage in the process of
> writing. If the process is to be wholly understood, if we are to
> know as much about writing as we possibly can, then we must
> bring to the study of it as many disciplines as are possible and
> appropriate (p. 337).

In other words, Klaus concludes, to be saved from "the appalling
state of our ignorance" (p. 338), and to prevent writing teachers from
being treated "like second-class citizens, like dedicated amateurs,
which we are, rather than genuine professionals, which we are not"
(p. 340), Practitioners must steep themselves in knowledge and
methods that are not their own.

These two themes have, quite naturally, shifted in form and
emphases over time. As the revolution has gathered momentum, the
invocation of crisis conditions seems to have worn a little thin. By
1980, say, the revolution's first phase is a *fait accompli*: lore and
Practitioner inquiry have been, for most official purposes, anyway,
effectively discredited. It is now a second-class sort of knowledge,
rapidly approaching the status of superstition—to be held or voiced
only apologetically, with deference to the better, new knowledges.
Still, though the Practitioners have thus been "conquered," the
making of lore goes on, its internal structure making it quite endlessly absorbent. It has been affected, of course: Practitioners have
probably found more to absorb in the past twenty years than in the
previous sixty, and one can now trace in lore often strange admixtures of ideas and jargon from a wider variety of sources. But while
it can be thus altered, lore is not the sort of thing that can be worn
down, let alone eradicated. Not unlike a native religion in a con-

quered or colonized territory, persecution only seems to make it grow.

As a result, impatience with Practitioners on the part of those who would reform them has gradually intensified. Presumably, such a development is inevitable. After all, a fair portion of the claims about crisis had rested on the belief that Practitioner inquiry had failed to produce knowledge adequate for the demands of teaching writing. This was still probably a tenable position into the late 1970s or so, but by then, with the other methodological communities more or less established, and ostensibly producing the required better-grade stuff, placing the blame on the *absence* of such knowledge was no longer possible. So if the crisis was to continue—and for the purposes of the non-Practitioner communities retaining their newly-won power, crisis conditions were a good thing—then emphasis had to shift away from the shortage of adequate knowledge toward the problem of dissemination, of getting the Practitioners to use it, and use it properly.

Given the nature of lore, this shift in emphasis turns out to be pretty well justified. Making a dent in lore seems to be a problem of crisis proportions. From the point of view of the purveyors of this new knowledge, anyway, Practitioners' apparent willingness to retain, on the one hand, what seem to be unenlightened, not to say primitive, beliefs and methods, and to ignore or distort, on the other, the new information they are given, smacks less of simple ignorance than of plain old intractability. A 1983 article in *College English*, Clinton Burhans Jr.'s "The Teaching of Writing and the Knowledge Gap," actually sets out to document this intractability:

> Surfing on the waves of books and articles dealing with theory, research, and application in writing and composition can be an exuberant experience: so much that is exciting in itself, so much that is rich and promising for the future. The teaching of writing seems to be sweeping and soaring in wondrous new patterns, and everyone seems to be rushing to join in the fun. And yet if you observe public-school, community-college, and university writing programs and talk to their teachers, the sobering reality is how few seem to know the surf is up or even that there is a sea there at all (p. 639).

But, as his metaphor suggests, this is not a benign simplicity. Even simple-mindedness ought not to be able to obscure the presence of such a "sea." Some other force must be involved, something that blocks the perceptions and won't let the "knowledge gap" be bridged. Burhans' account of the revolution in Composition, as it turns out, is much like Richard Young's, except that he would prefer to avoid the complications involved with granting especially current-traditional knowledge, but also its post-revolutionary replacement, paradigmatic status:

> It would be more exact, then, to speak not of paradigms but rather of current-traditional myths and emerging knowledge. Myths are beliefs accepted uncritically; they require neither evidence nor proof, neither research nor theory. Indeed they are impervious over long periods of time to rational inquiry, reasoned argument, or the claims of conflicting research or theory. . . . the slow and halting change this study reflects [in the way writing is handled in schools] is entirely consistent with the gradual process by which myth is replaced by knowledge (pp. 650–651).

In short, the natives seem to have minds of their own. The gum in the revolutionary works is turning out to be the current-traditional "myths" held by Practitioners; their allegiance to those myths makes it harder for the knowledge generated by what Burhans calls "different and more valid and reliable methodologies" (p. 650) to gain a foothold. As a term, of course, Burhans' "myth" is not very far from my own choice of lore. The main difference between us, whichever term one chooses, would lie in his pejorative, and perhaps methodologically chauvinist, usage. For revolutionary purposes both myth and lore are worse, deeper rooted and more tenacious, than plain old ignorance, which Burhans seems to think would be simply a void to be filled. What makes this such a discouraging discovery is that it means the revolution—as he conceives it, of course—will be longer and messier than maybe had been expected. In other words, Practitioners not only have ideas about how to do things, but they actually believe in them. Still, the revolutionary fervor, depicted by Burhans as myth-ocidal and driven by what amounts to a doctrine of manifest destiny, burns on:

> Myths die hard, and the current-traditional myths are no exception. In the perspective of this study the gleaming visions of a neat paradigm shift should give way to the sobering realization that the imperative of change will be longer and harder than many of us have hoped, that Lundsteen's gap [a twenty-five to thirty-year gap between knowledge and practice], at least in the study, conception, and teaching of writing, is far wider than even she had speculated (p. 652).

Aftermath: To the Rescue

The gradual increase of emphasis on what Burhans calls the "imperative of change" has manifested itself in two general patterns, two broad conceptions of how Practitioners might best be educated (or converted or corrected, etc.). The earliest and probably more virulent can be called the conservative model. In this model, the ability to generate and control knowledge resides permanently with the non-Practitioners—the Scholars and, especially, the Researchers. It is particularly strong among those who are adamantly pro-Researcher, though there is no reason that a Historian or a Philosopher can't support it, as well. It establishes what amounts to a science/technology relationship, with the Practitioners cast pretty much as technicians: the inquirers find out how the world works, and then tell the technicians, who behave accordingly. Versions of the conservative model may acknowledge that teaching writing is to some extent an art, but they are more likely to treat it more as a kind of technology, an applied science, as well, and to be far more attracted by the cumulative (and perhaps, by implication, Practitioner-proof) possibilities of that scientific dimension. The hallmarks of this perspective are easy enough to spot: Braddock et al.'s commission to assemble a "scientifically based" study of what is known and not known; the hopes and ambitions of the heralds of the new linguistics; Emig's ambition that "the learning and teaching of composition may someday attain the status of science as well as art" (p. 5); Young's insistence on a paradigmatic kind of knowledge; Burhans' myth-replaced-by-knowledge scenario, which implies a similar sort of transmission; and so on.

From the conservative perspective, then, the revolution that has successfully deposed the discredited and essentially helpless Practitioners from whatever position of power they may be said to have held has put in their place those, as Burhans so neatly puts it, with "more valid and reliable methodologies." What needs to cross communal borders is knowledge only—not method—and the traffic is pretty much one way. Researchers and Scholars find out what there is to know, and then pass that knowledge along to Practitioners. Indigenous Practitioner knowledge and method are a concern only insofar as they may obstruct the introduction and application of the new, imported knowledge. If lore and its production can be said to have a positive function at all, it is only as a starting point—a foil, almost—for investigations seeking real knowledge.

What we can call, by contrast, the liberal model represents a movement toward importing both knowledge *and* method as a means of rescuing the Practitioners. Although the potential for this

model has always been implicit in Composition's revolution, sur-
facing especially in the kind of professional self-flagellation offered
by Bryant and Klaus, my sense is that it has gained strength as non-
Practitioners have grown dissatisfied with the results of the conservative model. As I made clear in Chapter 2, the usual Practitioner
response to outside knowledge is simply to absorb it and transmute it
—pretty much without regard for origin—into lore, where it becomes
one more resource for Practitioner inquiry. This can obviously be
frustrating for the contributor, who has a considerable investment in
the context out of which the Practitioner seems, so irreverently, to
be ripping it. One solution, then, is to make the Practitioner aware
of—and if possible, a participant in—that context. It helps further
that this approach has found favor with some Practitioners, who
quite rightly see in it some chance for at least a minor enfranchisement in the new power structure of their field. If simply being a
Practitioner well versed in lore is not enough, then identification
with any other community can give them some membership, however peripheral, in the new elite.

There is thus something of a Peace Corps aura about the liberal
model. Its byword might be "empowerment." It sees a need not
merely to give Practitioners new and better knowledge, but to teach
them how to make this new and better knowledge themselves. The
conservative perspective, of course, does not directly preclude such a
possibility. The best and the brightest of the Practitioners—as judged
by Researcher or Scholarly standards, naturally—might be selected
for initiation into the mysteries of Experimental research or Historical inquiry. In the liberal model, however, such initiation is a top
priority.

Exactly where this model is first articulated, who should get
credit for it, is difficult to say. It is, as I say, implicit in some of the
up-by-our-bootstraps urgings quoted earlier in the chapter. Perhaps
its most visible and clearly articulated appearance—made the more
notable because it is offered by a writer whose strongest associations
are with Experimental research—is in Lee Odell's "Teachers of
Composition and Needed Research in Discourse Theory (1979)." He
begins by offering this pretty accurate characterization of the usual
relationship between Practitioners and the knowledge offered them
by other communities:

> Whether by preference or by necessity, teachers of composition
> tend to be pragmatists. Our response to any new theory is most
> likely to be: What does it imply for our teaching? What specific
> classroom procedures does it suggest? Are these procedures
> practical? Will they work for the sort of students we have in
> our classes? Underlying these questions is at least one major

assumption: our primary obligation is to have some influence on the way students compose, to make a difference in students' ability to use written language to give order and meaning to their experience (p. 39).

Except for his framing of the underlying assumption—the assertion that students need to learn to use language to give order and meaning to their experience might not gain universal acceptance—this is a pretty reasonable account, one that I expect would meet with Practitioner approval. It is made even more attractive when Odell, generally identifiable as a prominent Researcher, identifies himself as a Practitioner (*"Our* response . . ."). He maintains his rhetorical momentum with just a touch of commiseration even as he introduces his central contention:

> As though this obligation were not demanding enough, I want to argue that we have at least one other responsibility. We must not only influence our students' writing, but also help refine and shape the discourse theory that will guide our work with students. In addition to being teachers, we should also function as discourse theorists and researchers (p. 39).

That it should be Odell making such an argument is not entirely surprising; you will recall the discussion of his own dissertation research in Chapter 6. Here he echoes the sentiments of the reviewer who introduced the *RTE* article based on that study:

> Studies proposed in this article are relatively simple. They can be carried out by a single teacher or by a few colleagues in a single composition program. Because of their limited scope, it seems unlikely that any of these studies will be definitive. Considered individually, none will be able to generalize about all composition students in all circumstances; none will, once and for all, refute or confirm basic assumptions in discourse theory. Yet as a number of us begin to ask the same sort of questions and pursue related studies, we should be able to obtain information that will be useful in several ways (p. 44).

In other words, Odell is rejecting the conservative perspective. Practitioners are obligated, he argues, to be more than just consumers of Researcher knowledge. They must become, in at least some small way (that is, anyway, how I read "help refine and shape," "relatively simple," "limited scope," and so on), makers of that knowledge. From a Practitioner's point of view, of course, this invitation still rides roughshod over lore and its production. All the kinds of investigation Odell describes in the essay are what I would classify as Experimental or Clinical. It is an invitation to behave, and thus be enfranchised, paradigmatically: to ask the same sorts of questions, pursue related studies, in hopes that our individual investigations, in-significant by themselves, will gain cumulative power. The Practitioner remains cast primarily as an applications technician, only now the technician is being invited—even coerced—to do some lab work, too.

Odell's teacher-as-Researcher, however, is not the only version of the liberal perspective. Indeed, the most outspoken holders of the perspective seem to be reacting *against* what is construed as the tyranny of the conservative model. Ann Berthoff may be the most vociferous. Her central purpose in the collection of her writing and other materials called *The Making of Meaning* (1981) seems to be to define the proper relationship between what she calls, following con-ventional usage, theory and practice. Her definition is decidedly, radically, liberal in outlook, and diametrically opposed to that offered by, say, Richard Young. It is clear with whom she thinks the power over both knowledge and method ought to reside. This passage is from "The Teacher as REsearcher":

> Let me end my polemic with this assertion: educational research is nothing to our purpose, unless we formulate the questions; if the procedures by which answers are sought are not dialectic and dialogic, that is to say, if the questions and answers are not continually REformulated by those who are working in the classroom, educational research is pointless. My spies tell me that it's becoming harder and harder for researchers to get into the schools: I rejoice in that news because I think it might en-courage teachers to become researchers themselves, and once that happens, the character of research is bound to change (p. 31).

Berthoff's position may be even more rhetorically attractive than Odell's. She seems to have more to offer: in place of the teacher as technician being recruited to join, in a relatively minor role, the larger knowledge-generating Researcher communities, she hints that Practitioners can declare their autonomy—or, even more enticing, that they can regain the power they have had stripped away by the bad guys, the Researchers.

But what does this offer entail? It is not clear to what extent Berthoff might be willing to recognize a generic form of Practitioner inquiry or knowledge. She writes frequently about "recipe swapping," which seems to be her version of what Practitioners, left alone or at their typical worst, might do. In "Method: Metaphors, Models, and Maxims," it is characterized as "the result of rejecting theory," the polar opposite of her characterization of the Researchers' efforts, "the collocation and manipulation of data, which is the result of theory for theory's sake" (p. 4). "Recipe swapping" thus sounds as if it might be her account of lore and its production, but one can't be sure.

What is clear, however, as indicated by her insistence on "dialectic and dialogic," is her own preference for Philosophical inquiry and the kind of knowledge it produces. If Odell insists that all Practitioners are obliged to be, in some sense, Researchers, Berthoff insists they must be Philosophers:

> I want to do everything I can to persuade teachers, K–35, to become philosophers—to remind them that when they consider language and thought, theory and practice, intending and realizing, writing and re-writing; when they think about thinking; when, in Coleridge's wonderful phrase, they seek to know their knowledge, they are indeed philosophers, and their classrooms are philosophical laboratories. [From the bookjacket, quoted as "From the Preface"; however, the Preface version, for some reason, is without the last six words.]

Indeed, Berthoff seems to be saying that Practitioners are philosophers whether they want to be or not: that subject matter, not method, is at the heart of the philosophical enterprise.

For Practitioners, the implications of either the conservative or the liberal perspective are about equally demanding, not to say threatening. If they follow the conservative pattern, they (a) admit, in effect, to a second-class professional status as knowledge-users, not knowledge-makers; and (b) they become the recipients of an increasingly large, seldom very well sorted flow of information. Even if, as is increasingly unlikely, they are able to keep up with that new knowledge, there is no guarantee that it will be clear what they are to do with it: how what they are now reckoned to know should impinge on what they do. And even when they are able to make that connection, they cannot be at all sure that the new knowledge will not present them with contradictory or incompatible options.

Accepting the liberal model might be even worse. Under it, they acquire not merely a new body of information, but at least one and maybe more than one new mode of inquiry as well. Thus, if they accept Odell's challenge to become small-scale Experimental Researchers, it will no longer be enough for them to determine what to do in their classrooms, operating with and contributing to lore. In addition, they must spend some of their time trying to account for what they or their students do in terms of carefully monitored cause and effect relationships, in the hope that a large enough accumulation of such paradigmatically-directed small studies will lead to nomothetic explanations for what has happened.

Or they might become deliberately Philosophical, as Berthoff urges—although precisely how a classroom functions as whatever a "philosophical laboratory" is supposed to be is not very clear. In this mode, it would again not be enough for them to figure out what to do (with each class, for each student, and so on); they would be bound, in addition, to try to ground their actions in some philosophically defensible context—defer not to a pragmatic logic but a dialogic, and adopt dialectic in favor of (or, perhaps, as the preliminary to or basis for?) their ordinary mode of inquiry. Whether they opt for a Researcher or a Scholarly commitment, the irony of the liberal perspective remains the same: the rescued end up facing more demands than the rescuers.

11

The Revolution, Phase II:
To the Victors...

As the earlier chapters on these methodological communities have made clear, of course, the shift in the power structure of Composition has not been an entirely untroubled enterprise. Internal criticism, especially among the Researcher communities, has been frequent and sometimes severe. And all communities have had to deal with the frustrations of communicative breakdowns: being misunderstood, ignored, and so on. Still, apart from the concerted divestiture of the Practitioners, inter-communal conflicts have amounted to little more than occasional skirmishes, usually the sniping of a Practitioner or Scholar skeptical of naively accepted notions about the promise of systematic or "scientific" inquiry.

Thus it seems that so long as the Practitioners, characterized as hapless or helpless or malicious, have been available as the focal point of an alleged knowledge and method crisis, other inter-communal conflicts have been relatively muted. With academic acceptability as a primary goal, nearly any mode of inquiry other than the Practitioners' has been at least potentially acceptable. Moreover, with lore out of the way, the field has been roomy enough to accommodate all sorts of "pioneers" without any great danger of crowding. The whole territory was opened up, became ripe for the claiming. It's a standard sort of revolutionary logic: because whatever was known was known in the wrong way, nothing was known at all.

But communities constituted on the basis of such different modes of inquiry, with such divergent epistemological and ontological assumptions, can hardly be conceived as moving along parallel paths to some utopian conclusion. Thus, while the forces that unseated the Practitioners converged for that particular purpose, they converged from very different directions, and they have not evaporated. In that sense, while the revolution in Composition, conceived as the battle for methodological supremacy, may be said to have pretty nearly completed its first phase, it is far from over. In this second phase, the victors, as it were, must figure out how to divide the spoils; alliances of convenience must be reexamined, and conflicts that once seemed unimportant may begin to seem more serious. This chapter will consider this second phase of the revolution, and explore its impact on the dynamics of the field's inquiry.

One of the interesting features of inquiry in modern Composition has been its organization along topical lines. This would seem to be mostly a function of its origins in a concern about practice. The territory of inquiry has tended to be broken into topic areas which, not surprisingly, overlap, and the overall logic of which comes clear only in terms of lore: Invention, the Composing Process, Revision, Sentence Combining, Evaluating Writing, Responding to Student Writing, Writing in the Workplace, Writing about Literature, Talk about Writing, the Basic Writer, and so on. The major relevant effect of this pattern for our purposes is that it has provided the various methodological pioneers with a sense of shared mission, at the same time that it has disguised, at least for a time, what might otherwise be serious methodological differences.

We can see this effect at work, to take a familiar example, in Richard Young's proposal for a research agenda in "Paradigms and Problems." What he seems to have in mind is a multi-methodological, albeit paradigmatically directed, investigative assault on the general topic of invention. The assumption seems to be that "invention" is a paradigmatically-defined phenomenon, an identifiable thing that happens in the world, and that if enough kinds of inquiry are brought to bear on it, we can unlock its secrets. Given his paradigmatic bent, this process would boil down, finally, to one of elimination, with various hypotheses (presumably about how invention is best taught) to be ranked according to their relative effectiveness.

From a methodological perspective, of course, the central difficulty in this plan stems from his use of the term "invention." Inherited from classical rhetoric (*inventione*) it carries, and is even dominated by, connotations not particularly well suited to the other theories Young specifically mentions—Burke's dramatistic method, Rohman's prewriting, and Pike's tagmemic method—as comparable to the classical model, by which he primarily means the *topoi*. Thus, what Aristotle had in mind using *topoi* and what Rohman means by prewriting, and the modes of inquiry by which they reach and propose to test such meanings, are very different; and similar differences separate the meanings and validation procedures of the various investigators who would carry out Young's proposed research agenda.[1] Invention, then, serves as little more than a general rubric under which contributions from a variety of methodological perspectives can be loosely gathered; and which, for one reason or another, a particular commentator thinks are relevant to the generation of things to write about. What the term will actually *mean* in any given contribution—assuming that it is used at all—will depend on its methodological source.

Still, while there is obviously something awkward about an investigative agenda that would proceed along lines as loosely defined as this, it could be and really has been done. Where it gets terribly sticky—where, finally, the variant definitions begin to matter, and the disguised inter-methodological tensions begin to exert themselves —is at accumulation time. It's one thing for each member of a group of methodological communities to investigate some topically identified problem; it's another to say what it is the group "knows," collectively, when it reconvenes.

The best way to delineate the difficulties of this inter-modal accumulation is to look fairly closely at a topical area that has begun to fill up some—where, to push the analogy a little further, the pioneers have had time to explore enough that they have begun to get in one another's way. Revision is a logical choice, and I want to use, as a point of entry, Stephen P. Witte's "Topical Structure and Revision: An Exploratory Study." The essay is an impressive piece of Researcher work, winner of the Braddock award for the best essay in *CCC* for 1983 (and, incidentally, almost certainly the most heavily documented article in the history of the journal). Its central features are a discussion of the concept of topical structure, and a report on an exploratory Experimental study of its usefulness as a tool for studying revision. Equally important is the way in which Witte establishes the context within which he wants his exploratory study to acquire its meaning—in other words, the way in which Witte assumes that knowledge about the topic Revision accumulates in Composition.

I have quoted Witte's first two paragraphs and the first sentence of his third in full here, despite their length, to make it clear just how he goes about establishing that context. I have included his superscript numbers to indicate the density of his documentation. (It is also worth noting the ritual invocation of the scenario in which the bad or hapless Practitioner is rescued by the efforts of research):

> It is unfortunate that so many college teachers of writing and composition textbooks describe revision as the process by which a writer merely cleans up the mechanical and stylistic infelicities

of an otherwise completed text. This simplistic view presupposes something akin to the three-stage linear model of composing set forth by Rohman and Wlecke in the 1960s.[2] Research during the past decade, particularly that of Emig and Sommers, challenges the assumption underlying such a view of revision by demonstrating that revision is not the end of a linear process, but is rather itself a recursive process,[3] one which can occur at any point during composing. Recent research also shows that different groups of writers revise in different ways, a finding reflected in, for example, the work of Beach,[4] Bridwell,[5] Faigley and Witte,[6] Flower,[7] and Murray,[8] as well as Sommers. Finally, recent research has developed classification systems to explain those revisions. Such efforts appear, for example, in the work of Sommers,[9] Bridwell,[10], and Faigley and Witte.[11]

However much this body of research helps us to understand the results or effects of revision, it does considerably less to help us understand what causes writers to revise. The most promising research on the causes of revision, of course, is that of Flower and Hayes. Reporting on their use of composing-aloud protocols in a case-study format,[12] they conclude that when expert writers redefine or clarify the audience and goals of their texts they frequently revise.[13] This research offers the best hypotheses about the situational or contextual causes of revision. But while Flower and Hayes suggest that the "text produced so far" becomes part of the situational context, they do not adequately explore specific textual cues that may prompt revisions. Indeed, apart from what little can be gleaned from studies which look to errors[14] in the text for causes of revision, we know very little about the textual cues that prompt writers to alter texts to fit specific audiences and specific communication goals.

In the present study, I explore some of the textual causes and effects of revision which previous research has not examined (pp. 313–314).

Witte's object in this concise review of the literature, clearly, is to establish what is "known" about revision so that he can get on to what is not known and, subsequently, his own new contribution. He is not obliged to offer a comprehensive review of the literature on revision, nor, despite the heavy documentation, does he pretend to. I suppose it is even possible to argue that the whole passage could be deemed strictly ceremonial, and that he includes these titles simply by way of ritual salutation—so that a close analysis of the passage, like the genuine answering of the question "How are you?" is bad manners. But the seriousness of his tone, the careful documentation, and the essay's reception indicate otherwise. The studies cited may be, as his qualifiers suggest, exemplars and representatives, but they are deliberately and carefully chosen.

What concerns us here is the methodological mix. In the first paragraph, where he says most about what is known, Witte feels able to claim—on the basis of four Clinical studies (Emig, Sommers, Beach, Faigley and Witte), one quasi-Experimental study (Bridwell), two Formalist-based studies (Flower, Flower and Hayes), and the ruminations of a Practitioner (Murray)—that "recent research" has established that revision is a recursive process performed differently by different groups of writers, and rendered explicable by classification systems.

Now I want to be clear about this. The question here is not whether Witte *can* make such claims. He obviously does, and the fact of their publication in a leading journal, as well as the status of the essay as the *best* article in that journal for a full year, indicates that he does so with the blessing of at least that journal's editor, editorial board, and the Braddock Award committee. No: the question (or questions) are more like how, and why, and with what sort of logic can he make such claims? How can the products of such diverse kinds of inquiry be made to hang together? What happens to the inquiries— if there are any—that don't fit, that demonstrate or show or argue otherwise? To get at the answers, we need to begin by returning to the studies themselves.

We can begin with the first two citations: Janet Emig's *The Composing Processes of Twelfth Graders*; and Nancy Sommers' work, particularly her dissertation (*Revision in the Composing Process: A Case Study of College Freshmen and Experienced Adult Writers*) and "Revision Strategies of Student Writers and Experienced Adult Writers." All three are, in my scheme, Clinical studies; we reviewed them at some length in Chapter 7. And it may be safe to say that Emig, Sommers, and others have "challenged the assumption underlying" the alleged "unfortunate" simplistic view of revision, although it seems rather unfair to say that Rohman and Wlecke "set forth" such a model when it isn't clear whether the "akin"-ness makes their model unfortunate and simplistic, too, or just how they are implicated in fostering such a view.

However, it is another matter when Witte goes on to claim that the studies of either Emig or Sommers "demonstrated that revision is not the end of a linear process." Emig does suggest in her third chapter ("The Composing Process: Mode of Analysis") that the process she is trying to describe is "laminated and recursive," and that her narrative will try to "convey the actual density and 'blendedness' " (p. 33) of that process. But the "process" is composing, not revising *per se.* Moreover, she writes—as do the criticized Rohman and

Wlecke—of pre-writing, as well as planning, starting, stopping, and so on, all of which she seems to treat as temporally identifiable "stages" (or "moments" or "elements"), not recurring activities. Emig seems to view composing—as she must, presumably, since she claims to base her description on the work of her eight subjects—as a linear process within which there may be recurring activities. Thus she characterizes revising as one of three potential activities (along with correcting and rewriting) that are a part of what she calls "reformulation." As such, revising is identifiable as a "larger task [than correcting] involving the reformulation of larger segments of discourse and in more major and organic ways—a shift of point of view toward the material in the piece; major reorganizations and restructurings" (p. 43). Presumably such an activity could happen more than once during the composing of a piece, which would make it in some sense recursive.

But according to Emig's actual study, her subjects considered reformulation (in any of its three forms) at only one point during composing, and that after they had completed a fairly full draft. Moreover, none of them engaged in the "reformulating of pieces produced for this [Emig's] inquiry" (p. 87). In her discussion of Lynn, Emig writes that reformulation, stopping, and contemplating the product—the final three categories in her taxonomy—"take up so little chronological and psychological time that they almost coalesce into a single barely occurring experience" (p. 67). Emig offers explanations for this performance, ranging from the design of the study to Lynn's school-conditioned attitude, but the fact remains that Lynn does not revise. Thus, while certainly Emig argues that composing might be conceived as a recursive process, she definitely does not *demonstrate* that revising *is* such a process.

Sommers' argument is slightly different. What she claims, as she puts it in "Revision Strategies of Student Writers and Experienced Adult Writers," is that the experienced writers in her study "see their revision process as a recursive process—a process with significant recurring activities—with different levels of attention and different agenda for each cycle" (p. 386). This is no doubt an interesting finding, but what it actually represents is Sommers' generalized characterization of what 20 people told her about how they perceive something they do. While perhaps coming closer than Emig's study to the "demonstrating" Witte claims for them, it is nevertheless a demonstration about how a single researcher characterizes the individual perceptions of a small group.

But let's suppose, for the moment, that we grant Sommers the authority Witte affords her, and say that this characterization of how her experienced adult subjects perceived their revising constitutes a demonstration that revision is a recursive process. The methodological point would be essentially the same. How powerful a generalization can be made on the basis of her and Emig's 48 total subjects doing assigned tasks under what amounted to laboratory conditions, when a good number of those subjects did not, in the investigators' judgment, revise recursively, if at all? Clinical findings can be provocative, but these studies wouldn't seem to qualify as demonstrations that can provide the basis for Witte's Experimental study.

If Witte's handling of Emig and Sommers is interesting for the way in which Clinical findings are—well, let's say extended or amplified—the second set of six citations is interesting at least as much for the way various kinds of inquiry are pulled together. With this set, Witte wants to argue that recent research has shown that "different groups of writers revise in different ways." It isn't exactly clear why he opts for the locution that this finding is "reflected in" as opposed to, say, "supported by" different work, nor is it clear what research it then is that has demonstrated the truth of this finding so that these other studies could be said to reflect it. Whatever the case, the locution does seem to be deliberately chosen as less assertive than "demonstrating."

The first study—Richard Beach's "Self-Evaluation Strategies of Extensive Revisers and Nonrevisers"—rather fits the pattern of Witte's use of Emig and Sommers: it deals with revision, but not quite in the way suggested. In what might be described as a marginal Clinical study, Beach explicitly identifies his project as "an informal, exploratory study," the conclusions of which "should apply only to this group" (p. 160). The student subjects, all in the same class, were classified as extensive revisers or nonrevisers on the basis of "two short papers on topics of their choice," for which they wrote a mandatory initial draft in a "freewriting mode," followed by tape recorded self-evaluations, then revision, and so on (with two-day breaks between drafts) until they felt they were finished. It's an interesting, modestly framed study, on the basis of which Beach argues that students may benefit from work directly on their self-evaluation strategies.

What matters for our purpose, however, is that strictly speaking, Beach's study doesn't reflect what Witte says it does. That is, rather than reflecting the finding that "different groups of writers revise in different ways," it suggests only that writers can be grouped according to the different ways in which they revise. Unless Witte is offering a tautology, this can't be what he has in mind.

The second study, Lillian Bridwell's 1980 "Revising Strategies in Twelfth Grade Students' Transactional Writing," comes closer to doing what Witte says. This careful, considerably larger, quasi-Experimental study is based on the analysis of "6,129 revisions in 100

randomly selected sets of twelfth grade students' drafts of an inform-
ative/argumentative essay" (Abstract, p. 197). The student subjects—
171 of 195 twelfth graders in a Georgia high school—were asked to
write, in class, two drafts of an essay on a topic that provided them
with audience and purpose, but not subject. They were given the
assignment and "fact sheets" for note-taking the day before actual
writing (but forbidden to actually write).

One of the criteria by which these students were grouped for
analysis, then, was according to how well they wrote, the "quality
rating" of their single essay. So the study could be said, in accordance
with Witte's claim, to deal with "good" and "poor" twelfth-grade
writers as groups. However, this is obviously a fairly weak grouping criterion—a one-mode, in-class, forced-revision writing sample is hardly
grounds for a meaningful determination of good or poor writers, a
limitation of which Bridwell seems quite aware. Moreover, she is very
careful not to mistake statistical correlation for evidence of causation,
"not to assume cause-effect relationships between patterns [of revi-
sion] and quality [of final essay], but rather to describe possible
associations" (p. 212). In other words, she doesn't claim knowledge
of any causal connection between the ways the writers in these two
groups revised and the criterion by which they were grouped.

In the final analysis, then, Bridwell's study suggests that, for her
task and sample, the writers of poorly rated essays fell into two
"camps"—those who revised very little, and those who revised a great
deal, but in limited ways; but that the writers of highly rated essays
could not be so easily characterized, some revising little and some
extensively, with changes ranging "across the levels and stages investigated in the study" (p. 218). Thus, in Bridwell's study, a good
writer could be—and apparently was, in some instances—described
as revising like a poor writer, a finding which rather muddies the
waters for Witte's claim. That is, it suggests that different groups
of writers sometimes revise in different ways, but that sometimes
they revise in the same ways.

Not surprisingly, the study that, with Sommers', best supports
this second of Witte's contentions is reported in the article he co-
authored with Lester Faigley, "Analyzing Revision." This study, like
Emig's, Sommers', and Beach's, can be described as Clinical: 18
writers (six each of inexperienced students, advanced students, and
expert adults) were assigned a task in the same pattern as Bridwell's
subjects (three days, a mandatory first draft, a mandatory revision).
In addition, the expert adults were asked to revise the first drafts of
essays written by three of the inexperienced students, so that the
differences between the actual writers' and adult writers' revisions
could be analyzed.

The study's key feature was its analysis of textual changes. Faigley and Witte developed a taxonomy that they claimed enabled them to distinguish between "revisions that affect the meaning of the text ['Meaning Changes'] and those that do not ['Surface Changes']" (p. 402); and beyond that between Macrostructure and Microstructure changes (Meaning Changes that do and do not "affect the reading of other parts of the text," [p. 405]), and Formal versus Meaning Preserving Surface changes. This taxonomy was applied to the three stages of the assigned writings of all 18 writers, and to the extra revisions of the inexperienced writers' drafts by the expert adults.

The general results support Witte's claim: different groups of writers—in this case, groups identified according to the rather broad criteria of experience and ability—did revise in different ways, with the advanced student writers making the most changes, the inexperienced writers making mostly surface changes, and so on. Moreover, when given the inexperienced students' drafts and asked to revise them "as if they were their own" (p. 409), the expert adults made revisions of very different kinds from those offered by the actual authors.

The methodological catch here, of course, is that it is not clear in what way claims about groupings of this kind can be meaningful in a Clinical study. As the authors are careful to point out, they found "extreme diversity in the ways expert writers revise" (p. 410), and they briefly characterize four of the six in their study as highly idiosyncratic in their manner of revising. The result is to render the statistical profile generated by the taxonomy suspect, a suspicion that extends to the profiles of the other two groups as well. What this study indicates, then, is not so much that different groups of writers revise in different ways, as that individual writers revise in different ways, and that statistical profiles generated by the grouping of such writers will reflect those differences.

Similar sorts of problems arise for the rest of the work Witte cites, as I think can be made clear without carrying what is obviously an unusually close reading to obnoxious lengths. Linda Flower and John Hayes' investigations are offered in support of both the assertion about groups of writers and, later, as the most promising research on the causes of Revision. As should be clear from Chapter 8, however, it is a mistake to conceive of the results of Formalist inquiry as empirically-based in any Experimental sense: the connections between the Formalist's model and any real-world phenomenon are simply too problematic, at least without far more explanation than Witte offers. The Donald Murray essay cited, "Writing as Process: How Writing Finds Its Own Meaning," is a marvelous piece of Practitioner speculation, with Murray drawing in bits and pieces of knowl-

edge from all over and spinning a wonderful lor-ish argument about
what teachers and writers might do, but it's hard to see how it fits
here. At no point in that essay does Murray consider the revising of
different groups, let alone suggest that such groups revise differently.
If anything, he questions the usefulness of groups (except as audience
and communal support) as a focus of concern in Composition, insisting that "Individual conferences are the principal form of instruction
in the writing process approach" (pp. 15–16).

Somewhat less troublesome in terms of inter-modal blending of
inquiry is Witte's claim that Sommers, Bridwell, and Faigley and Witte
offer classification systems. All three are at least text-based—that is,
they classify identifiable changes made on the page—even if their
complementarity might pose some problems: Bridwell claims to offer
an "exhaustive and mutually exclusive scheme" (p. 203), apparently
subsuming Sommers', while Faigley and Witte want simply "to add a
research tool which can be used in combination with other research
tools such as protocol analysis" (p. 401). What is troubling, though,
is Witte's suggestion that these schemes can "explain those revisions,"
"those" apparently referring to the different revisions made by the
different groups of writers. These schemes did, in their various ways,
classify such changes. And in the Sommers and Faigley and Witte
studies the classified changes were, following Clinical usage, interpreted with more or less caution, while Bridwell, bound by Experimental rules, used them to seek correlative directions for further
inquiry. But in none of the three studies can the classifying itself
be construed as explaining.

This is an appropriate juncture at which to point out, once
again, that the object of this painstaking examination is not to im-
pugn Witte's scholarship. In this essay, and in his other writings, he is
energetic, wide-ranging, and stimulating. And, as I noted earlier, what
he has to say in "Topical Structure and Revision" has clearly been
sanctioned by the powers that be in Composition: This is what top-
flight inquiry in Composition is *supposed* to look like.

Nevertheless, my original question stands: By what sort of logic
are these studies being strung together? Witte seems to handle the
results of these methodologically diverse investigations as if they were
so many Lego blocks: standardized bits and pieces of "knowledge"
which, whatever their origins, sizes, or shapes, can be coupled together to form a paradigmatic frame within which his own exploratory Experimental study will fit. In the process, he is able to over-
look not only the less than direct connection between what these
studies actually offer and his claims about their impact, and some
substantive contradictions among the studies themselves, but to duck
as well the issue of methodological fit. Thus he argues that "recent

research" has demonstrated, shown, and explained various things about revision, but to whose satisfaction? By what standards? If, as I think is obviously the case, these studies cannot be offered as accumulating with any particular methodological integrity, what sort of integrity can they have? What forces are at work here that can override the otherwise powerful boundaries of methodological communities?

The answer lies in what Witte gains by establishing the context he does. His first step, you will recall, was to dissociate himself from the "simplistic view" allegedly held by so many Practitioners. But a preference for the complex over the simplistic doesn't provide much of a context within which revision can be defined or investigated. With the studies he has assembled, however, consider these three properties of the context he is able to claim:

(1) A context in which revision (and revising) is defined in textual terms. It might be put this way: revising is defined as the process which leads to revisions, the latter being identifiable, retrievable marks on a page (or, by extension, any medium for composing). The "recursive process" of revising—presumably a "mental" operation that results in these changes—is assumed to exist, but for operational purposes can only be said to have taken place after some addition, substitution, deletion or rearrangement (to use Sommers' terms, borrowed from Emig) has been made on a page.

Flower and Hayes are the only Researchers cited who might disagree. Their technique of asking for composing aloud purports to offer, in addition to and for their purposes more important than textual changes, a different sort of evidence for the occurrence of the assumed mental operation, so that they could claim to have indications of that process even in the absence of textual evidence. Witte gets around this potentially troublesome difference in definition by ignoring it. He rightly points out that the model Flower and Hayes derive from their analysis and interpretation of composing-aloud protocols suggests that writers may react to "situational" or "contextual" changes, and that such reactions may lead to textual changes. The point here, however, is that they don't have to, and then it becomes unclear whether such reconsiderations, and even the rehearsing aloud of possible alternatives that never get written down, constitute revising-the-mental-process or not. It may or may not be reasonable for him to criticize Flower and Hayes for their failure to "adequately explore specific textual cues that may prompt revision," depending upon how seriously they regard the texts people produce under composing-aloud conditions. What he seems not to understand, though, is that their definition for revision is, or at least can be, much broader than his own. (It is also worth noting that one of the four operations in Sommers' list, addition, is obviously troublesome given Witte's definition, because it can be hard to tell, from the evidence of a given draft, whether any portion of the text is the result of drafting —that is, first-time composing—or addition. If, for instance, I leave space for my introductory paragraph, and go back to write it in last, is that composing or revising? If it's composing, then how can adding *ever* be revising, and how does it come to be a category at all? As we shall see in his exploratory study, however, Witte also works around that problem by effectively removing the option to add to the text.)

(2) A context in which it is appropriate to study revision via prompted writings—under, as it were, laboratory conditions—and in which, moreover, second and even third drafts, written at assigned times, in assigned places, even with assigned instruments, are required of subjects. Only Murray of the sources named writes primarily about what could be called naturally occurring revision. Some of the others concede that forced writing (and revising) on assigned topics presents problems of artificiality: Emig and Sommers back up their forced writings with interviews, and Faigley and Witte say they "supplement" their work with the examination of the "actual revisions of practicing writers of various sorts" (p. 410). In none of the studies, however, is the artificiality deemed sufficient to invalidate the investigation.

(3) A context in which revisions are assumed to be for the purpose of making writing "better" or more "readable" as determined by a reader or readers. This is the weakest of the three features of this context because it is usually only implicit in the works cited. Flower (1979) is most explicit about it when she suggests that revision is the transformation of "Writer-Based prose" to "Reader-Based prose." Murray, in a rather puzzling formulation that nevertheless seems to fit here, argues that the end of revising is to help the writing say what it has to say "clearly and gracefully." Bridwell's inclusion of quality ratings suggests that she considered such improvement a possibility, and in fact found that there was significant improvement for her overall sample between first and second drafts in the General Merit and Mechanics segments of the rating scale applied (Diederich's nine-point scale excluding handwriting).

Of Witte's sources, only Sommers comes close to direct disagreement about the ends of revision. Sommers makes it clear that she thinks the greater range in her experienced subjects' revisions were desirable because they indicate a reaction to "the dissonance that both provokes revision and promises, from itself, new meaning" (p. 386). She doesn't really say for whose benefit or in what sense this writing will thus have changed, but the notion of "new meaning" indicates that it may be enough for the writer to like it better. On the other hand, she seems to have chosen the experienced writers ("journalists, editors, and academics") at least partly because they were known producers of publicly acceptable, readable writing—that is, because their composing processes produced "good," readable writing, for which, presumably, their "mature" revising habits were partly responsible.

We can get a better sense of how this context has been formed by considering alternatives to it, by looking at what gets left out. An alternative to (1), for example—revision defined in strictly textual terms—would be to define it, rather as Flower and Hayes do, as a process that may or may not be deduced from the existence of textual changes. So, for instance, if I were to consider two or three alternatives to this sentence, creating them aloud or silently, and then dispensing with one after the other, that activity could be conceived of as revising even though it produced no textual evidence.

Indeed, we might consider re-defining what or where a "text" is. In Witte's positivist-influenced context, a text is what Composition argot would currently call the "product": it has to be something that can be seen and measured. We would have no trouble generating support from literary theory, for instance, for a context in which the status and location of text was more variable than that. In such a context, obviously, the meaning of textual cues would have to change, and the role of the page-bound and in some sense writer- and reader-proof features that, by Witte's definition, currently constitute the only sort of textual cues, would have to change as well.

For (2)—the notion that revision can be studied under laboratory conditions—we need only adopt the Ethnographic position, and argue that while prompted writings and forced revisions no doubt tell us something about what people do under such conditions, that is all they tell us. That is, the idea of basing an investigation on the *a priori* conviction that there existed a discrete set of mental operations identifiable as revision—a set to which, by definition, not only the investigators but the subjects had no direct access—seems an unlikely way to proceed, to say the least. We would more likely be interested in what some of these investigators called their supplemental work, their interviews with and visits to real writers at work, even if their preoccupation with the idea of "doing over" did tend to distort what they could learn. In fact, we might even be sympathetic to some of these more intrusive investigative techniques if *they* were the supplements, concocted as ways to get insights we might then check with the writers studied. To accept and attempt to interpret the results of such odd tasks without that sense of the larger context, however, seems not simply irresponsible but almost absurd.

Similarly with (3), the idea that revising "improves" texts. There is surely no reason why revising, defined in any terms, shouldn't lead to more confused or less readable texts. Revisions can and presumably do go in any qualitative direction at all, can be said—depending, of course, on how a particular investigation chooses to measure such things—to make a text more, less, or equally readable. In fact, it should be possible to make space for all three of these categories of textual change without even going beyond Witte's restriction to traceable textual changes. We could, for example, posit things called *pro*visions as changes that make a text more readable, *anti*visions as those that make it less so, and *neu*visions as those that had no measurable effect. Indeed, we could even create categories that would chart a kind of second dimension of revision, one that might satisfy Sommers' concern for "new meaning": that is, we could create categories within which to classify changes that have been made to satisfy the writer's sense of what is true or accurate, regardless of their impact on readability. At any rate, it is clear that, even limiting its definition to changes traceable on the page in this way, revision still admits of a far greater degree of complexity than Witte allows here.

The importance of this context finally becomes fully clear when we see how Witte explains the exploratory study of textual cues by which he has sought to add to what is known about revision. Acknowledging that the "task may be somewhat artificial," he has given a 326-word passage from a published book called *Language and Community* to some 80 students. The subject of the passage is "something like 'language development in the vulnerable human infant'" (p. 320):

> The students were given 40 minutes in which to "read the passage carefully" and then to "revise it" so that it would be "easier to read and understand" but would retain "its character as a piece of informative discourse." The students were also asked to assume that they were revising for a "college-educated audience" that had a general knowledge of the subject matter of the text (p. 322).

Consider how far Witte has made the context he has established take him (or how far he has taken it) in constructing this study. Revision is still defined, as in (1), in terms of textual changes, but now—despite his earlier insistence that revision is a recursive process—those changes need not be made on a piece of the writer's own work-in-progress. Changes made by *any* writer on *any* text constitute revisions, apparently without the implied or assumed cognitive process—revising—losing its identity. How this can be true in the absence of the entire process of composing, and thus in the absence of opportunities for recursion, he doesn't say.

In keeping with (2), the revisions will take place on command in what amounts to a laboratory setting. The task is closest, perhaps, to the third day of the three-day Bridwell pattern, where writers are given their own work from the previous day and are free to mark up the original copy and then to produce a new one. Here, though, the subjects are given someone else's writing, and only the changes that actually appear in the rewritten versions are accounted for. What Witte particularly likes about this procedure, which again obviously stretches the boundaries of the context he has established, is its enhanced control over "both the text features and the content to which writers must respond during revision" (p. 322).

Finally, as the instructions indicate, revision here is defined as making the text easier for a specified (if not specific) audience to read. This definition raises something of a problem when Witte tries to interpret his data. He finds that both what he calls "high-score" and "low-score" revisions are both much shorter on average than the original: the former, 158.2 words shorter (sd = 46.1), the latter 93.9 (sd = 29.8). They were also considerably shorter in terms of two of his key measures: mean clause length, and T-unit length (p. 325). In other words, any findings he offers must be based on the different ways in which the two groups of essays have been *shortened*. The difficulty, as must be obvious, is that it would have been almost impossible for his subjects to make the passage substantively longer; they were not themselves experts on the subject matter. In short, they were forced to regard revision as reduction. It might still be interesting to compare how different writers shorten a passage when asked to make it more readable, but to do so is a long way from examining how they revise, at least in the sense of that term that Witte has established. What makes this particularly paradoxical, of course, is that Witte ends up fairly coercing his subjects into treating revision as something very close to what he condemns in his opening complaint about teachers and textbooks, "as the process by which a writer merely cleans up the mechanical and stylistic infelicities of an otherwise completed text."

The forces we see at work here, then, the only forces that could override methodological integrity and still claim to create a context within which Witte's study—a context-stretcher itself—still not only makes sense but in fact is rewarded for excellence, are political forces. Just as it has been useful to understand the revolutionary growth of Composition in essentially political terms, so here Witte's construction and deployment of an investigative context is best understood as a political act. We have seen how Richard Young dealt with invention in proposing his research agenda. Witte has tried to do the same by keeping the general rubric, Revision, intact—first, by actively ex-

cluding from consideration those approaches to it most inimical to
his own needs; and, second, by ignoring or passing lightly over the
contradictory features, and at the same time emphasizing the compatible features, of the approaches he does name. It is a strategy calculated to put him in a position to claim knowledge, and in this instance, anyway, it works. Those in position to say so have determined
that this is how Composition wants to define, investigate, and validate
claims concerning what is known about revision. Such approval,
barring either personnel changes in key positions or shifts in the
politics thereof, will no doubt prompt further study in more or less
the same context.

Witte's essay serves, in a microcosmic way, to exemplify what
has been the general pattern of inter-methodological accumulation of
knowledge for most of Composition's short history. Individual methodological communities, united in their drive to divest the Practitioners, and in any case lacking the wherewithal to establish any broad
power base, have gotten along tolerably well by pooling findings in
much the way that Witte pools them here. Faced with a relative
shortage of non-Practitioner knowledge, investigators have had to pile
together whatever they could find: a few Experimental hypotheses, a
little Clinical insight, a Formalist speculation or two, even an occasional Practitioner notion thrown in. So long as such a hodgepodge
has had the consent of most of the other producers and consumers—
which probably means, practically speaking, until one or more single
communities generate enough knowledge to operate independently—
it has held together.

However, this arrangement may be beginning to break down.
Not only the pace and volume but the variety of inquiry in Composition has accelerated rather dramatically. With more and more
knowledge of more and more kinds being cranked out by these communities, each one has more and more reason to be wary of the exchanges it is willing to make. And as this faith in the system erodes,
the field's idealized self-image of cumulative, multi-methodological
"progress"—so important in the first phase of the revolution—becomes harder and harder to maintain. The tensions constrained
beneath the surface are so great that that image is necessarily a distortion, and in such delicate balance that, under even the gentlest
probing, it threatens to shatter completely.

We might, by extending our conception of Composition in
political terms just a little further, characterize Witte's creation of an
investigative context by emphasizing, passing over, or suppressing
methodological points of view as it suits his purposes—all without
calling attention to, or perhaps being fully aware of, what he is doing
—as a kind of covert activity. There is a methodological war being

fought, but it takes place, as it were, behind the scenes. And this has been, except for some occasional sniping, as heated as the confrontation has been. As the supply of knowledge has grown, however, and with it the inter-communal tensions, there has begun to be overt activity, open conflict, as well. The general pattern tends to pit pro-Researcher positions against pro-Scholar ones. On one side are those commentators who, like Paul Bryant, Richard Young, Maxine Hairston, Janet Emig, James Kinneavy, Carl Bereiter and Marlene Scardamalia, Clinton Burhans, Jr., and others, argue that Composition has, ought to have, or soon enough will have some version of a paradigmatic structure. As Robert Connors, whose position we will review shortly, has objected, paradigm is not a term that has always benefited from terribly precise usage, with the result that some of its potency, gained from its prominence in Kuhn's widely read book, is a trifle bogus. Nevertheless, the pro-Researcher theme is fairly constant: in the post-revolutionary hierarchy, most of the power over knowledge and method in Composition is or ought to be accumulating in its Researcher communities; and the movement of the field as a whole ought generally to emulate what they perceive as the unidirectional, coherent, puzzle-solving sweep of paradigmatically-directed inquiry as it has worked in other fields.

The general outlines of this position are, I assume, clear enough by now. The exact nature and status of the paradigm varies from version to version: whether it is already in place or is just forming, for example; what sorts of methods are to be governed by it; how those methods might interact, and so on. The bottom-line problem every version faces, however, is the same one we have traced in Witte's essay: What shape will the cumulative, hybrid knowledge this paradigm produces take? What kinds of knowledge will be included, and how might they be altered? Which kinds will be left out, and how will their absence be explained? Young seems willing to include all sorts of inquiry, but he doesn't make it clear how they can come together; Witte is more selective, but silent about the principles governing his selection. It may be worthwhile to look here at a version that addresses these issues more directly.

What distinguishes the perspective that Carl Bereiter and Marlene Scardamalia set forth in their "Levels of Inquiry in Writing Research," then, is that it recognizes, in a way that most other paradigmatic scenarios do not, the inter-methodological conflicts at work in Composition:

> This chapter is concerned with providing a systematic way of viewing the varied forms of inquiry into the process of composition. Several motives lie behind this effort. On the one hand, we are impatient, as surely many others are, with the miscellaneous

character of much writing research, with its orientation toward topics or methods rather than toward goals, and with its general lack of cumulative force. On the other hand, we think that in this era of competing methodologies there is a special need to promote tolerance and a free spirit of inquiry. Writing research is new and there is not much of it. It is not easy and there are, as yet, no magic keys to an understanding of it. Writing research needs to be varied without being unfocused, guided by theory without being dogmatic, progressive without being mindlessly trendy. To achieve such balance, it seems desirable for research- ers to have conscious access to a scheme that allows them to conceive of their immediate activities within a larger pattern. In this chapter, we set forth such a scheme (p. 3).

What they offer is a scheme consisting of six "levels of inquiry": (1) reflective inquiry; (2) empirical variable testing; (3) text analysis; (4) process description; (5) theory embedded experimentation; and (6) simulation. These levels are not, they are careful to point out, best understood as steps or phases. They are connected by only a "weak sequentiality." We are asked to conceive of them, rather, as "ordered on a dimension of abstractness" (p. 4). Moreover, they are not ranked in an evaluative hierarchy: the higher levels are not inher- ently superior to the lower ones, so that a researcher would be wrong to seek Level 6 work only. Instead, "understanding of the composing process does not emerge from inquiry at any particular level but rather through synthesizing knowledge gained in the course of spi- raling through levels" (p. 4). The more levels an inquiry moves through, the more powerful the knowledge it produces ought to be. And, finally, this scheme does not itself constitute a paradigm; that can emerge only "as investigators come to recognize common prob- lems, to discover common ways of talking about them, and to agree on the relevance of certain kinds of data." Their scheme is *"a frame- work for the kind of interaction that should lead to a paradigm"* (p. 22, their emphasis).

So far so good; this approach seems inclusive in ways the others we have looked at were not. In fact, though, the kind of interaction they have in mind has a certain, fairly obvious bias to it; not every- one is invited to participate, and those who are invited can partici- pate only in certain ways. At base, what this scheme amounts to is a mustering of Formalist forces, with invitations offered to selected other communities to enlist, at varying prices, under the Formalist banner. Hence three of the levels, as conceived by Bereiter and Scardamalia at any rate, represent Formalist strongholds already: Level 3, textual analysis; Level 5, theory-embedded experimentation; and Level 6, simulation. Level 4, process description (as, e.g., Flower

and Hayes), is also conceived primarily as Formalist work, although
there is presumably an invitation at this level to Clinicians, who can
get in fairly cheaply: all they need is to be willing, as some seem to
be, to downplay the importance of depicting the individuality and
complexity of their subjects where such things are not Formally
relevant—relevant, that is, to the model under construction.

Other invitations appear to be more demanding. There seems to
be some room for Practitioners to gain entry at Level 1, reflective
inquiry, but it would mean a lot of work. So a Practitioner like Peter
Elbow (to pick one specifically named) would be expected to recon-
ceive his ordinary reflectiveness as "part of a more comprehensive
program of inquiry" (p. 5). He would thus move from thinking about
his own experience upward to the other levels—seeking variables to
test empirically, tracing in texts whatever lawfulness he could on the
assumption that it "must have its counterpart in the mind of the
writer" (p. 11), and so on—moving through all of the levels, finally,
if he sought the best knowledge. Similar mobility would be expected,
in theory, of all recruits.

Experimentalists would no doubt find the price of their inclusion in this interaction even higher, since it not only urges them
toward this mobility, but asks them to treat their own method as
little more than a research tool, a "supplement to—not replacement
for—Level 1 inquiry" (p. 7). From a Formalist perspective, apparently, the usual demands of Experimental inquiry are inappropriate
for the independent study of writing:

> It is not fair or reasonable to judge empirical variable testing
> against a standard of absolute certainty—to expect, for in-
> stance, that research on the relationship between good reading
> and good writing should finally yield us an answer that we can
> be sure of as we are sure that two plus two make four. We
> should ask instead whether the research has given us a sounder
> factual basis for Level 1 reflection than we would have had
> without it—that is, whether the factual basis is sounder than
> we could achieve through informal observations, study of iso-
> lated cases, or commonsense assumptions (p. 7).

The odd comparison aside—arithmetic is a formal system and doesn't
achieve certainty experimentally—the net result is, in effect, to ask
the Experimentalists to abandon their very powerful tradition,
severing the ties with the natural and social science disciplines from
which they derive such a large part of their prestige. What makes it
worth keeping without that heritage, argue Bereiter and Scardamalia,
is its superiority over Level 1 in terms of being able to reduce error.
What limits it, at least in the context of Formalist inquiry, is its

preoccupation with an apparently infinite set of variables and variable combinations, a preoccupation that the other levels of inquiry—for which we might read "Formalist inquiry"—escape by their concern for "the structures and processes lying behind them" (p. 10).

Ethnographers would be asked to make a similar surrender. The lack of sympathy that such holists, as they are called here, might have for Formalist goals apparently makes them rather rude and threatening extremists:

> Although holistic methods have much to offer in writing research, there is, on the other hand, a holistic ideology that poses an actual threat to writing research. The main feature of this ideology is opposition to any research (or instruction) that deals with less than the full act of writing carried out under natural conditions. One evident motive behind this ideology is to promote writing as a meaningful activity, but this laudable motive has gotten out of hand when it drives people to oppose any research procedure that they would not accept as an instructional procedure. . . . To hold strictly to a holistic ideology would mean giving up any hope of understanding writing as a cognitive process. The Levels of Inquiry framework, we hope, will make it possible for concerned humanists of a holistic persuasion to see that various methodologies, ranging from naturalistic observation to esoteric laboratory procedures, can be combined into a coherent effort to understand how human minds actually accomplish the complete act of writing (p. 21).

But of course it is precisely ideology—the politics of knowledge and method—that distinguishes the holists from the Formalists from the Experimentalists and so on. Ethnographers are surely as committed to understanding writing as Formalists. Given their fundamental assumptions, though, they might well be skeptical of inquiry that claims to "understand writing as a cognitive process," or at least of what "understand" might mean in such a context. Even assuming that the inter-communal hostility is not as severe as Bereiter and Scardamalia seem to think—so that a peaceful coexistence were possible—it seems hard to envision how there could be any more intimate relationship.

In the end, then, Bereiter and Scardamalia's conviction that "various methodologies . . . can be combined into a coherent effort" ends up looking a good deal like Witte's: the cumbersome ideological irregularities clinging to the results of inquiry as a result of their various methodological origins are assumed to be non-essential, so that, given the right spirit of compromise—or, better, sacrifice—they could be stripped away to leave basically uniform epistemological Lincoln

logs, from which a neat and coherent whole might be constructed.
And it just doesn't work that way.

Noteworthy by their absence from this framework for interaction, of course, are the Scholars. They might be conceived of as
fitting in somewhere on the margins of Level 1, reflective inquiry
(Aristotle's *Poetics* is offered as an example), although this first level
is characterized as beginning in and returning to personal experience,
with no indication that there might be either texts or dialectic in
between. Whether or not Bereiter and Scardamalia would place the
Scholars in this group, the inherent limitation of what they call
"armchair enquirers" no doubt extends to them: they don't get out
of the chair to check and see if what they figured out is *really* true.
Scholarly inquiry just doesn't fit very well in even a Formalist
paradigm.

So it makes sense at this point to introduce the other side in
this debate, a group consisting mostly of Scholars defending themselves against what amounts to this pro-Researcher power play. The
vocal membership in this group is smaller, and their arguments tend
to be directly in reaction to pro-Researcher pronouncements. What
they have in common, naturally, is an insistence that whatever
Composition is, it is not, cannot and should not be or become
paradigmatic in the pro-Researcher sense. They all point to the same
primary danger: that investigators are attracted to what they conceive of as paradigmatic inquiry by the power, prestige, and success
such methods have won their users in other fields, without regard for
their suitability to Composition.

These commentators, as we saw in Chapters 4 and 10 with Ann
Berthoff, are clear in their preference for Scholarly ways of making
knowledge, for inquiry founded on dialectic. They perceive Composition to be, or to be based on, what they are likely to label humanistic inquiry. Another example of such commentary can be found in
Michael Holzman's "Scientism and Sentence-Combining." In a
capsule account of the transformation of Composition very like the
one offered here in its tracing of the political motives for methodological choices, Holzman illustrates the dangers of scientism as manifested during the (then) sixteen-year history of sentence-combining
research and pedagogy. His purpose is not to undermine the promise
of sentence-combining as a pedagogical tool—it has already, he suggests, returned to a humbler, more appropriate status—but to speculate from the field's experience with it about the implications of
paradigmatic methods of inquiry for Composition's future. He is
particularly concerned with the role such methods might play as
Composition's hard-won and perhaps fragile professional identity
separates it from the larger English profession/discipline:

Sentence-combining research can be seen as an early indication of the growing methodological difference between the community of scholars concerned with literacy and the community of scholars concerned with literature. It contributed to the legitimacy of our organizational separation from English departments and associations; it pointed the way for us to achieve autonomy through the choice of research modes. No doubt other research targets will be developed; more sophisticated methods will be applied; a new generation of graduate students, even now being trained, will avoid the errors of their elders. The methodological difficulties of sentence-combining research will eventually, no doubt, be seen as a regrettable, but relatively unimportant, lapse in the development of an exciting new scholarly discipline, literacy research. A social scientific methodology eventually may be valuable in literacy research, but will not necessarily be superior to humanistic modes of research. Humanistic knowledge achieves intersubjective validity in a manner different from, but no less real than, that by which valid knowledge in the sciences is found. The humanities are the sciences of man; the nature and the extent of possible humanistic knowledge are themselves subjects of study by humanists. The humanities are fundamentally unlike the natural sciences, which seek to approach as close as possible to absolute knowledge. We often agree to a given interpretation of a cultural situation largely because we view events from within that culture (pp. 78–79).

The problem, however—for Holzman, and for the pro-Scholar position generally—is much the same as for his pro-Researcher counterparts: Just what might such a multi-modal body of knowledge look like? Berthoff would seem likely to deny non-Scholarly modes of inquiry admission to Composition altogether. Holzman is not quite so exclusive; when he suggests that "A social scientific methodology eventually may be valuable in literacy research . . . ," one senses he is leaving the door open for some version of Ethnography. Nevertheless, he does not seem to think any such method has yet proven its value. Moreover, not only will he not grant such methods the special status they ordinarily seem to demand (". . . will not necessarily be superior to humanistic modes of research"); he suggests that they must finally be subservient:

> It would be a serious mistake to allow the fascination of methodologies for social scientific research to bring us to doubt that literacy is primarily a humanistic attainment—not so much a special kind of knowledge as the necessary prerequisite for all knowledge. For a discipline as closely bound to classroom practice as composition research must be, the social scientific path

holds dangers as well as utopian possibilities. Quantification, no matter how necessary for analysis, is but the first movement in a dialectic that must return before its completion to humanistic notions of knowledge. Literacy—Rhetoric, Composition—is not necessarily the same type of discipline as Linguistics. If we employ social scientific methodologies in our research, we must be careful to do so in the service of a humanistic pedagogy (p. 79).

Robert Connors takes a similar position in his "Composition Studies and Science," where he confronts the pro-Researcher position head on. Proponents of that position, he argues, belied by their insistent borrowing from Kuhn, have been sending the same tacit message over and over again: ". . . *composition studies should be a scientific or prescientific discipline*" (p. 5). His aim is to beat such commentators at their own game; that is, to examine Composition's claims as a science against criteria derived from Kuhn and other sources, but derived more carefully and applied more critically. Connors' two questions, accordingly, are these: "Is the field of composition studies a scientific field? Can it become one" (p. 6)?

Not surprisingly, his answers are no and no:

> Methodologically rigorous, carefully controlled, and technically advanced though some aspects of psychologically-based research into composition may be, they do not make composition studies a mature scientific field with a paradigm of its own, and they do not even show conclusively that it is a preparadigmatic field—at least not one whose first paradigm is anywhere in sight. This survey of the branches and roots of composition studies has shown, I think, that Kuhn's terms, applied analogically as a claim for the essentially scientific or prescientific nature of the discipline, lead us only to blind alleys or to unrealistic expectations (p. 17).

Would Connors then banish what he calls "empirical research" from Composition? Isn't it finally a waste of time? Not quite: ". . . there must be room in composition studies for statistical or quantitative analyses or for science-based experimentation. We cannot cut our discipline off from verifiable knowledge" (p. 19). But again, it is very hard to tell just what role such inquiries, if they must finally surrender the power of their paradigmatic association, can play, or what status they can be assigned. Verification is precisely the central issue, and when there is more than one set of rules governing how it is done, there is bound to be trouble. And from Connors' perspective, rhetorical knowledge—by which he seems to mean something akin to knowledge derived by humanist methods—seems of a higher, or at least more encompassing, order, with breadth a virtue:

As Richard Weaver constantly reminds us, we as rhetoricians
must be concerned with a wider realm than are scientists—for
scientists are concerned only with facts and the relationships
between them, while rhetorical concerns must include both the
scientific occurrence and the axiological ordering of these facts.
We should not in our search for provable knowledge forget that
the essential use of all knowledge is in aiding humanity in the
search for consensually-arrived-at truth (p. 19).

An honorable enough sentiment, to be sure, but far from
undebatable; a fairly strong case can be made, even within the limited
confines of Composition, that an "essential" use of knowledge can be
to gain power. Truth, consensual or otherwise, seems as likely to
arrive via coercion or proclamation as cooperation. Nevertheless, by
framing the field in these terms, Connors manages to salvage for himself the open-endedness of dialectic, and with it the final superiority
of the pro-Scholar position. Thus he concludes as follows:

The enaction of imitation science cannot and should not be at
the heart of composition studies. Empirical research has much
to teach us, but it cannot teach us who or what we are. If we
surrender to the role-playing of scientism, to processing-
governed ameaning, our work can only result in a false objectivity that will "spew forth upon man a stream of ever more
degrading images of himself" (Koch, p. 675). The universe of
discourse is larger than the universe of science, and seductive
though the puzzle-solving of normal science may be, it has
always been the task of rhetoricians to try to solve problems
and not puzzles. It is the old burden of humanistic learning,
and every day we must shoulder it anew (p. 20).

VI

The Making
of Knowledge
in Composition

12

Futures

In the twenty years of its modern history, then, Composition has gone from being the least prestigious leg in the "tripod" of the English curriculum to a fairly substantial academic "society." In the first phase of this transformation, methodological differences were disguised or ignored in deference to unity towards a common goal, the divestiture of the Practitioners. During the second phase, those methodological differences have begun to clash, both above and below the surface of the society's public discourse—so far, along pro-Researcher versus pro-Scholar lines, but with the potential, clearly, for even further division along methodological lines. So, for example, Ethnography's phenomenological roots make it a threatening presence in the heavily positivist Researcher cluster of communities, and Formalists like Bereiter and Scardamalia threaten the status of Experimental inquiry. And there is always at least the remote threat of a Practitioner uprising.

The stakes remain much what they have been all along: power, prestige, professional recognition and advancement. It has thus far been a restrained confrontation; combatants on both sides seem to understand that, in the absence of an unlikely total victory, it is in their best interests that the field as a whole survive. Probably the most obvious indicator that this restraint is operating lies in the shared terms for characterizing Composition. For both sides, it is a "field," a "profession," and a "discipline," terms that seem to be treated interchangeably, as if in obedience to an unspoken rule: Characterize Composition as paradigmatic or dialogical, coherent or chaotic as you like, but it is to everyone's advantage to treat it as a legitimate academic discipline. Even Connors, whose attack on paradigmatic claims necessarily leads him to offer the harshest assessment of the field's coherence, uses all three terms freely. The furthest he goes toward suggesting that Composition might have internal inconsistencies is to call it a "mixed discipline" (p. 17)—something like history, presumably.

Still, it is not clear how long such restraints can endure. No doubt Composition can safely be termed a field, broadly defined as being concerned with the ways in which writing is done, taught, and learned. It may be, too, that those whose major academic interests lie within the loose boundaries of this field can be said to form a profession, although only its post-secondary members would seem able to declare full-fledged, full-time standing. And, as is true of teaching generally, it is a profession with relatively limited control over the training, licensing, and review of its members, at least by the standards of, say, the legal and medical professions.

But to consider Composition a discipline is to ask a good deal more; in effect, it demands that that term be reduced to a meaning little different from that of the already loosely construed "field." Training in a discipline ordinarily implies preparation for *doing* something, and in Composition, that something has been and in practice largely remains teaching writing. However, the modern version of the field is founded, really, on the subversion of that practical tradition. Indeed, both Holzman and Connors, presumably somewhat more sympathetic to that tradition than most of their paradigmatic counterparts, seem nevertheless to signal a break with it by suggesting new titles for the field—Holzman offering "literacy studies," Connors "composition studies," with the latter deliberately separate from "composition teaching." Surely when the field is conceived in these ways, or along the paradigmatic lines suggested by pro-Researcher proponents, the core of Composition as a discipline, and so the appropriate forms of training for its knowledge-makers, must lie in directions very different from those implicit in that practical tradition. If Composition is working its way toward becoming a discipline in any usual sense of that word, it is taking the long way around.

It might not be too much to claim, in fact, that for all the rhetoric about unity in pursuit of one or another goal, Composition as a knowledge-making society is gradually pulling itself apart. Not branching out or expanding, although these might be politically more palatable descriptions, but fragmenting: gathering into communities or clusters of communities among which relations are becoming increasingly tenuous. It is a process operating in accordance with what I would dub Diesing's law, from its formulation in Paul Diesing's *Patterns of Discovery in the Social Sciences*; to wit, "communication and co-operation occur primarily within the boundaries of a method, not within a field" (p. 11). That is, it is easier for an Experimentalist concerned with revision to get along with an Experimentalist studying reading instruction than with a Practitioner or a Philosopher studying revision; or for a Formalist studying the composing process to get along with a Formalist studying problem-solving than with an Ethnographer concerned with composing. Methodological sympathies cut across the boundaries of field, whereas methodological differences —disagreements over how knowledge is made, what knowledge can be—can create insurmountable barriers.

It is not difficult to envision what will happen if, as is most likely, these forces continue to operate unopposed in Composition. Quite simply, the field, however flimsily coherent now, will lose any autonomous identity altogether. Each of its constituent communities will be absorbed by some other field with a compatible methodology. It is the fate that seems to have awaited Composition's tripod counterpart, language, as embodied in linguistics. Linguistics hasn't disappeared, of course, but it has seemed unable to sustain an autonomous academic existence, appearing instead as psycho-linguistics, sociolinguistics, stylistics, linguistic anthropology, and the like. Composition's autonomy would dissolve in much the same way: Formalists concerned with the composing process would go off into cognitive psychology, Experimentalists into experimental psychology or schools of education, Ethnographers into anthropology, and so on. There they would find investigative contexts that could lend their findings the kind of methodological integrity they have not been able to provide for one another in Composition. Something closer to an integral Composition might surface as an institute or center, along the lines, say, of the Center for Applied Linguistics, or the Institute for Humanistic Approaches to Linguistic Analysis. However, such operations not only tend to embrace one or another methodological bias at the expense of others, but they represent a kind of institutional retreat, havens for inquiry that can find no more regular academic niche.

Probably the most striking feature of such a dissolution would be the fate of Composition in its academic birthplace, English. Currently, of course, Composition is still most often housed within English departments, usually as part of a writing program. But its presence there represents, as it nearly always has, mostly an administrative convenience—or, from some perspectives, inconvenience. The fact of the matter is that, despite longstanding pronouncements about the English tripod, and its continuing validity as a means of characterizing the English of elementary or secondary teachers, in postsecondary institutions both language and composition have given way to the overwhelming dominance of literature. With very few exceptions, the knowledge-making responsibilities of post-secondary English professionals lie in literary studies.

Some concessions have been made to a changing Composition. There are, for instance, a few dozen doctoral programs with Composition/Rhetoric tracks or concentrations. And, although these programs are often pretty heavy in literature requirements in a way that parallel literary studies programs are not laden with Composition requirements, it seems likely that there has been some reciprocity, doctoral programs in literary studies including more emphasis on Composition than has been their wont. In what is surely a related development, it is now possible, at least at some institutions, to receive tenure and promotion on the basis of work exclusively in Composition, although I suspect that in many settings a preference for Scholarly methods and a solid grounding in at least one specifically literary area are still good ideas. Finally, it seems certain that a higher percentage of college English department resources have gone to Composition instruction over the past ten years—in the form of writing courses, writing-across-the-curriculum programs, writing centers, and so on—than ever before.

For all that, it is clear that Composition has hardly taken its place as an equal third (or half, if language can be assumed to have departed) of English in terms of what matters most: knowledge-making. In some departments, now as always, all faculty are required to teach some Composition, just as they are required to serve on committees and do advisement work. I have no doubt that there are even departments in which this responsibility is accepted gracefully. But the professional identity of such faculty—as seems only proper, given their training and inclination—is based in literary studies. For the vast majority of them, Composition as a field remains a foreign and professionally unrewarding line of inquiry. Few, if any, English departments conceive of themselves as so responsible for knowledge-making in Composition that one-third to one-half of their full-time lines go directly to Composition professionals: 5 of 10, say, or 12 of 30, or even 20 of 60. Other patterns—the proportions of literature to writing courses, for example—may seem to reflect a greater commitment to Composition: 50%/50% splits, or even 40/60, with writing the larger number, are not uncommon. But commitment on this scale is strictly to instruction, not knowledge-making; and, in any case, such courses are usually staffed by teaching assistants and part-time instructors, who are generally not enfranchised as official knowledge-makers, and among whom a single faculty salary goes quite a long way.

If Composition's dissolution continues along the lines I have described, the continued dominance of literary studies, and the gradual enfeebling of Composition, seem inevitable. The sequence will go something like this. First, as I suggested above, the Researcher methods will be at once tugged and driven away toward more congenial surroundings. After all, one means by which literary studies has established the degree of academic autonomy it has achieved has been the maintenance of a fairly strict methodological homogeneity. Whatever the potential of Researcher modes of inquiry for investigating how literature is read, taught, and learned, the field has for the most part eschewed any other than Scholarly methods, remaining fundamentally a hermeneutical enterprise, supplemented by historical and philosophical inquiry. The same pressure for homogeneity would be, and indeed already has been, brought to bear on Composition as well.

Next, in keeping with both the prevailing pattern of literary studies and the development of their own field, the remaining Composition Scholars will try to increase their distance from practice. If, as Applebee argues, college English departments had insulated themselves from classroom practice for the fifty or so years before the academic reform movement, one might argue that in literary studies they have succeeded fairly well in establishing that insularity once again. With the exception of such minority positions as David Bleich's, literary studies has evolved into a community in which the gathering, testing, and validating of knowledge seem to generate and sustain a momentum more or less independent of the distribution of that knowledge outside of the methodological community. Thus, knowledge-making in literary studies all but excludes concern for how literature should be taught, or for how readers develop. There is inquiry into that sort of question elsewhere in the academy, yes, but outside of, and with little or no relevance for, literary studies. No doubt the vast majority of people who claim membership in the field actually teach for a living, operating according to a lore not so very different in structure from that developed by Composition's Practitioners. But teaching *per se* is nowhere near the heart of the field's interest, and inquiry is not—as it still tends to be in Composition— tied to practice by either internal or external demands for practical results. Freed from such fetters, of course, literary studies have soared off in some remarkable directions.

Composition Scholars will need and want to exercise a similar freedom. This is in part because they will want to fit in with their host knowledge-makers in literary studies. It is also, though, because such a tendency is a predictable byproduct of the operation of Diesing's law. That is, investigators are bound to want to be free to define their direction of inquiry—at least first, and perhaps completely—in their peculiar communal terms, and not the needs (real or imagined) of Practitioners. Indeed, we can see exactly such a motive already lurking, for example, behind Robert Connors' deliberate separation of "composition studies" from "composition teaching," with the former presumably identifiable by their allegiance to a particular non-Practitioner mode of inquiry.[1] For Composition Scholars trying to survive in the context of a field like literary studies, practicality can be a liability.

To a certain extent, these efforts by the Scholars to establish themselves in English will succeed. Departments will eventually stabilize their commitment to Composition as a knowledge-making field by affording it the same sort of coverage they now afford such "areas" as Milton or Nineteenth-Century American literature. One or two or more full-time positions—but only rarely, I should think, more than ten or fifteen percent of them, even in places with graduate programs—would be given over to Composition. The Composition Scholars who filled these lines would be expected to publish in that area. However, they would also be expected—and in this sense, there would probably always be some residual inequality— to handle whatever administrative work was necessary for the writing program the department retains.

The end result of this stabilization will be the slow strangulation of the English-based Composition that has emerged over the past two decades. Its designation as an "area" in English might be construed as an improvement. For a while, anyway, the people who run Composition programs might not regard it as professional penance. But this is obviously far short of the kind of equality the tripod metaphor holds out as a promise. Moreover, a Composition stripped of its methodological pluralism, and with its back turned more firmly than ever on the potential of practice as knowledge-making, promises to be a feeble Composition indeed.

This does not mean, of course, that Composition will suddenly— or ever—disappear. Strangulation need not be fatal, even though it's likely to do irreparable damage. The tradition of holding English responsible for the teaching of writing remains strong; the public and institutional demands that allowed composition, small "c," to become Composition, capital "C," in the first place are still potent. In addition, Composition professionals have become adept at extending their leverage, fostering a demand for Composition expertise that extends beyond departmental and even institutional lines. Writing-across-the-curriculum, writing centers and labs, writing in the workplace—all of these movements have intellectual and practical bases, but they also offer the obvious advantage of giving Composition a power base that transcends its ties to literary studies. Even these efforts, though, carry with them the seeds of an English-based

Composition's eventual demise, implying what English departments might already want to argue: that even if literacy, including writing, is to be construed as a peculiar disciplinary concern or a peculiar form of disciplinary expertise—and that issue remains in doubt—it certainly is not one that belongs especially to literary studies. And literary studies, after all, are what English departments do.

Is there any chance, then, for an academically full-fledged, autonomous, multi-methodological, knowledge-making Composition? Not, it would seem, without radical change. Composition faces a peculiar methodological paradox: its communities cannot get along well enough to live with one another, and yet they seem unlikely to survive, as any sort of an integral whole called Composition, without one another. Its long-term survival, then, will hinge on change of two kinds. First, Composition must break out of its constricting relationship with literary studies, either by taking a larger share of responsibility for knowledge-making in English departments, or by moving outside of such departments altogether.[2] Second, it must find some way to establish an internal, inter-methodological peace—to bypass or defy, in other words, the effects of Diesing's law, so that the methodological pluralism that was responsible for creating Composition in the first place can remain its vital core.

For the first, of course, it seems unlikely that literary studies will ever give over that much power to Composition. James Kinneavy makes a pretty good case in *A Theory of Discourse* for English conceiving of itself as involved with expressive, persuasive, and reference discourse as much as with literary discourse, but his argument seems to have had little impact or won much acceptance. Canons for literary studies are still, and look to remain, dominated by belles-lettres. And even if it met with wider acceptance, Kinneavy's position would have to be regarded as only limitedly representative of Composition as a whole. A fuller enfranchisement of Composition in English would demand changes in the pattern of inquiry far beyond his concerns about the breadth of the canon. They would have to include, also, concerns about how those texts, or any texts, were produced—a realm into which, except in literary biography, literary studies simply does not venture. Even if Composition could win such an expansion, then, it would still almost certainly run into impassable methodological barriers.

It looks, therefore, as if any autonomous Composition is likely to have to exist apart from literary studies. As I noted earlier, the dominant pattern is still for the writing programs, including graduate degrees and other professional activities, to be housed within English, reporting to English department chairs. Such departments have no doubt benefited from Composition's rapid growth, gaining both institutional and public visibility, with the attendant rewards. On the other hand, college English departments have long chafed under the burden of the Composition service courses, even when they may have been grateful for gains in institutional leverage. Such courses are traditionally small, eating up a disproportionate share of resources; and, also traditionally, few regular faculty have wanted to teach them. Advanced degrees in English have been and mostly are degrees in literary studies, so that most members of English faculties have denied any formal preparation in whatever it is that teaching Composition requires. Thus it might be that, under the right conditions, such departments could be convinced to relinquish the tradition, the duty, and the care of Composition, freeing them to declare without apology or demurrer what is already largely true: that literary studies are their disciplinary core.

And Composition probably still has the leverage to force such a break. Public concern over literacy seldom seems to flag, and institutions of higher education, already in some trouble because of demographic changes, are as vulnerable to the pressure generated by such concern as they have ever been. Given these conditions, a Composition based in its own departments might be founded. To house the autonomous sort of Composition I have described, these would obviously have to be more than the administrative convenience Composition programs tend to be now. They would have to be expected—and equipped—not only to disseminate knowledge, but to make and accumulate it in ways that would meet with academic approval. What such an entity would make possible—what, indeed, it would *force*— would be the methodological confrontation from which might emerge the second kind of change: the grounds for an inter-methodological coherence.

Exactly what sort of discipline might be forged in such an academic furnace is hard to say. Possibly, and perhaps even most likely, there would be no forging at all; Diesing's law would turn out to be essentially immutable, so that methodological differences would prove as immune to the effects of institutionalization, close quarters, and interdependence as they are to any other forces. In that case, Composition-as-department would simply repeat or continue the process by which Composition-as-field has pulled itself apart, with the majority Practitioners at the bottom of a hierarchy governed by an increasingly divisive minority of Scholars and Researchers.

It is also possible, however, that the close quarters and interdependence could do what twenty-odd years of revolution have not. Three conditions, I think, would have to be met. First, there would have to be heightened methodological consciousness. Members of each methodological community would have come to understand not only their own, but each others' mode of inquiry. Obviously, one of my objects in offering this study has been to lay the groundwork for such understanding. Much of the squabbling and dissension in Composition, it seems to me, arises out of cross-methodological misunderstanding: Philosophical arguments misread as Practical ones, Formalist arguments misread as Experimental ones, and so on. Composition acquired its precocious methodological breadth so quickly that it has not had time to sort itself out very well. Even what seem to be its key or universal terms, as we have seen with invention and revision, change radically across communal borders.

Second, there would have to be a spirit of methodological egalitarianism. Understanding one's own method, and then other methods, is an important first step, but it is not enough. All methods, and all kinds of knowledge, would have to be assumed to be created equal. This may be hardest for Researcher communities with positivist assumptions, which tend to be the most tyrannical in their claims about validation, but it will be no easy feat for those more militantly committed to dialectic, either. The key, presumably, will lie in what Peter Elbow calls, in another context, disciplined believing: a genuine and in this case mutual embracing of the perspective and assumptions of other inquirers as the basis for further relations. Even if, as seems likely, certain methodological polarities cannot be reconciled, there can at least be the beginnings of a new bridge mode of inquiry, a sort of deliberative rhetoric by which—as in a town meeting, say—very un-like minded individuals can find ways to cooperate. If a Composition housed in these departments is to survive, it will need the cooperation of every member. The prosperity of all will finally depend on the prosperity of each.

Third, it would require the re-establishment of Practice as inquiry. This is implied, of course, in both of the previous conditions, but the stock of Practitioners has sunk so low that they need specific mention. Given the sort of treatment they have suffered, it may seem a little ironic to argue here that, in fact, Practitioners have been responsible for Composition holding together as long as it has. But they have been, and remain, just that: at the center of the field's knowledge-making explosion, exerting a sort of epistemological gravitational pull, there has always been the enormous inertial mass of lore.

As we have seen, the other communities tend to think of lore in less kindly terms. It has been the thing to be changed, to be wiped out—faulty paradigm, damaging myth, swapped recipes—and Practitioners, therefore, have been ripe for vilification, rescuing, conversion, and so on. What is required here, however, as the basis for a transformed Composition, is a full recognition of and appreciation for lore: an understanding of what it is and how it works such that other kinds of knowledge can *usefully* interact with it.

Initially, this will require an understanding of its absorbency—lore's power, that is, to reshape the results of Researcher or Scholar inquiry equally well in its own image; and the extent to which, therefore, it is effectively impervious to the kind of direct assault Burhans, for example, suggests with his myth versus knowledge confrontation. No matter what you do to it, lore isn't going to go away; it only gets bigger. It will also mean recognizing its predominantly oral nature, with the kinds of limits that orality places on the possible impact of written materials, on the one hand, and the extent to which it empowers talk, on the other—a difference in preferred medium that has always separated Practitioners from the other communities.

But perhaps most important, it will mean coming to grips with the communal allegiances Practitioners hold. For the dominant knowledge-making communities in Composition, first allegiance tends to be to their inquiry community, then to Composition as a whole, and then somewhere, third or fourth, to their institutional colleagues and their classrooms. This tends not to be the case for Practitioners. Their first allegiance, rightly, is to their classrooms, their second to their immediate colleagues, and then their third— often a distant third, at that—to their profession, with some portion of that being Composition. The other communities' traditional response to these different priorities has been to try and strengthen their relationship with Practitioners by creating a dependency: selling a brand of knowledge that Practitioners cannot produce for themselves, and at the same time ignoring or devaluing lore. Professional preparation, then, tends to be top-down: the spoon-feeding of the lowly Practitioners with whatever they can handle of the findings of other communities. The end result, of course, is that the little that is spoon-fed gets absorbed into lore in a form likely to be rejected by its contributor, and neither side is any richer for the contact.

For an autonomous Composition to survive, this pattern has to change, and at both ends. Practitioners will have to make the same efforts as other communities to become methodologically aware and egalitarian, while the other communities must treat practice with much greater respect. And there are, in fact, some signs that such changes are possible, and maybe even underway. What I earlier called the liberal model, where Practitioners are enfranchised by being trained to make knowledge other than lore, suggests at least a recognition of the problem, even if it still devalues practice as inquiry. And Ethnography has at least the potential to recognize and value the order of Practitioner allegiances, although it is too soon to tell whether in fact it will do so, and whether, in the process, it will honor practice as inquiry.

Even more interesting, though, has been the National Writing Project, a teachers-teaching-teachers effort with 125 sites across the country. Between 1974 and 1984, the Project involved some 3000 teachers in intensive summer seminars, and reached another 300,000 or so with in-service workshops run during the school year. Its success and durability stem, I think, from its at least tacit recognition of the features of lore I have listed here: absorbency, orality, and order of allegiances. Practitioners are treated with dignity, as people who already know a good deal about what they do. They work, face to face, with their peers; there is little of the old top-down, theoretician to practitioner hierarchy. And, finally, the classroom is recognized as the community of first importance.

The Project is not without its problems. There are obviously limits on how fully, and with how much integrity, other kinds of inquiry can be represented. Beyond the 3000 intensively trained and proselytizing teacher/consultants, especially, it seems inevitable that these other kinds of knowledge will get distorted much as they always have. And, too, there is a sort of balance of trade difficulty, with the non-Practitioner communities taking far less in lore than they dispense in knowledge of their own making. Nevertheless, if ever there is an autonomous Composition, the Project could well turn out to be an important prototype.

Conclusion: Of Happy Endings

These are not, obviously, the happiest of happy endings. Ideally, I suppose, Composition should live happily ever after. It would remain a happy part of English, it would find the secret of inter-methodological peace, and Practitioners would find a place of honor as knowledge-makers. Instead, I end up predicting that either (a) Composition as we know it will essentially disappear, reverting to something much like its pre-1963 form; or that (b) it might survive, but probably only by breaking its institutional ties with literary studies and, hence, English departments.

There are, I am certain, those who would say that the stabilizing of a stunted Composition represents a happy ending—a perfectly acceptable, even natural development. From their perspective, its emergence as an independent field has been a mistake from the outset, a product of economic and political forces, but without sufficient intellectual substance or focus to survive very long. As a kind of academic hype, calling attention to one component of literacy, it has served a useful purpose, but it will soon give way to other crisis-bred drives—for reading, say, or listening and speaking, or mathematics

and computers. Its continuing existence in a handful of graduate programs, or schools of education, or the National Institute for Education's Center for the Study of Writing, is as much or more than the
formal academic space it warrants.

And it's not a bad argument. Worse, my urge to reject it is made
somewhat suspect by my own ten-year professional commitment to
the field. Nobody wants to admit a mistake after that sort of investment. Can Composition really muster enough coherence to justify an
autonomous academic existence, or is that just wishful thinking? It
is, after all, a damned awkward sort of subject, reflexive in the way
that psychoanalysis is reflexive, with inquiry and practice bound
together in an academically untraditional way. And to make matters
worse, it has spent much of its energy over the last twenty years
trying to run away from that reflexiveness, to deny its inextricable
entanglement with practice. The spectacle of so many once and
future Practitioners scrambling to find academic respectability by
invoking the authority of any mode of inquiry *except* their own,
except practice, can hardly be described as dignified. For anyone
looking to discount the field, it might well be comic.

For all that, I find myself unwilling to settle for a stunted
Composition. I have seen and felt too strongly the excitement produced by studies like, say, Janet Emig's *The Composing Processes of
Twelfth Graders*, James Britton et al.'s *The Development of Writing
Abilities (11–18)*, Linda Flower and John Hayes' models of composing or, more recently, C. H. Knoblauch and Lil Brannon's
Rhetorical Traditions and the Teaching of Writing. True, the excitement is often as much political as intellectual, the struggle for
knowledge-power very raw, rough and ready, and polemical, very
much of a piece with the sometimes comic scrambling. But it is
tremendously vital, too, and holds the tantalizing promise of
future excitement, if only the right arena can be found.

Which leaves me pleading the cause of a Composition either
fully partners with, or separate from, literary studies. I would prefer
the partnership, and maybe my sense of probable futures is too dark.
Maybe Composition is simply growing into a fuller share of English
knowledge-making in increments I don't see; maybe the pressures
for methodological homogeneity are fading. I hope so. Secessions
are always risky business, hard to pull off amicably. And Composition is surely richer for having grown up in the humanities, gaining a
dialectical dimension that seems unlikely to have emerged anywhere
else in the academy. But it still seems unlikely that any lasting
peaceful co-existence with literary studies is possible—nothing else
under the English rubric has ever managed it for very long. So, sad as
it may be, I would rather take my chances on a fully vital Composition that fails than to settle for one that is never quite free to try.

But then, there's no need to be gloomy in advance, either. If Composition's short modern history teaches us nothing else, it is that, as one of the traditional three "Rs," 'ritin' tends to be far more vulnerable to non-academic influences than most other academic fields. Our national preoccupation with literacy seems to be a peculiarly American phenomenon, with deep roots in our Puritan heritage and our love affair with free enterprise—in general, with our commitment to the ideal of a society in which *Poor Richard's Almanac*, and Poor Richard's Rhetorik, too, can be the handbooks for unlimited social mobility. We want to believe that every American needs to know how to read and write. The result is that no academic topic seems quite so durable a legislative—and media and popular—concern as America's apparently chronic literacy crisis: the real or imagined breakdowns in the reading and writing that we consider so central to the successful operation of our democracy. With that sort of presence always looming over Composition, anything can happen.

Notes

Preface

1. See "Standing on One's Head: Composition Now" (*CCC* [1978], pp. 177-80).

Introduction

1. This approach obviously requires a conception of knowledge a little different from some of our workaday notions, but I don't think it's all that new or radical. First, then, knowledge is conceived as a social construct, the truth value of which is a function of a given community's commitment to it. It follows that kinds of knowledge are not automatically interchangeable; knowledge cannot cross communal borders, as it were, with impunity. Thus, the image of a two-part knowledge characteristic of Composition (and education in general)—i.e., that knowledge consists of theory, which then informs practice—won't serve. Each mode of inquiry, including practice, can produce its own brand of theory. The issue, therefore, is not how theory informs practice, but how these different brands of knowledge relate to one another: which can claim what kind of authority, and why.

Chapter 1

1. Quoted in *Research in Written Composition*, p. 1.

Chapter 2

1. Conspicuously missing from this community, of course, is that other sort of "practitioner," writers, people whose primary interest is in the doing, not the teaching, of writing. Paradoxical though it may seem, writers *qua* writers are not considered members of the Practitioner community, nor members of the larger society of Composition at all. Composition journals, for example, rarely publish work that is not more or less directly related to writing as a subject of study. Obviously, some members of Composition do a good bit of writing that falls outside the boundaries of "composition writing" (e.g., poetry, fiction, literary scholarship) and may even gain some measure of respect by doing so; Donald Murray, for example, is often introduced as a Pulitzer Prize winner. The written work itself, though, is of little interest to those in Composition. What may be of interest is the doing of such writing—the practice, and the writer's reflections about it. These are considered to be potential resources, and to offer possible lines of inquiry. There has come to be an axiom that those who teach writing should do writing, and even that they should write along with their

students. But "doing writing" in this sense and "being a writer" mean very different things, and no set of credentials as a writer of prose or poetry has, so far as I know, gained anyone much more than guest speaker status in the Practitioner community. Only classroom duty—and that preferably in teaching the writing of non-fiction prose—has done that.

2. That is, Britton et al. had presumably hoped to find a wide range of audiences represented, but found instead that more than 92% of the texts fell into only two of ten possible audience sub-categories, a result they describe as "something of an anticlimax" (p. 192). And in terms of function, 63% fell into the "transactional" category, with very few—about 5%—in the "expressive" category for which the authors had had much higher expectations.

3. They explain their system for computing the raters' reliability in Appendix II, pp. 206–08. The figures I have given are those for the raters alone, without corrective ratings provided by the investigators.

4. See, e.g., Mike Rose's "Sophisticated, Ineffective Books—The Dismantling of Process in Composition Texts" (*CCC*, 32 [1981], pp. 64–74); or Clinton S. Burhans Jr.'s "The Teaching of Writing and the Knowledge Gap" (*College English*, 45 [1983], pp. 639–56). We'll return to the latter—for other reasons—in Chapter 10.

5. Given this sort of system, some textbooks eventually acquire, as catechetical texts will, a certain totemic power. How better to account for what has happened with books like Strunk and White's *The Elements of Style*, or Macrimmon's *Writing with a Purpose*, or Ken Macrorie's more "heretical" *Uptaught*? A master tries to codify the principles of his practice. In the hands of disciples, these serve a catechetical pupose, become the articles of faith. After two or three generations, these principles lose touch almost entirely with the experience that informed them, and acquire power of a different kind: Strunk and White is invoked as synonymous with literacy by people who have never even read it; people talk about writing in "inverted pyramids," believing that they really do; or they scorn "Engfish" as a kind of language-bogey genuinely loose in the world. The authority of the images or catch-phrases of the master take on a life of their own. Within the Practitioner community, then, and with the greater public, too, these books become totems—symbols or emblems which evoke fear or admiration or loathing. For an argument along similar lines, see C. H. Knoblauch's "Composition Textbooks and the Myth of Literacy," a paper presented at NCTE, 1985.

6. For a fairly comprehensive review of the field's journals, see Robert Connors' "Journals in Composition Studies" in *College English* (46 [1984], pp. 348–65).

7. Fuller treatments of this issue can be found, among other places, in two essays in NCTE's 1981 *The Nature and Measurement of Competency in English*: editor Charles R. Cooper's "Competency Testing: Issues and Overview," and Miles Myers' "The Politics of Minimum Competency." I also recommend Chapter 7 of C. H. Knoblauch and Lil Brannon's *Rhetorical Traditions and the Teaching of Writing*, "The Development of Writing Ability: Some Myths about Evaluation and Improvement." Probably the most comprehensive treatment of these issues to date is Edward M. White's *Teaching and Assessing Writing* (Jossey-Bass, 1985).

Section III

1. The "Report of the Committee on Future Directions" can be found in *CCC* 11(1) 1960, 3–7.

Chapter 3

1. First generation in terms of modern Composition, that is. There was certainly historical inquiry by composition teachers before 1963. Kitzhaber, as we shall see shortly, is perhaps the best known, but the Dec. 1954 issue of *CCC*, for example, features Karl W. Dykema's "Historical Development of the Concept of Grammatical Proprieties," J. E. Congleton's "Historical Development of the Concept of Rhetorical Proprieties," and James B. McMillan's "Summary of Nineteenth Century Historical and Comparative Linguistics."

2. In his paper, Prof. Connors follows a more traditional three-part framework for Historical inquiry: external criticism, "which establishes what sources are available" and whether they are appropriate and/or adequate; internal criticism, in which sources are examined to be sure they are understood correctly; and synthesis of materials, which covers most of what I have listed here under "Interpretive Stage" (pp. 16–17).

3. Kitzhaber argues as follows: "They [the modes] represent an unrealistic view of the writing process, a view that assumes writing is done by formula and in a social vacuum. They turn the attention of both teacher and student toward an academic exercise instead of toward a meaningful act of communication in a social context. Like Unity-Coherence-Emphasis—or any other set of static abstractions concerning writing—they substitute mechanical for organic concepts and therefore distort the real nature of writing." (From Kitzhaber, pp. 220–21, as quoted in Connors' "The Rise and Fall of the Modes of Discourse," p. 454.)

Chapter 4

1. The four pieces appeared in *CCC* between 1970 and 1972, and full citations can be found in the Works Cited. For convenience here, I have used the page numbers from Ross Winterowd's (ed.) *Contemporary Rhetoric: A Conceptual Background with Readings* (Harcourt, 1975), where they are printed together.

Section IV

1. For examples of each kind of survey suggested in this paragraph, see the following, simply pulled in a cluster from my files: G. W. Redman, Jr., "The Philosophy of Teaching Composition Held by Selected Teachers and Students at the University of Northern Colorado, Winter Quarter, 1973" (*DAI*, 1974, 35, 932A); B. J. Honeycutt, "An Analysis and Prognosis of the Technical Report Writing Curriculum in Texas Public Junior Colleges" (*DAI*, 1973, 34, 1587a); P. W. Willis, "A Study of Current Practices in Freshman English in Oklahoma Colleges" (*DAI*, 1974, 34, 4806A); Ron Smith, "The Composition Requirement Today: A Report on a Nationwide Survey of Four-Year Colleges and Universi-

ties" (*CCC*, 25 [1974] pp. 138-48); B. K. McKee, "Types of Outlines Used by Technical Writers" (*Journal of English Teaching Techniques*, Winter 1974/1975, pp. 30-36); and Charles Schaefer, "Young Poets on Poetry" (*Elementary School Journal*, 1973, 74, pp. 24-27).

Chapter 6

1. The studies given in this paragraph, in order: I. O. Ash, "An Experimental Evaluation of the Stylistic Approach in Teaching Written Composition in the Junior High School" (*Journal of Experimental Education*, 4 [Sept. 1935], cited in *Research in Written Composition*); Samuel Becker, et al., *Communication Skills: An Experiment in Instructional Methods* (Iowa City: U of Iowa P, 1958; reviewed in *Research in Written Composition*); B. S. Moore, "The Impact of a Workshop Approach on the Process of Composing Expository Writing for Twelfth Grade Inner City College-Bound Students" (*DAI* 44, 976A); R. F. Shannon Jr., "A Small Group, Personal Growth Method for the Teaching of Writing" (*DAI*, 44, 1714A); M. L. Perry, "A Study of the Effects of a Literary Models Approach to Composition on Writing and Reading Achievement" (*DAI*, 1980, 40, 6137A); A. C. Armstrong, "A Comparison of the Garrison Method and the Traditional Method of Teaching Composition in a Community College" (*DAI*, 1980, 40, 6127A); R. M. Reynolds, "The Design and Testing of a Focused and Sequenced Free Writing Approach to a First Year Course in Composition for Two Year College Students" (*DAI*, 1981, 42, 989A).

2. Examples of these kinds of studies, again in order: N. L. Benson, "The Effects of Peer Feedback During the Writing Process on Writing Performance, Revision Behavior, and Attitude Toward Writing" (*DAI*, 1979, 40, 1987A); M. Caroselli, "The Effect of Parental Involvement on the Writing Skills and Attitudes of Secondary Students (*DAI*, 1980, 41, 1915A); Dora Smith, *Class Size in High School English: Methods and Results* (Minneapolis: U of Minnesota P, 1931; reviewed in *Research in Written Composition*); J. E. Johnson, "The Effect of Beginning Shorthand on Learning in Selected Language Arts Skills" (*DAI*, 1976, 37, 708A-709A); E. R. P. DeHaven, "The Effect of Typewriting on Seventh Grade Students' Ability to Recognize Composition Errors" (*DAI*, 1970, 30, 4871A); S. L. Liggett, "Preparing Business Writing Students to Use Dictational Systems: An Experimental Study" (*DAI*, 1983, 43, 3831A); P. G. Ackerman Jr., "The Effect of Paper Size on College Freshman Course Writing" (*DAI*, 1976, 36, 5266A); J. Ziviani, "Effects of Pencil Shape and Size on Motor Accuracy and Pencil Posture of 8 Year Old Children" (ERIC ED 218 658); G. A. Lindsay and D. McLennan, "Lined Paper: Its Effects on the Legibility and Creativity of Young Children's Writing" (*British Journal of Educational Psychology*, 53 [1983], pp. 364-68).

3. We will consider Bereiter and Scardamalia's essay at some length in Chapter 11.

4. Justification and verification are also candidates, and there are no doubt others. I like certification because it provides the best etymological fit with my sense of the Experimentalist drive toward *cert*-ainty.

5. His justification for this is that "a relatively thorough description of a few students' work seemed more valuable than a partial description of the work

of a larger number of students" (p. 232). While it's hard to say just how this affects validity or reliability—although it seems a shame to discard any data in a study this small—it is a good example of the economic forces I mentioned before. What it sounds like is that he was limited in what he could afford in terms of rater time.

6. So, for example, her study is cited at some length in a note in Sheridan Blau's "Invisible Writing: Investigating Cognitive Processes in Writing" (*CCC*, 34 [1983] p. 310); and her "Reflection: A Critical Component of the Composing Process" (*CCC*, 30 [1979], pp. 275-78), based on her dissertation, is cited in George H. Jensen's "The Reification of the Basic Writer" (*Journal of Basic Writing*, 5.1 [Spring 1986], p. 54ff).

7. It's important to keep in mind, though, that no single subject had to be an under-21, male, remedial student, balanced off by an over-21, male, traditional student, or any other such equation. These characteristics were simply distributed somewhere throughout the sample of 24. Pianko never does account for their possible "interaction."

8. The most recent addition to the literature on sentence combining is *Sentence Combining: A Rhetorical Perspective*, edited by Daiker, Kerek and Morenberg (Southern Illinois UP, 1985).

9. In his dissertation, Odell cites "the sign test which appears in Barry F. Anderson's *The Psychology Experiment* (Belmont, California: Brooks/Cole Publishing Co., 1966)" [p. 140]. It may be that the results he refers to in his article are from that test.

10. From the announcement for the award, printed in *Research in the Teaching of English*, 13 (1979), p. 95.

11. So, e.g., it may be that the structure of the universe that has made positivist inquiry in the natural sciences as productive as it has been is an essentially local—and accidental—set of conditions.

Chapter 7

1. See, e.g., Ralph Voss's "Janet Emig's *The Composing Processes of Twelfth Graders*: A Reassessment," in *CCC*, 34 (1983), pp. 278-83.

2. The researcher who has probably come closest to a Piagetian influence in terms of writing is Donald Graves, supplemented by the work of his various colleagues (e.g., Nancie Atwell and Lucy Calkins). Because of his concern for the school context, however, I have placed Graves in Chapter 9, "The Ethnographers." I should also note that Joan Pettigrew reviews some research on the composing process in *The Research in Composition Newsletter*, Fall 1981. However, the analysis is necessarily pretty sketchy, nor is it restricted to what I am calling Clinical studies.

3. I find it interesting that Emig's dissertation, on which the monograph is based and from which it does not differ all that much, is titled a little more modestly: *Components of the Composing Process Among Twelfth-Grade Writers*.

4. Perl does try to examine the effects of what she calls the talk-write pedagogy, and reports her findings in her Dissertation, pp. 331-34. In their last two sessions, she asked her subjects to do their planning for the essays aloud, so that she could see what effect, if any, such planning aloud had on either composing or text. This is interesting, but it hardly qualifies as teaching.

5. Emig actually designates dimension 6, "Composing Aloud: A Characterization," as explicitly dealing with this specialized talk. It is clear, though, that other portions of her outline draw from the tapes, as well.

6. Lynn has in fact generated five subjects by this point. For some reason, Emig decides to combine the bus ride and the two old ladies into a single topic.

7. I should note that Voss approaches this same section on Lynn's topic choice—with a similar skepticism—to illustrate the possible effects of Emig's presence as observer.

Chapter 8

1. See, e.g., the list of studies they offer in their "Counterstatement" (*CCC*, 36 [1985], p. 96) response to Michael Holzman and Marilyn Cooper, whose essay we'll consider shortly.

2. See, however, Flower's "Response to Anthony Petrosky, review of Linda Flower, *Problem-Solving Strategies for Writing*, CCC, 34 (May, 1983), 233-35" (*CCC*, 35 [1984], pp. 96-97).

Chapter 9

1. Two prominent publications: *Ethnography in the Classroom*, a special issue of *The English Record* edited by Thomas Reigstad (34 [1983]); and Sondra Perl and Nancy Wilson's *Through Teachers' Eyes: Portraits of Writing Teachers at Work* (Heinemann, 1986).

Chapter 10

1. See his footnote on p. 29: "Although 'paradigm' has several meanings in Kuhn's work, I am treating it as synonymous with what he calls a 'disciplinary matrix'. . . ."

2. We will treat Connors' work on the subject in some detail in the next chapter. Knoblauch's paper, delivered at MLA, 1985, is "The Current-Traditional Paradigm: Neither Current, Nor Traditional, Nor a Paradigm."

3. For a very interesting and readable analysis of the most recent "crisis," conceived in its broadest terms, see Harvey Daniels' *Famous Last Words: The American Language Crisis Reconsidered* (Carbondale: Southern Illinois UP, 1983).

Chapter 11

1. In a footnote on p. 32, Young recognizes that the term has had many meanings: " 'Invention' here refers not only to classical invention (which provides formal procedures for determining the status of an argument, discovering possible ways of developing it, and adapting it to specific audiences), but also to other formal methods designed to aid in retrieving information, forming concepts, analyzing complex events, and solving certain kinds of problems." Nevertheless, as his language here suggests, he regards them as essentially interchangeable.

Chapter 12

1. It is made even more explicit by Bereiter and Scardamalia, who hope that their Levels of Inquiry will free researchers "from the pressure to show that their work is leading toward improvements in the teaching of writing." Their notion is that "significant improvements in teaching writing will depend on gaining a deeper understanding of the process, but gaining this understanding promises to be a long and difficult effort." One of their ambitions for their scheme, then, is that it will insulate Composition researchers much as literary scholars are insulated, acting "as an intellectually sound replacement for the now largely discredited notion of the basic-to-applied [research] continuum" (p. 23).

2. I am hardly the first to point out this sort of secession as an option, of course. Its most recent and visible appearance was as the subject of Maxine Hairston's Chair's address to CCCC in Minneapolis, 1985, which appears in *CCC*, 36 (1985) as "Breaking Our Bonds and Reaffirming Our Connections" (pp. 272-82). However, Hairston does not, I think, account for the methodological implications of her arguments fully enough. For other recent treatments of the same general issue, see Richard Lanham's *Literacy and the Future of Humanism*, especially Chapter 7, "Should English Departments Take an Interest in Teaching Composition?" (New Haven: Yale UP, 1983); or Jay Robinson's biting "Literacy in the Department of English" (*College English*, 47 (1985), pp. 482-98).

Works Cited

Ackerman, Paul G. Jr. "The Effect of Paper Size on College Freshman Course Writing." *DAI* 36 (1976): 5266A.

Allport, Gordon. *The Use of Personal Documents in Psychological Science.* New York: Social Sciences Research Council, 1942.

Applebee, Arthur N. *Tradition and Reform in the Teaching of English: A History.* Urbana: NCTE, 1974.

Armstrong, Anne C. "A Comparison of the Garrison Method and the Traditional Method of Teaching Composition in a Community College." *DAI* 40 (1980): 6127A.

Ash, I. O. "An Experimental Evaluation of the Stylistic Approach in Teaching Written Composition in the Junior High School." *Journal of Experimental Education.* 4 (1935): 54–62.

Beach, Richard, and Lillian S. Bridwell, eds. *New Directions in Composition Research.* New York: Guilford, 1984.

Beach, Richard. "The Effects of Between-draft Teacher Evaluation Versus Student Self-evaluation on High School Students' Revising of Rough Drafts." *Research in the Teaching of English.* 13 (1979): 11–19.

————. "Self-Evaluation Strategies of Extensive Revisers and Nonrevisers." *College Composition and Communication.* 27 (1976): 160–63.

Beaugrande, Robert de. *Text, Discourse, and Process: Toward a Multidisciplinary Science of Texts.* Norwood: Ablex, 1980.

Becker, Samuel L., et al. *Communication Skills: An Experiment in Instructional Methods.* Iowa City: U of Iowa P, 1958.

Benson, Nancy L. "The Effects of Peer Feedback During the Writing Process on Writing Performance, Revision Behavior, and Attitude toward Writing." *DAI* 40 (1979): 1987A.

Bereiter, Carl, and Marlene Scardamalia. "Levels of Inquiry in Writing Research." *Research on Writing.* Ed. Peter Mosenthal, Lynne Tamor, and Sean A. Walmsley. New York: Longman, 1983. 3–25.

Berkenkotter, Carol, and Donald Murray. "Decisions and Revisions: The Planning Strategies of a Publishing Writer, and Response of a Laboratory Rat—or, Being Protocoled." *College Composition and Communication.* 34 (1983): 156–72.

Berlin, James A. "Contemporary Composition: The Major Pedagogical Theories." *College English.* 44 (1982): 765–77.

————. *Writing Instruction in Nineteenth-Century American Colleges.* Carbondale: Southern Illinois UP, 1984.

Berthoff, Ann E. *The Making of Meaning.* Montclair, NJ: Boynton, 1981.

————. "The Problem of Problem Solving." *College Composition and Communication.* 22 (1971): 237–42. (Rpt. in *Contemporary Rhetoric: A Conceptual Background with Readings.* Ed. W. Ross Winterowd. New York: Harcourt, 1975. 90–97.)

————. "Response to Janice Lauer, 'Counterstatement.'" *College Composition and Communication.* 23 (1972): 414-15. (Rpt. in *Contemporary Rhetoric: A Conceptual Background with Readings.* Ed. W. Ross Winterowd. New York: Harcourt, 1975. 100-03.)

Bizzell, Patricia. "Thomas Kuhn, Scientism, and English Studies." *College English.* 40 (1979): 764-71.

Blau, Sheridan. "Invisible Writing: Investigating Cognitive Processes in Composition." *College Composition and Communication.* 34 (1983): 297-312.

Bleich, David. *Subjective Criticism.* Baltimore: Johns Hopkins UP, 1978.

Booth, Wayne. *The Rhetoric of Fiction.* Chicago: U of Chicago P, 1961.

————. "The Rhetorical Stance." *College Composition and Communication.* 14 (1963): 139-145.

Braddock, Richard. "The Frequency and Placement of Topic Sentences in Expository Prose." *Research in the Teaching of English.* 8 (1975): 287-302.

Braddock, Richard, Richard Lloyd-Jones, and Lowell Schoer. *Research in Written Composition.* Champaign: NCTE, 1963.

Brannon, Lil, Melinda Knight, and Vara Neverow-Turk. *Writers Writing.* Montclair, NJ: Boynton, 1982.

Brannon, Lil, and C. H. Knoblauch. "On Students' Rights to Their Own Texts: A Model of Teacher Response." *College Composition and Communication.* 33 (1982): 157-66.

Bridwell, Lillian S. "Revising Strategies in Twelfth Grade Students' Transactional Writing." *Research in the Teaching of English.* 14 (1980): 197-222.

Britton, James, et al. *The Development of Writing Abilities (11-18).* London (Eng.): Macmillan Education, 1975.

Bruffee, Kenneth. "Peer Tutoring and the 'Conversation of Mankind.'" *Writing Centers.* Ed. Gary Olson. Urbana: NCTE, 1984. 3-15.

Bryant, Paul. "A Brand New World Every Morning." *College Composition and Communication.* 25 (1974): 30-33.

Burhans, Clinton S. Jr. "The Teaching of Writing and the Knowledge Gap." *College English.* 45 (1983): 639-56.

Burke, Virginia. "The Composition-Rhetoric Pyramid." *College Composition and Communication.* 16 (1965): 3-6.

Burton, Dwight. "Research in the Teaching of English: The Troubled Dream." *Research in the Teaching of English.* 7 (1973): 160-89.

Calkins, Lucy. "Children Learn the Writer's Craft." *Language Arts.* 57 (1980): 207-13.

Campbell, Donald T., and Julian C. Stanley. *Experimental and Quasi-Experimental Designs for Research.* Boston: Houghton, 1966.

Caroselli, Marlene. "The Effect of Parental Involvement on the Writing Skills and Attitudes of Secondary Students." *DAI* 41 (1980): 1915A.

Christensen, Francis. "A Generative Rhetoric of the Sentence." *College Composition and Communication.* 14 (1963): 155-61.

Christensen, Francis, and Bonnijean Christensen. *Notes Toward a New Rhetoric.* Second ed. New York: Harper, 1978.

Clark, Christopher M., and Susan Florio, et al. "Understanding Writing Instruction: Issues of Theory and Method." *Research on Writing.* Ed. Peter Mosenthal, Lynne Tamor, and Sean A. Walmsley. New York: Longman, 1983. 236-64.

Cohen, Jacob. *Statistical Power Analysis for the Behavioral Sciences.* New York: Academic, 1969.

Congleton, J. E. "Historical Development of the Concept of Rhetorical Proprieties." *College Composition and Communication.* 5 (1954): 140-44.

Connors, Robert J. "Composition Studies and Science." *College English.* 45 (1983): 1-20.

————. "Historical Inquiry in Composition Studies." Ms. given at CCCC, 1984.

————. "Journals in Composition Studies." *College English.* 46 (1984): 346-65.

————. "The Rise and Fall of the Modes of Discourse." *College Composition and Communication.* 32 (1981): 444-63.

Connors, Robert J., Lisa S. Ede, and Andrea A. Lunsford, eds. *Essays on Classical Rhetoric and Modern Discourse.* Carbondale: Southern Illinois UP, 1984.

Cooper, Charles R. "Competency Testing: Issues and Overview." *The Nature and Measurement of Competency in English.* Ed. Charles R. Cooper. Urbana: NCTE, 1981. 1-20.

Cooper, Charles R. and Lee Odell. "Considerations of Sound in the Composing Process of Published Writers." *Research in the Teaching of English.* 10 (1976): 103-15.

Cooper, Charles R. and Lee Odell, eds. *Research on Composing: Points of Departure.* Urbana: NCTE, 1978.

Cooper, Marilyn, and Michael Holzman. "Talking About Protocols." *College Composition and Communication.* 34 (1983): 284-93.

Corbett, Edward P. J. *Classical Rhetoric for the Modern Student.* Second ed. New York: Oxford UP, 1971.

————. "Hugh Blair: A Study of His Rhetorical Theory." Diss. Loyola 1956.

————. "John Locke's Contributions to Rhetoric." *College Composition and Communication.* 32 (1981): 423-33.

————. "Some Rhetorical Lessons from John Henry Newman." *College Composition and Communication.* 31 (1980): 402-11.

————. "The Usefulness of Classical Rhetoric." *College Composition and Communication.* 14 (1963): 162-64.

Crowley, Sharon. "Response to Robert J. Connors, 'The Rise and Fall of the Modes of Discourse.'" *College Composition and Communication.* 35 (1984): 88-90.

Daiker, Donald A., Andrew Kerek, and Max Morenberg, eds. *Sentence Combining: A Rhetorical Perspective.* Carbondale: Southern Illinois UP, 1985.

Daiute, Colette. "Psycholinguistic Foundations of the Writing Process." *Research in the Teaching of English.* 15 (1981): 5-22.

Daly, John. "Broadening the Apprehension Construct." Paper presented at NCTE Post-Convention Research Conference. Cincinnati, 1980.

Daly, John A., and Anne Hexamer. "Statistical Power in Research in English Education." *Research in the Teaching of English.* 17 (1983): 157-164.

D'Angelo, Frank. *A Conceptual Theory of Rhetoric.* Cambridge: Winthrop, 1975.

————. "The Evolution of the Analytic *Topoi:* A Speculative Inquiry." *Essays on Classical Rhetoric and Modern Discourse.* Ed. Robert J. Connors, Lisa

S. Ede, and Andrea A. Lunsford. Carbondale: Southern Illinois UP, 1984. 50-68.

Daniels, Harvey. *Famous Last Words: The American Language Crisis Reconsidered*. Carbondale: Southern Illinois UP, 1983.

DeHaven, Edna R. "The Effect of Typewriting on Seventh Grade Students' Ability to Recognize Composition Errors." *DAI* 30 (1970): 4871A.

Diederich, Paul B. *Measuring Growth in English*. Urbana: NCTE, 1974.

Diesing, Paul. *Patterns of Discovery in the Social Sciences*. New York: Aldine, 1971.

Dillon, George. *Constructing Texts*. Bloomington: Indiana UP, 1981.

Dixon, John. *Growth Through English: A Report Based on the Dartmouth Seminar*. Reading (Eng.): National Association for the Teaching of English, 1967.

Dykema, Karl W. "Historical Development of the Concept of Grammatical Proprieties." *College Composition and Communication*. 5 (1954): 135-39.

Dyson, Anne Haas. "Learning to Write/Learning to Do School: Emergent Writers' Interpretations of School Literacy Tasks." *Research in the Teaching of English*. 18 (1984): 233-64.

————. "The Role of Oral Language in Early Writing Processes." *Research in the Teaching of English*. 17 (1983): 1-30.

Elbow, Peter. *Writing with Power*. New York: Oxford UP, 1983.

————. *Writing Without Teachers*. New York: Oxford UP, 1973.

Emig, Janet. *Components of the Composing Process Among Twelfth-Grade Writers*. Diss. Harvard U., 1969. Ann Arbor: UMI, 1970. 7012418.

————. *The Composing Processes of Twelfth Graders*. Urbana: NCTE, 1971.

————. "The Tacit Tradition: The Inevitability of a Multi-Disciplinary Approach to Writing Research." *Reinventing the Rhetorical Tradition*. Ed. Aviva Freedman and Ian Pringle. Conway: L&S Books, 1980. 9-18. (Rpt. in *The Web of Meaning*, Upper Montclair: Boynton, 1983. 145-56.)

Faigley, Lester, and Stephen Witte. "Analyzing Revision." *College Composition and Communication*. 32 (1981): 400+.

Florio, Susan, and Christopher M. Clark. "The Functions of Writing in an Elementary Classroom." *Research in the Teaching of English*. 16 (1982): 115-30.

————. "Occasions for Writing in the Classroom: Toward a Description of Written Literacy in School." Paper presented at American Anthropological Association. Cincinnati, Dec. 1979.

Flower, Linda. "Response to Anthony Petrosky, Review of Linda Flower, *Problem-Solving Strategies for Writing*." *College Composition and Communication*. 35 (1984): 96-97.

————. "Writer-Based Prose: A Cognitive Basis for Problems in Writing." *College English*. 41 (1979): 19-37.

Flower, Linda, and John Hayes. "Images, Plans, and Prose: The Representation of Meaning in Writing." *Written Communication*. 1 (1984): 120-60.

————. "Problem Solving Strategies and the Writing Process." *College English*. 39 (1977): 449-61.

————. "Response to Marilyn Cooper and Michael Holzman, 'Talking About Protocols.'" *College Composition and Communication*. 36 (1985): 94-99.

Foster, David. *A Primer for Writing Teachers: Theories, Theorists, Issues, Problems.* Upper Montclair: Boynton, 1983.

Fowler, Robert J. *An Analysis of the Composing Processes of Three Black Adolescents.* Diss. U of Pittsburgh, 1979. Ann Arbor: UMI, 1979. 7910664.

Frederikson, Carl H., and Joseph F. Dominic, eds. *Writing: The Nature, Development, and Teaching of Written Communication.* 2 vols. Hillsdale: Erlbaum, 1981.

Freedman, Sarah Warshauer, and Robert C. Calfee. "Holistic Assessment of Writing: Experimental Design and Cognitive Theory." *Research on Writing.* Ed. Peter Mosenthal, Lynne Tamor, and Sean A. Walmsely. New York: Longman, 1983. 75-98.

Freedman, Sarah Warshauer. "Comparative Evaluation of Student and Professional Prose." Paper presented at AERA. San Francisco, April 1979.

————. "Student Teacher Conversations About Writing: Shifting Topics in the Writing Conference." ERIC ED 214 181.

Freedom and Discipline in English: Report on the Commission on English. New York: CEEB, 1965.

Fulkerson, Richard P. "Kinneavy on Referential and Persuasive Discourse: A Critique." *College Composition and Communication.* 35 (1984): 43-56.

Gage, John. "An Adequate Epistemology for Composition: Classical and Modern Perspectives." *Essays on Classical Rhetoric and Modern Discourse.* Eds. Robert J. Connors, Lisa S. Ede, and Andrea A. Lunsford. Carbondale: Southern Illinois UP, 1984.

————. "Teaching the Enthymeme: Invention and Arrangement." *Rhetoric Review.* 2.1 (1983): 38-50.

————. "The 2000 Year-Old Straw Man." Review of *Rhetorical Traditions and the Teaching of Writing,* C. H. Knoblauch and Lil Brannon. *Rhetoric Review.* 3.1 (1984): 100-04.

Geertz, Clifford. *The Interpretation of Cultures.* New York: Basic, 1973.

Gerber, John. "Explosion in English." *The Shape of English: NCTE Distinguished Lectures, 1967.* Champaign: NCTE, 1967. 1-14.

Golden, James L. "Plato Revisited: A Theory of Discourse for All Seasons." *Essays on Classical Rhetoric and Modern Discourse.* Ed. Robert J. Connors, Lisa S. Ede, and Andrea A. Lunsford. Carbondale: Southern Illinois UP, 1974. 16-36.

Gorrell, Robert M. "Very Like a Whale—A Report on Rhetoric." *College Composition and Communication.* 16 (1965): 138-43.

Graves, Donald H. *Children's Writing: Research Directions and Hypotheses Based upon an Examination of the Writing Processes of Seven Year Old Children.* Diss. SUNY Buffalo, 1973. Ann Arbor: UMI, 1974. 748375.

————. "An Examination of the Writing Processes of Seven Year Old Children." *Research in the Teaching of English.* 9 (1975): 227-41.

————. *A Researcher Learns to Write.* Exeter: Heinemann, 1984.

————. "What Children Show Us About Writing." *Language Arts.* 56 (1979): 312-319.

Graves, Richard L., ed. *Rhetoric and Composition: A Sourcebook for Teachers and Writers.* Second ed. Upper Montclair: Boynton, 1984.

Greenberg, Karen, Harvey Weiner, and R. A. Donovan, eds. *Writing Assessment: Issues and Strategies.* White Plains: Longman, 1986.

Hairston, Maxine. "Breaking Our Bonds and Reaffirming Our Connections." *College Composition and Communication.* 36 (1985): 272-82.

————. "The Winds of Change: Thomas Kuhn and the Revolution in the Teaching of Writing." *College Composition and Communication.* 33 (1982): 78-86.

Halloran, S. Michael. "The Birth of Molecular Biology: An Essay in the Rhetorical Criticism of Scientific Discourse." *Rhetoric Review.* 3.1 (1984): 70-83.

————. "On the End of Rhetoric, Classical and Modern." *College English.* 36 (1975): 621-31.

————. "Rhetoric in the American College Curriculum: The Decline of Public Discourse." *Pre/Text.* 3 (1982): 245-69.

Harris, Roland J. "An Experimental Inquiry into the Functions and Value of Formal Grammar in the Teaching of English, with Special Reference to the Teaching of Correct Written English to Children Aged Twelve to Fourteen." Diss. U of London, 1962. (Reviewed in *Research in Written Composition.*)

Hartwell, Patrick. "Grammar, Grammars, and the Teaching of Grammar." *College English.* 47 (1985): 105-27.

Hayes, John, and Linda S. Flower. "Identifying the Organization of Writing Processes." *Cognitive Processes in Writing.* Ed. Lee Gregg and Erwin Steinberg. Hillsdale: Erlbaum, 1980. 3-30.

Heath, Shirley Brice. *Ways with Words.* New York: Cambridge UP, 1983.

Herman, Jerry. *The Tutor and the Writing Student: A Case Study.* Curriculum Publication no. 6. Berkeley: U of California, 1979 (ERIC ED 192 324).

Hilgers, Thomas L. "Training College Composition Students in the Use of Free-writing and Problem-Solving Heuristics for Rhetorical Invention." *Research in the Teaching of English.* 14 (1980): 293-307.

Hillocks, George. *Research on Written Composition.* Urbana: NCRE, 1986.

Hirsch, E. D. Jr. *The Philosophy of Composition.* Chicago: U of Chicago P, 1977.

Hobbs, James H. *The Poetry-Composing Processes of Proficient Twelfth-Grade Writers.* Diss. U of Colorado/Boulder, 1981. Ann Arbor: UMI, 1982. 8200791.

Holzman, Michael. "Scientism and Sentence Combining." *College Composition and Communication.* 34 (1983): 73-79.

Honeycutt, B. J. "An Analysis and Prognosis of the Technical Report Writing Curriculum in Texas Public Junior Colleges." *DAI* 34 (1973): 1587A.

Hook, J. N. "The Importance of the Conference to Project English." *Needed Research in the Teaching of English: Proceedings of a Project English Research Conference May 5-7, 1962.* Ed. Erwin R. Steinberg. Washington: U.S. Government Printing Office, 1963.

Horner, Winifred B., ed. *Composition and Literature: Bridging the Gap.* Chicago: U of Chicago P, 1983.

————, ed. *The Present State of Scholarship in Historical and Contemporary Rhetoric.* Columbia: U of Missouri P, 1983.

Horner, Winifred B. "Rhetoric in the Liberal Arts: Nineteenth-Century Scottish Universities." *The Rhetorical Tradition and Modern Writing.* Ed. James J. Murphy. New York: MLA, 1982. 85-94.

Hughes, Richard E. "The Contemporaneity of Classical Rhetoric." *College Composition and Communication.* 16 (1965): 157-59.

Hunt, Kellogg W. *Grammatical Structures Written at Three Grade Levels.* Champaign: NCTE, 1965.

Irmscher, William F. *Teaching Expository Writing.* New York: Holt, 1979.

Jacobs, Suzanne, and Adela Karliner. "Helping Writers to Think: The Effect of Speech Roles in Individual Conferences on the Quality of Thought in Student Writing." *College English.* 38 (1977): 489-505.

Jensen, George. "The Reification of the Basic Writer." *Journal of Basic Writing.* 5.1 (Spring, 1986): 52-64.

Johnson, Jack E. "The Effect of Beginning Shorthand on Learning in Selected Language Arts Skills." *DAI* 37 (1976): 708A-709A.

Johnson, Nan. "Ethos and the Aims of Rhetoric." *Essays on Classical Rhetoric and Modern Discourse.* Ed. Robert J. Connors, Lisa S. Ede, and Andrea A. Lunsford. Carbondale: Southern Illinois UP, 1984. 98-114.

Judy, Stephen. "The Experiential Approach: Inner Worlds to Outer Worlds." *Eight Approaches to Teaching Composition.* Ed. Timothy R. Donovan and Ben W. McClelland. Urbana: NCTE, 1980. 37-52.

Kameen, Paul. "Rewording the Rhetoric of Composition." *Pre/Text* 1 (1980): 73-93.

Kantor, Kenneth J., Dan R. Kirby, and Judith P. Goetz. "Research in Context: Ethnographic Studies in English Education." *Research in the Teaching of English.* 15 (1981): 293-310.

Kinneavy, James L. "Contemporary Rhetoric." *The Present State of Scholarship in Historical and Contemporary Rhetoric.* Ed. Winifred Bryan Horner. Columbia: U of Missouri P, 1983. 167-213.

―――. *A Theory of Discourse: The Aims of Discourse.* New York: Norton, 1971.

Kinney, J., et al. "What Do Teachers Think About Composition?―A Qualitative Research Project." Paper presented at CCCC. Washington, March, 1980.

Kirby, D. R., and Kenneth Kantor. "Toward a Theory of Developmental Rhetoric." Paper presented at the Canadian Council of Teachers of English Conference on Learning to Write. Ottawa, May 1979.

Kitzhaber, Albert R. "4C, Freshman English, and the Future." *College Composition and Communication.* 14 (1963): 129-38.

―――. "The Government and English Teaching." *College Composition and Communication.* 18 (1967): 135-41.

―――. "Rhetoric in American Colleges, 1850-1900." Diss. U of Washington, 1953.

―――. *Themes, Theories, and Therapy: The Teaching of Writing in College.* New York: McGraw, 1963.

Kraus, W. Keith. *Murder, Mischief, and Mayhem: A Process for Creative Research Papers.* Urbana: NCTE, 1977.

Klaus, Carl. "Public Opinion and Professional Belief." *College Composition and Communication.* 27 (1976): 335-39.

Knoblauch, C. H. "Composition Textbooks and the Myth of Literacy." Ms., delivered at NCTE 1985.

————. "The Current-Traditional Paradigm: Neither Current, Nor Traditional, Nor a Paradigm." Ms., delivered at MLA, 1985.

Knoblauch, C. H., and Lil Brannon. *Rhetorical Traditions and the Teaching of Writing.* Upper Montclair: Boynton, 1984.

————. "Teacher Commentary on Student Writing: The State of the Art." *Freshman English News.* 10 (Fall, 1981): 1-4.

Kuhn, Thomas S. *The Structure of Scientific Revolutions.* Second ed. Chicago: U of Chicago P, 1970.

Lamb, Mary. "Just Getting the Words Down on Paper: Results from the Five-Minute Writing Practice." *The Writing Center Journal.* II, 2 (1982): 1-6.

Lamme, Linda Leonard, and Nancye M. Childers. "The Composing Processes of Three Young Children." *Research in the Teaching of English.* 17 (1983): 31-50.

Lanham, Richard A. *Literacy and the Future of Humanism.* New Haven: Yale UP, 1983.

Lauer, Janice. "Composition Studies: Dappled Discipline." *Rhetoric Review.* 3.1 (1984): 20-29.

————. "Heuristics and Composition." *College Composition and Communication.* 21 (1970): 396-404. (Rpt. in *Contemporary Rhetoric: A Conceptual Background with Readings.* Ed. W. Ross Winterowd. New York: Harcourt, 1975. 79-89.)

————. "Response to Ann E. Berthoff, 'The Problem of Problem Solving.'" *College Composition and Communication.* 23 (1972): 208-10. (Rpt. in *Contemporary Rhetoric: A Conceptual Background with Readings.* Ed. W. Ross Winterowd. New York: Harcourt, 1975. 97-99.)

Liggett, Sarah L. "Preparing Business Writing Students to Use Dictation Systems: An Experimental Study." *DAI* 43 (1983): 3831A.

Lindsay, G. A. and D. McLennan. "Lined Paper: Its Effects on the Legibility and Creativity of Young Children's Writing." *British Journal of Educational Psychology.* 53 (1983): 364-68;

Linett, Deena S. *Studies in Process: Writing and Architectural Design.* Diss. Rutgers, 1982. Ann Arbor: UMI, 1983. 8301589.

Lunsford, Andrea A. "Essay Writing and Teachers' Responses in Nineteenth Century Scottish Universities." *College Composition and Communication.* 32 (1981): 434-43.

Macrorie, Ken. *Searching Writing: A Contextbook.* Rochelle Park: Hayden, 1980.

————. *Uptaught.* New York: Hayden, 1970.

————. *Writing to Be Read.* New York: Hayden, 1968.

Mandell, Barrett. "The Writer Writing Is Not at Home." *College Composition and Communication.* 31 (1980): 370-77.

Matott, Glen. "The Importance of Making Distinctions between Kinds of Writing." *College Composition and Communication.* 27 (1976): 355-58.

Matsuhashi, Ann. "Pausing and Planning: The Tempo of Written Discourse Production." *Research in the Teaching of English.* 15 (1981): 113-34.

————. *Producing Written Discourse: A Theory-Based Description of the Temporal Characteristics of Three Discourse Types from Four Competent*

Grade 12 Writers. Diss. SUNY Buffalo, 1979. Ann Arbor: UMI, 1980. 8005689.

McKee, Blaine. "Types of Outlines Used by Technical Writers." *JETT.* 7 (Winter 1974/75): 30-36.

McMillan, James B. "Summary of Nineteenth Century Historical and Comparative Linguistics." *College Composition and Communication.* 5 (1954): 145-49.

Mellon, John C. *Transformational Sentence Combining.* Champaign: NCTE, 1969.

Mersand, Joseph. *Attitudes Toward English Teaching.* Philadelphia: Chilton, 1961.

————. "What Has Happened to Written Composition?" *The English Journal.* 50 (1961): 231-37.

Metzger, Elizabeth. *Causes of Failure to Learn to Write: Exploratory Case Studies at Grade Seven, Grade Ten, and College Level.* Diss. SUNY Buffalo, 1977. Ann Arbor: UMI, 1977. 7726313.

Milic, Louis. "Theories of Style and Their Implications for the Teaching of Composition." *College Composition and Communication.* 16 (1965): 66-69.

Miller, Susan. "Is There a Text in This Class?" *Freshman English News.* 11 (1982): 22-33.

Mischel, Terry. "A Case Study of a Twelfth-Grade Writer." *Research in the Teaching of English.* 8 (1974): 303-14.

Moffett, James. *Teaching the Universe of Discourse.* Boston: Houghton, 1968.

Moore, B. S. "The Impact of a Workshop Approach on the Process of Composing Expository Writing for Twelfth-Grade Inner City College-Bound Students." *DAI* 44 (1983): 976A.

Moran, Michael G., and Ronald F. Lunsford, eds. *Research in Composition and Rhetoric: A Bibliographic Sourcebook.* Westport: Greenwood, 1984.

Morenberg, Max, Donald Daiker, and Andrew Kerek. "Sentence Combining at the College Level." *Research in the Teaching of English.* 12 (1978): 245-56.

Morgan, Betsy. "A Case Study of a Seventh-Grade Writer." *The English Record.* Fall 1975: 28-39.

Mosenthal, Peter. "On Defining Writing and Classroom Competence." *Research on Writing.* Ed. Peter Mosenthal, Lynne Tamor, and Sean A. Walmsley. New York: Longman, 1983. 26-71.

————, Lynne Tamor, and Sean A. Walmsley, eds. *Research on Writing.* New York: Longman, 1983.

Moss, Sidney P. "Logic: A Plea for a New Methodology in Freshman Composition." *College Composition and Communication.* 20 (1969): 215-22.

Muller, Herbert J. *The Uses of English.* New York: Holt, 1967.

Murphy, James J. "The Four Faces of Rhetoric: A Progress Report." *College Composition and Communication.* 17 (1966): 55-59.

Murphy, James J., ed. *The Rhetorical Tradition and Modern Writing.* New York: MLA, 1982.

Murray, Donald. "Writing as Process: How Writing Finds Its Own Meaning." *Eight Approaches to Teaching Composition.* Ed. Timothy R. Donovan and Ben W. McClelland. Urbana: NCTE, 1980. 3-20.

Myers, Miles, "The Politics of Minimum Competency." *The Nature and Measurement of Competency in Writing.* Ed. Charles R. Cooper. Urbana: NCTE, 1981. 165–74

———. *The Teacher-Researcher.* Urbana: ERIC/NCTE, 1985.

The National Interest and the Teaching of English: A Report on the Status of the Profession. Champaign: NCTE, 1961.

Nelson, M. W. "Writers Who Teach: A Naturalistic Investigation." Diss. U of Georgia, 1981.

Ney, James W. "Notes Towards a Psycholinguistic Model of the Writing Process." *Research in the Teaching of English.* 8 (1974): 157–69.

Nichols, James W. "Julian Huxley: The Specialist as Rhetorician." *College Composition and Communication.* 16 (1965): 7–13.

Nold, Ellen W., and Brent E. Davis. "The Discourse Matrix." *College Composition and Communication.* 31 (1980): 141–52.

Nold, Ellen W. and Sarah Warshauer Freedman. "An Analysis of Readers' Responses to Essays." *Research in the Teaching of English.* 11 (1977): 164–74.

North, Stephen. "Composition Now: Standing on One's Head." *College Composition and Communication.* 29 (1978): 177–80.

———. "Writing in a Philosophy Class: Three Case Studies." Ms. (Also in *Research in the Teaching of English.* 20 (1986): 225–62.)

Odell, Lee. *Discovery Procedures for Contemporary Rhetoric: A Study of the Usefulness of the Tagmemic Heuristic Model in Teaching Composition.* Diss. U of Michigan, 1970. Ann Arbor: UMI, 1971. 7115255.

———. "Measuring Changes in Intellectual Processes as One Dimension of Growth in Writing." *Evaluating Writing: Describing, Measuring, Judging.* Ed. Charles R. Cooper and Lee Odell. Urbana: NCTE, 1977. 107–34.

———. "Measuring the Effect of Instruction in Pre-Writing." *Research in the Teaching of English.* 8 (1974): 228–41.

———. "Teachers of Composition and Needed Research in Discourse Theory." *College Composition and Communication.* 30 (1979): 39–44.

Odell, Lee, and Dixie Goswami. "Writing in a Non-Academic Setting." *Research in the Teaching of English.* 16 (1982): 201–23.

O'Hare, Frank. *Sentence-Combining: Improving Student Writing Without Formal Grammar Instruction.* Urbana: NCTE, 1973.

Oliver, Kenneth. "The One-Legged, Wingless Bird of Freshman English." *College Composition and Communication.* 1.3 (1950): 3–6.

Ong, Walter J. "The Writer's Audience Is Always a Fiction." *PMLA.* 90 (1975): 9–21.

Perl, Sondra. *Five Writers Writing: Case Studies of the Composing Processes of Unskilled College Writers.* Diss. NYU, 1978. Ann Arbor: UMI, 1979. 7824104.

———. "The Composing Processes of Unskilled College Writers." *Research in the Teaching of English.* 13 (1978): 317–36.

Perl, Sondra, and Nancy Wilson. *Through Teachers' Eyes: Portraits of Writing Teachers at Work.* Portsmouth: Heinemann, 1986.

Perry, Marden L. "A Study of the Effects of a Literary Models Approach to Composition on Writing and Reading Achievement." *DAI* 40 (1980): 6137A.

Perry, William G. Jr. *Forms of Intellectual and Ethical Development in the College Years.* New York: Holt, 1968.

Petrosky, Anthony R. Review of *Problem-Solving Strategies for Writing*, by Linda Flower. *College Composition and Communication.* 34 (1983): 233-35.

Pettigrew, Joan. "Studies of the Composing Process: A Selective Review." *Research in Composition Newsletter.* 3.1 (1981): 1-28.

Pettigrew, Joan, Robert A. Shaw, and A. D. Van Nostrand. "Collaborative Analysis of Writing Instruction." *Research in the Teaching of English.* 15 (1981): 329-42.

Phelps, Louise Wetherbee. "Foundations for a Modern Psychology of Composition." *Rhetoric Review.* 3.1 (1984): 30-37.

Pianko, Sharon. *The Composing Acts of College Freshman Writers.* Diss. Rutgers, 1977. Ann Arbor: UMI, 1977. 7727956.

——— . "A Description of the Composing Processes of College Freshman Writers." *Research in the Teaching of English.* 13 (1979): 5-22.

——— . "Reflection: A Critical Component of the Composing Process." *College Composition and Communication.* 30 (1979): 275-78.

Price, Gayle B. "A Case for a Modern Commonplace Book." *College Composition and Communication.* 31 (1980): 175-82.

Raymond, James. "Enthymemes, Examples, and Rhetorical Method." *Essays on Classical Rhetoric and Modern Discourse.* Ed. Robert J. Connors, Lisa S. Ede, and Andrea A. Lunsford. Carbondale: Southern Illinois UP, 1984. 127-39.

——— . "Rhetoric: The Methodology of the Humanities." *College English.* 44 (1982): 778-83.

Redman, George W. Jr. "The Philosophy of Teaching Composition Held by Selected Teachers and Students at the University of Northern Colorado, Winter Quarter, 1973." *DAI* 35 (1974): 932A.

Reigstad, Thomas J. *Conferencing Practices of Professional Writers: Ten Case Studies.* Diss. SUNY Buffalo, 1980. Ann Arbor: UMI, 1981. 8104233.

Reigstad, Thomas J., ed. *Ethnography and the English Classroom* Vol. 4 (4) of *The English Record*, 1983.

Reither, James A. "Writing and Knowing: Toward Redefining the Writing Process." *College English.* 47 (1985): 620-28.

"Report of the Committee on Future Directions." *College Composition and Communication.* 11.1 (1960): 3-7.

Reynolds, H. M. "The Design and Testing of a Focused and Sequenced Free Writing Approach to a First Year Course in Composition for Two Year College Students." *DAI* 42 (1981): 989A.

Robinson, Jay L. "Literacy in the Department of English." *College English.* 47 (1985): 482-98.

Rogers, Louise. *The Composing Acts of College Freshman Writers: A Description with Two Case Studies.* Diss. Rutgers, 1977. Ann Arbor: UMI, 1977. 7727956.

Rohman, D. Gordon. "Pre-writing: The Stage of Discovery in the Writing Process." *College Composition and Communication.* 16 (1965): 106-12.

Rohman, D. Gordon and Albert O. Wlecke. *Pre-Writing: The Construction and*

Applications of Models for Concept Formation in Writing. USOE: Cooperative Research Project No. 2174.

Rose, Mike. "Sophisticated, Ineffective Books—The Dismantling of Process in Composition Texts." *College Composition and Communication.* 32 (1981): 65-74.

————. *Writer's Block: The Cognitive Dimension.* Carbondale: Southern Illinois UP, 1984.

Sanders, Sara E. and John H. Littlefield. "Perhaps Test Essays Can Reflect Significant Improvement in Freshman Composition: Report on a Successful Attempt." *Research in the Teaching of English.* 9 (1975): 145-54.

Schaefer, Charles. "Young Poets on Poetry." *Elementary School Journal.* 74 (1973): 24-27.

Schultz, John. *Writing from Start to Finish: The 'Story Workshop' Basic Forms Rhetoric-Reader.* Montclair: Boynton, 1982.

Schuster, Charles I. "Mikhail Bakhtin as Rhetorical Theorist." *College English.* 47 (1985): 594-607.

Scott, Fred Newton. "Rhetoric Rediviva," ed. Donald Stewart. *College Composition and Communication.* 31 (1980): 413-19.

Scott, Patrick. "Jonathan Maxcy and the Aims of Early Nineteenth-Century Rhetorical Teaching." *College English.* 45 (1983): 21-30.

Seaman, Ann. "Exploring Early Stages of Writing Development: A Fourth Grader Writes." *The English Record.* Fall 1975: 40-46.

Searle, Dennis and David Dillon. "The Message of Marking: Teacher Written Responses to Student Writing at Intermediate Grade Levels." *Research in the Teaching of English.* 14 (1980): 233-42.

Selfe, Cynthia. *The Composing Processes of Four High and Four Low Writing Apprehensives.* Diss. U of Texas/Austin, 1981. Ann Arbor: UMI, 1981. 8128686.

————. "The Predrafting Processes of Four High- and Four Low-Apprehensive Writers." *Research in the Teaching of English.* 18 (1984): 45-64.

Selzer, Jack. "The Composing Processes of an Engineer." *College Composition and Communication.* 34 (1983): 178-87.

Shannon, Richard F. Jr. "A Small Group, Personal Growth Method for the Teaching of Writing." *DAI* 44 (1983): 1714A.

Shaughnessy, Mina P. *Errors and Expectations: A Guide for the Teacher of Basic Writing.* New York: Oxford UP, 1977.

Siegel, Sidney. *Nonparametric Statistics for the Behavioral Sciences.* New York: McGraw, 1956.

Smith, Dora. *Class Size in High School English: Methods and Results.* Minneapolis: U of Minnesota P, 1931. (Reviewed in *Research in Written Composition.*)

Smith, James Steel. "H. G. Wells' Tonic." *College Composition and Communication.* 13.2 (1962): 14-17.

Smith, Ron. "The Composition Requirement Today: A Report on a Nationwide Survey of Four-Year Colleges and Universities." *College Composition and Communication.* 25 (1974): 138-48.

Sommers, Nancy. *Revision in the Composing Process: A Case Study of College*

Freshmen and Experienced Adult Writers. Diss. Boston U, 1978. Ann
 Arbor: UMI, 1979. 7905022.
———. "Revision Strategies of Student Writers and Experienced Adult
 Writers." *College Composition and Communication.* 31 (1980): 378-88.
Sommers, Nancy, and Donald McQuade, eds. *Student Writers at Work: The
 Bedford Prizes.* New York: St. Martin's, 1984.
Sowers, Susan. "A Six Year Old's Writing Process: The First Half of First
 Grade." *Language Arts.* 56 (1979): 829-35.
Stallard, Charles K. "An Analysis of the Writing Behavior of Good Student
 Writers." *Research in the Teaching of English.* 8 (1974): 206-18.
Stalnaker, Bonny Jean. *A Study of the Influences of Audience and Purpose on
 the Composing Processes of Professionals.* Diss. RPI, 1981. Ann Arbor:
 UMI, 1982. 8200472.
Steinberg, Erwin R., ed. Introduction. *Needed Research in the Teaching of
 English: Proceedings of a Project English Research Conference May 5-7,
 1962.* Washington: U.S. Government Printing Office, 1963. 1-4.
Steinhoff, Virginia. "The Phaedrus Idyll as Ethical Play." *The Rhetorical Tradi-
 tion and Modern Writing.* Ed. James J. Murphy. New York: MLA, 1982.
 31-45.
Stewart, Donald. "Two Model Teachers and the Harvardization of English
 Departments." *The Rhetorical Tradition and Modern Writing.* Ed. James
 J. Murphy. New York: MLA, 1982. 118-29.
———. "The Status of Composition and Rhetoric in American Colleges,
 1880-1902: An MLA Perspective." *College English.* 47 (1985): 734-45.
Sweeder, John J. *A Descriptive Study of Six Adult Remedial Writers: Their
 Composing Processes and Heuristic Strategies.* Diss. Temple, 1981. Ann
 Arbor: UMI, 1981. 8124589.
Talbert, Carol. "Anthropological Research Models." *Research in the Teaching
 of English.* 7 (1973): 190-211.
Tate, Gary. *Teaching Composition: 10 Bibliographical Essays.* Forth Worth:
 Texas Christian UP, 1976.
Voss, Ralph. "Janet Emig's *The Composing Processes of Twelfth Graders*: A
 Reassessment." *College Composition and Communication.* 34 (1983):
 278-83.
Warfel, Harry R. "Structural Linguistics and Composition." *College English.*
 20 (1959): 205-13.
Warner, Paul C. and W. S. Guiler. "Individual vs. Group Instruction in
 Grammatical Usage." *Journal of Educational Psychology.* 34 (1933):
 140-51.
Warnock, John. "New Rhetoric and the Grammar of Pedagogy." *Freshman
 English News.* 5 (Fall 1976): 1-4.
White, Edward M. *Teaching and Assessing Writing.* San Francisco: Jossey-Bass,
 1985.
Whiteman, M. F. "What We Can Learn from Writing Research." *Theory into
 Practice.* 19 (1980): 150-56.
Wigginton, Eliot. *Foxfire.* 3 Vols, bks. 1-3. New York: Doubleday, 1975.
Williams, J. D. "Covert Language Behavior During Writing." *Research in the
 Teaching of English.* 17 (1983): 301-12.

Willis, Phyllis W. "A Study of Current Practices in Freshman English in Oklahoma Colleges." *DAI* 34 (1974): 4806A.

Winterowd, W. Ross. *Rhetoric: A Synthesis.* New York: Holt, 1968.

Witte, Stephen. "Topical Structure and Revision: An Exploratory Study." *College Composition and Communication.* 34 (1983): 313+.

Witte, Stephen P., and Lester Faigley. *Evaluating College Writing Programs.* Carbondale: Southern Illinois UP, 1983.

Worsham, S. E. "A Naturalistic Study of a Basic Writing Program." Unpublished Ed. S. Project, U of Georgia, 1980.

Wozniak, John Michael. *English Composition in Eastern Colleges, 1850–1940.* Washington: UP of America, 1978.

Young, Richard E., and Alton L. Becker. "Toward a Modern Theory of Rhetoric: A Tagmemic Contribution." *Harvard Educational Review.* 35 (1965): 450-68. (Rpt. in *Language and Learning.* Ed. Janet A. Emig, James T. Fleming, and Helen M. Popp. New York: Harcourt, 1966. 195-215. Also in *Contemporary Rhetoric: A Conceptual Background with Readings.* Ed. W. Ross Winterowd. New York: Harcourt, 1975. 123-43.)

Young, Richard E. "Arts, Crafts, and Knacks." *Visible Language.* 14 (1980): 341-50.

————. "Paradigms and Problems: Needed Research in Rhetorical Invention." *Research on Composing: Points of Departure.* Ed. Charles C. Cooper and Lee Odell. Urbana: NCTE, 1978. 29-48.

Ziv, Nina. *The Effect of Teacher Comments on the Writing of Four College Freshmen.* Diss. NYU, 1981. Ann Arbor: UMI, 1982. 8225619.

Ziviani, Jenny. "Effects of Pencil Shape and Size on Motor Accuracy and Pencil Posture of 8 Year Old Children." ERIC ED 218 658.

Zoellner, Robert. "Talk-Write: A Behavioral Pedagogy for Composition." *College English.* 30(1969): 267-320.

Index

Academic reform movement, the, 9–13
Applebee, Arthur, *Tradition and Reform in in the Teaching of English*, 9–10, 11–12, 324, 367

Beach, Richard, "Self-Evaluation Strategies of Extensive Revisers and Nonrevisers," 340–41, 343
Bereiter, Carl, and Marlene Scardamalia, "Levels of Inquiry in Writing Research," 353–57, 363, 383 n. 1
Berkenkotter, Carol, "Decisions and Revisions: The Composing Strategies of a Publishing Writer," 198, 209, 237
Berlin, James, 64; "Contemporary Composition: The Major Pedagogical Theories," 95; *Writing Instruction in Nineteenth-Century American Colleges*, 68, 77, 78, 95
Berthoff, Ann, 64, 357; *Making of Meaning, The*, 94, 144–45, 334–36; "Problem of Problem Solving, The," 108–09; "Response to Janice Lauer, 'Counterstatement,'" 110–11
Booth, Wayne C., 64; *Rhetoric of Fiction, The*, 63; "Rhetorical Stance, The," 63, 93
Braddock, Richard, Richard Lloyd-Jones, and Lowell Schoer. *See Research in Written Composition*
Brannon, Lil, Melinda Knight, and Vara Neverow-Turk, *Writers Writing*, 31
Brannon, Lil, and C. H. Knoblauch. *See* Knoblauch, C. H., and Lil Brannon
Bridwell, Lillian, 273; "Revising Strategies in Twelfth Grade Students' Transactional Writing," 144, 153, 340–41, 343–44, 346, 348
Britton, James, Tony Burgess, Nancy Martin, Alex McLeod, and Harold Rosen. *See Development of Writing Abilities (11-18), The*
Bruffee, Kenneth, 118; "Peer Tutoring and the 'Conversation of Mankind,'" 99–100
Bryant, Paul, "Brand New World Every Morning, A," 326–27, 332, 353
Burhans, Clinton Jr., "Teaching of Writing and the Knowledge Gap, The," 329–30, 331, 353, 378 n. 4.
Burke, Virginia, 64; "Composition-Rhetoric Pyramid, The," 93–94

Case studies, forms of, 200–02
Christensen, Francis, 64; "Generative Rhetoric of the Sentence, A," 63; *Notes Toward a New Rhetoric*, 63
Clark, Christopher, and Susan Florio. *See* Florio, Susan, and Christopher Clark
Clinical community, 137, 197; problems in, 199–203, 233, 236–37
Clinical inquiry: collecting and analyzing data for, 218–26; designing studies for, 210–18, 226, 230; drawing conclusions from, 233–37; identifying problems for, 208–10; idiographic authority of, 207, 217–18, 219, 230–32, 237; interpreting data in, 226–32; levels in, 204; nature of, 137–38; outline of, 207; range of, 198; in relation to Ethnographic inquiry, 202, 205, 207, 208, 220; in relation to Experimental inquiry, 137–38, 199–200, 205, 206, 207–08, 220, 343, 345; in relation to Formalist inquiry, 206–07, 355; reliability in, 219–26; technical eclecticism of, 218–20; validity in, 219–26; value of, 203, 207
Clinical knowledge: advantages of, 205–06; disadvantages of, 206–07; logic of, 203–05, 226; structure of, 203–05, 206, 210, 226, 381 n. 2
College Composition and Communication, 31, 136
Composing aloud, 347; in Clinical inquiry, 211, 213, 216, 220–26; in Formalist inquiry, 245, 259–66, 347
Composing Processes of Twelfth Graders, The (Emig), 2, 135, 145, 331, 348, 374, 381 n. 3, 382 nn. 5, 6; composing aloud in, 220–21, 222–23; design of, 210–12, 215; drawing conclusions in, 233, 234, 326; indictment of Practitioners in, 234, 326; interpretation of data in, 226–30; published criticism of, 381 n. 1, 382 n. 7; on revision, 340–41, 341–43; as seminal Clinical study, 197, 199–202, 208–209, 236–37
Composition: academic base for, 13; autonomous departments of, 369–73, 374, 383 n. 2; coherence of knowledge in, 337–39, 341, 346–47, 351–52; connections with Rhetoric, 63–65; crises in the teaching of, 321–24, 382 n. 3; in departments of English, 365–70, 373–75; as a "discipline," 363–64;